The Civil War

100

The Stories Behind the Most Influential Battles, People and Events in the War Between the States

Michael Lee Lanning

SOURCEBOOKS, INC.
NAPERVILLE, ILLINOIS

Published by Sourcebooks, Inc.
P.O. Box 4410, Naperville, Illinois 60567–4410
(630) 961–3900
Fax: (630) 961–2168
www.sourcebooks.com

Library of Congress Cataloging-in-Publication Data
Lanning, Michael Lee.
The Civil War 100 : the stories behind the most influential battles, people and events
in the war between the states / Michael Lee Lanning.
    p. cm.
Includes bibliographical references and index.
ISBN-13: 978–1-4022–0659–7
ISBN-10: 1–4022–0659–3
1. United States—History—Civil War, 1861–1865—Anecdotes. I. Title. II. Title:
Civil War one hundred.
E655.L36 2007
973.7—dc22
2006012428

Printed and bound in the United States of America
BVG 10 9 8 7 6 5 4 3 2 1

To

Allyanna Maeve Corcoran, David Garland Neary,

and Michael Thomas Neary

CONTENTS

INTRODUCTION

One hundred and forty years after it ended, the American Civil War still rivets and polarizes historians, scholars, and "buffs" as does no other event. The country's most divisive, violent, and costly conflict took the lives of more than 615,000 Union and Confederate soldiers—the equivalent of 5.5 million if compared to today's population. We continue to preserve many battlefields, maintained and opened to the public by the National Parks Services. Monuments to the war's dead and surviving veterans occupy prominent places on courthouse squares in both the North and South today.

It is a war that still divides. It is a war that still creates great controversy. Currently, colleges and schools have more Civil War scholars teaching about the conflict than the war had generals. Historians, intrigued laymen, and interested readers studying about the events between 1861 and 1865 outnumber the combined total of actual soldiers and sailors who served under both the Stars and Stripes of the Union and the Stars and Bars of the Confederacy.

More than seventy thousand books have been published about the Civil War during the century and a half since the war ended—more than have been written on any other event in American history. Most of these books chronicle the war by combining the divergent political and social issues with battlefield actions. A myriad of others focus on the lives of individual military and civilian leaders of the time or cover specific units, battles, or campaigns. Yet, none of these works to date has attempted to rank the war's leaders, battles, and events according to their influence on the conflict and the future of the country.

This book takes the unique approach of presenting the war by first identifying, and then ranking by order of influence, its most significant leaders, battles, and events. It is difficult, of course, to compare these three aspects, but the key to understanding these rankings is focusing on the influence of each on the war. This includes beginnings and outcome rather than only immediate impact, decisiveness, popularity, or reputation. In some instances, the accomplishments of an individual, the immediate results of a battle, or the enormity of an event stand alone to justify the ranking, while in other cases, placement on the list is the result of comparisons to contemporaries.

For the ease of comparison, when one leader, battle, or event references another included on the list, the ranking of the referenced entry follows its name, e.g., U. S. Grant (3), Battle of Fort Sumter (50), and the Missouri Compromise (78).

AUTHOR TO READER

Comparisons of the leaders, battles, and events of the American Civil War must be within the context of the entire war. Each side had both advantages and disadvantages at the beginning of the conflict. Neither the North nor the South were prepared for the war, but resources to man and sustain their armies were far from equal. Many factors, however, interceded to provide the balance between the two opponents that produced a long and bloody war.

If one looks only at statistics, the North entered the war at a great advantage. The population of the Union states totaled twenty-two million compared to only nine million in the Confederacy—and fully a third of this latter population were black slaves. While the slaves produced food and other supplies for the rebels, they were not a source of manpower for the military. In fact, the threat of runaways and slave rebellions required white overseers to maintain security rather than join the troops at the front.

More than three-fourths of the existing manufacturing, financial, and shipping assets remained within the boundaries of the Union. Foundries for casting cannons and armories for manufacturing small arms lay almost entirely in the Northern states. The Confederacy never advanced beyond a rudimentary level of weapons manufacturing, remaining dependent on stocks seized at the war's outbreak, those captured in battle, and whatever could be procured from Europe. Gunpowder manufacturing also lay almost exclusively in the North in 1861, but the Confederate states began to produce an adequate supply of their own shortly after the war began.

The Union also possessed a huge advantage in naval assets, which it increased as the war continued. The U.S. Navy expanded from sixty-nine vessels in 1861 to a total of more than two hundred ships, including seventy-four ironclads, over the next three years. This naval superiority allowed the Union to blockade the Confederacy and greatly reduce the export of crops and import of weapons and supplies. The Confederate navy numbered only a few ships captured in port at the beginning of the conflict and, later, a dozen or so built or bought from England.

Advantages in transportation and communications also lay within the Union. More than two-thirds of the thirty thousand miles of rail network were in the North, as were the mills and factories to produce and maintain tracks, engines, and railcars. Telegraph lines mostly paralleled rail lines, and the superior resources of the Union allowed it to extend an additional fifteen thousand miles of telegraph wire during the war. This gave the Union an even greater advantage in communications.

The North also went into the war with the advantage of the stated purpose of preserving the Union. Although slavery was an unstated cause of the war, President Abraham Lincoln did not declare abolition to be an objective of the conflict. This secured the slaveholding border states of Missouri, Kentucky, Maryland, Delaware, and West Virginia—which contained a white population of more than half that of the Confederacy—from joining the rebellion. When Lincoln later added ending slavery as a war aim with the Emancipation Proclamation on January 1, 1863, the border states remained neutral. The Proclamation also gained the moral high ground in relations with European countries and prevented their overt support of the South.

Despite all the resources and factors favoring the North, the South also had its advantages. First and foremost, the Confederacy did not have to "win" the war. All it had to do was "not lose." To maintain its independence, the South had to defend its territory and repulse any invasions from the North. The patriotic zeal of the Confederates for their independence and self-government—including the right to preserve slavery—filled the ranks with volunteers willing to fight for their country and cause.

Both sides had an abundance of experienced officers, including those who had fought in the Mexican War. The Confederacy initially had the advantage in military leadership because it selected its commanders based on their abilities. In the war's early years, Union generals—most who proved ineffective—gained their positions on political connections rather than on leadership skills.

To counter the Northern advantages in manufacturing war materials, the Confederacy outfitted much of its armed forces with materials taken from U.S. armories located in the South at the war's outbreak and then from arms and supplies captured in battle. Blockade runners carried raw materials out of Southern ports to Europe where they exchanged them for arms and other equipment to bring back into Confederate ports.

Early in the war, the advantages and disadvantages of the North and South were relatively balanced. The patriotism and belief in their respective causes lengthened the war and increased its carnage. Ultimately, however, the Union placed able generals in command, and this leadership—combined with numerically superior manpower, naval power, and manufacturing resources—shifted the balance and defeated the rebellion.

The conflict that divided America in the nineteenth century has always had several different names, including the War of Rebellion and the War Between the States. Over the years, the most commonly accepted name has become the American Civil War, and that is the primary label used in this book. Likewise, the names of battles also differ, as do designations of armies, definitions of casualties, and ranks of officers. The following basic explanations are provided for the reader's understanding.

Battle Names: Generally the North named battles for nearby terrain features, such as rivers, while the South assigned names based on proximity to towns or villages where or near where they occurred. As a result, the first major battle of the war carries the name First Bull Run in the North and Manassas in the South, while the most influential battle is either Antietam for the creek or Sharpsburg for the town. Sometimes the two sides agreed on names such as Gettysburg and Chambersburg; then they differed for no apparent reason on naming the battle Shiloh or Pittsburg Landing. Over the years, the names generally used by historians have been those of the war's victor, and this book follows that policy.

Military Organization: Both armies organized their forces into structures of squads, platoons, companies, battalions, regiments, divisions, corps, and armies. Two to five or more of each of these elements combine to form the next level. Various reorganizations and transfers of all size units occurred throughout the conflict. The most often referred-to organization in these rankings, and the largest operational unit in the war, is an army. Armies composed of two or more corps generally took the name of the territories in which they operated or originated. Again, the North and South differed on how to name their armies and followed the general procedures they used to name battles. The Federals designated their armies for rivers while the Confederate armies took their names from the region of their assignment. Thus, the Union Army of the Potomac opposed the Confederate Army of Northern Virginia. This becomes even more confusing when the Union organization was the Army of *the* Tennessee as opposed to the Confederate-named Army *of* Tennessee.

Officer Ranks: Officers of both sides often had two ranks—one awarded by their state militia and another by the regular army. Even more confusion arises from the practice of both sides to award "brevet" promotions. These ranks, awarded for gallantry or meritorious action, were strictly honorary and had none of the authority or pay of the actual rank. Regular ranks are the ones most used in this work. Both armies followed the traditional ranks of lieutenant, captain, major, lieutenant colonel, colonel, and general. The two sides differed, however, in the rankings of their general officers. The Union maintained three ranks—brigadier general, major general, and lieutenant general, with only the most senior officer achieving this last rank. The Confederacy promoted officers to brigadier general, major general, lieutenant general, and general. Several officers achieved the designation of general with their seniority based on the date of their promotion.

Casualties: During the Civil War, the definition of casualty included losses in numerical strength as a result of death, wounds, capture, desertion, sickness, or discharge. Casualty figures for battles and campaigns often differ according to the source; the numbers included in this book are those generally accepted as accurate. Some writers and readers assume casualty numbers equal the number of those killed in combat. This grossly overstates the loss of life. This book uses the above definition for casualties.

Author's Disclosure: Born, reared, and educated in the South—and with the middle name coming from the Confederacy's most influential officer—I have at least a dozen kin who fought in the Civil War. All were enlisted; all were rebels. The most information I have on any individual is on a distant uncle who left behind a brief journal of his participation in the campaign around Corinth, Mississippi, in 1862. He mentions little combat but writes on and on about how many miles he marched and how much his feet hurt. As an infantry veteran of more than twenty years in the U.S. Army who proudly served under the Stars and Stripes in the Vietnam and Cold Wars, I understand his woes.

I have given much thought about which side I would have chosen to serve if my time in uniform had been in the mid-nineteenth century rather than the latter part of the twentieth. It is impossible to be certain, but if the Civil War had begun before I joined the U.S. Army, I would have probably remained loyal to my state and the South. If already in the U.S. Army, I believe I would have stood faithful to my oath "to protect and defend the United States against all enemies, foreign and domestic" and remained in blue.

As the author who identified, ranked, and then wrote about these leaders, battles, and events, I have endeavored to present fair findings biased only by the ultimate rule that the winner takes all. The North had heroes and incompetents; the South had heroes and incompetents. The war had the whole array in between.

1

ANTIETAM

September 16–18, 1862

The Battle of Antietam, the bloodiest day in American military history, is the single most influential occurrence of the Civil War. It was here that General George McClellan (51) and his Union forces first blocked General Robert E. Lee (5) and his Confederate army in their move northward. The Union victory, although far from complete, was pivotal for several reasons. First, the defeat discouraged European countries from recognizing the rebel states and providing needed aid and support to them. It also provided the opportunity for President Abraham Lincoln (2) to issue the Emancipation Proclamation (22) that verified that one of the war's objectives had become to free the slaves. Later battles at Gettysburg (4) and Vicksburg (7) would seal the fate of the Confederacy, but the long road to defeating the rebellion began along Antietam Creek, Maryland, in mid-September 1862.

Even before the United States gained its independence from Great Britain in 1781 at the Battle of Yorktown, conflict between states of the North and South was inevitable because the two regions differed so dramatically on geographical, political, and social issues. Beliefs about slavery and states' rights were the primary differences, however. While several agreements—including the Missouri Compromise of 1820 (78)—had staved off open hostilities for many years, the election of the Republican Lincoln in November 1860 was the spark that ignited the final explosion.

Although Lincoln had made no campaign promises to outlaw slavery, Southerners, as well as Northerners, viewed him as an abolitionist who would end the institution. Some Southern states, whose agriculture and industry depended on slave labor, demanded independence from the North—a state's right they believed to be guaranteed in the U.S. Constitution. Only a month after the Lincoln election, South Carolina voted to secede. During the first three months of 1861, seven additional states left the Union to join the South Carolinians in forming the Confederate States of America.

Few on either side believed that secession would lead to war. Northerners thought that diplomatic efforts, supported by a sea blockade of the southern coast, would return the rebel states to the fold. However, chances for a peaceful settlement ended when Confederate artillery batteries bombarded Fort Sumter, South Carolina (50), during April 12–14, 1861. Four more states joined the Confederacy a few days later.

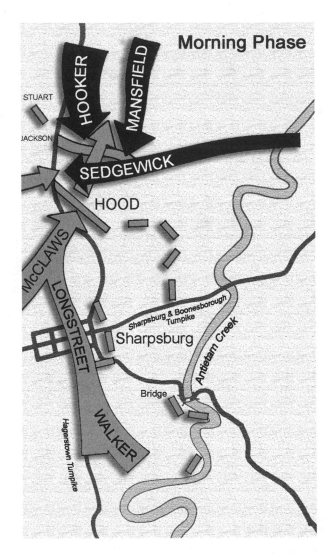

Both the North and South mobilized quickly, and aggressive Confederate commanders initially achieved success over more reluctant, cautious Union generals. Warfare on land, fought mostly on their own territory, favored the rebels; however, they lacked an effective navy, which allowed the U.S.—using its Anaconda Plan (27)—to blockade its shores. The blockade prevented the South from exporting its cash crop of cotton and importing much-needed arms, ammunition, and other military supplies that the meager Southern industrial complex could not provide.

The remainder of 1861 and the early months of 1862 brought a series of battles and skirmishes. The first major fight occurred at Bull Run, Virginia (10), on July 21,

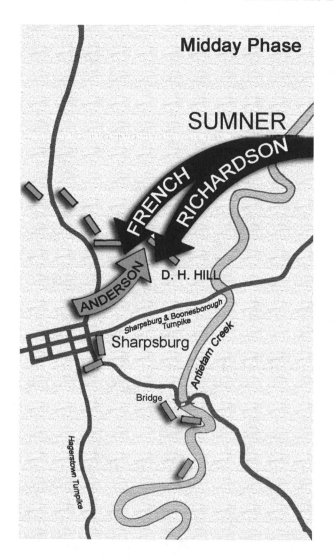

1861, and proved the war would be bloodier and lengthier than many had anticipated. Then on August 10, 1861, Union and Confederate forces met at Wilson's Creek, Missouri (70), and demonstrated that the war would extend far beyond the Atlantic Coast.

In May 1862, Robert E. Lee took command of what he renamed the Army of Northern Virginia and soon became one of the most revered and beloved commanders in military history. Lee often had difficulties controlling his subordinate leaders, but his overall leadership and tactical expertise far overshadowed his shortcomings, enabling him to outmaneuver and out-general his opponents during his initial battles.

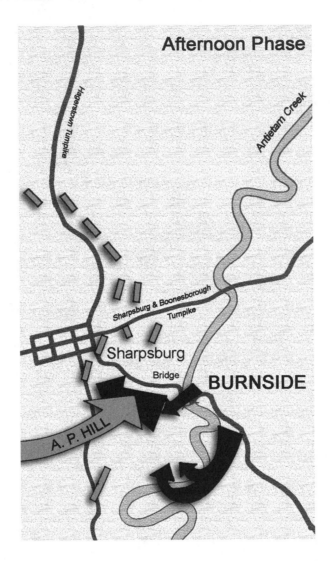

He stopped a numerically superior army's threat against the Confederate capital of Richmond and then turned north to achieve victory at Second Bull Run (40) near Manassas, Virginia, on August 29–30, 1862.

Despite the early successes in Virginia, both Lee and Confederate president Jefferson Davis (9) understood that the South could not defeat the more populous and industrialized North in a prolonged war by simply defending their own territory. Although the war had been ongoing for only a year, the Southerners were already experiencing shortages in arms and other war materials that they could not produce themselves. To break the Union blockade and receive needed supplies and naval support, the Confederate States had to obtain the support of European countries, especially Great Britain, France, and even Russia. While these and other countries were sympathetic with the cause of Southern independence, they were not prepared to risk bad relations, or even war, with the United States until the Confederacy proved that its rebellion would likely succeed.

The victory at Second Bull Run sufficiently stabilized the defensive security of the South for Lee and Davis to plan to take the war into the Northern states. Their planned offensive would accomplish immediate goals of demoralizing the North and securing supplies for the South. More importantly, a victory in the North would further the long-range goal of gaining recognition and support from Europe.

On September 6, 1862, Lee's army marched out of Virginia into Maryland with the intent of continuing its invasion into southern Pennsylvania. Union general George McClellan (51)—who had assumed command of the Union army after Lincoln relieved General Irwin McDowell (80) for his reluctance and poor performance in the Peninsular Campaign (32) and at Second Bull Run—paralleled the Southern advance, keeping his army between the rebels and Washington, D.C. Three days later Lee issued Order Number 191 that sent half his army to Harrisburg, Pennsylvania, to control the region's primary rail center while the other half, led by General Thomas J. "Stonewall" Jackson (36), moved to capture the musket factories at Harpers Ferry. This latter move would also secure Lee's lines back to Virginia.

Four days later, a Union soldier discovered a copy of the order, wrapped around three cigars, which had been dropped on the rebel's march northward. The order was soon in the hands of McClellan and his staff. The Union general now possessed Lee's entire maneuver plan as well as the revelation that his army outnumbered the rebels seventy-six thousand to forty thousand. McClellan, however, did not take immediate advantage of this rebel intelligence failure. Instead he heeded warnings from his own intelligence officers that the rebel force was far larger than the order indicated and advanced cautiously.

McClellan's caution, combined with delaying actions by Confederate forces at passes in South Mountain, cost the Union army the element of surprise and allowed Lee to deploy his force in defensive positions along Antietam Creek, just east of Sharpsburg, Maryland. The Union army finally began its attack on the morning of September 17, with the plan of striking both of Lee's flanks and then committing the reserve against the middle once the initial advances were successful.

What actually occurred was far from the plan. Hesitation by McClellan and his subordinates, combined with poor communications, resulted in three uncoordinated attacks rather than a single effort. At dawn, following a murderous artillery barrage,

Union infantry commanded by General Joseph Hooker (48) attacked the Confederate left flank. Attacks and counterattacks continued for the next two hours with neither side gaining an advantage.

Meanwhile, at mid-morning the Union center struck rebel troops, commanded by General James Longstreet (13), who were defending a sunken road that would become known as the "Bloody Lane." Again repulsed, the Union attempted another advance in the early afternoon against the South's right flank. Despite the fact that most of Antietam Creek was easily fordable, infantrymen under General Ambrose Burnside (57) concentrated their attack at a narrow bridge over the waterway. After yet more bloodshed, the Union troops pushed across the bridge and were about to cut off Lee's route back to Virginia when additional rebel troops arrived from Harpers Ferry, causing still another stalemate along the battle lines.

By sundown the entire battlefield was quiet except for the sounds of each side attending to its wounded and preparing to bury its dead.

With McClellan's army blocking his advance northward, Lee withdrew back to Virginia on the morning of September 18. McClellan, overcautious as usual, did not pursue and resume his attack. Although Lee claimed victory in the battle because he had not been forced to retreat, it is extremely possible that McClellan might have defeated Lee and brought an end to the war if he had continued the fight.

The single day of battle along Antietam Creek killed or wounded more than twenty-three thousand Americans—more casualties than suffered by the United States in the entire Revolutionary War, the War of 1812, the Mexican War, and the Spanish American War combined. Casualties at Antietam outnumbered those suffered by Americans on the "Longest Day" of World War II during the Normandy Invasion by nine to one.

Influence of the Battle of Antietam reached far beyond the many graves and hospital tents. For the first time the Union army had stopped, if not defeated, Lee and his Army of Northern Virginia, ending a threat against Maryland and Pennsylvania and providing a tremendous morale boost to the North in general. More importantly, when Britain and France learned of the battle's outcome, they no longer believed the South would win and decided that recognition of the Confederacy would not be to their advantage. They would remain neutral; the South would stand alone in its quest for independence.

Antietam also significantly changed Lincoln's objectives for the war. Previously he had stated that his one and only purpose was to "preserve the Union" and claimed that slavery was not an issue. Five days after the battle he met with his cabinet and delivered a draft of the Emancipation Proclamation. Although the document—not issued until the following January 1, 1863—did not free slaves in Northern states, and, of course, had no power to do so in Southern-controlled areas, it did advance emancipation as an objective of the war.

While the conflict took two and a half more years of bloody battles, including Gettysburg and Vicksburg, before the Confederate surrender at Appomattox Court House, the Confederate States were doomed from the time Lee began his withdrawal back to Virginia from Antietam Creek. An improving Union army, the rise of more efficient leaders—including Ulysses S. Grant (3)—and a refusal of recognition and support from European countries sealed the fate of the rebellion. No other event in the American Civil War was so pivotal in influencing the war's outcome and the future of the United States of America.

2

ABRAHAM LINCOLN

Sixteenth President of the United States

1809–1865

The history of the American Civil War and the presidency of Abraham Lincoln are intertwined to the point of being indistinguishable. Lincoln's election sparked the secession of the Southern states, and his efforts to resupply and maintain Fort Sumter, South Carolina (50), ignited the beginnings of military hostilities. For his efforts throughout the war, Lincoln collected an assortment of epitaphs. For his personal selection of generals to lead the Union army in the field and his assumption of many governmental powers, including the suspension of the writ of habeas corpus, many labeled him a tyrant. For his proclamation that added freeing the slaves as an objective of the war, he gained the title of the "Great Emancipator." For his address shortly after the Battle of Gettysburg (4), he earned the title of one of the world's most eloquent writers and great orators. Of all the leaders of the Civil War, Lincoln is the one who promised and then delivered the preservation of the Union. To that end, he produced the united nation that acts as today's single world superpower.

Lincoln was born on February 12, 1809, in a log cabin in Hardin (now Larue) County, Kentucky, to a family of farmers. In 1816, the Lincolns moved to Indiana because of the difficulty in securing land titles in Kentucky. Lincoln would later relate that his family also moved "partly on account of slavery."

The young Lincoln grew up on the frontier with only a basic education. Except for a trip down the Mississippi River to New Orleans aboard a flatboat in 1828, his teenage experiences were limited to farming and survival. The Lincoln family moved to Illinois in pursuit of more land in 1830 and Abraham made a second visit to New Orleans the next year. Despite the hardships and lack of opportunity, Lincoln, perhaps inspired by the trips to New Orleans, made every effort to learn on his own. He read the few books and periodicals available and actively pursued provocative discussions with his neighbors. The ambitious Lincoln, having no desire to remain on the farm, held several clerking jobs and then joined a partner in an unsuccessful grocery business.

Lincoln experienced no great success until he enlisted in his local militia to participate in the Black Hawk War of 1832. Although his military service was mostly uneventful, the fellow members of his volunteer company elected him captain. His time in the military and the recognition of his leadership abilities by his comrades gave new direction to the ambitious Lincoln. After returning home from the military, he ran unsuccessfully for the Illinois legislature before winning in his second attempt in 1834. He remained in the legislature for the next four terms while he also studied law to become a licensed attorney with his own practice in Springfield in 1836. In 1842, Lincoln married Mary Todd, who bore him four sons.

Elected to the U.S. House of Representatives in 1847, Lincoln took the unpopular stance of opposing the Mexican War as being unconstitutional and spoke against the annexation of the slave state of Texas. At the end of this two-year term, he did not run for reelection, choosing instead to return to his law practice in Springfield.

In 1856, Lincoln reentered politics by joining the Republican Party in its opposition to the Kansas-Nebraska Act that allowed new U.S. territories self-determination on slavery based on popular sovereignty. Two years later he ran against Stephen A. Douglas for the U.S. Senate. During a series of debates, Lincoln made clear his stance on slavery and the necessity for the preservation of the Union when he declared on June 16, 1858, "A house divided against itself cannot stand." He continued, "I believe this government cannot endure permanently half slave and half free."

Douglas won the election but Lincoln emerged from the debates as a national figure and a leader of the Republican Party. In 1860, the Republicans selected Lincoln as their presidential candidate. Lincoln further declared his beliefs in a February 27 speech when he said, "Let us have faith that right makes might; and in that faith, let us to the end dare to do our duty as we understand it."

Northern supporters called Lincoln "Honest Abe," while Southerners who supported states' rights referred to him as a "baboon." The Southerners interpreted Lincoln's "dare to do our duty as we understand it" as the declaration of an abolitionist. Although Lincoln hated slavery, he was not, in fact, an abolitionist. However, he made no statements to reassure the South that he would not end the practice. By election time, those in the South who favored secession declared that if Lincoln were elected, they would leave the Union.

On November 6, 1860, Abraham Lincoln won the presidency. Despite the fact that his Republican Party did not control the House, the Senate, or the Supreme Court—meaning Lincoln and his government could not end slavery without a constitutional amendment that would be impossible to pass—representatives of the

Southern states met to discuss secession. Led by South Carolina, the state that depended the most on slavery to maintain its agricultural economy, seven states agreed to leave the Union and form the Confederacy.

Lincoln quickly initiated the Anaconda Plan (27) to blockade Southern ports and to extend diplomatic efforts to prevent war. However, he also ordered that U.S. forts in the South be resupplied and held for the Union. When Union forces refused to evacuate Fort Sumter, South Carolina, rebel artillery batteries shelled it on April 12, 1861. Two days later, despite only two men killed and one wounded, the Union commander surrendered the fort. The American Civil War had begun.

Lincoln called for the loyal states to enlist seventy-five thousand militiamen. The response was so heavy that volunteers had to be turned away. He also made it clear that he would go to any means to preserve the Union and assumed powers that made him more a dictator than a democratic president. On April 27, 1861, Lincoln suspended many legal rights, including habeas corpus, and ordered martial law to replace previous civilian rights and powers. When newspapers opposed him or the war, he ordered them closed. When generals failed to achieve victory, he relieved them of command and replaced them with new generals—again and again until he found his chosen leader in U. S. Grant (3).

Lincoln could be unforgiving with those who opposed his objectives, but at the same time he was generous in pardoning soldiers convicted by court martial. He was also extremely adept in appointing subordinates to manage the manpower and supply needs of the extended war.

Although Southern secessionists claimed that Lincoln's abolitionist leanings were one of the reasons they left the Union, the president did not make slavery an issue in the war's first year. In the summer of 1862, he again made clear his war purposes when he wrote, "My paramount objective in this struggle is to save the Union, and is not either to save or destroy slavery. If I could save the Union without freeing any slave I would do it; and if I could save it by freeing all the slaves I would do it; and if I could save it by freeing some and leaving others alone I would also do that."

Even though Lincoln wrote this statement, he personally held strong objections to slavery. He knew that continuous Confederate victories were demoralizing the Union, and recruits were becoming more difficult to enlist. Lincoln believed he could accomplish two objectives by ending slavery. First, freed slaves could be a great source of manpower for his cause and, second, the abolishment of slavery would provide moral clarity to the efforts to preserve the Union by making it an aim of the war.

When the Union army stopped Robert E. Lee's (5) invasion of the North at the Battle of Antietam (1) in September 1862, Lincoln announced plans to his cabinet to issue the Emancipation Proclamation (22) to become effective January 1, 1863. The Proclamation did not end slavery, and, in fact, declared something neither it nor Lincoln could enforce—the freeing of slaves in rebel-held territory. However, despite its shortcomings, the Proclamation gained Lincoln the title of Great Emancipator and opened the way for thousands of blacks to don the blue uniform of the U.S. Army.

Not everyone in the North was happy with this or other decisions made by Lincoln. In the election of 1864, Northern Democrats nominated George B. McClellan (51), an army general Lincoln had relieved from command for being too cautious. McClellan ran on a platform of ending the war by giving back to the South all rights it had enjoyed previous to 1860, including slavery, in return for peace.

Lincoln did not yield to political pressures. He had already promised in his masterful Gettysburg Address (66) on November 19, 1863, that "we here highly resolve that these dead shall not have died in vain." In August 1864 he restated his war aims when he said there would be "no bargaining, no negotiating, no truces with the rebels except to bury their dead, until every man shall have laid down his arms, submitted to the government, and sued for peace."

McClellan had many supporters, but victories in 1864 by Grant in Virginia, William T. Sherman (6) in Georgia, and Phillip Sheridan (8) in the Shenandoah Valley (29) raised the spirits in the North and sent them to the ballot boxes to reelect Lincoln.

The war was nearing its end when Lincoln made his second inaugural address on March 4, 1865. Grant surrounded Lee at Petersburg, Virginia (46), and other rebel armies were in full retreat across the South when Lincoln's speech demonstrated that he was already planning for a reunited nation, saying, "With malice towards none; with charity for all; with firmness in the right, as God gives us to see the right, let us strive on to finish the work we are in; to bind up the nation's wounds; to care for him who shall have borne battle, and for his widow, and his orphan—to do all which may achieve and cherish a just and lasting peace among ourselves, and with all nations."

A little more than a month later, Lee surrendered his army. Lincoln had preserved the Union, but he had little time to enjoy his victory or to bring the country back together. On April 14, 1865, Southern sympathizer John Wilkes Booth (75) shot Lincoln while he attended a play at Washington's Ford Theater. The next morning at 7:22 a.m., the president died.

The long shadow cast by Abraham Lincoln extends over all aspects of the Civil War. Although the South would have likely seceded regardless of the outcome of the election of 1860, Lincoln symbolized the reason for the separation and the eventual war and then stood firm as probably the only American who could have held the

Union States together and led them to victory. His freeing of the slaves ended the darkest chapter in American history.

Without Lincoln, the Confederacy would have probably maintained its independence, creating two weak nations in North America rather than a single strong country. Perhaps the U.S.A. and C.S.A. would have reunited against the threat of Spain in 1898 or during the First World War. Even a reunified United States would not have so quickly achieved its position of global influence, nor assumed its role today as the single world power. Lincoln, as the most influential individual of the Civil War, is exceeded in influence only by the many events and leaders that emerged at the Battle of Antietam.

3

ULYSSES SIMPSON GRANT

Union General

1822–1885

Ulysses Simpson Grant proved himself the most influential military commander of the Civil War through his victories in the west and his final campaign where he showed superior strategic and tactical maneuvers over Robert E. Lee (5). Although described by his critics as a drunkard and a butcher for the heavy casualties he experienced, Grant understood the importance of committing entire military and economic assets to total warfare. Of all the Union generals, he was the one most responsible for the final victory that preserved the Union of the United States of America.

Neither Grant's civilian nor military beginnings were remarkable. Born the oldest of six children to a Point Pleasant, Ohio, tannery owner on April 27, 1822, Grant received an appointment to the U.S. Military Academy in 1839. Upon reporting to West Point, Grant decided to change his birth name from Hiram Ulysses to Ulysses Hiram to avoid the embarrassing initials "HUG." An administrative error on the part of the congressman who nominated him for the academy recorded the name as Ulysses Simpson. The young cadet made no effort to correct the error and readily became U. S. Grant.

Grant displayed no great potential at West Point, graduating twenty-first among thirty-nine cadets in the Class of 1843. Although horsemanship had proven to be Grant's most outstanding talent at the academy, the new lieutenant's commission was in the infantry, and he reported to the Fourth Regiment at Jefferson Barracks, Missouri, after graduation.

At the outbreak of the Mexican War in 1846, Grant and his regiment joined Zachary Taylor along the Rio Grande border. Grant participated in the early battles of the war, earning praise for his valor at the Battle of Monterrey. In 1847 his unit transferred south to join the Winfield Scott (30) invasion at Vera Cruz. Grant participated in battles at Cerro Gordo in April, Churubusco in August, and Molino del Rey and Chapultepec in September. By the time Mexico City fell, Grant had earned brevet promotion to captain and a Regular Army advancement to first lieutenant.

Grant returned to Missouri in 1848 and married Julia Dent, a local planter's daughter whom he had met during his earlier assignment to Jefferson Barracks. Frequent transfers

took the Grants to Mississippi, New York, Michigan, and the Pacific Northwest. In 1854, Grant, now a Regular Army captain, reported to Fort Humboldt, California. Unable to have his wife join him at his new assignment, Grant began—or, according to some accounts, continued—to drink heavily and shortly thereafter resigned his commission.

During the next six years Grant tried farming and various business ventures back in Missouri. None proved successful. In 1860 he moved his family to Galena, Illinois, and worked as a clerk in his father's leather store.

At the outbreak of the Civil War, Grant attempted to regain his commission in the Regular Army, but despite the massive mobilization, senior military officials showed little interest in him. Grant finally secured a militia appointment as a colonel in command of the 21st Illinois Volunteer Infantry Regiment and within two months advanced to the rank of brigadier general in command of the District of Southeast Missouri.

Grant's first combat against the rebellion produced a limited victory at Belmont, Missouri. He did not gain the attention of President Abraham Lincoln (2) and the War Department until his brilliant coordination of naval and land forces resulted in the capture of Forts Henry and Donelson (35) in northern Tennessee in February 1862. Grant's demand to the rebel commander at Fort Donelson led to his nickname "Unconditional Surrender" Grant.

In the spring of 1862, Grant received a promotion to major general and command of the Army of the Tennessee. On April 6, the Confederate army of General Albert Sidney Johnston (85) surprised the Union defenders of Shiloh, Tennessee (18), but Grant rallied his troops to beat back the rebel attack.

After Shiloh, Grant conducted several maneuvers that displayed his mastery of battlefield tactics. Using rapid movement and aggressive action, Grant fought and won a series of five battles against numerically superior forces in Mississippi as he moved his army toward Vicksburg (7). Grant again coordinated his land offensive with the U.S. Navy fleet on the Mississippi River and by June had Vicksburg surrounded on the water and on land. The city surrendered to Grant on July 4, giving the Union complete control of the Mississippi River and effectively dividing the Confederate States into two geographic, non-supporting sectors.

Following Vicksburg, Grant finally received an appointment to the Regular U.S. Army, promotion to major general, and command of the newly formed Military Division of Mississippi. In short order he took control at Chattanooga (12) and broke the rebel siege of the city. Grant did not rest after his victory; rather, he pursued the retreating rebels.

For three years, Lincoln had been looking for a general who could end the war and preserve the Union. In 1864, he determined that Grant was that man and on March 9 promoted him to lieutenant general and general in chief of the Union forces. To complaints from Regular Army officers who disliked Grant and to civilians who revived stories of Grant's drinking, Lincoln simply responded, "I need this man. He fights."

And that is exactly what Grant did. He immediately took charge, directing the entire Union war effort from the field and by telegraph. Aware that the Southerners could not match the North's manpower and other resources, Grant pursued a course of action based on attrition. He ordered William Sherman (6) to march on Atlanta (20) and Phil Sheridan (8) to neutralize the rebel forces in the Shenandoah Valley (29), while he himself accompanied George Meade's Army of the Potomac against Richmond and Robert E. Lee (5). Although a series of bloody battles at the Wilderness (62), Spotsylvania (65), and Cold Harbor (59) resulted, Grant did not achieve total victory in his initial campaign. Lee matched and, on occasion, out-generaled him, but the Confederates continued to sustain casualties they could not replace. The Confederates now had to react to Grant rather than assume any initiative of their own.

By June 1864, Grant had Lee's army besieged at Petersburg (46), twenty miles south of Richmond. The siege lasted until April 1, 1865, when Grant's victory at Five Forks, southwest of Petersburg, compromised Lee's right flank and forced him to withdraw from the city. Grant paralleled Lee's westward retreat and ordered Sheridan to cut off the withdrawal route. At Appomattox Court House on April 9, Lee recognized that he could no longer continue to fight and surrendered to Grant. The remainder of the rebel forces across the South followed suit over the next several weeks.

Grant remained in the army following the war, and in 1866 Congress authorized his promotion to the rank of full general, the only such promotion since that of George Washington in 1799. In 1868 Grant won the first of two elections as president of the United States. Marred by several scandals involving fraud by political appointees—though not by Grant himself—his presidency certainly demonstrated that he was a more successful general than statesman.

After an unsuccessful third-term campaign in 1879, Grant moved to New York City, where he soon proved that his business skills had not improved with time. He lost his entire fortune in a banking venture. Diagnosed with throat cancer, Grant spent his final days writing his autobiography, finishing it only four days before his death on July 23, 1885, at Mount McGregor, New York. The book was very successful, and its revenues adequately provided for his family's future.

Grant—short, stocky, and round-shouldered—never impressed anyone with his military bearing. A failure in nearly everything else he ever attempted, he nevertheless ranks as the most influential military commander of the Civil War. His casualty lists were long, and he did indeed, on occasion, drink to excess. Not as beloved as Lee or as flamboyant as Sheridan, Grant proved Lincoln correct that he could and would fight. He was exactly the right general at the right time. Modern "total warfare" and the survival of the Union of the United States are his legacy. Only the Battle of Antietam (1) and Lincoln exceed his influence on the outcome of the American Civil War.

4

GETTYSBURG

July 1–3, 1863

The successful stand by the United States army at Gettysburg, Pennsylvania, in July 1863 marked the "high tide" of the Confederate States of America. By turning back the second and final invasion of the North by General Robert E. Lee (5) and his Army of Northern Virginia, the Federals opened the way for the final defeat of the rebellion and the preservation of the Union.

Following the battle of Antietam (1), which had stopped Lee's first invasion of the North the previous September, the Confederate army fought a series of successful battles in Virginia, including Fredericksburg (53) and Chancellorsville (31). Despite these victories, the long war was exhausting the limited resources available within the Southern states, and the Union blockade (25) of Confederate ports continued to further limit the import of arms and supplies from Europe. Lee and President Jefferson Davis (9) decided that it was once again time to invade the North. They hoped that the invasion would permit the Army of Northern Virginia to forage the countryside and factories of Maryland and Pennsylvania to find supplies for their immediate use and to stockpile for future operations. Lee believed that he could defeat any Union army sent to intercept him, and that a victory in Federal territory would strengthen the Northern peace movement that was demanding an end to the war. The Southern leaders also still hoped a great victory might win recognition and support from European nations, despite the slavery issue.

Lee crossed the Potomac River in June 1863 and marched north into southern Pennsylvania. As with his invasion the previous year, he aimed his army toward the rail center of Harrisburg. Meanwhile in Washington, Abraham Lincoln (2), concerned about the recent Confederate victories in Virginia, fretted over the inability of his generals to defeat the rebels. When he learned of Lee's move northward, Lincoln promoted General George Meade (24), who then became the fifth commander of the Army of the Potomac in only ten months.

As soon as he assumed command, Meade maneuvered his force to intercept the Confederates. The ultimate clash between the two armies came by chance rather than by design when Confederate general A. P. Hill (26) learned about the possibility of a Gettysburg factory where he might find much-needed shoes for his infantrymen. On

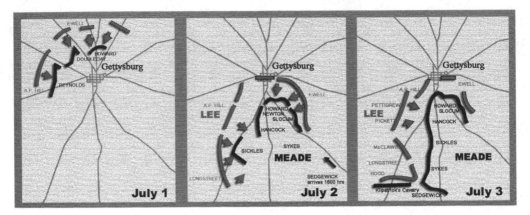

July 1, just west of town, a Union cavalry patrol came upon the advancing rebels and, although badly outnumbered, held the line until additional rebel troops under General Richard Ewell arrived and pushed them back through Gettysburg and onto Cemetery Ridge and Culp's Hill. Ewell, who had replaced the famous Stonewall Jackson (36) after Jackson was killed, was not as aggressive as his predecessor and failed to act on the opportunity to roll up the exposed Union flank. Lee arrived in time to order Ewell to attack "if practicable," but the reluctant general felt it was not practical and conceded his assault against the enemy flank.

During the late afternoon and evening of July 1, the remaining Confederate and Union units converged on Gettysburg. Unfortunately for Lee, his cavalry commander J. E. B. Stuart (23) was off on a raid of his own and unaware of the developing battle around the Pennsylvania town. Without Stuart, Lee had little reconnaissance and intelligence-gathering capability.

By the morning of July 2, Meade had his Union army of ninety thousand arrayed in a fishhook pattern running from "the hook" on Culp's Hill in the north for three miles southward along Cemetery Ridge to Little Round Top. Across an open field three-quarters of a mile to the west stood Lee's seventy-six thousand-man army along the high ground of Seminary Ridge.

Previous Civil War battles had validated what military commanders had learned throughout the ages—the advantage lies with the defense, especially when the defenders outnumbered the attackers. In recognition of this adage and his observations of the Union defenses to his front, General James Longstreet (13), the commander of Lee's right flank, advised against an attack. Lee nevertheless ordered Longstreet to advance toward Little Round Top, believing that if he could secure this high ground, the Confederate artillery could place enfilade fire on the Union lines and easily turn their flank.

The initial Union line in front of Little Round Top was out of position and gave way early to the assault; however, other regiments quickly filled the gap and occupied the coveted high ground. After a bloody, close battle, the Federal infantry forced Longstreet's advance to withdraw.

Having failed in the attacks on both the Union's left and right flanks, Lee now decided to assault the enemy center. When Longstreet again expressed his opposition, Lee responded, "The enemy is there, and I am going to attack him there."

On the morning of July 3, Lee ordered a division led by George Pickett (93) from Longstreet's command and two additional divisions from A. P. Hill's corps to advance against the Union center. Although all three divisions made this move, it would forever be known as Pickett's Charge.

A preparatory Confederate artillery barrage proved mostly ineffective against the Union defenses spread along the long ridge line. The fifteen thousand rebel soldiers began their long march at 3 p.m. across the open field. For three-quarters of a mile, the two hundred guns of the Federal artillery shredded the long gray line. At two hundred meters, the Union infantrymen poured musket shots into the advancing rebels as they shouted "Fredericksburg! Remember Fredericksburg!" Despite the carnage, the disciplined Confederates made it to the Union defenses and even broke through briefly before reinforcements threw them back from what became known as "the high tide of the Confederacy."

Less than half of the assault force staggered back to Seminary Ridge. Lee met the survivors saying, "It's all my fault...I'm sorry." The three-day fight left more than twenty-three thousand of Lee's best troops dead, wounded, captured, or missing. Meade's casualties totaled about the same.

Lee anticipated a Union counterattack on the morning of July 4, but Meade, both cautious and uncomfortable in a command that he had held for mere days, was satisfied with a partial victory. He did not pursue Lee's army as it retreated back to Virginia, even though the flooded Potomac would have aided an attack.

Some accounts blame the loss at Gettysburg on Stuart for his being absent and not providing Lee with sufficient information early in the battle. Others point at Longstreet for his reluctance. The real blame, however, belongs to Lee for piecemealing his attack and for assaulting across open ground into the heart of the Union defenses. Even accounts that Lee was ill or suffering heart problems cannot excuse his flawed tactics and deplorable decisions.

After Gettysburg, the South was never again able to resume effective offensive operations. Although fighting continued for nearly two more years, the Confederacy took its first steps down the road to becoming a Lost Cause when it suffered defeat at Gettysburg.

Gettysburg is the best-known battle of the Civil War, and it was more influential on the war's outcome than Vicksburg (7), which was fought at the same time. Yet it remains less pivotal than Antietam, which was fought the previous year. Antietam established that the Confederacy would have to stand alone without support from Europe; Gettysburg proved that it could not.

5

ROBERT EDWARD LEE

Confederate General

1807–1870

Robert Edward Lee, through strategic brilliance and inspired leadership, turned the Confederate States from a hollow boast into a viable threat to the Union of the United States. His innovations in the use of field fortifications and in maneuvers—nearly always against larger, better equipped armies—allowed him to consistently achieve victories. The loyalty and affection he received from his soldiers and his Southern compatriots extended beyond the war and the Lost Cause, earning Lee the reputation as the most influential leader of the Confederacy and one of America's most revered military commanders.

Lee was born on January 19, 1807, at Stratford, Virginia, the son of a Revolutionary War hero and one of the state's most distinguished families. He graduated second in his West Point class of 1829 with the distinction of having never received a single demerit. An officer of tremendous discipline and presence, Lee, who stood nearly six feet tall, did not smoke, drink, or swear; he placed his honor and religion above all else.

During his initial army assignments as an engineer, Lee performed well in building forts and harbors but exhibited no exceptional talents. It was not until the Mexican War began in 1845 that he experienced his first combat that foreshadowed his future brilliance. As a member of General Winfield Scott's (30) staff, Lee led a reconnaissance that discovered a flanking route through which the Americans could defeat the Mexicans at Cerro Gordo in April 1847. The following September, Lee planned the artillery support for the battle of Chapultepec that opened the way for victory at Mexico City. By the end of the war Lee had been wounded once and had earned three brevets for gallantry. Scott later wrote that Lee "was the best soldier I ever saw in the field."

Following the Mexican War, Lee served in several cavalry regiments before his appointment as superintendent of West Point in 1852. While at the Military Academy, he improved the academic curriculum and instructional methods that influenced future graduates who occupied important positions on both sides in the

Civil War. His three-year tenure was also noteworthy for his dismissal of future artist James McNeill Whistler for academic deficiencies.

Lee was in Washington, D.C., in 1859 and led the small force that ended John Brown's (54) raid on Harpers Ferry and the abolitionist's hopes of igniting a slave rebellion. A year later he assumed command of the army in the Department of Texas and remained there until the outbreak of the war in 1861. In April of that year, Winfield Scott, now in overall command of the U.S. Army, recalled Lee to Washington where President Abraham Lincoln (2) offered him command of the Union field forces. Despite more than thirty years' service in the U.S. Army and his personal objections to secession and slavery, Lee turned down the offer, stating that he could not take up arms against his native state of Virginia.

Lee resigned from the U.S. Army on April 25, 1861, to accept an appointment as commander of Virginia's forces, but he did not immediately become involved in combat operations. For several months he supervised the mobilization of his state's militia and the fortification of key sites. In August he joined the staff of President Jefferson Davis (9) as a personal advisor. It was not until the wounding of Joseph E. Johnston (17) in May 1862 that Lee assumed command of what he renamed the Army of Northern Virginia.

During the next four years Lee demonstrated his extraordinary talents in maneuvering his forces and in recognizing his enemy's intentions and weaknesses. He orchestrated the deployment of his advance forces, the commitment of his limited reserves, the use of interior lines of communications, and the distribution of supplies with such skills that military students still study his techniques today. Lee also used his engineering expertise to develop and employ field fortifications to gain defensive advantages and to force his opponents to move against his strengths.

Lee's greatest asset was his demeanor as a calm man who rarely raised his voice or expressed his anger—he even referred to the enemy as "those people" rather than "Yankees" or in other negative terms. "Marse Robert," as he was called by many of his men, inspired loyalty, confidence, and affection among his soldiers who held him in near godlike esteem. This same leadership style, however, was also one of Lee's greatest liabilities. It limited his control over his subordinate generals such as James Longstreet (13) and J. E. B. Stuart (23), whose insubordination and independence occasionally caused Lee's plans to go awry or to fail.

Soon after taking command of the Army of Northern Virginia, Lee turned back George McClellan's (51) numerically superior force that threatened Richmond. He then moved north and routed the Union force at Second Bull Run (40) on August

28–30, 1862. Lee then decided not to attack heavily defended Washington, D.C., but rather to take the war into the Northern states.

Lee's first venture into Northern territory failed miserably. The North and South met in the war's single bloodiest day at Antietam Creek (1) on September 16–18, 1862. Although neither side achieved a clear-cut victory and Union and Confederate casualties were about equal, the battle forced Lee to withdraw back to Virginia.

Lee's skills in fortifications and use of terrain gained a decisive victory at Fredericksburg (53) in December 1862, and his brilliant counterattack, led by Stonewall Jackson's (36) flanking movement, again defeated the Union army at Chancellorsville (31) the following spring. Boosted by his victories in spite of the mortal wounding of Stonewall Jackson at Chancellorsville, Lee decided to once again invade the North. At Gettysburg, Pennsylvania (4), Lee, out of contact with his cavalry and without the total support of his subordinate generals who were reluctant to attack, ordered his army across a three-quarter-mile-wide open field into the strength of the Union defenses.

By the end of the three-day-long battle on July 3, more than twenty-eight thousand Confederates were dead, wounded, or missing. Lee admitted to one of his subordinates, "All this has been my fault, it is I that have lost this fight." He turned his army back toward Virginia where he offered his resignation to President Davis, who refused it.

The Confederacy had reached its "high water mark" at Gettysburg, but the South and Lee were far from defeated. In a brilliant series of defensive actions during 1864 at the Wilderness (62), Spotsylvania (65), and Cold Harbor (59), Lee made successful stands against the new Union commander, U. S. Grant (3). Lee's skills in anticipating Grant's moves and in deploying the diminishing Confederate resources prolonged the war and the life of the Confederacy—and added to the death toll.

By April 1865, the Union controlled the Mississippi River, occupied Atlanta (20), and surrounded Lee's army at Petersburg (46). Although Lee managed a breakout and withdrew to the west, Grant paralleled the rebel army before finally blocking its retreat at Appomattox Court House. On April 9, Lee told his staff, "There is nothing left for me to do but to go and see General Grant, and I would rather die a thousand deaths." Within a month after Lee's surrender, all the remaining rebel forces also capitulated. The Confederacy was no more.

Under the generous terms of the surrender, Lee returned home. In the fall of 1865, he assumed the presidency of Washington College, now Washington and Lee University, in Lexington, Virginia. He died there of heart disease at age sixty-three on October 12, 1870. In 1975, more than a century later, the U.S. Congress voted to posthumously restore Lee's citizenship.

Undoubtedly, Lee was the most influential of the Confederate leaders, including President Davis, both during and after the war. He remains a military hero respected and studied for his strategic skills in fighting larger, better supplied armies and for his personal appeal in generating the adoration and near worship of his army. He is an icon for military proficiency and dignity. Yet, despite the South's immortalization of their leader, Lee ranks below the victors—Grant, who ultimately defeated him on the battlefield, and Lincoln, who demanded and insured that the Union be preserved. Lee well earned his legacy as the symbol of the South and its pride, but the cause he so brilliantly represented was truly a lost one.

6

WILLIAM TECUMSEH SHERMAN

Union General

1820–1891

William Tecumseh Sherman was one of the few Civil War commanders who proved a better strategic than tactical commander. He excelled in leading large rather than small commands. He rightfully earned the reputation as one of the war's best and most famous generals—usurped only by his friend and mentor U. S. Grant (3)—for introducing the concept of "total war" to the Confederacy and to the world.

Born on February 8, 1820, at Lancaster, Ohio, into a family of judges and statesmen, Sherman was orphaned at age nine and reared by U.S. senator and cabinet officer Thomas Ewing, whose daughter he eventually married. Only five of the forty-two cadets in the West Point Class of 1840 graduated ahead of Sherman, who accepted a commission in the artillery. During the next thirteen years he served honorably but without distinction in the Seminole War and in California during the Mexican War.

Sherman resigned from the army in 1853 to remain in California, first as a banker and then as a lawyer. Neither career proved particularly successful. In 1859 he accepted the position of superintendent of a military school that later became Louisiana State University. Sherman liked the South but made his loyalties clear when the state seceded from the Union in 1861. In a letter of resignation to the governor of Louisiana, he wrote, "On no earthly account will I do any act or think any thought hostile to the United States."

Sherman moved to St. Louis, where he worked briefly as the head of a streetcar company before accepting an appointment as an infantry colonel. He led a brigade at First Bull Run (10) and then transferred to Kentucky where he became first the deputy and then the commander of the Department of the Cumberland. In this position, he expressed differences with Lincoln's administration about how the war was being fought, quarreled with his superiors concerning the lack of replacements, and made enemies with the press, whom he saw more as spies than journalists.

By early 1862, Sherman's enemies, both in uniform and in the press, cast doubts about the general's sanity. Sherman did indeed have frequent emotional outbursts, but in an army having difficulties finding commanders who would fight, he continued to

advance in rank. He commanded a division at Shiloh (18) in April 1862, even after being wounded.

During this period Sherman came to the attention of U. S. Grant, who recognized that, despite his reputation as "crazy," the general was the kind of leader who could win the war. Grant used Sherman in the assault against Vicksburg (7). By the end of the battle and siege, the Union had captured the city and blocked the rebels' use of the Mississippi River; Grant had earned command of all the U.S. Army. Sherman took charge of the Military Division of the Mississippi, effectively assuming the leadership of all Union operations in the Western Theater.

Sherman's leadership had been notable, but his overall results were mixed before this assumption of command. He quickly, however, proved to be a master of large unit operations and displayed his strategic abilities in forming plans to end the war. In May 1864, he began a one-hundred-mile march toward Atlanta (20). Over the next two and a half months, Sherman consistently outmaneuvered the Confederate army units he encountered and then captured the prize. Understanding the value of the city as well as the need to break the resolve of the Southern people, Sherman ordered Atlanta evacuated and then burned. When the city's mayor wrote a letter requesting the order be revoked, Sherman replied that his orders were not "to meet the humanities of the case" but rather were issued in order "to prepare for future struggles."

Continuing this philosophy of total war, Sherman deployed blocking positions to protect his gains and then led the rest of his army eastward in what became known as the March to the Sea (16). In a letter to Grant on September 9, Sherman promised to "make Georgia howl." He then issued Special Field Order Number 120 in preparation for the march, stating, "In districts and neighborhoods where the army is unmolested, no destruction of property should be permitted; but should guerrillas or bushwhackers molest our march, or should the inhabitants burn bridges, obstruct roads, or otherwise manifest hostility, then army commanders should order and enforce a devastation more or less relentless.... The army will forage liberally on the country."

Along the way Sherman and his army were indeed "more or less relentless," covering a path forty to sixty miles wide from Atlanta to the sea. They destroyed rebel units, devastated farms and industries that supplied the Confederates, freed slaves they found, and generally terrorized the civilian population. Sherman's army captured Savannah in time for the general to telegraph Abraham Lincoln (2) that he was presenting the city to the president as a "Christmas present."

Sherman continued his march of destruction to Columbia, South Carolina, and captured that city on February 16, 1865. Confederate commander Wade Hampton (69) later accused Sherman of being responsible for burning the city to the ground, but in reality the destructive fires probably spread from burning cotton that the withdrawing rebels set ablaze to prevent its capture. From Columbia, Sherman pursued the remnants of the Confederate army. Two weeks after Grant's victory at Appomattox, Sherman accepted the surrender of the remaining rebel forces in the eastern theater.

By all accounts, Sherman was a careful planner with a powerful sense of orderliness. Despite these characteristics, photographs usually show him unkempt and wild-eyed. During the final weeks of the war, Union staff officer Theodore Lyman described Sherman as "the concentrated quintessence of Yankeedom...tall, spare, sinewy, with a very long neck, and a big head. All his features express determination, particularly the mouth."

"He is a very homely man, with a regular nest of wrinkles in his face, which play and twist as he eagerly talks on each subject; but his expression is pleasant and kindly," Lyman's description continued.

Sherman remained in uniform after the war. He succeeded Grant as commander in chief of the army in March 1869, a position he held for the next fourteen years. He increased his reputation for toughness as he enforced Reconstruction policies in the South and led the war against the Native Americans on the western frontier. During this period he made many public speeches, including one at Columbus, Ohio, on August 12, 1880, where he is attributed with saying, "War is hell." In 1884 he established the Command School at Fort Leavenworth, Kansas, that continues today to train military commanders.

Sherman retired to New York City on February 8, 1884, and refused all offers to enter politics. Shortly after his retirement, the Republican Party pursued him as a presidential candidate. In a statement typical of the general he responded, "If nominated I will not accept. If elected, I will not serve."

In 1885 he published his memoirs and then the following year moved back to St. Louis. He died there on February 14, 1891, and is buried in Cavalry Cemetery. Among those attending his funeral was Joseph E. Johnston (17), the Confederate general who had opposed Sherman in his final battles.

Sherman's March to the Sea generated such hatred against the general that the feelings continue to this day. Despite what his detractors say, Sherman and his harsh measures certainly shortened the war and achieved victory for the North. He introduced a method of waging combat that gained the attention of military planners around the world. In the Franco-Prussian War in the 1870s, both sides, particularly the Prussians, studied and applied many of Sherman's concepts of "total war." These measures have continued in every conflict since. Warfare has never been the same.

Following only Grant and Robert E. Lee (5), Sherman is by far the most influential military leader of the war. In terms of lasting influence, Sherman may even exceed his friend and mentor Grant and his opponent Lee. Sherman had both the understanding and willingness to conduct war with nothing but victory as the goal.

7

VICKSBURG

May 18–July 4, 1863

The victory by the Union army at Vicksburg on July 4, 1863, eliminated the primary obstacle to its control of the Mississippi River and divided the Confederacy into two non-mutually supporting sectors. Vicksburg also established U. S. Grant (3) as a superior general, a step that led to his eventual overall command of the Union army which, in turn, led to the defeat of Robert E. Lee (5) and the end of the rebellion.

Most of the major battles fought during the first two years of the Civil War took place in the East, but the western Confederate States were vital as a source of manpower and supplies. The Confederates moved much of these resources by watercraft along the part of the Mississippi River they controlled from northern Tennessee to the Gulf of Mexico. Union leaders recognized the need to sever this transportation line as well as the advantages of controlling the river for their own transfer of troops and supplies.

To control movement on the Mississippi, the U.S. Navy blockaded its Gulf entrance and dispatched low-draft gunboats northward to open the waterway. At the same time, Union vessels moved southward from Illinois to occupy the northern portion of the vast river. These warships were mostly unopposed on the water as the South had few boats of their own. However, rebel fortifications armed with heavy cannons dominated high ground along the river, blocking the navigation of the Union flotillas. As a result, the Union had to coordinate its naval operations with ground operations to neutralize these enemy strongholds.

In February 1862, Union forces led by Grant captured Forts Henry and Donelson (35) to take command of the Tennessee and Cumberland Rivers, blocking the Confederates' water access into the Tennessee interior. Captain David Farragut (14) captured New Orleans the following April. The United States now held both ends of the Mississippi River, but the Confederate States still controlled its interior by way of a series of forts along its banks, with the strongest perched high on the cliffs of Vicksburg, Mississippi. President Abraham Lincoln (2) understood the city's importance, declaring, "Vicksburg is the key! The war can never be brought to a close until that key is in our pocket."

Lincoln, always looking for aggressive generals, awarded Grant a promotion to command the Army of the Tennessee after his capture of Fort Donelson. Grant then moved

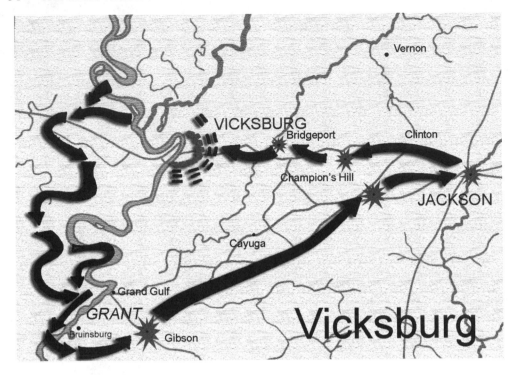

south but quickly discovered that he faced a formidable foe. Not only did he encounter the powerful guns on the Vicksburg bluffs, but also Confederate forces, commanded by Generals Joseph Johnston (17) and John Pemberton, equal in size to his own.

Despite the strong opposition, from January through March 1863, Grant made four unsuccessful attempts to capture or at least isolate Vicksburg. These operations even included an attempt to dig a canal across the bend of the river below the city to bypass its defenses. Confederate raids on the Union supply lines further delayed Grant's offensive.

Finally in April, Grant devised an elaborate plan integrating the land and naval forces that would spread out and weaken the Confederate defenses. Under the cover of darkness on the night of April 16, Admiral David Porter sailed south past the Vicksburg batteries with twelve vessels, losing one to enemy fire. The next day, General Benjamin Grierson led a Union cavalry division out of La Grange, Tennessee, on a sixteen-day raid through central Mississippi toward Baton Rouge, Louisiana. On April 22, a supply flotilla slipped past the Vicksburg guns and joined the Union fleet south of the city. Another diversionary attack took place against Haines's Bluff, northeast of Vicksburg, on April 29–30. Confederate units deployed to counter these actions, but in doing so they fragmented their defenses, just as Grant had hoped.

Meanwhile, Grant moved the bulk of his army by land down the western bank of the Mississippi past Vicksburg to the village of Hard Times, Louisiana. There, under the protection of Porter's gunboats, he transported his army across the river into Mississippi. By May 7, Grant had assembled an army of forty-one thousand men who were prepared to move against the southern and eastern approaches to Vicksburg. Before advancing against the city, Grant ensured the security of his rear by first attacking the Confederate forces defending Jackson, Mississippi, fifty miles east of the river, on May 14. He quickly routed the rebels and forced them to retreat.

Grant left a small detachment in Jackson to destroy captured Confederate supplies while he turned the bulk of his army west toward Vicksburg. The rebels briefly delayed his advance on May 16 at Champion's Hill, but the Union army reached the outskirts of Vicksburg on the 19th.

Pemberton had only about thirty thousand soldiers to oppose Grant's seventy thousand, but the Confederates had the advantage of nine miles of defensive trenches surrounding the city. On May 17 and again on May 22, Grant assaulted the defenses, only to be beaten back. After the second attack failed, Grant decided to settle into a siege. With Porter's gunboats preventing any resupply by water and his army blocking land access to the city, Grant planned to starve Vicksburg into submission. To hasten their surrender, he initiated a sustained artillery bombardment.

The cannon fire, combined with hunger and disease, forced Pemberton to surrender on July 4. Over the next few days, the other Confederate fortifications along the river also gave up or withdrew. Grant sent word to Washington that the Mississippi River was now open from the Union states in the North all the way to the Gulf of Mexico. It would remain so for the rest of the war.

During the final days of Vicksburg, the much more publicized Battle of Gettysburg (4) was concluding in Pennsylvania with a Union victory. Gettysburg ended Confederate offensive operations in the East while Vicksburg opened the way for the defeat of the rebels in the West and Deep South. Gettysburg was more influential in that it stopped Robert E. Lee's threat against Washington, D.C., but Vicksburg hastened the end of the war by dividing the Confederacy into Eastern and Western sections. Equally important, it provided the Union with a route for men and supplies to push the war into Georgia. While neither Gettysburg nor Vicksburg were as influential as Antietam (1), they helped form the triad of major battles that saved the Union and defeated the Confederacy.

8

PHILIP HENRY SHERIDAN

Union General

1831–1888

Philip Henry Sheridan earned the title of the war's greatest cavalryman and joins U. S. Grant (3) and William Sherman (6) as one of the trio of military leaders who saved the Union. Besides leading horsemen, Sheridan planned and spearheaded the operation into Virginia's Shenandoah Valley (29) that defeated the region's Confederate army. While there, he destroyed crops and other resources that fueled the rebellion.

In his postwar memoirs, Sheridan claimed he was born in Albany, New York, on March 6, 1831, to recently arrived Irish immigrants. The date and parental information may be correct, but the exact place of his birth is a mystery, for in his lifetime, he claimed not only Albany but also Boston and Somerset, Ohio, as his birthplace. It is, however, confirmed by records that he lived in Somerset as a boy and worked briefly as a clerk in a country store before securing an appointment to West Point.

Sheridan's career at the military academy was less than distinguished. He was accepted only because the original appointee failed the entrance examination. He spent an extra year at the Academy as punishment for threatening an upperclassman with a bayonet and then assaulting him with his fists.

After finally graduating as an infantry second lieutenant and thirty-fourth of fifty-two in the Class of 1853, Sheridan reported to Texas for duty on the Rio Grande. Three years later he transferred to the Oregon Territory where he performed well in several engagements with hostile Indians. He advanced to first lieutenant only when officers leaving the U.S. Army for the newly formed Confederacy in 1861 resigned.

After the outbreak of the war, Sheridan held several administrative and logistical positions in St. Louis and the surrounding region. Despite being threatened with court martial for issuing vouchers in exchange for supplies taken from Southern sympathizers, he was promoted to captain. Over the next year he earned the friendship and trust of several senior officers, including Sherman and Gordon Granger. When Granger was promoted in the spring of 1862, he recommended Sheridan as his replacement in command of the 2nd Michigan Cavalry. On May 25, 1862, Sheridan jumped from infantry captain to cavalry colonel and began his rapid advance in command of Union horse soldiers.

A month later, using superior repeating rifles and deception about the size of his force, Sheridan defeated a rebel force at Booneville, Mississippi, that outnumbered him more than six to one. The fight earned him command of a division and the star of a brigadier general at the age of thirty-one. He continued his stellar leadership in the fall of 1862 at the battles of Perryville, Kentucky, and Murfreesboro, Tennessee. In 1863, Sheridan fought with Grant and Sherman in the battles of Chickamauga (74), Missionary Ridge, and Lookout Mountain near Chattanooga, Tennessee.

The young general's performance so impressed Grant that, after he assumed command of all of the Union army, he called Sheridan east to lead the twelve thousand-man cavalry corps of the Army of the Potomac in April 1864. A month later on May 7, Sheridan defeated the leading Confederate cavalry commander General J. E. B. Stuart (23) at Todd's Tavern. Four days after that his troops mortally wounded the rebel general at Yellow Tavern.

Sheridan's Irish temper made him few friends among his fellow generals, but Grant greatly respected him and, recognizing the warrior ethos of Sheridan, continued to add to his responsibilities. In August, Grant gave Sheridan command of the Middle Military Division which contained all Union forces in the Shenandoah Valley. After a month of planning and preparation, Sheridan defeated the army of Jubal A. Early (19) at Winchester on September 19. Instead of pursuing Early, Sheridan began a "scorched-earth" campaign to destroy the rich area known as the "breadbasket of the Confederacy." He later claimed that a crow flying over the region would have to carry its own provisions.

In a report written in October, Sheridan explained, "I would rather win by burning a man's farm than by killing his sons."

He also claimed, "I have destroyed over two thousand barns filled with wheat, hay, and farming implements, over seventy mills filled with flour and wheat; have driven in front of the army over four thousand head of stock; and have killed and issued to the troops not less than three thousand sheep. The people here are getting sick of war."

By "the people here" he meant the Virginia civilians of the Valley. Sheridan, like Sherman in Georgia, understood that the war would be won not only on the battlefield but also in the countryside by the destruction of the enemies' supplies, morale, and supporters. In the midst of one of his final Valley campaigns, Sheridan wrote, "I will soon commence on Louden County and let them know there is a God in Israel."

Sheridan did not only take the war to the civilian residents of the Valley, but also he continued to defeat the rebels on the field of battle. When Early counterattacked at Cedar Creek on October 19, Sheridan was on his way back from a visit to Washington. In a mad dash to rally his army against the attack, he rode at full speed for more than fifteen miles in what was later immortalized in verse as "Sheridan's Ride" by Thomas Buchanan Read.

In February 1865, Sheridan joined Grant in the assault of Lee's positions in the Petersburg Campaign (46). It was Sheridan's defeat of George Pickett (93) at Five Forks on April 1 that cut off rail supplies to Lee and forced the Army of Northern Virginia to retreat westward. Sheridan also participated in the defeat of rebels at Saylor's Creek on April 6 and then raced to block the rebels at the Appomattox Court House, which forced Lee's surrender to Grant.

Sheridan was appreciated, if not liked, by his troops, who called him "Little Phil," an apt title for the five foot, five inch tall general. Staff officer Theodore Lyman described him near the end of the war as "a small, broad-shouldered, squat man with black hair and a square head."

Following the war, Sheridan led a "show-of-force" expedition to the Texas-Mexico border to deter any expansion thoughts of Maximilian's French occupation government. He then headed Reconstruction efforts in Texas and Louisiana until reassigned in September 1867 because of his harsh enforcement of government regulations.

In 1867–1868 Sheridan commanded the Department of Missouri during campaigns against the Plains Indians. He offered his opinion of warfare of this period when he said, "The only good Indians I ever saw were dead." Conversely, Sheridan showed a compassionate side when he led efforts to have Yellowstone declared a national park.

In 1870 Sheridan sailed to Europe, where he acted as an official observer of the Franco-Prussian War. Shortly after returning home, he commanded the U.S. troops who fought the Great Chicago Fire and guarded against looting in October 1871. He then returned to duty in the West before succeeding Sherman as the army's commanding general in 1884.

Sheridan died on August 5, 1888, at Nonquitt, Massachusetts, shortly after publishing his memoirs. He is buried in Arlington National Cemetery.

As the Union's youngest senior commander, Sheridan earned the loyalty of his men and the respect of his superiors for his aggressive tactics and detailed use of reconnaissance and intelligence. His influence as the war's best cavalry commander was confirmed by the defeat and death of Stuart. His understanding and execution of the concept of taking the war to the civilian population gained him control of the Shenandoah Valley and ultimately helped end the war.

Only Grant and Sherman exceeded Sheridan's influence on the Union side. Lee outranks Sheridan, not in battlefield performance but rather in sainthood status in the South during the war and Lee's elevation to a godlike figure in the postwar period.

9

JEFFERSON DAVIS

President, Confederate States of America

1808–1889

Jefferson Davis was the first, last, and only president of the Confederate States of America. No one ever questioned his courage, integrity, loyalty, or sincerity. However, he was never popular during his time in office, garnering criticism for his dictatorial and autocratic leadership as well as for the mismanagement of his generals. Ultimately hailed as a hero of the Lost Cause, Davis performed as well as anyone could have in the same circumstances.

Born on June 3, 1808, on a farm in Christian County, Kentucky, Davis was the youngest of ten children. As a small boy he moved with his family to St. Mary Parish, Louisiana, in 1811 and on to Wilkinson County, Mississippi, the following year. He attended Jefferson College at Washington, Mississippi, and Transylvania University in Lexington, Kentucky, before accepting an appointment in 1824 to the U.S. Military Academy. Davis, commissioned into the infantry, graduated number twenty-three of thirty-three cadets in the Class of 1828.

For the next seven years Davis served at various posts on the northwest frontier and saw his first combat in the Black Hawk War. In 1835, Davis married Sarah Taylor, daughter of his commander Zachary Taylor, who would later become a general and president of the United States. Davis resigned his commission two weeks after his marriage and returned to Mississippi. Three months later Sarah Davis contracted malaria and died. Davis also had the disease but recovered to take charge of Bierfield Plantation in Warren County, Mississippi. Over the next eight years, Davis became a wealthy planter while he read and studied political science. After an unsuccessful campaign for a seat in the Mississippi House in 1843, he won election to the U.S. Senate the following year. In 1845, he married Varina Howard, the daughter of a socially prominent Mississippi family.

Davis resigned his Senate seat in 1846 to accept a commission as colonel of Mississippi volunteers in the Mexican War. Joining his former father-in-law Zachary Taylor, Davis fought with distinction at Monterrey, where he was wounded, and at Buena Vista. When offered a promotion to brigadier general in the federal army,

Davis declined, stating that the power of promoting militia officers belonged solely to the states, not to the federal government.

Davis returned to the U.S. Senate in 1847, and in 1852 he was appointed secretary of war as a reward for his support in the successful presidential campaign of Franklin Pierce that year. When Pierce failed to win reelection four years later, Davis once again ran for and won a Senate seat. Davis became known in the Senate as a great supporter and spokesman for the Southern states, advocating the expansion of slavery, even the resumption of importing slaves that Congress had banned in 1808.

Despite these views, Davis spoke against secession and believed that the South could exist as "a country within a country." He stood by this position even after the election of Abraham Lincoln (2) and the departure of South Carolina from the Union. Not until January 21, 1861, when Mississippi seceded, did Davis resign his Senate seat. In an eloquent departure speech, he expressed his regrets for any hard feelings and wished his Northern counterparts well.

Back home in Mississippi, Davis accepted an appointment as a major general in the state militia. Before he could assume his duties, representatives meeting in Montgomery selected him to be the provisional president of the Confederacy. Davis was not the group's first choice, but rather a compromise candidate between the extremists and moderates.

Davis was not happy about the appointment and his wife described his reaction as "so grieved that I feared some evil had befallen our family."

Despite his misgivings, Davis accepted and was later elected to a six-year term. On February 22, 1861, at his inauguration in Richmond, Davis voiced hopes that there would be no war between the North and South, stating, "All we ask is to be left alone."

One of Davis's first actions as president was to appoint a Peace Commission with the objective of preventing an armed conflict. Knowing, however, that peace was unlikely, he also appointed military leaders. From the beginning, Davis faced difficulties. He knew that a well-organized central government would be necessary to defend the Confederacy, but he was also aware that the states had seceded to escape such a governing force. The Confederate Constitution, much like the document of the United States that it copied, contained the same provisions for states' rights that had been the South's legal basis for secession.

When the war began, Davis found some state governors unwilling to dispatch their militias anywhere outside their own borders. The governor of Georgia even declared that his state would secede from the Confederacy and fight both the North and South if his militia was removed from his control.

The states finally yielded to a degree of central control when they realized that the survival of the Confederacy depended upon joint action. As the war progressed, Davis assumed additional responsibilities in running the government and the military. Complaints about his concentration of powers became so widespread that some Southerners discussed impeachment because of Davis's violation of states' rights. They were unhappy to realize that they had traded one central government for another. Others railed against him for his continued support of his old Mexican War friend Braxton Bragg (60), because he lacked of control of his generals, and for granting Lee permission to invade the North twice.

General Pierre G. T. Beauregard (43) summarized the problems of both Davis and the Confederate States after the war was finally over when he said, "We needed for president either a military man of high order, or a politician of the first-class without military pretensions. The South did not fall crushed by the mere weight of the North; but it was nibbled away at all sides and ends, because its executive head never gathered and wielded its great strength under the ready advantages that greatly reduced or neutralized its adversary's physical superiority."

Neither Beauregard nor others who opposed Davis admitted that the very basis on which the Confederacy stood—states' rights—was exactly the factor that prevented Davis or anyone else as its president from leading the South to victory. Also, despite the general's claims of being "nibbled away," the reality was that the South faced an enemy far superior in manpower, industry, and manufacturing supported by a U.S. president who vowed to preserve the Union.

Davis mostly ignored the criticism throughout the war, remaining unyielding, dour, and humorless. Although an excellent orator and a frequent visitor to the field to bolster troop morale, he remained unwilling and unable to pander to his electorate or to public opinion. He did not have to consider reelection because the Confederacy did not complete his first term. Davis, despite illness that reduced his strength and eyesight, remained passionately committed to the Confederacy until the very end. He refused to consider surrender and remained in Richmond until Union troops neared the city on April 3, 1865. Fleeing south, he reached Irwinsville, Georgia, before his capture by Union troops on May 10.

Davis's captors took him to Fort Monroe, Virginia, where he was imprisoned in an unheated, damp cell. For a brief time they placed him in irons while the U.S. Supreme Court considered charges. A year after his capture, the U.S. finally charged Davis with treason, but the Court never set a trial date. Leaders in both the North and the South lobbied for his release. Two years after his capture, Union officials released Davis on bail, and in February 1869, the United States dropped all charges against the former Confederate president.

In 1869, Davis accepted a position as president of the Carolina Insurance Company in Memphis, Tennessee. The following year he presided at the memorial for Robert E. Lee in Richmond. In 1881 he returned to Mississippi where, at his residence near Biloxi, he spent his final years writing about the Confederacy.

Davis died on December 6, 1889, in New Orleans. After ceremonies in Louisiana, a special train conveyed his body across the South, stopping many times for additional honors and ceremonies, before his final burial in Richmond's Hollywood Cemetery.

Although still blamed by many for the failure of the Confederate States, by the time of his death Davis had become a hero of the Lost Cause, ranking only behind Lee as the most beloved leader of the South.

Davis has only one contemporary head-of-state on this list. While he did about as well as anyone could have under the circumstances, his influence on the war pales in comparison to that of Abraham Lincoln. Lincoln's election help start the war, but his leadership also helped to end it. On the other hand, Davis opposed the war in the beginning and then did his best to ensure the survival of the Confederacy. He failed, but it is questionable that he could have handled his challenges better.

10

FIRST BULL RUN

July 21, 1861

When the Union army assaulted the Confederate lines along Bull Run Creek outside Manassas, Virginia, on July 21, 1861, its leaders were confident of an easy victory that would lead to a quick conclusion to the Southern rebellion. By the end of the day, the Northern troops were in a chaotic retreat back toward Washington and the rebels were celebrating a victory that they thought foreshadowed the guarantee of their independence.

After the Confederate takeover of Fort Sumter (50) led to further division of the former United States, President Lincoln (2) called for volunteers to preserve the Union. Meanwhile, in the South, men flocked to join the militias with fantasies of defending their states and relishing what they thought would be the glory of a short war. After a few brief battles that were little more than skirmishes over the next few weeks, both sides avoided a major confrontation because neither had yet organized an army of any size.

To consolidate their control of Virginia and to protect their newly established capital in Richmond, Confederate leaders placed Joseph E. Johnston (17) in command of its troops around Harpers Ferry in what is now West Virginia. Johnston's second in command, Pierre Beauregard (43), took part of that army to prepare defenses along Bull Run Creek in order to protect the rail center at Manassas.

By the end of July, thousands of soldiers in blue uniforms were camped on the outskirts of Washington. All shared a zeal for fighting the rebels but few had any battlefield experience. Most of the militiamen had enlisted for only three months and were nearing their discharge dates. Despite the army's lack of preparedness and stability, Northern newspapers called for revenge for Fort Sumter and declared their goal in their headlines: "On to Richmond." Lincoln—faced with pressure from the press and politicians and keenly aware that most of his army would soon be returning to civilian life—gave orders to assume the offensive.

On July 18, 1861, the Union army of about thirty-five thousand under General Irwin McDowell (80) marched toward Manassas. Civilians, both men and women, accompanied the army on horseback and in carriages. They brought their picnic lunches thinking they would watch the battle from the hillsides like a sporting event.

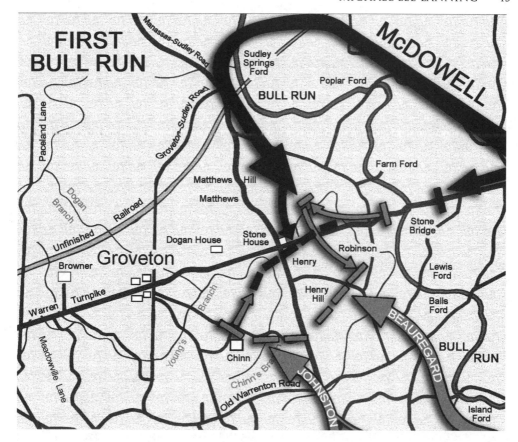

Beauregard, with twenty thousand men, prepared for the attack along a fourteen-mile front on Bull Run Creek. An additional nine thousand troops, dispatched via rail by Johnston from Harpers Ferry, joined Beauregard's troops in the first strategic use of railroad transportation in military history.

McDowell planned for his main attack to swing northward, attacking the rebels' flank while his secondary force advanced westward against the enemy front. He used a feint southward to hold the rebel right flank and keep it from reinforcing the north and center. His plan was more than adequate to produce victory; however, its execution was far from satisfactory. The poorly trained militiamen fought bravely but coordination and communication between units was almost nonexistent, and officers—both senior and junior—were either not willing or not able to exert the necessary leadership.

Despite great confusion, the main attack did turn the rebel flank. They were within reach of victory before a Virginia brigade led by Colonel Thomas Jackson (36) held the line near Henry House Hill. Confederate Bernard Bee encouraged his own men to hold, shouting, "Look at Jackson's brigade; it stands like a stone wall! Rally behind the Virginians!"

Bee shortly fell to a fatal wound, but the Confederates did indeed rally behind Jackson to stop the Union advance. From that time on Jackson would be known as "Stonewall" and his command the Stonewall Brigade.

After holding "like a stone wall," the Confederates began a counterattack that threatened McDowell's exposed right flank, forcing him to order a withdrawal with intentions of regrouping at Centerville. His inexperienced troops fled toward Washington. Officers lost control of their units and soon the road eastward was jammed with running soldiers as well as panicked civilian observers who no longer saw battle as a spectator sport.

Union commanders immediately offered excuses for their failure. Brigadier General William B. Franklin, commander of the 1st Brigade of the U.S. 3rd Division, was one who blamed the loss on inferior musketry. Franklin stated, "It is my firm belief that a great deal of the misfortune of the day at Bull Run is due to the fact that the troops knew very little of the principles and practice of firing. In every case I believe that the firing of the rebels was better than ours."

Franklin was correct in his observation about the lack of training his men had in the use of their muskets, but what he did not say was that the Confederates were no better armed or trained. His biggest omission was that he and his fellow officers were also inexperienced in the horror and deadliness of the modern battlefield and did not take the initiative of leadership required to get brave men to perform great deeds. The most common comment from observers of the battle was that the Union soldiers were in "want of orders."

On the other side of the lines, Jackson, Bee, and others did take charge and lead their men to victory. Good leadership turned the battle's tide, but superior performance on the Confederate side was not the major influence on the battle. Simply stated, both sides were ill trained, poorly led, and unprepared for the fight. Throughout history, when two forces are equal, prepared or not, the victory goes to the defense, and that is exactly what occurred along Bull Run Creek.

The Confederates did not pursue the Union army toward Washington, even though they might have been able to capture the U.S. capital. The lack of training and unity of command, combined with a shortage of supplies, prevented the exploitation of their victory.

At the end of the day on July 21, the Union had sustained more than 2,700 casualties, including 418 dead. Confederate losses totaled nearly 2,000, with 387 killed.

The battle's influence, however, reached far beyond the dead, wounded, and missing.

Northerners now realized that the war would not be won quickly or easily, and they began to seriously focus on attaining superior numbers and resources for a long war. Many in the South looked at Bull Run as proof of the superiority of their soldiers and doubted if Lincoln would continue the war. Some of the Southern veterans of Bull Run accepted their discharges and returned home. Others simply deserted, thinking the war was as good as over.

First Bull Run easily rates its ranking for its status as the war's first great battle. It secures a high position because of its influence in revealing to the North just what it would take to preserve the Union and what unification was necessary to accomplish that aim. Antietam (1), Gettysburg (4), and Vicksburg (7) rate higher because of their particular influences on the outcome of the war, but First Bull Run certainly set the stage for the remainder of the conflict.

11

GEORGE HENRY THOMAS

Union General

1816–1870

Although born and reared in the middle of Southern slave country, George Henry Thomas honored his oath as an officer in the U.S. Army and earned distinction as one of the Union's most successful generals. He refused to seek or accept personal glory, but his loyalty to his superiors and his battlefield victories significantly influenced the war.

Born on July 31, 1816, in Southampton County, Virginia, Thomas was barely a teenager when he, his sisters, and his widowed mother fled their home to hide from harm during Nat Turner's slave rebellion. In 1836, Thomas gained an appointment to West Point where he graduated twelfth of forty-two in the Class of 1840 that included William Sherman (6).

For the next fifteen years, Thomas served as an artillery officer and saw action in the Seminole and Mexican Wars. After four years as an instructor at West Point, he finally was promoted to major in 1855 in the newly formed 2nd Cavalry where his colonel was Albert S. Johnston (85) and his lieutenant colonel was Robert E. Lee (5). On November 1, 1860, Thomas began what would become a one-year leave of absence from his regiment to recover from an arrow wound in the face that he had suffered in an Indian battle.

At the outbreak of the Civil War, Thomas faced the difficult decision of whether to remain in Union blue or to resign his commission and join the rebellion. After much deliberation over an offer from the governor of Virginia for him to assume the command of that state's ordnance department, Thomas decided to remain in the Union army.

In April 1861, Thomas returned to the 2nd Cavalry from his convalescence to assume the rank and position Robert E. Lee vacated when he resigned and left for Virginia. The next month he advanced to colonel in command when Johnson followed Lee to the South. With the 2nd Cavalry decimated after so many of its officers and men joined the rebel army, Thomas assumed command of a brigade of Pennsylvania volunteers in the campaign leading to First Bull Run (10). His performance in the

Shenandoah earned him promotion to brigadier general of volunteers and command of a division in the Army of the Ohio.

Thomas' division was instrumental in the Union victory at Mill Springs in January 1862 that secured eastern Kentucky for the Federals. It also provided the Union its first victories in the West and raised the morale of the people in the North who thus far in the war had experienced mostly defeat.

At Shiloh (18), Perryville, and Stone's River, Thomas proved to be a successful and loyal subordinate as he advanced to become second in command of the Army of the Ohio. At Stone's River on December 31, 1862, Thomas displayed both his fighting ability and his resolve when he said to his staff, "This army can't retreat. Gentlemen, I know of no better place to die than right here."

When officials in Washington became disenchanted with his commander Don Buell and offered the position to Thomas, the ever-loyal deputy turned down the promotion, explaining orders had already been issued and a change in command would be disruptive.

During the several reorganizations of the Union army in early 1863, Thomas accepted a promotion to major general of volunteers in command of a corps. At Chickamauga (74) in far northwestern Georgia on September 18–20, 1863, Thomas delivered his greatest performance and earned the nickname that made him forever famous. When more than half the Union army, including its commander William Rosecrans, fled their defenses and retreated from the battlefield back toward Chattanooga, Thomas rallied parts of broken regiments and divisions to cover the retreat that had turned into a rout. Thomas held the line long enough for the rest of the army to reach safety and then fought a rearguard action that extracted his own troops in an orderly withdrawal. For his heroic stand, Thomas advanced to the rank of brigadier general in the Regular Army and carried the name of "Rock of Chickamauga" for rest of his life.

At the Battle of Chattanooga (12) the following November, Thomas led the attack that broke the lines of Braxton Bragg (60) on the heights of Missionary Ridge. In the Atlanta Campaign (20) that followed, Thomas commanded nine infantry and three cavalry divisions in the Army of the Cumberland—about half of William Sherman's (6) entire force.

When Sherman began his March to the Sea (16), Thomas turned back to Tennessee to protect Union supply lines and to stop an offensive led by John Bell Hood (45). By this time, Thomas' troops had been reduced in number and power by battle, disease, and fatigue. Grant and Lincoln pushed for Thomas to immediately attack the Confederate army, but Thomas took his time as he trained newly arrived replacements and rested his veterans. Before he finally assumed the offense, his superiors feared that he had become just another too-careful, reluctant commander.

On November 30 at the Battle of Franklin (15), however, Thomas proved them wrong when he defeated Hood in one the most decisive encounters and clear-cut victories of the war. Continuing fights over the next few weeks assured that Hood and his army would never again be an effective fighting force. Thomas accepted promotion to regular major general and received a "Thanks of Congress."

Thomas remained in command of the Army of the Department of the Tennessee for the remainder of the war and during Reconstruction. In 1869 he transferred to the Army of the Pacific in San Francisco, where he died of a stroke on May 28, 1870. Because his native state of Virginia still viewed him as a traitor, he is buried in Oakwood Cemetery at Troy, New York, his wife's home.

Six feet in height and two hundred pounds in weight, Thomas was an impressive figure. From the time he was a West Point cadet, he maintained a reputation for being studious and deliberate, carrying nicknames of "Old Tom" and "Slow Trot." His own troops respectfully called him "Pap Thomas" before he won the well-deserved moniker of the "Rock of Chickamauga."

Thomas is one of the few generals on either side to have been successful in every endeavor and battle in which he participated. Had he been born in New York or elsewhere in the Union rather than in Virginia, he might have risen to even higher command. Because of his birthplace, some of his fellow Union officers distrusted him, while Southerners came to hate him. Even his own sisters disowned him and never spoke to him again after the war began.

Despite the emotion and hostility he instilled in many Southerners, Thomas knew where he stood and never wavered in his dedication to the preservation of the Union. While attending the burial of some of his soldiers after the Battle of Orchard Knob, Tennessee, on October 24, 1863, Thomas answered a subordinate who asked if the dead should be buried in groups by state of origin by saying, "No, mix 'em up, mix 'em up. I'm tired of states' rights."

Thomas ranks below only Union generals Grant, Sherman, and Sheridan in his influence on the war. He outranks many of the Confederate generals on this list, including Hood, for besting them on the battlefield. In the long war, Thomas achieved an early victory at Mill Springs, saved much of the Union army at Chickamauga, and soundly defeated the Confederate army at Franklin (15), effectively ending the war in the western theater.

12

CHATTANOOGA

November 23–25, 1863

The Battle of Chattanooga in November 1863 broke the Confederate siege of this important transportation center and opened the way for the Union advance into Georgia. This encounter displayed the military skills of George Thomas (11) and once again demonstrated the teamwork of U. S. Grant (3) and William Sherman (6). It also brought the much overdue relief of Braxton Bragg (60) from further field command.

Union success at Gettysburg (4), at Vicksburg (7), and in Tennessee during the summer of 1863, encouraged the federal army to push into Georgia to further divide and defeat the Confederacy. In September 1863, the Union army led by William Rosecrans advanced on Chattanooga, where the Confederates under Braxton Bragg withdrew without a fight. Bragg thought he could more easily defeat the Union army in the mountains and forest of northwest Georgia and made his stand at Chickamauga (74). In a confused, mostly unorganized battle, Bragg succeeded in forcing Rosecrans to retreat. By the end of September, the Union army occupied the important rail and transportation center of Chattanooga while Bragg besieged the city from Missionary Ridge, the prominent high ground that dominated the city.

Bragg made no attempt to retake Chattanooga other than to restrict supplies reaching the town. Confederate soldiers resented Bragg's harsh discipline, his officers doubted his competence, and the Southern public was concerned about his failures. Within the army and on the streets in the South, people said that Bragg retreated whether he won or lost. A story went through the camps that Bragg would never get to heaven because as soon as he reached the Pearly Gates he would fall back.

Jefferson Davis (9) was so worried about Bragg that he traveled from Virginia to meet with his general. Despite recommendations from nearly every quarter, Davis decided to leave Bragg in command.

Abraham Lincoln was not so complacent. He understood the importance of the Union positions and previously had stated that "taking Chattanooga is as important as taking Richmond." Now that it was in Union hands, Lincoln emphasized the importance of holding the city and appointed U. S. Grant as commander of all Union troops west of the Allegheny Mountains.

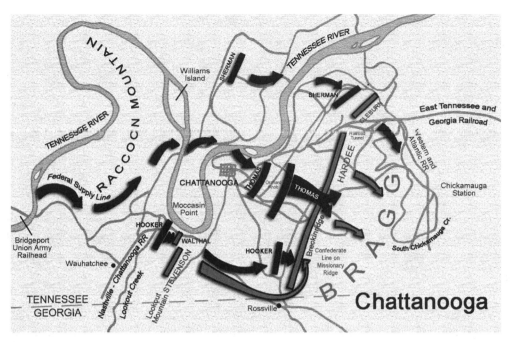

Many in the Union felt about Rosecrans the same way their opponents did about Bragg. Lincoln even remarked that his general acted "stunned and confused like a duck hit on the head." Upon his arrival in Chattanooga, Grant relieved Rosecrans from command and replaced him with Thomas, the hero at Chickamauga. When asked about the lack of supplies that were reaching the city, Thomas responded, "I will hold the town till we starve."

Grant began operations to bring additional supplies to Chattanooga while also planning to break the siege. During the final week of October, Grant moved Sherman's army down the Tennessee River to take positions on the city's eastern border near the Confederate right flank. General Joseph Hooker (48) maneuvered from the west to approach the Confederate left flank. This opened a supply route known as "the Cracker Line," which delivered food and ammunition to Thomas within the city.

With his supply lines secure, Grant planned his attack. On November 23, Grant ordered Thomas to take Orchard Knob between the city and Missionary Ridge in order to provide a "demonstration" to hold Bragg's army in place. The next morning, both Sherman and Hooker attacked the Confederate flanks in a double envelopment. Hooker's first objective was the 1,100-foot-tall Lookout Mountain that anchored the Confederate right flank. The Southern detachment of about twelve hundred men provided little resistance before withdrawing. Although hardly more than a skirmish, the Battle for Lookout Mountain would later be widely hailed and promoted as "The Battle Above the Clouds."

Despite their progress at Lookout Mountain, Hooker as well as Sherman were stopped when they assaulted the main Confederate flank positions. During the evening of the 23rd, Grant moved his headquarters to Orchard Knob and ordered another attack on the enemy flanks the next morning. Once again both Hooker and Sherman were turned back.

Grant now ordered Thomas forward against the Confederate center to take pressure off the flanks. Having been the target of taunts by Hooker's and Sherman's soldiers for the past month about their defeat at Chickamauga, Thomas's men were ready for the fight. Ordered to take the Confederate first line of defense at the base of Missionary Ridge, Thomas's men quickly accomplished their mission. While occupying the Confederate positions, they came under fire from other defensive lines on higher elevations of the Ridge. Without orders—and knowing Hooker's and Sherman's men were observing the battle—they took the initiative and continued their attack as they shouted, "Chickamauga, Chickamauga."

The Confederate lines briefly held and then began to fold under the charge of Thomas's army. Soon the entire rebel line was in general retreat until they finally regrouped and entrenched near Dalton, Georgia, twenty miles to the southeast.

The Union victory broke the siege of Chattanooga and secured the supply routes into the city. Grant, Sherman, and Thomas added to their growing reputations while Bragg failed once again. He was soon relieved of command. Chattanooga lived up to its title of "Gateway to the Lower South," as it became the Union center for the invasion of Georgia, the capture of Atlanta (20), and Sherman's March to the Sea (16). Only the Union victories at Antietam (1), Gettysburg, and Vicksburg had greater influence on the war's outcome than Chattanooga.

13

JAMES LONGSTREET

Confederate General

1821–1904

James Longstreet was the best tactical commander on either side in the war, yet he did not do well in independent command. He believed that the Confederacy should fight a strategic offensive-tactical defensive war and opposed the two Confederate invasions of the North. These ideas, a resistance to following orders with which he did not agree, and his postwar support of the Republican Party made him a controversial figure without equal. Longstreet is often blamed for the failures of his superior, Robert E. Lee (5), and even for the South's loss of the war. In reality, the Confederacy would have endured for a longer period and possibly not have lost the war if it had followed Longstreet's advice.

Born on January 8, 1821, in Edgefield District, South Carolina, into a farm family, Longstreet grew up in Augusta, Georgia, and Somerville, Alabama, from where he accepted an appointment to the U.S. Military Academy. Longstreet graduated number fifty-four of sixty-two cadets in the Class of 1842, and he was commissioned into the infantry. He earned two brevets for gallantry in the Mexican War before suffering a serious wound from a musket ball at Chapultepec on September 13, 1847.

After that war, Longstreet served in routine assignments on the western frontier, advancing to the rank of major and acting as a paymaster in several assignments. When the Civil War began, Longstreet resigned his commission and traveled to Richmond where he volunteered to be a paymaster in the new Confederate army. Jefferson Davis (9) ignored the request and appointed Longstreet a brigadier general in command of an infantry brigade on June 17, 1861.

In a period of only weeks, Longstreet trained his three regiments in close drill and battlefield maneuvers. As a result, his brigade stopped the lead Union division in its march toward Manassas at Blackburn's Ford and then fought well at First Bull Run (10) in July. Promoted to major general in October, Longstreet led a division against the Union's Peninsular Campaign (32), where he earned the confidence of Lee. Joining Stonewall Jackson (36) at Second Bull Run (40) in August 1862, Longstreet again showed his superiority in battlefield maneuver.

Longstreet, promoted to lieutenant general on October 11, 1862, opposed Lee's idea for his first invasion of the North but performed well in the battles that led up to Antietam (1) and in the bloody fight itself near Sharpsburg. Upon their withdrawal back to Virginia, Longstreet's corps held the Confederate center, including Marye's Heights, in their defeat of the Union attack against Fredericksburg (53) the following December. When Lee expressed fears that the Confederate line might be broken, Longstreet confidently replied, "I will kill them all."

Lee dispatched Longstreet and his corps back to the Virginia Peninsula after their victory at Fredericksburg, to protect Richmond and to gather food and other supplies. Longstreet accomplished both missions but was later criticized for not aggressively attacking Union positions in the area. Longstreet, always careful and fully aware of Confederate shortages in manpower and war supplies, simply responded that he did not think they could "afford to spend the powder and ball."

Lee ordered Longstreet to rejoin his Army of Northern Virginia for the Battle of Chancellorsville (31) in May 1863, but the general arrived after the battle had already concluded with a victory for the Confederates. Despite some complaints about his corps moving too cautiously and slowly to join the fight, Lee advanced Longstreet to the position as his principal lieutenant when Stonewall Jackson died.

Longstreet again opposed Lee's plans for another invasion of the North aimed at Pennsylvania, believing that all the South had to do to endure was successfully remain on the battlefield defending its territory. Any offensive, especially into the North, he argued, would endanger the army and the survival of the rebellion. Longstreet finally capitulated but thought that he had an agreement with Lee in which the Confederate army would advance as a strategic offensive and then, when confronted with the Union army, would maneuver into a defensive position, requiring the enemy to attack.

When the two armies maneuvered around Gettysburg (4) in early July 1863, Longstreet still recommended that the army assume the defensive and make the Union attack. Lee disagreed and on both the second and third days of the battle ordered Longstreet forward. On both occasions Longstreet advanced only to be severely beaten back. Although his troops performed magnificently, critics blamed Longstreet for the loss because of his resistance to attacking and his reticence once ordered to do so.

After their return to Virginia in September, Longstreet moved his entire corps by rail in only nine days to reinforce Braxton Bragg's (60) army at Chickamauga (74) in northwest Georgia. By exploiting a gap in the Union lines, Longstreet's corps broke the Union defenses and pushed them back to Chattanooga (12) in one of the most successful and well-executed attacks of the war.

Following the victory at Chickamauga, Longstreet once again departed on an independent mission to expel the Union army from Knoxville, Tennessee. However, the recent battles and problems with subordinate generals weakened his forces, and the operation failed.

In May 1864, Longstreet rejoined the Army of Northern Virginia for the Battle of the Wilderness (62). Again serving under Lee, Longstreet arrived in time to significantly contribute to the Confederate victory. Ironically, almost a year from the date that Jackson had been killed by friendly fire, Longstreet was also wounded by his own men a short distance from the same spot where Jackson fell during the second day of fighting.

Longstreet remained out of action until the following October as he recovered from a mine ball that had entered near his throat and penetrated into his right shoulder. Despite a paralyzed arm and a voice limited to a whisper, Longstreet joined Lee's defense of Petersburg (46). He accompanied the army when it withdrew from Petersburg in early April and surrendered with Lee at the Appomattox Court House a week later.

In the early postwar days, Southerners, bitter about the defeat of their Lost Cause, sought someone to blame. They continued to believe that the victory should have been theirs, even though the lack of manpower and industry had doomed the rebellion from its beginning. Having elevated Lee to sainthood, they needed a villain to hold responsible for their circumstances.

Longstreet was their man. Many already held him responsible for the pivotal loss at Gettysburg. Then Longstreet aggravated them further when he became a personal friend of U. S. Grant (3) and joined the Republican Party. His vilification was complete when he spoke out for civil and voting rights for former slaves.

For the rest of his life, Longstreet remained the center of the debate on how the South had lost the war. After the surrender, he made his first postwar home in New Orleans, where he worked as an insurance company president, but his employment opportunities soon became limited to appointments from Republican administrations. These included positions as a postmaster, U.S. marshall, and the ambassador to Turkey in 1880. In 1884 Longstreet settled in Gainesville, Georgia, tending a small farm and writing his memoirs before returning to Washington in 1896 as the U.S. commissioner of railroads. He died while on a visit back to Gainesville on January 2, 1904, and is buried in the city's cemetery.

Longstreet, called "Old Pete" by his men and "my old war horse" by Lee, proved again and again that he was the superior tactician and best general on any battlefield where he fought. Although it is true that he did not perform well in independent operations, the blame placed on him for "losing" the war is baseless. Lee himself never made any postwar criticism of Longstreet. In fact, if Lee had followed his advice and not invaded the North, the Confederacy would not have suffered the defeats at Antietam and Gettysburg that proved disastrous to their cause. At the very least, if the South had adopted Longstreet's rather than Lee's war strategy, the Confederacy would have existed for a longer period of time.

The debate on Longstreet continues today and remains so controversial that a true picture of his contributions and influence is difficult to access. It is clear, however, that Longstreet made a great difference in the war—regardless of which side one supports. Only the victorious Union high command generals and Lee exceed his individual influence on the conflict. Had he survived longer, Jackson might have proven himself the better of the two generals on all counts, but Stonewall's death curtailed his influence, leaving Longstreet with the higher ranking.

14

DAVID GLASGOW FARRAGUT

Union Admiral

1801–1870

David Glasgow Farragut actively served in the U.S. Navy for sixty years. He earned the status of his country's best-known nineteenth-century sailor and most influential naval leader of the Civil War. He captured New Orleans and then assisted U. S. Grant (3) in his victory at Vicksburg (7) which established Union control of the Mississippi River and divided the Confederacy. Farragut later planned and led the attack on the important Confederate port of Mobile Bay (56), winning the most famous naval battle of the conflict.

Born into a naval family as James Glasgow Farragut near Knoxville, Tennessee, on July 5, 1801, he was adopted by the family of U.S. Navy captain David Porter when his mother died of yellow fever in 1808. In honor of his adoptive father, Farragut changed his first name to David.

At the age of only eight, Farragut became a midshipman and went to sea. During the War of 1812 he served aboard the *Essex* and participated in raids against the British whaling fleet in the Pacific Ocean. At the age of twelve he captained a captured vessel to port in 1813, and a year later in February he was briefly a prisoner of war after the defeat of the *Essex* by the HMS *Phoebe* off the coast of Chile.

Farragut worked hard after the War of 1812 to remedy his lack of formal education by studying languages and naval history. Despite the austerity of the peacetime navy, Farragut, because of his seamanship and leadership abilities, moved steadily up the ranks as he served in the Mediterranean, the Caribbean, and the Atlantic off the Brazilian coast. During the war with Mexico, he participated in the blockade of Mexican ports and in 1854 established the Mare Island Naval Yard in San Francisco.

After the outbreak of the Civil War in the spring of 1861, Farragut, born a Southerner and married to a Virginian, said, "God forbid that I should have to raise my hand against the South." However, he also declared that he was "sticking to the flag" and moved his family north. Soon in command of the West Gulf Blocking Squadron, Farragut received orders to capture New Orleans and take control of the southern portion of the Mississippi River. In the spring of 1862, Farragut repeatedly attempted, with gunfire from his ships, to destroy the Confederate stronghold blocking the channel from the Gulf to New Orleans at Fort Jackson. Unable to neutralize the enemy fortifications, Farragut used the cover of darkness to sail past the fort. He then easily defeated the small Confederate flotilla guarding New Orleans. In coordination with the army commander General Benjamin Butler (71), he occupied the city on April 24.

In July the navy promoted Farragut to the newly created rank of rear admiral. Farragut then moved up river to block the approaches to Vicksburg and in 1863 joined Grant to besiege the city. The city surrendered on July 4, effectively cutting the Confederate States into two unsupportable portions. For the remainder of the war the Union navy exercised full control of the Mississippi River.

With the major inland waterway secured, Farragut next turned his attention to the primary rebel port still receiving supplies from Europe via blockade runners (25).

Mobile Bay presented a formidable objective. Mines known as torpedoes protected the narrow entrance to the bay, and guns from Fort Morgan covered the shoreline. A Confederate fleet centered around the CSS *Tennessee* was also present.

Farragut sailed into the bay with intentions of directing his primary attack against the *Tennessee,* but before he could close on the enemy vessel, one of his own ships, the USS *Tecumseh* struck a mine and sank along with most of its crew. The Union attack was faltering before Farragut rallied his fleet with the order, "Damn the torpedoes, full speed ahead."

Farragut's gamble that most of the wooden encased mines would be ineffective because of their long exposure to salt water paid off. No more of his ships exploded mines, and after a brief battle, the *Tennessee* and the shore defenses surrendered. Farragut's victory at Mobile Bay earned him promotion to vice admiral and the praise of the Union.

Advancing age and failing health restricted Farragut's further service in the war. Nonetheless, near the end of the conflict, he went from Washington to join the lead ground elements in their march to Richmond. As a result, he was the first sailor, and one of the first Northerners, to enter the captured Confederate capital. On July 25, 1866, he accepted promotion to the rank of full admiral, the first U.S. naval officer to hold that rank.

Following the war, Farragut recovered sufficiently to take command of a U.S. Navy squadron and sail to Europe to show the flag and to receive the congratulations of foreign nations for the defeat of the rebellion. Shortly after his return to the United

States, Farragut died on August 14, 1870, during a visit to the Portsmith Naval Yard in New Hampshire.

Farragut's victories at New Orleans, Vicksburg, and Mobile Bay contributed significantly to the conclusion of the Civil War and the preservation of the Union. Farragut is the most influential naval figure of the conflict, having no other navy officer of either side rivaling his influence or stature. Brave, resourceful, and aggressive, Farragut served the U.S. Navy for more than sixty years. He is one of the greatest heroes of the Civil War as well as one of most influential military leaders of all times.

15

FRANKLIN

November 30, 1864

The Battle of Franklin, Tennessee, on November 30, 1864, was the bloodiest fight in the West. Often compared to Gettysburg (4) for its part in ending the war, this battle actually stalemated with the Union army withdrawing and the Confederates declaring victory. It was as costly a win for the rebels as Gettysburg was a defeat. The rebels lost leaders and men they could not replace.

After William Sherman (6) captured Atlanta (20) on September 1, 1864, Confederate leaders knew they had to prevent Sherman from marching eastward to join U. S. Grant (3) and the Army of the Potomac. John Bell Hood (45) decided that the best course of action was to attack Sherman's 140-mile supply and communications route back toward Chattanooga and beyond. Hood moved northward, pausing only to skirmish with Union rear-detachments at Allatoona on October 5 and at Resaca on October 12.

On October 31, Hood and his army of thirty-eight thousand crossed the Tennessee River west of Chattanooga. Sherman, who had been pursuing the Confederates, decided that there were sufficient troops in Tennessee to stop the rebels' march, and so he returned to Atlanta to begin his March to the Sea (16), placing George Thomas (11) in charge of defending Tennessee. Thomas consolidated half his army at Nashville and ordered his principal subordinate John Schofield, with thirty-two thousand men, to fall back and join him.

Hood realized that if Schofield and Thomas united, they would outnumber him by two to one. In late November he attempted to cut off Schofield's route of march toward Nashville. On November 29, the rebels almost blocked the Union retreat, but an all-night march allowed Schofield's army to withdraw to Franklin, about eighteen miles south of Nashville, where Schofield discovered the bridge over the Halpeth River so badly damaged it could not handle his supply wagons. He ordered his engineers to repair the bridge and his infantry divisions to occupy and improve defenses left over from a minor battle in the same area the previous year.

When Hood discovered, on the morning of November 30, that the Union force had slipped by his army, he assembled his subordinate generals and issued orders for a frontal attack against Franklin. Immediately thereafter—and since—accusations

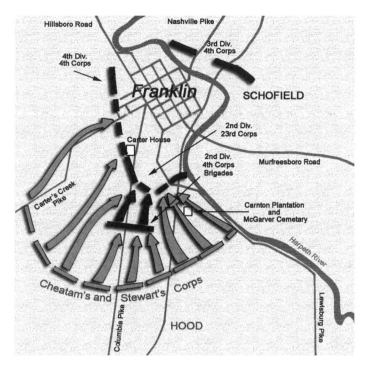

reigned upon Hood, claiming that he was so angry at his subordinates over their failure to block the Union force at Spring Hill that he ordered the frontal assault as punishment. This theory is absurd. While Hood was aggressive and not always as competent as he might have been, his only purpose in ordering the attack was to achieve victory. Hood knew that time was of the essence because the Federals had had little time to prepare their defenses. He hoped to drive them toward the river and destroy them. Furthermore, he knew he had to defeat the Union army around Nashville, and he preferred to fight Schofield before he could unite with Thomas.

It is true that several of Hood's generals recommended against the frontal assault, suggesting instead that they make an attempt to flank the Union positions. When Hood insisted, they saluted and prepared their units. Patrick Cleburne, one of those most outspoken in opposition to the plan, willingly followed Hood's orders. As he mounted his horse to prepare his command for the assault, he promised Hood, "We will take the works or fall in the attempt."

It was not until 4 p.m. that Hood was fully prepared for the assault. The light in the late fall day was already fading but the weather was clear and unusually warm for the time of year. The initial Confederate charge, twice the size of "Pickett's Charge" at Gettysburg, broke the Union defensive position and opened a gap for follow-on regiments. Union

General Emerson Opdycke observed the gap from his reserve position and, without orders, launched a determined counterattack that restored the line. Over the next hours Hood ordered repeated attacks into the Union defenses, only to be repeatedly beaten back. After a final assault at nine that night also proved unsuccessful, the fighting was reduced to occasional sniper and artillery fire.

About midnight Schofield began his withdrawal across the repaired bridges toward Nashville. The exhausted Confederates occupied Franklin but did not immediately give chase to the retreating army.

On the field and in the trenches lay twenty-five hundred Federal casualties. Confederate dead, wounded, and missing totaled three times that number—nearly seventy-five hundred. Only one Union general was wounded in the fight, none killed. Of the twenty-eight Confederate generals in the battle, five were killed and another ten wounded. Among the dead was Patrick Cleburne.

Hood reorganized his force and continued toward Nashville, but what was left of his army was too weak to attack the combined forces of Thomas and Schofield. Southeast of the city he went into defensive positions to await replacements and reinforcements. They never arrived. By the end of the year, Thomas attacked and destroyed most of Hood's remaining army.

The Battle of Franklin had two unique features. It was one of the few night battles of the Civil War, and it was also one of its smallest major battlefields, at only two miles long by a mile and a half wide. One of its participants, Sam Watkins of the 1st Tennessee Infantry, later wrote, "[Franklin] is the blackest page in the history of the War of the Lost Cause. It was the bloodiest battle of modern times in any war. It was the finishing stroke to the Independence of the Southern Confederacy. I was there. I saw it."

Watkins's evaluation may be a bit exaggerated, but the Battle of Franklin was extremely influential. Many historians later compared it in tactics and bloodshed to Gettysburg; while Franklin was not as important, the result of the two battles did have similarities. Gettysburg was Lee's and the South's last offensive in the East; Franklin was the last Confederate offensive in the West. Both significantly contributed to the ultimate end of the rebellion.

While Franklin does not rank as high as Gettysburg, the battle in front of the Harpeth River marked the final rebel victory, as expensive as it was, in the West. Until the end of the war, the Confederate army there would be either on the defensive or on the run.

16

MARCH TO THE SEA

November 15–December 21, 1864

By late fall of 1864, the Union army in the West, commanded by William Sherman, (6) had captured Atlanta (20) and secured Tennessee and Kentucky. To shorten his lines of resupply, Sherman advanced on Savannah, where he would join the Union fleet already at anchor. By the time Sherman reached the Confederate port on December 21, his Union forces had created a wake of destruction 60 miles wide and 225 miles long.

Upon taking command of the Union army in March 1864, U. S. Grant (3) intended to reduce the numbers of Confederate soldiers by direct combat. He also planned to destroy the rebel economic structure and to erode the Southern civilian population's continued support for the war. By the fall of 1864, Grant had Robert E. Lee (5) retreating toward Petersburg (46), Phil Sheridan (8) neutralizing the Confederate forces and agricultural support in the Shenandoah Valley (29), and Sherman occupying Atlanta.

Despite the approach of winter, Grant and Sherman continued their offensives while Sherman prepared for his march through Georgia to the port of Savannah. From there he could be supplied by the Union fleet before continuing his march into South Carolina. He would then move northward to join Lee in the final offensive against Richmond.

After Sherman captured Atlanta in September 1864, he took the next eight weeks to secure the city, rest his men, and reorganize his army of about one hundred thousand. On November 15, he marched out of the city with sixty thousand of his best troops divided into two columns headed toward Macon and Augusta. General Oliver O. Howard commanded the right wing, and General Henry W. Slocum led the left.

Sherman's written orders for the campaign, dated November 9, stated that the columns were to move fifteen miles per day. They would include ammunition carriers and ambulances but were to be unencumbered by supply wagons. Paragraph four of the order stated, "The army will forage liberally on the country during the march."

Subsequent paragraphs gave corollary instructions. Towns that did not defend themselves were to be spared. Mills, houses, cotton gins, and other structures were to be destroyed only in those regions where the army met resistance. Sherman ordered his

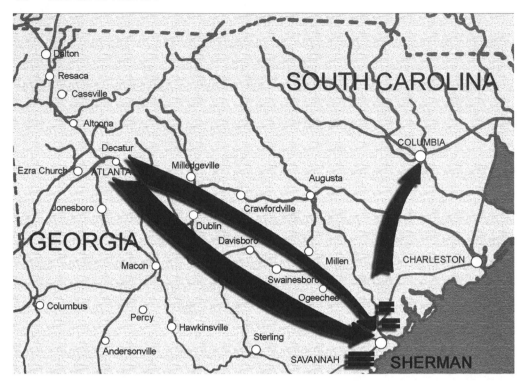

corps commanders to "enforce a devastation more or less relentless" in those locations of resistance. Other sections of the order granted permission for the army to forage all needed food and to appropriate any animals needed to replace worn-out horses and draft animals. Slaves were to be freed and organized into engineer battalions when possible.

Sherman faced little resistance on the march. Fewer than thirteen thousand Confederates defended the region, and many of those were inexperienced local militiamen. Only after the advancing Union army secured the rail junction near Milledgeville did it become apparent to the Confederates that Sherman was on his way to Savannah.

Skirmishes increased as the Union army neared the port city, but the Confederates could do no more than briefly delay Sherman's advance. The Federal columns reached Savannah on December 9 to find it defended by ten thousand men commanded by William J. Hardee. Sherman used artillery to attack the city and sent word to Hardee, "Should I be forced to assault…I shall then feel justified in resorting to the harshest measures, and shall make little effort to restrain my army." Not waiting to find out what "harshest measures" meant, Hardee evacuated the city on December 21 and crossed the Savannah River into South Carolina. The next day, Sherman marched into the town and sent a telegram to President Abraham Lincoln (2), "I beg to present you as a Christmas gift the City of Savannah, with one hundred and fifty guns and plenty of ammunition, also about twenty-five thousand bales of cotton."

Sherman's March to the Sea accomplished his mission of decimating what remained of the Confederate forces in Georgia, trouncing the state's morale, and debilitating the ability to provide provisions to any remaining rebel army. It also did more than any other campaign to generate Southern hatred toward the Union army at the time, and to prolong sectional resentment that still lingers today. Both sides are correct in their interpretations of the campaign, but the reasons behind the bitterness are not plain or simple.

It is a fact that some of the subordinate Union commanders encouraged their troops to loot and destroy regardless of the opposition they faced. A few leaders simply could not control their soldiers. Still others, most deserters called "bummers," took whatever they wanted, more like bandits than soldiers. Some regular soldiers were not above stealing silver utensils, jewelry, or any other valuables they could haul away. Pillaging became so rampant near the end of the march that Howard issued an order to his wing threatening to shoot anyone found destroying or looting without justification.

Another practice of the Union soldiers on their march to the sea that continues to anger Georgia residents was the burning of courthouse records. Justification for this act was based on the belief that the destruction of property records would prevent large land and slave owners from later reclaiming their property. In reality it destroyed marriage, birth, and death records that still cause difficulties to family genealogy researchers.

Sherman later admitted that his men destroyed $80 million worth of property for which they had no use. He never apologized, however, for "making Georgia howl." There was no need to, for he had indeed brought the war to the people and ended any desire on the part of Georgia to experience more warfare. Sherman had introduced "total war"; no future conflict would ever be simply fought between armies without the civilian population sharing the dangers, hardships, and destruction.

Sherman understood that his tactics could help bring an end to the war and that his soldiers welcomed the opportunity to engage in total war. Before advancing northward into the state where the rebellion began, Sherman wrote, "The truth is the whole army is burning with an insatiable desire to wreck vengeance upon South Carolina. I almost tremble for her fate."

Across much of white Georgia today, Sherman remains the most vilified participant in the war. Black Georgians remember him as a liberator.

Sherman himself would later say words to the effect that "war is hell," and he certainly proved his point in his march to Savannah. Despite—or perhaps because of—

its harshness, the campaign helped to shorten the war and bring a final end to the rebellion. These ends and the beginning of "total war" make the March to the Sea one of the conflict's most influential events.

17

JOSEPH EGGLESTON JOHNSTON

Confederate General

1807–1891

Joseph Eggleston Johnston served as one of the highest ranking Confederate officers in the Civil War. Although deemed overly cautious by President Jefferson Davis (9), Johnston established himself as one of the war's most brilliant defensive commanders. He had a better understanding of just what it would take for the Confederacy to survive than most any other military or civilian leader.

Born on February 3, 1807, at Farmville, Virginia, Johnston joined the West Point Class of 1829, where he was a classmate of Robert E. Lee (5). Upon graduating number thirteen of forty-seven cadets, Johnston accepted a commission in the artillery. He then served in the Black Hawk Expedition, on the frontier, and in the Seminole War before resigning in 1837 to become a civil engineer in Florida. As a civilian there, Johnston spent as much time fighting Indians as working in construction and, after only a year, returned to active duty as a topographical engineer.

During the Mexican War he won three brevet promotions and suffered five separate wounds. He remained with the engineers after the war to serve in Texas and Kansas. He took part in the Utah Expedition under Albert S. Johnston (85), with whom he shared a name but no direct family relation. In 1860 Johnston became the head quartermaster of the army at the rank of brigadier general.

When the Civil War began, Johnston had served in the U.S. Army for more than thirty years. He reluctantly submitted his resignation on April 22, 1861, explaining, "I must go with the South, though the action is in the last degree ungrateful. I owe all that I am to the government of the United States. It has educated me and clothed me with honor. To leave the service is a hard necessity, but I must go. Though I am resigning my position, I trust I may never draw my sword against my flag."

Commissioned a brigadier general in the Confederate army, Johnston assumed command of Harpers Ferry. Only three months after leaving the U.S. Army with hopes of never drawing his sword against the flag, Johnson moved his force to Manassas to join P. G. T. Beauregard (43) in First Bull Run (10). Although Johnston was the senior officer in the battle, he deferred leadership to Beauregard, who was more familiar with the territory.

As a result of the victory at Bull Run, President Jefferson Davis promoted Johnston to full general. Johnston, however, was unhappy that three other officers, including Lee, were promoted with an earlier date of rank. Johnston believed that, since he had been the senior officer in the U.S. Army to join the Confederacy, he should be the ranking general. Johnston further alienated Davis by complaining that the lack of supplies from Richmond prevented his army from advancing against Washington from Bull Run. This discord initiated a strain between Johnston and Davis that lasted for the remainder of the war.

In addition to their disagreement over rank, Johnston and Davis differed on how the war should be conducted. Davis wanted aggressive commanders who would take the war to the enemy. Johnston much more accurately understood that the South was short of manpower and supplies and that it should trade space for time and conduct mostly defensive operations.

Johnston displayed these defensive tactics against the Union's Peninsular Campaign (32), when he fell back before George McClellan (51) in the spring of 1862. The rebel general did not assume the offensive until he believed he had the advantage when McClellan split his army into two columns. The rebels attacked the Federals on May 31, 1862, at Fair Oaks, but the Confederate assault soon broke apart in confusion. Johnston attempted to rally his troops by riding up and down his lines, only to be seriously wounded and forced to leave the field.

While Johnston recovered from his wounds, Lee replaced him in command. By the time Johnston fully healed the following November, Lee was thoroughly in charge of the Army of Northern Virginia and Johnston was placed in charge of the western theater. Again Johnston favored the defensive over the offensive but was overruled by Davis. Johnston wanted to evacuate Vicksburg rather than continue the fight until the army there had to surrender.

After Braxton Bragg's (60) debacle at Chattanooga in November 1863, Johnston assumed command of the Army of Tennessee to defend Atlanta (20) from the advancing army of William Sherman (6). Johnston's defenses were brilliantly planned and executed, but Sherman recognized the genius of the positions and flanked the Confederates. The Confederates maneuvered again to block Sherman but the larger enemy force again flanked their defenses, forcing them to withdraw.

Davis used Johnston's withdrawal as rationale to replace him with John B. Hood (45) on July 17, 1864. Hood proved even less successful than Johnson. Atlanta fell on September 8, and then Hood lost much of his army in an ill-fated offensive into Tennessee that found defeat at Franklin (15) and Nashville (87).

Lee recommended to Davis that Johnston return to the Army of Tennessee. On February 23, 1865, Johnston resumed command with the mission of stopping Sherman's march northward from Savannah, Georgia, into the Carolinas. Outnumbered, short of supplies, and aware that Lee had given up on April 9, Johnston surrendered to Sherman on April 26, 1865, near Durham Station, North Carolina.

Johnston worked in the insurance business in Savannah and then Richmond after the war. He served as a congressman from Virginia from 1879 to 1881 and then remained in Washington, where he became a railroad commissioner. Johnston died on March 21, 1891, of complications developed from pneumonia that he contracted when he went hatless to show his respect at the funeral of his former opponent Sherman. He is buried at Baltimore's Green Mount Cemetery.

Although small and graying, Johnston had a distinct military bearing and displayed confidence to the point of arrogance. His skills on the battlefield, particularly on the defense, were unmatched by generals on either side and rivaled only by those of his fellow engineer, Lee. His differences with Davis, mostly petty, prevented him from having an even greater influence on the war, and his ranking is deservedly high on this list.

18

SHILOH

April 6–7, 1862

The Battle of Shiloh commenced on a Sunday, and received its name from a country church in the midst of the battlefield. Despite the setting, compassion was absent from the scene and death ruled in one of the war's bloodiest fights. By the end of the battle, the Union knew that ending the rebellion would not be easy. However, U. S. Grant (3) had begun his operation that would divide the Confederacy by controlling the Mississippi River. He would not be stopped.

During the winter of 1862, Union forces commanded by Grant moved southward from St. Louis to capture Forts Henry and Donelson (35) on the Cumberland and Tennessee Rivers. These relatively easy victories gained the Federals' control of Kentucky and most of Tennessee, forcing the retreating Confederates into defenses around Corinth in the northeastern corner of Mississippi. From Corinth the rebel commander Albert S. Johnston (85) established defenses along the Memphis and Charleston Railroad, which provided the only all-weather link from the East Coast to the Mississippi River.

Grant leisurely followed the Confederates on their retreat southward and concentrated his army at Pittsburg Landing on the Tennessee River, about twenty-five miles northeast of Corinth. Neither Grant nor his subordinate generals thought there was any danger of a Confederate attack, and they did little to fortify their camp. They conducted daily drills for their soldiers, but they also allowed plenty of time for the men to relax and enjoy camp life as much as possible. While Grant's Army of the Tennessee idled, he planned a summer offensive toward the Mississippi River. He also awaited the arrival of the Army of the Ohio led by Don Carlos Buell to reinforce his numbers.

The Union and Confederate armies each numbered about forty thousand, and Johnston knew he had to attack before Buell arrived with his twenty thousand additional men. The Confederate army moved toward Pittsburg Landing with the intention of attacking in the predawn hours of April 6. The lack of roads, most being little more than cow paths, delayed the march, but the majority of men were almost in position by daylight. Before Johnston could completely coordinate his units, Union pickets spotted the advancing rebels. When a few shots rang out, Johnston ordered a general assault, telling his officers, "Tonight we will water our horses in the Tennessee."

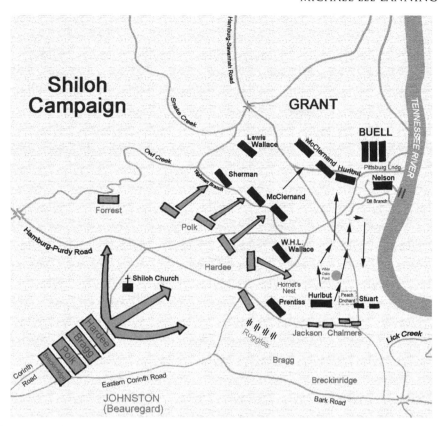

The Union divisions were arrayed in camps rather than in formal defenses and quickly gave way to the charging Confederates. By mid-morning, Johnston's men had advanced more than two miles and were about halfway to Pittsburg Landing when the Union western flank finally held around Shiloh Church. Just to the east, other Union troops delayed the attack in a peach orchard and in a dense oak thicket that became known as the "Hornet's Nest" because of the volume of bullets that buzzed through the air.

Union defenders took advantage of the natural defenses of a sunken road to make another stand. The Confederate infantry launched eleven separate charges against the Sunken Road. Only after concentrating sixty-two cannons, the largest firing of artillery to that point in the war, did the rebels force the Union defenders backward.

During the battle a bullet struck Johnston in the leg while he was directing the fight on the eastern flank. Although the wound was minor and could have been treated with a tourniquet, Johnston refused medical care. About two-thirty in the afternoon he bled to death, leaving P. G. T. Beauregard (43) in command.

Darkness and the six-hour delay by the Union defenders at Shiloh Church and at the Sunken Road brought an end to the first day of the battle. Cries of the wounded on both sides echoed across the battlefield. Later reports claimed injured rebel and Federal alike crawled to a small pool of water between the Peach Orchard and the Sunken Road to drink and bathe their wounds in what became know as Bloody Pond.

During the night Buell arrived with his army. Grant ordered the fresh divisions to counterattack and, despite a tenacious defense by the rebels, began to regain the ground lost the previous day. Beauregard hoped for reinforcements from Arkansas, but, when he realized they would not arrive in time, he retreated back toward Corinth. The exhausted Federals reclaimed their original positions. A limited pursuit was turned back by the cavalry of Nathan Bedford Forrest (21).

Union casualties included 1,754 dead, 8,408 wounded, and 2,885 missing for a total of 13,047 of their more than 62,000 combatants. Confederate losses included 1,723 dead, 8,012 wounded, and 959 missing of their 40,335 soldiers.

The Battle of Shiloh was the largest fight of the war to date. Most of its participants had little combat experience prior to the battle. Small unit commanders, taking the initiative in the absence of overall orders or coordination, conducted much of the fight. Both sides claimed to win the battle but the Union was the clear, but narrow, victor by holding Pittsburg Landing and forcing the Confederates to retreat.

The ease of the previous Union victories in Tennessee had persuaded many that the war in the West and perhaps defeat of the entire rebellion could be quickly achieved. Shiloh, with its combined total of more than twenty-three thousand casualties, convinced both Union and Confederate leaders that there were many more bloody battles to be fought.

Their loss at Shiloh took the initiative away from the Confederates, forcing them back into the defensive. It would be more than another year before Grant captured Vicksburg (7), securing the Mississippi River for the Union and dividing the Confederacy into two, nonsupporting geographical regions, but Shiloh provided a critical step to that important goal. Ultimately, Vicksburg would exceed the influence of Shiloh, but the battle around the rural Tennessee church that began on a Sunday morning was one of the most influential in the West and in the entire war.

19

JUBAL ANDERSON EARLY

Confederate General

1816–1894

Jubal Anderson Early was an aggressive, fearless commander who led from the front regardless of the size of the opposition. His independent actions in raids against Washington, D.C., in the summer of 1864 reduced pressure on the Army of Northern Virginia, and his actions extended the war for six to nine months.

Born on November 3, 1816, in Franklin County, Virginia, Early grew up on his father's four thousand-acre tobacco plantation at the foot of the Blue Ridge Mountains. In 1837 he graduated from the U.S. Military Academy, ranking number eighteen in a class of fifty. After brief service in the Seminole War as an artillery lieutenant, he resigned his commission and returned home to study law. Early joined the Virginia militia as a major during the Mexican War, but saw little combat as he performed mostly garrison duty.

By 1861, Early had a well-established law practice and an active role in Virginia politics. As a delegate to his state's Secession Convention, he vigorously opposed Virginia's leaving the Union. However, once Virginia seceded, he enthusiastically supported the Confederacy. As a colonel in the 24th Virginia, he fought at First Bull Run (10) and advanced to brigadier general during the Peninsular Campaign (32). Wounded at Williamsburg on May 1862, he recovered sufficiently to fight at Second Bull Run (40) the following August.

At both battles of Bull Run, and again at Fredericksburg (53) in May 1863, Early led assaults and counterattacks that significantly influenced the fights. Early also participated in the battles of Antietam (1), Chancellorsville (31), Gettysburg (4), and Mine Run. By the summer of 1864, Robert E. Lee (5) considered him to be his best on-the-battlefield commander, rivaled only by Stonewall Jackson (36).

During the summer of 1864 the Union army closed on Lee's Army of Northern Virginia near Richmond and Petersburg (46). To take pressure off his army and to divert Union corps that were attempting to surround him, Lee ordered Early to conduct an offensive into the Shenandoah Valley. With an army of only fourteen thousand, Early drove through the Union army in the valley and then marched into Maryland, headed for Washington. His offensive accomplished exactly what Lee had intended. U. S. Grant (3) had to divert troops to stop Early, allowing Lee to consolidate his forces and prepare defenses at Petersburg.

On July 9, 1864, Early defeated a Union force at Monocacy, Maryland, and then advanced farther toward Washington. Early's army was on the outskirts of the federal capitol before Grant's reinforcements arrived to save the city. Reluctantly, Early turned his force back into Maryland on July 12 and dispatched a message stating, "We haven't taken Washington, but we've scared Abe Lincoln like hell!"

Even as the Union troops pursued the retreating Confederate raiders, Early resumed offensive operations. On July 30, 1864, he dispatched his cavalry to Chambersburg, Pennsylvania, with demands that the town pay more than a half-million dollars in restitution for Union destruction of communities and farms in Virginia. When the Chambersburg officials failed to come up with the money, Early ordered the town burned.

Early continued operations in the Shenandoah Valley where Phil Sheridan (8) and George Custer (52) defeated him in a series of battles over then next eight months. On March 2, 1865, the Union army finally cornered Early's force, now reduced to only about a thousand men, at Waynesboro, Virginia. Early and a few dozen of his men managed to escape; the rest were killed or captured.

By the time of the Battle of Waynesboro, Early was vilified in the North for burning Chambersburg and in the South for causing Sheridan to retaliate. When Lee surrendered a few weeks later, Early was already heading west and eventually escaped to Mexico. By 1868 he had relocated to Canada, where he was living when old friends in Washington convinced President Andrew Johnson to grant him a pardon.

Early never surrendered and never took the oath of allegiance to the United States. He resumed his law practice in Lynchburg, Virginia, and published articles and books on the history of the war. Early was a great supporter of Robert E. Lee, believing the general could do no wrong, and was instrumental in the near deification of Lee and the Lost Cause. In his later years, he served as the president of the Southern Historical Society and managed the Louisiana state lottery.

Early died on March 2, 1894, and is buried in the Lynchburg cemetery. At his funeral, Senator John W. Daniel, who had served on Early's staff in the war, eulogized, "Virginia holds the dust of many a faithful son, but not one of whom loved her more, who fought for her better, or would have died for her more willingly."

Six feet tall and 170 pounds, Early lacked a military bearing because his posture was stooped by arthritis. Generally described by his peers as outspoken, direct, eccentric, and caustic, he was also known to be extremely profane. Lee, who did not swear or care for those who did, forgave him and referred to Early as his "bad old man."

"Old Jube" or "Jubilee" influenced many of the war's early battles with his direct leadership and personal bravery. His raid against Washington with less that two thousand troops forced Grant to divert more than fifty thousand men to protect the capital, prolonging the ultimate surrender of Lee by at least a half year. Early's burning of Chambersburg and destruction of other Union property was no different than the actions of Sheridan and William Sherman (6). Although it made him unpopular on both sides of the lines, Early, like his Union opponents, was one of the first to understand total war and the importance of taking the carnage to the civilian population.

Early's influences with a pen were equal to, if not greater than, his talents with the sword. The unreconstructed general did much to embellish the reputation of Lee and to encourage the glory and nobleness of the Lost Cause.

This influence on the battlefield and in the postwar peace gain Early a ranking exceeded only by his allies Lee, James Longstreet (13), and Joe Johnston (17), and by his enemies Grant, Sherman, Sheridan, and George Thomas (11).

20

ATLANTA CAMPAIGN

May 1–September 8, 1864

In the summer of 1864, General William Sherman (6) and his Union army forced the Confederates to retreat along the railway line from southeast of Chattanooga for more than 140 miles. The offensive led to the fall of Atlanta and opened the way for Sherman's March to the Sea (16), ensuring the North's domination of the Deep South for the remainder of the war.

At the conclusion of the Battle of Chattanooga (12) in November 1863, the Confederate army commanded by Braxton Bragg (60) withdrew twenty-five miles southeast and prepared defensive positions around Dalton, Georgia. U. S. Grant (3) departed the battle area to assist Union forces at Knoxville and then to direct the actions against Robert E. Lee (5) in Northern Virginia. For the next few months both the Union and Confederate armies near Chattanooga rested and refitted. In December, Joseph E. Johnston (17) replaced Bragg in command of about sixty-two thousand soldiers facing about one hundred thousand Union men led by Sherman.

The following spring, Grant ordered Sherman "to move against Johnston's army, to break it up, and to get into the interior of the enemy's country as far as you can, inflicting all the damage you can against their war resources." Sherman took these general orders and made them specific. He devised a plan to destroy Johnston's army in the field and to capture the region's key transportation, manufacturing, and medical center: Atlanta. Sherman understood that the railway from Chattanooga offered the best route to Atlanta and the best source of supplies during the campaign.

After several weeks of reconnaissance and probes, Sherman flanked the Confederate position on Dalton's western side on May 7, 1874, because he realized that a frontal assault would be extremely costly. This maneuver forced Johnston to withdraw further southeast down the railway to Resaca, where Sherman again flanked Johnston's defenses on May 15 after heavy fighting. Over the next month the Confederates continued to stand and then withdraw at Rome, New Hope Church, and Allatoona Pass.

By June 27, Sherman had marched to within twenty-five miles of Atlanta, but the Confederates blocked his farther advance at Kennesaw Mountain. Sherman

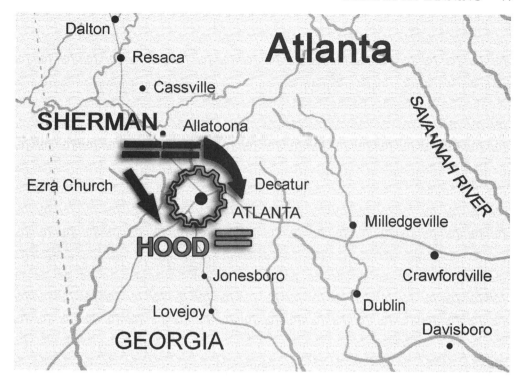

attempted a direct attack into the Confederate defenses, but they beat him back and inflicted heavy losses. Once again Sherman flanked the rebels, forcing Johnston to withdraw even farther toward Atlanta. The Confederates crossed the Chattahoochee River at the edge of northwest Atlanta and once again prepared defenses.

Throughout the campaign, Johnston had stated, "As the enemy has double our number, we must be on the defensive. My plan of operations, therefore, must depend on that of the enemy."

Jefferson Davis (9) was not pleased with Johnston's continued plans for defense, and after conferring with Lee, replaced him with John Bell Hood (45) on July 17. Davis, aware of Hood's reputation for aggressiveness, encouraged him to take the offensive. Sherman also knew Hood's reputation and, when he learned from Atlanta newspapers of the change of command, ordered his own commanders to be prepared for a Confederate assault. When Hood attacked at Peach Tree Creek on July 20, the Union soldiers were ready and beat him back. On July 28, Hood attacked at Ezra Church, only to be defeated once again.

On August 4, Sherman surrounded Atlanta. He also dispatched a cavalry raid by George Stoneman (89) toward Macon to cut Hood's supply line. Sherman then began an artillery bombardment of the city that continued for the next three weeks. When the artillery failed to force Hood to surrender, Sherman dispatched another force south of Atlanta to Jonesboro to block the last rail resupply route into the city. When the Jonesboro fell on September 1, Hood, with his lines of communications and supply cut, withdrew from Atlanta southward to positions around the village of Lovejoy. On September 2, lead elements of Sherman's army marched into Atlanta and accepted the city's surrender from Mayor James Calhoun.

The cost of the Atlanta Campaign was high on both sides. Union losses totaled more than twenty-one thousand; Confederate casualties numbered over twenty-seven thousand.

Much of Atlanta was in ruins from Sherman's artillery and the resulting fires. Atlanta officials, as well as others in both the South and the North, complained about Sherman's tactics. In a letter written on September 4 from Atlanta to General Henry Halleck (63) in Washington, Sherman explained his actions as well as his ideas on how to conduct a war. Sherman wrote, "War should be 'pure and simple' as applied to the belligerents. I would keep it so, till all traces of the war are effaced, till those who appealed to it are sick and tired of it, and come to the emblem of our nation, and sue for peace. I would not coax them, or even meet them halfway, but make them so sick of war that generations would pass away before they would again appeal to it."

Grant showed his opinion of Sherman's actions in a letter written the same day. To his old comrade, he wrote from Petersburg (46), "In honor of your great victory I have ordered a salute to be fired with shotted guns from every battery bearing on the enemy. The salute will be fired within an hour amidst great rejoicing."

In order to defend the captured city with the fewest number of troops, Sherman ordered the evacuation of all civilians from Atlanta. When Mayor Calhoun wrote a letter of protest, Sherman responded on September 12, stating, "I have your letter of the 11th, in the nature of a petition to revoke my orders removing all inhabitants from Atlanta. I have read it carefully, and give full credit to your statements of the distress that will be occasioned, and yet shall not revoke my orders, because they were not designed to meet the humanities of the case, but to prepare for the future struggles."

Hood unsuccessfully attempted to cut Sherman's supply route back to Tennessee in November. Mid-month, Sherman departed Atlanta with the bulk of his army for the "future struggles" that included his March to the Sea. In addition to taking the war farther into the Georgia countryside, his march would make it possible for supplies for his army to be delivered more easily through Atlantic ports.

The destruction of Atlanta introduced Sherman's concept of "total war" that he would expand in his March to the Sea. In Georgia he would forever be considered a monster, but doubtlessly Sherman's actions helped bring the war to conclusion.

Atlanta had been the South's main source of manufacturing and medical supplies, as well as the region's primary transportation hub. With Sherman's capture of the city, the rebellion lost these resources. Where Antietam (1) and Gettysburg (4) in the East and Vicksburg (7) in the West served notice to the end of the Confederacy, the Atlanta Campaign did the same for Georgia and the Deep South. Within six months after the fall of the city, the entire rebellion would collapse.

21

NATHAN BEDFORD FORREST

Confederate General

1821–1877

Although he had little formal public education and no training in the art of warfare, Nathan Bedford Forrest advanced from private to lieutenant general during the Civil War, earning the reputation of one of the conflict's finest cavalry leaders. Forrest promoted fear in his opponents and ire from his superiors, but respect and love from his men.

Born near Chapel Hill in Bedford County, Tennessee, on July 13, 1821, Forrest attended less than six months of school in order to help provide for his widowed mother and siblings. As a young man he earned a fortune in real estate, cotton, livestock, and slave trading. At the outbreak of the Civil War, he enlisted in a cavalry unit as a private, even though he was only a month from his fortieth birthday. A few months later, with the encouragement of the governor of Tennessee, he accepted a commission as a lieutenant colonel and spent his own money to arm and fit a mounted battalion.

Forrest may have been uneducated, but he was well-read and a quick study. Not limited by military dogma that taught the principles of past wars, he was open to acquiring and inventing new tactics and maneuvers. When his reading and experience failed to provide battlefield solutions, Forrest relied on his personal bravery and leadership to carry the day.

In February 1862, Forrest's cavalry was in northwestern Tennessee where the unit took part in the battle for Fort Donelson (35). Forrest argued with his superiors' decision to surrender the fort and troops until he received permission to lead a breakout. At the head of fifteen hundred of his cavalrymen and a few infantry volunteers from other units, Forrest managed to escape without firing shot.

Forrest then covered the Confederate retreat out of Nashville and rode into northern Mississippi to support the attack against Shiloh (18) in April. Because of the heavily wooded terrain surrounding the Union defense, his cavalrymen played only a minor role in the battle, but they did contribute to covering the Confederate withdrawal.

Wounded in the retreat from Shiloh, Forrest recovered to assume command of a cavalry brigade as a brigadier general in the Army of Tennessee. With his new command, Forrest began a series of raids behind Union lines that earned him widespread reputation and fame. It was also during this time that he feuded over the use of his command with his superiors, including Braxton Bragg (60) and Joe Wheeler (77). Confederate leaders soon learned that Forrest contributed the most as an independent commander rather than as a direct subordinate.

On his first raid against Murfreesboro, Tennessee, on July 13, 1862, Forrest captured more than a thousand Union prisoners and seized a much-needed store of arms and supplies. For the rest of 1862 and on into the new year, Forrest operated mostly in the Union rear as he cut lines of communications and disrupted supply deliveries. His operations slowed the Union advance against Chattanooga (12) and delayed U. S. Grant's (3) overland advance to Vicksburg (7).

In September 1863, Forrest, now a major general in command of a cavalry corps, rejoined the regular Confederate army for the Battle of Chickamauga (74). After the battle he again clashed with Bragg and, as a result, resumed his operations as an independent raider. In April 1864, units of Forrest's cavalry attacked and captured Fort Pillow on the Mississippi River north of Memphis. The Confederates easily won the battle, but in its aftermath many of the fort's black defenders were killed. The complete truth about the incident remains a mystery. Northern investigators claimed Forrest's men murdered unarmed black soldiers after they surrendered; they renamed the battle the Fort Pillow Massacre. Southern officials claimed the black soldiers refused to surrender in what was simply an overwhelming victory against an enemy that refused to give up.

While debate over Fort Pillow continued, the general conceded that unarmed blacks were, in fact, killed. Whether this took place in the heat of battle or on the direct orders of Forrest or others remains unknown. All Forrest would ever admit was that "the river was dyed with blood of the slaughtered troops for two hundred yards."

Regardless of what really happened at Fort Pillow, the battle added to Forrest's fame in the South and increased the hatred of him in the North. Forrest then turned to raiding behind the lines of the Union advance against Atlanta (20). He was so successful that Union general William Sherman (6) said, "That devil Forrest…must be hunted down and killed if it costs ten thousand lives and bankrupts the Federal treasury." Sherman added that "there will never be peace in Tennessee till Forrest is dead."

Sherman was unsuccessful in eliminating Forrest, who extended his operations to harass Union rear areas in the Franklin (15) and Nashville (87) campaigns of late 1864.

Southern newspapers continued their near worship of Forrest and, with Stonewall Jackson (36) dead, the cavalryman was second in popularity only to Robert E. Lee (5).

In early 1865, Forrest advanced in rank to lieutenant general while continuing his bold raids. Not until the war's final weeks did the general experience his first defeat. With worn-out horses and dwindling manpower, Forrest attempted to cut off an advance of three divisions led by James H. Wilson (64) south from Tennessee toward Selma, Alabama, one of the South's last surviving centers of war supply manufacturing. Forrest resisted the Union advance and then fell back to defenses around Selma. On April 2, Forrest retreated with what was left of his command, leaving the city to the Union army.

Forrest maintained limited operations even after Lee's surrender at Appomattox, but finally gave up on May 9. He returned to Memphis to find his slaves free, his plantations destroyed, and his fortune gone. Over the next years he farmed successfully and served several years as a railroad president. It was also during this period that he assisted in the organization of what became the Ku Klux Klan and, according to some reports, became its first Grand Dragon. To just what extent he participated in Klan activities is unknown, and some apologists for Forrest claim he led the efforts in 1869 to break up the organization. Forrest died on October 29, 1877, likely of diabetes, and is buried in Memphis.

There is no doubt that Forrest believed in his state and the Confederacy. For him, it was a personal war. He had much at stake in a conflict that threatened to end his ownership and trade of slaves. Forrest was not the only member of his family to support the South. Two of his brothers died in the war, one of wounds, one of disease, and two more fell to serious wounds.

Forrest's abilities as a battlefield tactician were rivaled only by his personal bravery. He was wounded at least four times and had twenty-nine horses killed or wounded beneath him. On June 14, 1863, one of his junior officers, Lieutenant A. Wills Gould, took a comment by Forrest as a personal insult and drew his pistol and fired. Although wounded, Forrest grabbed his assailant's pistol hand, took out his pocketknife with his other, opened it with his teeth, and stabbed the young man to death.

One of the most important indicators of Forrest's stature is the respect he received from Confederate infantrymen. In every war in history, foot soldiers have thought little of those who ride instead of walk. Usually infantrymen greeted passing cavalry with jeers or profanity. When Forrest and his men rode by, rebel infantrymen cheered.

Forrest's personal toughness was never in doubt. Those who did not think an uneducated, non-West-Point-trained officer could achieve military greatness were mistaken. He fought with a simple of mantra, "I always make it a rule to get there first with the most men. War means fighting, and fighting means killing. Get them scared, and keep the scare on them."

These tactics are usually misquoted as "get there firstest with the mostest" but regardless of how they are worded, they summarize the reasons for Forrest's success. Since the war, many, especially in the South, have proclaimed Forrest the conflict's leading cavalry leader, with some declaring him the best of all times.

Despite the controversy that still surrounds Forrest, his long series of successes were remarkable. Considering his lack of resources, he very well may have been the war's best commander of cavalry. Sherman's words alone are enough to gain Forrest a high ranking on this list.

22

EMANCIPATION PROCLAMATION

January 1, 1863

The Emancipation Proclamation did not free a single slave, but it did transform the Union objectives of the Civil War. Prior to the proclamation, the United States fought to preserve the Union; after the proclamation, the end of slavery was an aim of the conflict as well. The document provided the U.S. a moral force in relations with other countries and opened the way for African Americans to fill the depleted ranks of the Union army and navy.

Abraham Lincoln (2), considered pro-abolition prior to his election in 1860, maintained even after the war began that preserving the Union—and not abolishing slavery—was the reason he sent his armed forces against the Confederacy. Despite pressure from antislavery factions in the North, Lincoln confirmed his objectives as late as the summer of 1862, stating, "My paramount object in the struggle is to save the Union, and is not either to save or destroy slavery. If I could save the Union without freeing any slave I would do it; and if I could save it by freeing all the slaves I would do it; and if I could save it by freeing some and leaving others alone I would also do that."

Even as he made the statement, the progress of the Confederacy forced him into taking a more decisive position. After more than a year of almost continuous victories by the rebels on the battlefield, the demoralized Union army had begun to experience difficulties in attracting sufficient numbers of volunteers to fill its rapidly depleting ranks. Continued Confederate success also attracted support from European countries interested in Southern agricultural exports and trade if their rebellion was successful.

Lincoln believed that emancipating the slaves would provide a new source of military manpower and would secure a moral advantage in negotiations with foreign countries that had already ended slavery. In June 1862, the president drafted a document that he presented to his cabinet on July 22. His proposal declared "that all persons held as slaves" within the rebellious states "are, and henceforward shall be, free." It also included a provision that those freed and who met enlistment standards "will be received into the armed service of the United States to garrison forts, positions, stations, and other places, and to man vessels of all sorts in said service."

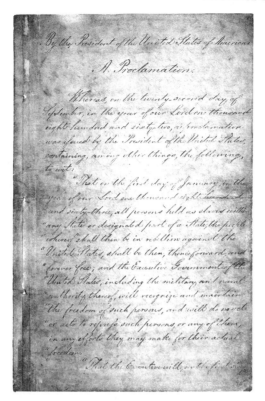

Some of Lincoln's cabinet favored the proposal; others opposed it; all feared the political ramifications in the approaching fall elections and the reaction of Confederate officials. They debated for several hours and then continued discussions with Lincoln and other staff members over the next few days. Finally, the president announced his decision to issue the proclamation, but he agreed with members of his cabinet who recommended he not do so until the Union army gained an advantage on the battlefield. Without a combat victory, they felt the proclamation would be seen as little more than a plea for support from a government in danger of losing the war.

The Battle of Antietam (1) on September 16–18 was not a clear-cut Union victory, but it was the first great battle in which the U.S. had forced Robert E. Lee (5) to retreat and to terminate his invasion of the North. Less than a week after the battle's last shots, on September 22, Lincoln issued the Emancipation Proclamation to take effect on January 1, 1863.

Reaction to the Proclamation varied widely. Some damned it for doing too much; others protested it did not do enough. The antislavery editor of the New York *Tribune* declared, "God bless Abraham Lincoln." Others, particularly in the border states where slaves were numerous, feared that even though the Proclamation did not include their territory, it would lead to the eventual loss of their property. In the South, slave owners and their supporters condemned the Proclamation as an open invitation for a slave revolt.

Those who read the Proclamation closely realized that what Lincoln ordered was more political than practical, more style than substance. In reality, it did not free a single slave. The Proclamation did not apply to slaves in Union-held territory and freed only those in areas held by the Confederacy over which the Union had no authority. Provisions even exempted those parts of the Confederate States currently occupied by Union forces. In essence, where Lincoln could free those held in slavery he did not; in areas where he did extend emancipation, he had no means to enforce freedom.

An immediate result of the Proclamation was the loss of several Republican congressional seats to the Democrats in the fall election of 1862. The Democrats, many of whom favored a peaceful end to the war and recognition of the Confederacy, even carried Lincoln's home state of Illinois, but the Republicans maintained their overall advantage in Congress.

The positive outcomes of the Proclamation became evident immediately. European countries, including Great Britain and France, no longer considered supporting the Confederate States because they were discouraged by Lee's failure at Antietam and encouraged by the Union's support of the moral cause of freeing the slaves. The Confederacy lost all hope for help from Europe in breaking the Union blockade and for export of their agricultural products and import of needed war supplies.

Just as importantly, runaway slaves and those slaves freed by Union offensives into Southern territory flocked to recruitment centers. The liberated now fought as part of the liberators. Before the Emancipation Proclamation, only a few thousand African Americans served in the Union army and navy. By the end of the war almost two hundred thousand blacks had served in the Union armed forces—about 10 percent of the total in uniform.

Not until eight months after the war ended in 1865 did the U.S. Congress enact the 13th Amendment that ended slavery throughout the newly re-United States. However, Lincoln's Emancipation Proclamation provided the opening that ultimately led to freedom for all. It also influenced the war by discouraging European support for the Confederacy and opening the door for blacks to earn and defend their own newly found freedoms.

Lincoln's wisdom in handling the issues and the contents of the Emancipation

Proclamation were remarkable. If he had gone farther to immediately free the slaves in the United States, he very well might have lost support from the border states and others in the North. While doing little, he ultimately accomplished much. The Emancipation Proclamation endures as one of the greatest documents in American history, rivaled only by the Declaration of Independence and the Constitution. It began the righting of the greatest wrong in American history by providing the beginning of the end of human bondage. For these reasons it gains the highest ranking on this list of any event during the war, being eclipsed and exceeded only by the few battles and leaders that provided the ultimate differences in the war's outcome.

23

JAMES EWELL BROWN (J. E. B.) STUART

Confederate General

1833–1864

James Ewell Brown Stuart was the South's most famous cavalry commander for his flamboyance in dress, his boldness in battle, and his classic use of horse soldiers to gather intelligence and disrupt enemy rear areas. Robert E. Lee (5) considered him one of his most trusted subordinates. Stuart became a symbol of Southern chivalry during the war and a legacy of the Lost Cause afterward.

Born on February 6, 1833, in Patrick County, Virginia, Stuart attended Emory and Henry College for two years before accepting an appointment to West Point as a member of the Class of 1854. After graduating thirteenth of forty-six cadets, Stuart served as a cavalry officer on the western frontier, where he was seriously wounded in a skirmish with Native Americans.

He then participated in the army's efforts to maintain peace in "Bleeding Kansas" before traveling back east for a family visit. Stuart was on leave in Washington, D.C., in 1859 when word came of the raid on Harpers Ferry, and he volunteered to act as Lee's personal aide in the expedition to capture John Brown (54).

On May 3, 1861, Stuart resigned his commission as a captain in the U.S. Army to become a lieutenant colonel in the Confederacy. He initially served in the Shenandoah Valley and then rode to Manassas to participate in First Bull Run (10) in July. Stuart's early performance in the war was marked by those characteristics that defined his future successes. While known for his boldness, he was not reckless. He thoroughly understood that the mission of cavalry was to perform reconnaissance and to disrupt enemy lines of supply and communications. His actions were aggressive, but he recognized the importance of survival. He knew that cavalry was ineffective in fighting infantry in defensive positions. He supported his speed and audacity by careful planning.

In his early battles, Stuart exhibited personal bravery along with superior tactical abilities. By the end of 1861 his performance had earned him the star of brigadier general and leadership of the cavalry brigade of the Army of Northern Virginia.

During the Union's Peninsular Campaign (32) in the spring of 1862, he covered the retreat from Yorktown, fired the first shots at Williamsburg, and gained a personal commendation from James Longstreet (13) for his actions at Seven Pines.

In preparation for the Battle of Mechanicsville in June, Lee directed Stuart to scout the Union right flank and rear to determine enemy dispositions. Stuart departed Hanover Court House on June 12 with a thousand horsemen. Over the next three days—going far beyond his orders—he rode more than 150 miles and completely circled the Union army with the loss of only one man. The "ride around McClellan" delivered needed intelligence to Lee, added to the Confederate general's confidence in his cavalry commander, and put Stuart on every front page in the South and many in the North.

Stuart again completely circled the Union army in another reconnaissance prior to Second Bull Run (40) in August 1862. He then covered Lee's advance to Antietam (1) by delaying Union reinforcements in the passes of South Mountain. By the end of 1862, Lee had become so dependent on Stuart's intelligence-gathering that he called the cavalry leader the "eyes of the army."

At Fredericksburg (53) the following December, Stuart demonstrated his effectiveness in defense tactics by successfully shifting his artillery to support Stonewall Jackson (36). The following May, Stuart moved with Jackson in the masterful march to turn the Union flank at Chancellorsville (31). When Jackson was wounded, A. P. Hill (26) assumed his command until he was also injured. Stuart then took the lead through the end of the battle.

Between these major battles Stuart continued to lead raids behind Union lines that captured prisoners and much-needed supplies. In one operation he even penetrated the headquarters of Union general John Pope, capturing several staff officers as well as the general's personal property. During this period Stuart's cavalry—and indeed all of the Southern horse units—were far superior to those of the North, and able to raid almost at will behind enemy lines. Stuart and his fellow rebel horsemen wisely avoided Union infantrymen but felt mostly unthreatened by enemy cavalry.

On June 9, 1863, Stuart and his ten thousand men chanced upon eleven thousand Union cavalrymen led by General Alfred Pleasonton at Brandy Station, Virginia. Although he was surprised by the presence and size of the Union force, Stuart had little respect for the horsemen wearing blue. Instead of avoiding a fight, he charged and quickly discovered that Pleasonton and the Union cavalry had learned much over the past months. During the next several hours both sides charged and counter-charged in what became the war's largest cavalry battle.

Neither side gained the advantage until Confederate infantry arrived to reinforce Stuart. Pleasonton withdrew, but neither side could claim victory. Although Stuart ultimately held the field, he was criticized for not being prepared for the battle and also for revealing that Lee was marching northward.

Stuart was humiliated by criticism from the Southern press that previously had treated him as a hero. When Lee gave him general orders to advance in front of the Army of Northern Virginia into Pennsylvania, Stuart saw it as an opportunity for personal and public redemption.

Stuart found raiding so easy in Pennsylvania that he ranged far from Lee's army. When he tried to return, the Union cavalry delayed him and prevented his discovery and reporting of the Union build-up at Gettysburg (4). As a result, Lee approached one of his most important battles without his "eyes" and, accordingly, misjudged the terrain and the enemy. By the time Stuart rejoined Lee on the second day of the battle, he had little impact on the remainder of the fight.

Despite more criticism from the Southern press, as well as some historians who continue today to blame Lee's defeat at Gettysburg on the absence of his cavalry, Stuart continued to perform bravely and well for the remainder of 1863 and on into 1864.

His reconnaissance and intelligence-gathering at the battles of Spotsylvania Court House (65) and the Wilderness (62) once again significantly influenced their outcomes.

Although Stuart was only thirty-one years old, he had been in the midst of nearly every major action in the eastern front. As the months passed, he was finding that quality horses, arms, and replacements were becoming more difficult to acquire, while the Union cavalry was increasing in size and abilities. On May 10, 1864, expressing feelings about his own vulnerability and the possibility of defeat, Stuart wrote to Major Andrew Vanable from Beaver Dam Station, Virginia, "I don't expect to survive the conflict, I do not want to survive if the South is conquered."

When Stuart wrote his letter, the South was already in retreat before U. S. Grant (3), with Phil Sheridan's (8) cavalry riding toward Richmond. Lee dispatched Stuart to stop Sheridan. The cavalry leader moved to Yellow Tavern, where he prepared defenses along the main route to the Confederate capital. Outnumbered twelve thousand to forty-five hundred, Stuart fought on the front lines. He rode to a point where the Union was about to break through his defense and emptied his pistol at the advancing enemy. Stuart was still on his horse when a dismounted Union soldier fired his pistol at a range of about ten meters into the general's stomach.

Stuart's men evacuated him to Richmond, where he died of his wound the next day. Among his final words was the statement, "I would rather die than be whipped." After great honors and ceremony, his grateful nation buried him in the city's Hollywood Cemetery.

At five feet, nine inches in height with a massive, almost square body, Stuart let his West Point classmates satirically nickname him "Beauty." As a man, he was known for his religious piety as well as his good humor. During the war he wore a flowing beard to cover a weak chin and to camouflage his youth. His personal vanity included wearing a large plume in his hat.

Stuart's death in battle, like that of Jackson, fueled his fame and legend in the extensive press coverage that reported on the eastern theater. Criticisms of Stuart for Brandy Station and especially for Gettysburg are certainly warranted, but these actions do not distract from Stuart's abilities and accomplishments as a cavalry leader. Stuart did not lose Gettysburg; it was lost because Lee made bad decisions.

Stuart is deserving of his high rating on this list. He refined cavalry tactics, and invented new ones when necessary, to perfect the classic use of cavalry in the role of reconnaissance and intelligence-gathering. He also proved he could lead in battle, and his personal bravery was outstanding in every manner. Forrest, although not a recipient of the publicity because he fought in the West, outranks the more famous Stuart because of his continued service until the end of the war. Sheridan also ranks ahead of Stuart, first because he was on the winning side and second because he defeated Stuart at Yellow Tavern.

24

GEORGE GORDON MEADE

Union General

1815–1872

George Gordon Meade significantly influenced the American Civil War, but he is neither as well-known nor as well-respected as are many of the war's "great captains." Major factors hindered his reputation, including his decreasing responsibilities in the final year of the conflict, his caustic disposition with his fellow officers, and his hostility toward the press. Despite his flaws, Meade's victory at Gettysburg (4) proved a turning point in the war and his loyal service later to U. S. Grant (3) significantly aided ending the rebellion.

Meade was born on December 31, 1815, in Cadiz, Spain. At the time, his American merchant parents were in the process of losing their wealth in the aftermath of the Napoleonic Wars. Upon his entry into the United States, the young Meade earned an appointment to West Point where he graduated nineteenth of fifty-six members of the Class of 1835. After brief service in the Seminole War in Florida, he resigned his commission to work as a civil engineer in surveying boundaries from Maine to Texas.

After four years as an engineer, Meade had difficulty finding lasting employment and returned to the army in 1842. He earned a brevet for gallantry at Monterrey in the Mexican War and then served throughout the East Coast and Great Lakes supervising the construction of lighthouses and breakwaters.

He continued service as a captain of engineers during the early months of the Civil War until August 31, 1861, when he accepted appointment as a brigadier general in command of a Pennsylvania volunteer brigade. Meade ably led his brigade in the Peninsular Campaign (32) where he was severely wounded. He recovered to command divisions at Antietam (1) and Fredericksburg (53) and then a corps at Chancellorsville (31).

When Lincoln decided to replace Joseph Hooker (48) for his failure to achieve victory at Chancellorsville, the president passed over the more qualified John F. Reynolds in favor of Meade. This decision may well have been based on Meade's foreign birth, which excluded him from the presidency and from becoming a rival of Lincoln's in the election of 1864.

Meade assumed command of the Army of the Potomac on June 28, 1863, as it maneuvered to stay between Robert E. Lee's (5) army and the capital in Washington. The new commander immediately sought ground favorable for engaging and halting the rebel invasion of the North. After only three days in command, Meade positioned his army at Gettysburg where he developed a strong defense line along Cemetery Ridge from Culp's Hill to Little Round Top.

During three days of some of the war's most intense fighting, the Army of the Potomac turned back each Confederate assault. Late on July 3, Lee and his army retreated southward for the safety of Virginia. Meade, satisfied with his victory but unsure if his new command could successfully purse the rebels, did not press the fight. Rather, Meade kept his force in the Gettysburg area so his troops could rest and receive supplies.

Meade received a "Thanks of Congress" for Gettysburg, but Lincoln was not happy that the general had failed to pursue and defeat Lee's army. The president, however, did not replace the hero of Gettysburg; instead, he created a new senior command position to lead all of the Union ground forces, including the Army of the Potomac, with U. S. Grant (3) in charge.

While Lincoln had found his general whom he believed would win the war, Meade accepted the role of subordinate, even permitting Grant to co-locate his headquarters with him. The combination proved extremely successful in the final campaigns of the war from the Battle of the Wilderness (62) to the ultimate victory at Appomattox Court House.

Despite his competency and loyalty, Meade did have more than his share of flaws. Several of his subordinates referred to him as "a damned old google-eyed snapping turtle" because of his appearance and temperament. General Meade often argued with his own generals but saved his greatest anger for the news media that followed his headquarters. He ran several reporters out of his camp for writing uncomplimentary or intelligence-compromising dispatches. He even had one correspondent tied on a mule facing backwards and ridden out of his camp. These antics certainly did not endear Meade to the press, who finally became so frustrated with him that they banded together and agreed to mention the general's name in their articles only when they reported a Union defeat.

Meade's own aide, Theodore Lyman, wrote to his wife about him, "I don't know any thin old gentleman with a hook nose and cold blue eye, who, when he is wrathy, exercises less of Christian charity than my well-beloved chief."

In his memoirs, Grant wrote of his subordinate, "General Meade was an officer of great merit, with drawbacks to his usefulness that were beyond his control. He was brave and conscientious, and commanded respect of all who knew him. He was unfortunately of a temper that would get beyond his control at times. No one saw this better that he himself, and no one regretted it more. This made it unpleasant at times, even in battle, for those around him to approach him even with information."

Meade served on Reconstruction duty in the South following the war before assuming command of the Division of the Atlantic headquartered in Philadelphia. He died there on November 6, 1872, of pneumonia, likely a lingering effect of the wounds he had received early in the war. He is buried in the city's Laurel Hill Cemetery.

Gettysburg alone earns Meade a place on this list. He is even more worthy for his continued loyal service to Grant even after he became subordinate to the general. However, Meade's decreasing responsibility after Gettysburg, his temperament throughout the war, and his lack of good press from the angry news correspondents decrease his overall influence. He easily ranks above fellow Union generals Hooker (48) and Burnside (57) but did not nearly exert the influence of Grant (3), Sherman (6), and Sheridan (8) on the war's outcome.

25

BLOCKADE AND BLOCKADE RUNNERS

1861–1865

The blockade of the Confederate States' major ports by the Union navy was a two-sided knife that cut the South both ways. It significantly reduced the amount of exports the South could sell to secure funds for purchasing weapons and other war materials. At the same time, the blockade prevented the import of what arms and equipment that they could afford to purchase. While regular shipping in and out of Southern ports diminished to almost nothing, blockade runners using small, swift craft did take goods from the South across the Atlantic to Europe to exchange for needed materials in what became known as the "lifeline of the Confederacy."

President Abraham Lincoln (2) and his senior military commander Winfield Scott (30) drafted plans to preserve the Union as soon as Southern states seceded in late 1860 and early 1861. When the first shots were fired at Fort Sumter (50) in April, Lincoln immediately initiated part of Scott's Anaconda Plan (27) to strangle the South by ending its exports and imports. On April 19, 1861, Lincoln issued a proclamation outlawing the "entrance and exit of vessels" from ports of the states that had seceded up to that time. Lincoln issued another proclamation on April 27 that extended the blockade to states that left the Union after the firing on Fort Sumter.

Lincoln did not make his blockade decision in a vacuum. He was aware that stopping foreign ships from entering Southern ports might be considered an act of war, and he by no means wanted other powers supporting the Confederacy. Not until Lincoln received word from the British ambassador that his country would honor the blockade did the president act. With the world's strongest sea power recognizing the U.S. blockade, other countries would also honor the proclamation.

Lincoln quickly gained the support of foreign governments, but he still had a problem in enforcing the blockade. At the outbreak of the Civil War, the U.S. Navy had a total of only sixty-nine ships, and all of these were wooden—half depending on sail power alone. To enforce his blockade, Lincoln ordered a massive ship-building operation that launched two hundred steam vessels, seventy-four of which were ironclads.

To close the four thousand miles of Southern coastline, the president organized the fleet into the Atlantic Blockading Squadron (ABS) and the Gulf Blockading Squadron (GBS), with the dividing line being the southern tip of Florida. He further divided the ABS into North and South sectors and the GBS into the East and West.

Lincoln took additional measures to accomplish the blockade by having his navy capture the primary Confederate ports including Hampton Roads, Virginia; Key West, Florida; Port Royal, South Carolina; and New Orleans, Louisiana. With the capture of Mobile Bay (56) in August 1864, the only major port still in Confederate hands was the remote Galveston, Texas.

The Confederates had little naval assets except for a few vessels captured in port at the beginning of the war. Southern planners attempted to break the blockade by converting the Union wooden warship *Merrimack* into the Confederate ironclad *Virginia*. The *Virginia* caused little damage to the Union fleet before the recently launched USS *Monitor* fought it to a draw off Hampton Roads (72) on March 9, 1862. The *Virginia* returned to port only to be captured later by Union land forces.

Unable to break the blockade with traditional vessels, the Confederates turned to using smaller, faster boats with lower drafts that could cross sandbars and enter more limited ports where the Union warships could not pursue. These blockade runners challenged the blockade to take cotton to England and exchange the revenue for weapons and other material desperately needed both at home and on the battlefield. As the war progressed, English businessmen met the blockage runners "halfway," bringing their money and goods to exchange for cargoes at Bermuda and the Bahamas.

The blockade experienced only limited success early in the war, but as more Union warships were launched and their captains and crews gained experience, they tightened their grip. In 1860, the year before the war began, an estimated six thousand ships had entered and cleared Southern ports. To replace this number, the South launched about sixteen hundred vessels as blockade runners. Most were privately financed and proved to be extremely profitable for their owners. Cotton could be purchased in the South for three cents a pound and sold in England for forty cents to a dollar. Even a small steamer could haul enough cargo to earn a profit of nearly a quarter million dollars for only a few week's work.

Much of these profits went into the pockets of the ship's owners and investors. The money from the sales of exports went to buying weapons and other materials to import into the Confederacy, the return haul adding another layer of profits for blockade runners.

Early in the war, blockade running was reasonably safe as well as profitable. In 1861 the Union navy caught only one of every ten blockade runners. This increased to one in eight in 1862, one in four in 1863, and one in two in the last years of the war. Northern sailors confiscated cargoes worth $22 million along with the vessels with an estimated value of $7 million.

Even these losses did not stop profits for Confederate investors. The average blockade runner made five round trips before capture or destruction, more than paying for its construction and any lost cargo. Importance of these blockade runners cannot be measured only in dollars. In a year's time, beginning in September 1862, the entire manufacturing network in the South produced only thirty-five thousand rifles and pistols. During this same period, blockade runners delivered four times that number from Europe.

Guns were not the only cargo of the blockade runners. Although their numbers were dwindling, in 1864 the small vessels still brought in more than eight million pounds of food and a half-million pounds of coffee, earning the blockade runners the title of "the lifeline of the Confederacy."

The Union blockade of the South played a critical role in its final victory. One of the greatest limitations of the Confederacy was its lack of an industrial base to produce weapons, equipment, and uniforms for those in the field and to produce other sufficient supplies for the army and the civilian population. Because of the blockade, by the end of the war the Confederate army was in rags and short of ammunition while many of their families back home were hungry. At the same time, without the blockade runners, their situation would have been worse and defeat might have come even quicker.

From the first days of the war, the blockade proved influential in bringing the rebellion to an end. Its influence, as well as that of the blockade runners who penetrated the net, earn it a high ranking as a critical factor in the conduct and conclusion of the war. If the North had been able to successfully blockade the entire South, it would rank even higher on this list.

26

AMBROSE POWELL HILL

Confederate General

1825–1865

Ambrose Powell Hill was a magnificent combat officer and the best division commander in the Confederate army. His abilities to train his men and lead them into combat significantly influenced several major battles and saved Robert E. Lee (5) from total defeat at Antietam (1). As a corps commander, Hill did not fare so well due to the responsibilities of the larger organization and personal illness.

Born on November 9, 1825, in Culpeper, Virginia, A. P., or Powell Hill, as he was known, graduated number fifteen of thirty-eight in the West Point Class of 1847. Upon receiving his commission in the artillery, Hill joined the U.S. Army in Mexico and then served in the campaign against the Seminoles in Florida and on the Texas frontier. Hill was a captain attached to the U.S. Coast Survey in Washington, D.C., when he resigned his commission in March 1861.

Two months later Hill was a colonel in command of a Confederate regiment and stood in reserve at First Bull Run (10) in July. Promoted to brigadier general in February 1862, Hill performed well at Williamsburg and Fair Oaks the following May and by the end of the Union's Peninsular Campaign (32) was a major general in command of a division.

Hill's methods of organization, training, and discipline quickly developed his division into one of the South's finest. Although it was larger than most divisions with its six brigades, it earned the name of the Light Division for its speed in march and rapid maneuver on the battlefield.

During the summer of 1862, Hill's Light Division was in the midst of the heaviest fighting during the Seven Days' Campaign before joining Stonewall Jackson (36) for the battles of Cedar Mountain and Second Bull Run (40) in August. Jackson and Hill did not get along personally but performed wonderfully as a team on the battlefield. Hill's division was instrumental in the capture of Harpers Ferry in September. When ordered to reinforce Lee at Antietam in October, Hill force marched his division to join the fight and arrived in time to prevent the Union army from turning the Confederate flank, and then he covered Lee's withdrawal southward.

Hill was at Fredericksburg (53), but played only a minor role in the Confederate victory. At Chancellorsville (31) in May 1863, he joined Jackson in the rapid march that flanked the Union defenses. When Jackson was hit with a bullet, Hill helped dress his wounds and then replaced the general only to become a casualty himself a short time later.

Upon recovery, Hill accepted promotion to lieutenant general and command of the III Corps in the Army of Northern Virginia. Elements of Hill's command initiated the Battle of Gettysburg (4) in July 1863, and his army fought the main battle of the first day. Hill was not well during the invasion of Pennsylvania and continued to have health problems of undetermined origins for the remainder of his command tenure. Some accounts indicate that his difficulties were psychosomatic rather than physical. Whatever the source, his illness diminished his leadership abilities at Bristoe Station in October 1863, where he unsuccessfully assaulted the Union strength without first performing a proper reconnaissance. He again suffered heavy casualties in the Battle of the Wilderness (62) in May 1864.

Hill seemed his old self during the bloody Battle of Cold Harbor (59) in June 1864 and in the defense of Petersburg (46) that fall, which was key to the defense of Richmond as well as the survival of the Confederacy. Hill well understood the importance of the defense and on several occasions remarked that he did not want to survive the surrender of the Confederate capital. He remained at Petersburg where, a week before the war ended, he was in a conference with Lee when a Union assault broke through the defenses. Hill rushed to rally the defenses but rode so far forward that a Union rifleman shot him in the heart. He died on April 2, 1865. Hill is buried in Richmond.

Described as easy to get along with and approachable in his private life, Hill was restless, brash, and impulsive in battle. No one ever doubted his personal bravery. Throughout the war Hill wore a red battle shirt as an inspiration to his men and for easy identification to his officers. As a division commander he was unmatched. Lee declared him the best major general in the army.

Lee never commented on Hill's performance as a corps commander but, by all measures, it did not match his accomplishments leading the Light Division. Some of this may have been due to Hill's inability to grasp and lead the larger-sized unit; however, his illness must also have been a factor. Whether this was a mental or physical disability is not important; the fact remains that Hill was never as effective after his promotion to lieutenant general.

Hill's influence as the commander of the Light Division is more than sufficient to gain him a high place on this list. While his influence does not equal that of Lee, Jackson, Forrest (21), and other Confederate leaders, or that of Union generals Grant (3), Sherman (6), and Sheridan (8), the name A. P. Hill is synonymous with effective division command.

Hill was the type of commander whom senior leaders depended upon. When Stonewall Jackson lay dying in delirium in 1863, some of his last words were to call for A. P. Hill to advance his division. In 1870, seven years after Jackson's death and five years after the war had concluded, Robert E. Lee made a similar request to Hill from his deathbed.

27

ANACONDA PLAN

1861

Known as the Anaconda Plan, General Winfield Scott's (30) strategy to defeat the Southern rebellion included blockading the sea ports, controlling the Mississippi and Tennessee Rivers, and establishing a line of strong Union army camps to isolate and disorganize the Confederacy. Scott believed this strategy would bring the Confederate States to peaceful terms without fighting a long war of attrition, but Northern generals, newspapers, and the public ridiculed the plan and demanded an immediate offensive against Richmond. Only after nearly a year of bloody warfare did the North fully implement Scott's plan that eventually led to the preservation of the Union.

As the clouds of war gathered and it appeared that political measures would be unsuccessful in preventing the secession of many Southern states, Scott, as Union general in chief, met daily with President Abraham Lincoln (2) to discuss military options. The aged and physically disabled Scott could no longer take to the field on horseback, but he still possessed the mental facilities that had earned him the title of "father of the U.S. Army" and one of America's most influential military leaders.

Scott's planning sessions with the president began several weeks before the firing on Fort Sumter (50). Although Scott was a Virginian, he made it clear that his loyalties remained with the Union. However, he also believed that the nation would again be united some day and that the rebellion should be defeated with as little bloodshed as possible in order to expedite the reunification.

Scott presented his plan to Lincoln shortly after the rebels fired on Fort Sumter and then communicated it to the Union field commander George McClellan (51) on May 3, 1861. The first part of the plan, the blockade of the Atlantic and Gulf coasts of the Southern states, had already been ordered by Lincoln on April 19, six days after Fort Sumter. This action would prevent the exchange of agricultural goods for war materials while also depriving the South of imports and goods from foreign countries.

The second part of the plan called for a joint army and naval force of sixty thousand men to push down the Mississippi River from Cairo, Illinois, to take control of the waterway all the way to New Orleans and the Gulf of Mexico. Meanwhile, another operation would move up the Tennessee and Cumberland Rivers to take control from the Ohio River to the transportation center of Nashville. While these two

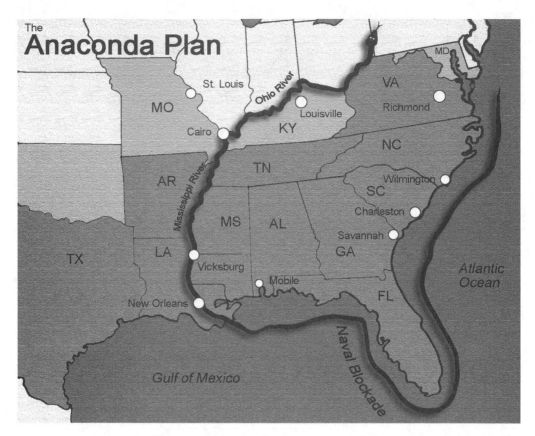

The **Anaconda Plan**

St. Louis · Ohio River · MO · VA · Richmond · Louisville · KY · Cairo · MD

Mississippi River · NC · TN · AR · Wilmington · SC · Charleston · MS · AL · Savannah · GA · Vicksburg · LA · TX · Mobile · Atlantic Ocean · FL · New Orleans · Naval Blockade

Gulf of Mexico

water operations were being implemented, Scott proposed the Northern army establish a series of forts along the border states to further isolate the South and to serve as a "show of force."

Scott believed that many Southerners did not actually want war with their brothers from the North. By passively isolating the Confederacy rather that directly attacking its capital and cities, the Union could quell the fire of rebellion and the conflict could be resolved peacefully.

Lincoln understood the merits of Scott's strategy, but few others appreciated the possibility of a "peaceful solution." When McClellan received a letter from Scott outlining the plan, he remarked that it looked like a "boa constrictor" meant to squeeze the South into submission. Newspapers picked up on McClellan's statement and labeled the proposal the Anaconda Plan after the large snake. The media and the public wanted immediate revenge for Fort Sumter, not a long, peaceful campaign. Demands of "On to Richmond" soon filled headlines and public meetings.

Except for continuing the sea blockade, the Anaconda Plan was shelved while thousands of volunteers came forward to destroy the Confederate army and to capture their capital of Richmond. Within weeks, with the debacle at First Bull Run (10), they discovered that victory would not be easily achieved. During the Peninsular Campaign (32) in the spring of 1862, the Union army and McClellan realized that the war would be long and costly.

Scott, ignored and criticized, retired in November 1861, but his Anaconda Plan began to make more sense with time. Lincoln ordered the sea blockade to remain in place, and it soon prevented all but the swiftest and most daring blockade runners from entering or leaving southern ports. Manufactured goods along with foreign-produced military supplies entering the South by sea dwindled to nearly nothing.

In early 1862, the Union river fleet and army captured Forts Henry and Donelson (35), gaining control of the Tennessee and Cumberland Rivers and of Nashville itself. The capture of this important rail center and supply depot cut off an important source of war materials to the Confederate army in the East—one of the reasons Robert E. Lee (5) made the fatal decision to invade Pennsylvania to secure supplies the next year. While Lee was at Gettysburg (4), the Union army, led by U. S. Grant (3) who had also been the victor at Fort Donelson, captured Vicksburg (7), opening the way for control of all of the Mississippi.

By mid-1863, the key provisions of the Anaconda Plan had been accomplished. The South was blockaded at sea and the Union controlled the Mississippi, Tennessee, and Cumberland Rivers, effectively cutting the Confederacy in half and disrupting resupply and movement of troops and materials.

The war, however, had progressed far beyond Scott's original hope for a peaceful settlement. Bloody battles and full cemeteries marked the past and only offered a glimpse of the carnage to come—but Lincoln had finally found generals who could win the war and preserve the Union. The final part of the original Anaconda Plan was replaced with a two-front offensive with Grant in Virginia and William T. Sherman (6) in Georgia. Ultimately, the "squeeze" from the blockade and the control of the major waterways, combined with attrition caused by the Union army, brought Lee and the South to the surrender table.

Shortly before Lee's capitulation at Appomattox Court House, Grant's forces finally occupied Richmond. The victory was symbolic rather than significant. Other than being the capital and sentimental center of the rebellion, Richmond had no particular military importance. Had the original Anaconda Plan prevailed, rather than the fevered call of "On to Richmond," the massive number of casualties and the widespread destruction of property from the war could have been reduced, if not prevented.

With the addition of the final offensives in Virginia and Georgia, the Anaconda Plan provided the strategy that won the war. Although Scott was long retired before the Union fully implemented his plan that carried a name he disliked, the old general's ideas ultimately preserved the Union. Both before and after the Civil War, the United States entered conflicts with no real plan for victory or for their end. Not so with the Civil War. Scott's Anaconda Plan provided a clear, logical, and conservative way to achieve victory. As with any plan, modifications were necessary once combat actually began, but it nevertheless is one of the most brilliant and complete strategies for winning a conflict that anyone has ever devised. For that reason it stands high on this list and serves as a guide to future generations as an example of how to enter and end a war.

28

JOHN BUCHANAN FLOYD

Confederate General

1806–1863

As secretary of war of the United States from 1857 to 1860, John Buchanan Floyd transferred more than one hundred thousand muskets and rifles from armories in the North to those in the South in anticipation of secession. Knowing that rebels would confiscate Federal supplies in the event of war, he quietly moved this armament over a period of time. The majority of the arms and ammunition that the Confederate army used in its early days came from these stockpiles. Thus did Floyd significantly influence the war.

Born near Blacksburg, Virginia, on June 1, 1806, Floyd grew up in a family of privilege where his father served as a U.S. congressman and then governor of his state. Floyd graduated from South Carolina College in 1826 and gained admission to the bar. He soon moved to Helena, Arkansas, where he practiced law and managed a cotton plantation. Floyd, however, did not find success in the West, and after only three years returned to Virginia broke and in poor health.

Back home he quickly established a successful law practice and became a leader in state politics. After serving three terms in the Virginia legislature, he won election as governor in 1850. During his tenure, Floyd championed legislation that enacted an import tax on all products from states that refused to surrender fugitive slaves owned by Virginia masters. Three years later he returned to the legislature and in 1856 was a delegate to the Democratic National Convention where he supported James Buchanan for the presidential nomination.

In March 1857, President Buchanan rewarded Floyd for his support by appointing him secretary of war. Despite his previous support of slavery in his home state, Floyd spoke openly against the secession movement that was growing in the South. His views changed, however, with the election of Abraham Lincoln (2) in 1860. Floyd, never known as a particularly good administrator, drew scrutiny and criticism for his supervision of the War Department.

Accusations were made that Floyd had honored drafts of nearly a million dollars from contractors before they actually performed their work. Floyd resigned his cabinet

post on December 29, 1860, and demanded a trial based on the accusations. A month later a congressional committee cleared Floyd of all charges.

Floyd, however, had an agenda, and he would have resigned even without the corruption charges. Accusations, this time true, began to surface that Floyd had used his position as secretary of war to transfer arms and ammunition from the North to the South where they could be confiscated by states seceding from the Union.

Later audits showed that Floyd transferred 115,000 muskets and rifles, enough to arm at least ten infantry divisions, to the South from Northern armories between November 1859 and February 1860. This supply of arms totaled more than one-sixth of the military equipment under federal control at the time. The audit also revealed that during his final months as secretary, Floyd had transferred many of the regular U.S. Army units from duty in the East to remote assignments in the West.

The South did not officially acknowledge what Floyd had done for the war effort as secretary of war when he returned to Virginia. However, President Jefferson Davis (9) rewarded him with an appointment as a brigadier general when the war began. Despite his previous lack of military service, Floyd performed adequately as a brigade commander in the skirmishes that made up the West Virginia campaign of mid-1861.

In December 1861, Floyd transferred to the West under command of Albert S. Johnston (85), who gave him the responsibility for the defense of Fort Donelson (35) on the Cumberland River. Floyd's command withstood land and river assaults on February 14, 1862, from a Union army led by U. S. Grant (3). The next day the

Confederates attempted to break out of the Union encirclement, but Grant's men stood to force them back into their trenches.

That evening Floyd and about three thousand of his men escaped across the river, leaving Simon B. Buckner to hand over more than ten thousand men to "Unconditional Surrender" Grant. To excuse his absence, Floyd stated that he feared he would be returned to Washington and executed as a traitor for his actions while secretary of war. President Davis did not think there was any excuse for a commander to desert his post and relieved Floyd from command on March 11.

Floyd returned to Virginia, where on May 17 the legislature appointed him as a major general in the state militia. After brief service in southwestern Virginia, Floyd resigned his commission due to his failing health and retired to his home in Abingdon. He died there on August 26, 1863, and is buried in the town cemetery.

Most officers in the Union army who aligned with the South resigned their commissions to fight for their states. Some simply abandoned their posts and exchanged their blue uniforms for gray ones. None, regardless of how they left the U.S. Army, was ever charged or tried for any related offense. Neither was there ever a threat to do so. With that in mind, it is doubtful that Floyd would have faced charges of treason had he been captured—and there is no evidence of any plans for such consequences. In a war where both sides, and particularly the South, emphasized loyalty, honor, and chivalry, Floyd deserves criticism for his departure from Fort Donelson as well as his "underhanded" dealings while secretary of war.

Still, there is no evidence of Floyd ever exhibiting any cowardice, and he did manage to extract part of his original command from Fort Donelson. It is likely that Floyd did believe he would not be treated as an ordinary prisoner of war, and that is the reason he did not surrender. However, Davis relieving him from command does make a statement that the Confederate president thought his general should have remained at Donelson regardless of the circumstances.

Floyd's defection from the battlefield and relief of command, along with his failing health, ended any opportunity for him to directly influence the war. He had, however, already established himself as one of the conflict's most influential individuals. The South, both before and during the war, was woefully short of any industry capable of manufacturing arms. With the Union blockade (25) preventing the export of cotton for funds and the import of arms with which to fight, the Confederate army greatly depended upon muskets and arms marked as coming from U.S. armories rather than C.S. factories.

Floyd's transfer of more than one hundred thousand small arms to the South only months before the war began is one of the most significant and influential events of the conflict. This act, more than any other, impacted the early successes of the Confederate army. His actions, however, were not in keeping with the traditions and myths of the great and honorable Lost Cause. Instead of being honored as a hero, Floyd remains a minor, obscure character in Confederate history.

29

SHENANDOAH VALLEY CAMPAIGN

August 7, 1864–March 2, 1865

By the end of the summer of 1864, Union forces had surrounded Robert E. Lee (5) at Petersburg (46), and William Sherman (6) was marching to capture Atlanta (20). The only continued Confederate strength remained in Virginia's Shenandoah Valley, where rebel forces secured supplies and from which they conducted diversionary attacks. In August, U. S. Grant (3) put Phil Sheridan (8) in charge of neutralizing the Valley. By March 1865, Sheridan had defeated the remaining Confederates and had destroyed the rebel supply base to the point that, according to the general, "A crow would have had to carry its rations if it had flown across the valley."

In June 1864, Grant had Lee on the run and Sherman was making his way toward Atlanta. The end of the war seemed to be in sight, but daring Confederate commanders were still able to take the offensive from their strongholds and supply centers in the Shenandoah Valley. On June 27, Jubal Early (19) led a Confederate army of ten thousand men out of the Valley on a raid into the North that threatened Baltimore and the U.S. capital. Early made it to the outskirts of Washington before Union forces finally turned him back at Silver Spring, Maryland, July 11. He returned to the Valley.

Early's raid caused Grant and President Lincoln (2) to accept the fact that they had to end the Confederate presence in the Shenandoah Valley and cut off food and supplies provided to the rebels from there. On August 7, Grant combined the four commands around the valley into Middle Military Division with Sheridan in command. In addition to defeating Early's army, Grant instructed Sheridan: "In pushing up the Shenandoah Valley…it is desirable that nothing should be left to invite the enemy to return. Take all the provisions, forage, and stock wanted for the use of your command; such as cannot be consumed, destroy."

On September 19, Sheridan attacked Early at Winchester and forced the rebels to retreat to Fisher's Hill. Sheridan's attack on September 22 again drove the rebels from their defenses. With Early's army now dispersed, Sheridan withdrew to Winchester to consolidate his force and to dispatch smaller forces to defeat the remaining Confederates. His orders to his subordinates were simple. To one cavalry commander he ordered, "Either whip the enemy or get whipped yourself."

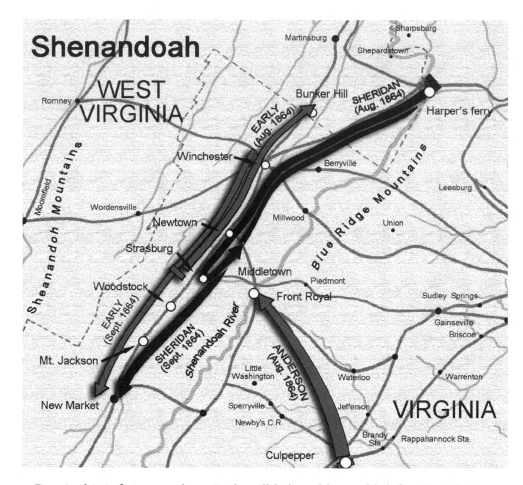

Despite his inferior numbers, Early still believed he could defeat Sheridan's army and began to concentrate his own. On October 19 he attacked the thirty thousand Federals defending Cedar Creek with his force of eighteen thousand. Early drove the defenders back from their initial lines of defense and appeared to be near victory before Sheridan showed up on the battlefield from a visit to Washington. Sheridan, whose troops welcomed him with cheers, showed his leadership, as well as his use of profanity, when he ordered a counterattack, shouting, "Goddamn you, don't cheer me! If you love your country, come up to the front! Goddamn you, don't cheer me! There's lots of fight in you men yet! Come up, goddamn you! Come up!"

Sheridan's troops answered his call and soon Early withdrew in defeat, leaving behind nearly three thousand Confederate casualties and almost all his artillery. The Battle of Cedar Creek marked the end of major military action in the Valley. That is not to say, however, that Early was defeated. For five more months he conducted raids and harassing attacks against Union outposts and patrols. It was not until March 2, 1865, at Waynesboro that Union cavalry led by George Custer (52) thoroughly defeated Early's remaining force. Although Early and a few of his men escaped, the Confederate army was no longer viable in the Shenandoah Valley.

Sheridan not only succeeded in his mission of defeating Early, but also he was successful in his other mission of ending the capability of the Valley to provide food and supplies to the Confederacy. Sheridan, like Sherman in Georgia, realized that defeating the rebel army in the field was not sufficient; they also had to destroy the logistical base of the Confederacy and the morale of the supporters of the rebellion.

Sheridan made known his plan in a telegram to Henry Halleck (63) on November 26, 1864. He wrote, "Those who live at home in peace and plenty want the duello part of this war to go on; but when they have to bear the burden of loss of property and comforts, they will cry for peace. I will soon commence on Louden County and let them know there is a God in Israel."

With more than five infantry and cavalry divisions spreading destruction across the Shenandoah Valley, the devastation was nearly complete. One of the cavalry divisions commanded by Wesley Merritt reported that in Louden County alone they had seized or destroyed "3,772 horses; 545 mules; 10,918 beef cattle; 12,000 sheep; 15,000 swine; 250 calves; 435,802 bushels of wheat; 77,176 bushels of corn; 20,397 tons of hay; 20,000 bushels of oats; 10,000 pounds of tobacco; 12,000 pounds of bacon; 2,500 bushels of potatoes; 1,665 pounds of cotton yarn; 874 barrels of flour; 500 tons of fodder; 450 tons of straw; 71 flour mills; one woolen mill; eight saw mills; one powder mill; three saltpeter works; 1,200 barns; seven furnaces; four tanneries; one railroad depot; and 947 miles of rail."

Sheridan's destruction of the Shenandoah Valley brought him the same hatred from Southerners that Sherman earned in his March to the Sea. Regardless of the harsh feelings, some of which still linger today, Sheridan had neutralized the Valley, and a crow would indeed have had to carry his lunch if he had flown across the region. With Early's army defeated and the safe havens and supplies cut off in the Valley, Grant's defeat of Lee and the rebellion was now insured.

The Shenandoah Valley was important to the Confederacy throughout the war. Although Sheridan's actions were extreme, they were exactly the kind of operations required to end the conflict. Unfortunately, Sheridan had to lay waste to the countryside, punishing the civilian population as well as destroying the rebel army, to achieve victory. It was a lesson that would be remembered in future wars as well.

The Union would have prevailed even without the destruction of the Shenandoah and if Early had been only contained rather than defeated. The combination of the two, however, shortened the war and hastened the final victory. As a result, the Shenandoah Valley Campaign ranks in the middle of this list rather than sharing the high-ranking battles that dramatically turned the tide and changed the outcome of the war, like Antietam (1), Gettysburg (4), and Vicksburg (7).

30

WINFIELD SCOTT

Union General

1786–1866

At the outbreak of the Civil War, Winfield Scott had already served in the military for a half-century and had been the army's senior officer for more than two decades. Although well past his prime, Scott had been responsible for the professional development of most of the officers who led both sides in the war. His Anaconda Plan (27), while not initially well received, proved to be the outline for the defeat of the rebellion.

Born on June 13, 1786, on his family estate of Laurel Branch near Petersburg, Virginia, Scott attended the College of William and Mary before independently studying law. After a brief legal career, Scott joined a local cavalry troop in 1807 to begin a military career that would last more than fifty-four years. Scott's early years in uniform led to a commission as an artilleryman in the Regular Army, but so frustrating were his experiences that on at least two occasions, because of conflicts with his superiors, he considered returning to civilian life.

From 1809 to 1810, Scott served in New Orleans, where he accused his commander, General James Wilkinson, of being "a traitor, liar, and scoundrel." Although Scott's accusations ultimately proved true, he was court-martialed for the accusations, and he received a one-year suspension from active duty.

Upon return to active service, Scott advanced to the rank of lieutenant colonel and participated in the invasion of Canada early in the War of 1812. He was captured during the Battle of Queenston Heights on October 13, 1812, but released three months later. He then participated in the unsuccessful offensive against Montreal where he concluded that the U.S. Army was limited by poor training and inferior leadership from officers who gained their positions socially rather than militarily.

By March 1814, Scott was a brigadier general and had established the style of leadership that would sustain him for the next quarter-century. He initiated rigorous training composed of a series of drills repeated over and over again. Scott also selected and promoted officers on the basis of merit rather than social position.

For the reminder of the War of 1812, Scott achieved success through the performance of his unit and his personal bravery that included sustaining serious wounds

while leading his command. By the end of the war, Scott, now a major general, had earned the respect of those within the military as well as acclaim as a hero by America's civilian population.

During the ensuing peace, Scott reorganized the postwar military and wrote the army's first standard drill book, incorporating the many lessons he had learned on the battlefield. He also made two visits to Europe to study their military organizations and training methods. Scott earned the reputation as a superior negotiator in solving problems with various Indian tribes and in mediating border disputes between the U.S. and Great Britain. Throughout this period, Scott remained outspoken, often clashing with the political agendas of congressmen and presidents. However, his reputation for total honesty and his military skills held him in good stead. On July 5, 1841, Scott assumed command of the entire army, a position he would hold for the next twenty years as he continued to advocate discipline and to standardize drill and tactics.

At the outbreak of the Mexican War in 1846, Scott initially remained in Washington. Once the lines were stabilized in Northern Mexico, Scott led an invasion force on the Mexican eastern coast at Vera Cruz. His advance into the interior against Mexico City is one of the most brilliant and successful campaigns in U.S. military history. Scott, despite being heavily outnumbered, captured the Mexican capital and ended the war. The resulting peace agreement expanded U.S. territory from Texas to California, increasing the country's size by one-third.

In Mexico, Scott led and trained many of the future leaders of the Civil War, including U. S. Grant (3) and Robert E. Lee (5). He also enhanced his fame and popularity among the American people who selected him as the Whig candidate for president in 1852. Scott, however, lost the election to Democrat Franklin Pierce, primarily because he failed to maintain the backing of his own party in the South, where there were doubts about his support of slavery.

By the time the rebellious Southerners fired on Fort Sumter in 1861, Scott had served his country for more than a half-century. Many of his fellow Virginians encouraged him to resign his commission and lead the Confederate army. Scott responded, "I have served my country, under the flag of the Union, for more than fifty years, and so long as God permits me to live, I will defend that flag with my sword, even if my native state assails it." Scott stood by his exclamation and ultimately was the only senior non-West Point graduate of Southern origin in the Regular Army to remain with the Union.

Not everyone in the North was happy with Scott's retaining control of the army. His advancing age, his weight of over three hundred pounds on his six foot, five inch frame, and his gout and vertigo no longer permitted him to mount a horse. Many criticized him as "Old Fuss and Feathers," a nickname he had earned early in his career for his elaborate uniforms and attention to pomp and protocol.

Scott received even more ridicule for not sharing the belief of many Northern leaders that the war would be short. Instead of promising a quick victory, Scott anticipated the possibility of a long, grueling, and bloody war. He proposed a massive mobilization, a sea blockade of the South, and a general offensive to split the Confederacy along the Mississippi River. The Northern press, politicians, and young military officers viewed his Anaconda Plan (27) with cynicism and ridicule. Newspaper caricatures portrayed Scott as a fat old senile man who often fell asleep at his desk.

When everyone looked for a reason for the debacle at First Bull Run (10) on July 21, 1861, many placed the blame on Scott. Unable to influence the army in the field, Scott offered his resignation to Lincoln. The president turned down the offer, but Scott left it on the table for acceptance at Lincoln's discretion. In October, the Federal army suffered another humiliating loss at Ball's Bluff, Virginia, and Lincoln finally accepted Scott's departure from the army.

Scott officially retired on November 1, 1861, and over the next few years wrote his memoirs and once again visited Europe. The series of Union commanders who took his place did not solicit his advice on how to conduct the remainder of the war. Scott lived to see the defeat of the rebellion, mostly as a result of his Anaconda Plan, before he died at West Point on May 29, 1866. He is buried in the Military Academy's cemetery.

If this list were rating the most influential military commanders of all time, Scott would rank above any and all of the generals who led the U.S. and the C.S.A. His long-term tenure advanced the army from the postcolonial militias to the efficient army that defeated Mexico. Scott's plan for the defeat of the South, while not well-received early in the war, proved to be the guide for final victory. If Scott had been younger, or in better health, it is likely he would have led the Union to a much earlier, less bloody victory. Perhaps he could have done the same for the South if he had joined his fellow Virginians rather than remaining loyal to his oath as an officer in the U.S. Army. Unfortunately, Scott's day had passed before the war began, and the leading officers of both sides, including U. S. Grant, William Sherman (6), Phil Sheridan (8), Robert E. Lee, Stonewall Jackson (36), James Longstreet (13), and their like exceed the old warrior in direct influence in the war's progress and outcome.

31

CHANCELLORSVILLE

April 30–May 6, 1863

At the Battle of Chancellorsville, the Union army commander Joseph Hooker (48) had a brilliant plan to defeat the Confederate army. On the other side, Robert E. Lee (5)—with help from Stonewall Jackson (36) and J. E. B. Stuart (23)—executed nearly perfect maneuvers to defeat Hooker's plan. Chancellorsville became known as "Lee's greatest victory." In the end though, both sides suffered not only the loss of soldiers but also of leaders. Hooker was relieved of command, and Jackson was killed.

After his disastrous defeat at Fredericksburg (53) late in 1862, Ambrose Burnside (57) relinquished his command to Hooker. For the remainder of the winter, the Union army remained north of the Rappahannock River while the Confederates manned their positions south and southeast of Fredericksburg. Hooker used the time to develop a plan to resume the offensive to defeat Lee. The Confederate commander rested his army but was forced to dispatch James Longstreet (13) and two divisions to gather food and supplies in southeastern Virginia.

By the end of April 1863, the Union forces outnumbered their rebel opponents by 130,000 to 60,000. Hooker had used the winter months to reorganize his army, including the formation of a cavalry corps, and prepare them for the offensive. Morale of the Union soldiers, so broken in the charges against Marye's Heights at Fredericksburg, had been restored to the point that Hooker bragged that he had "the finest army on the planet."

Hooker was proud of his soldiers and rightfully confident about his plan. Not only was it sound tactically, but also it was the aggressive kind of action that President Abraham Lincoln (2) had been seeking. Hooker boasted, "My plans are perfect, and when I start to carry them out, may God have mercy on General Lee, for I will have none."

To defeat the Confederates, Hooker dispatched his ten thousand-man cavalry corps around Fredericksburg to cut Lee's line of communication and supply from Richmond. Meanwhile, he marched most of his infantry about forty miles upstream to where they could cross the Rappahannock and Rapidan Rivers and turn back east to attack Lee's western flank. When this attack began, the remainder of the Union

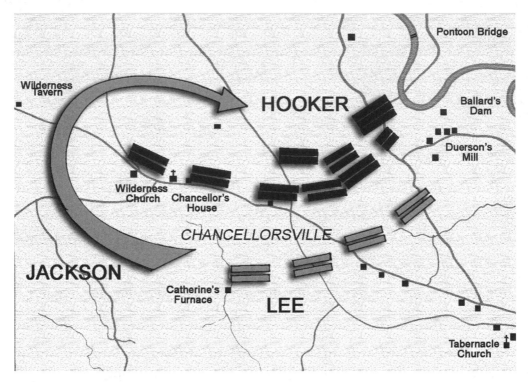

army was to attack Marye's Heights to hold the Confederate defenders in position. With these pressures on the Confederate rear, flank, and front, Hooker anticipated Lee would be forced to retreat. Then he could defeat the withdrawing army in detail.

By April 29, the Union maneuver elements were in place, but Lee did not retreat. Although outnumbered two to one, he left a division on Marye's Heights to hold the high ground while he marched the rest of the army westward. Lee, aided by reconnaissance reports on the location of the Union army from Stuart's cavalry, approached the advancing Union elements near Chancellorsville around mid-afternoon on April 30. Although Hooker had the advantage of momentum and numbers, he decided to halt until more of his soldiers arrived in a densely wooded area known as the Wilderness. After a daylong, indecisive battle in the thick underbrush, Hooker, in what even he later admitted was a loss of nerve, decided to go onto the defensive.

Hooker chose the crossroads at Chancellorsville for the center of his defenses. While the crossroads were important, the village of Chancellorsville was no more than a brick tavern that lent its name to the following battle.

Lee, aware that an attack into a much larger defensive force would be futile, decided on maneuver rather than direct assault. Early on the morning of May 2, Lee further divided his army by sending Jackson on a sixteen-mile forced march around the Union western flank. Stuart had discovered that the Union flank was "in the air"—meaning that it was not tied to a natural or artificial obstacle and, therefore, was vulnerable.

By late afternoon Jackson's men were in position and his two-mile-wide attack inflicted heavy losses as he drove the Union flank back. At sunset Jackson halted his offense to regroup so he could press forward in a night assault before the Union lines could reform. In preparation for the renewed attack, Jackson rode forward of his lines to determine the best route of advance. When he returned to his own lines in the mounting darkness, his soldiers thought he was Union cavalry and fired. Jackson was mortally wounded.

A. P. Hill (26) assumed command of Jackson's corps, but before he could resume the attack he, too, fell to enemy artillery fire. Stuart assumed command and decided that a night attack would no longer be wise.

On the morning of May 3, each side battled the other with artillery and infantry assaults. Hooker, who was slightly wounded by an artillery fragment, withdrew his army northward. Lee was preparing for another attack against Hooker's main army when word reached him that the Union force remaining at Fredericksburg had finally forced the Confederate defenders off Marye's Heights and were approaching his eastern flank. Late on May 3, Lee maneuvered still another portion of his army to block the new Union threat.

Once his flank was secure, Lee ordered a counterattack to retake Marye's Heights to secure his flank. This was accomplished on May 4, and the following day Lee prepared to resume his attack against Hooker, but the Union army was already in the process of withdrawing back north of the Rappahannock.

The Battle of Chancellorsville showcased all of Lee's talents. At a time when communications between units were conveyed almost entirely by foot or horse messengers, Lee had masterfully coordinated his cavalry, artillery, and infantry. When every rule of warfare called for a withdrawal, Lee attacked and won.

However, "Lee's greatest victory" loses much of its luster when Hooker's ineptitude and lack of nerve become apparent and when one learns that fully a third of the Union army never engaged in the battle. While Lee's tactics and leadership were nothing short of magnificent, he did not destroy the enemy. Hooker's casualties totaled about seventeen thousand, or 13 percent of his men. Lee lost thirteen thousand men, about 22 percent of his army—a number the limited manpower of the South could not replace.

The Confederate victory at Chancellorsville increased the confidence and lifted the morale of the Army of Northern Virginia. The need for supplies and the desire to once again take the war into the Northern states led to Lee's invasion of Pennsylvania in June and the Battle of Gettysburg (4) in July. Neither decision proved to be wise.

Chancellorsville deserves a ranking above many battles if for no other reason than it remains today a fight studied by military leaders of the present. Hooker's plan was a good one; Lee's counter and execution were even better. Chancellorsville was a classic maneuver, countermaneuver, and exposition of the will to fight and win.

While it was a great victory for Lee and the South, Chancellorsville took away men Lee could not replace, especially Stonewall Jackson, and opened the way for the Confederate's last great offensive. The failure of the Confederate army, and the ultimate destiny of the rebellion that came to the forefront at Gettysburg, began around a single brick tavern in Virginia named Chancellorsville.

32

PENINSULAR CAMPAIGN

April–July 1862

The first extended offensive of the war in the East was the Union advance toward Richmond that became known as the Peninsular Campaign. Moving westward from the Atlantic between the York and James Rivers, this massive effort was a continuum of poor organization, missed opportunities, and hesitancy. Instead of ending the war, the campaign set the stage for three more years of bloody fighting.

From the firing on Fort Sumter (50) in April 1861 through the Confederate rout of the Union army at First Bull Run (10), the Confederate army ruled in the East during the first year of war. While Union forces thus far had fared better in the West with the capture of Fort Donelson (35) in February 1862, the Union army in the East, concentrated around Washington, D.C., added recruits and prepared for battle under commander General George McClellan (51).

McClellan and the Union authorities agreed that taking Richmond would be the objective of the campaign, but they differed on the best route to use to capture the rebel capital. They also differed on when the attack should begin. Lincoln and his cabinet wanted the army to move immediately, but the always careful McClellan kept postponing the departure date in order to continue to enlarge and train his army.

Finally, after Lincoln accused him of having "the slows," McClellan launched his campaign. Instead of marching directly south toward Richmond, McClellan decided to exploit the Union superiority at sea that was secured when the ironclad USS *Monitor* forced the Confederate ironclad *Virginia* back into port in the Battle of Hampton Roads (72) in early March. Using naval transportation, he moved his army down the Potomac into Chesapeake Bay to land at Fort Monroe. He then marched westward inland between the York and James Rivers with his army of more than 120,000.

McClellan faced no more than seventy thousand rebel troops on the entire peninsula and fewer than seventeen thousand directly to his front. He had only begun his march when his advance units encountered Confederate defenses commanded by John Magruder along the Warwick River on April 4. Magruder's defenses were part of a series of protective belts around Richmond under the overall command of Joseph Johnston (17). The Confederates had the assistance of Robert E. Lee (5), who had

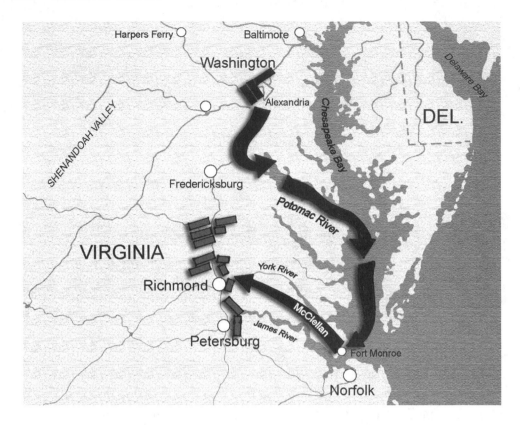

recently joined President Jefferson Davis (9) as a military advisor.

Despite his superior numbers, McClellan decided to conduct a siege of the Confederate capital instead of attacking. Johnston, happy with the delay, knew the weaknesses of his defense line and remarked, "No one but McClellan could have hesitated to attack."

McClellan was also influenced by two other factors. Part of his army had been held in Washington to maintain its defenses; therefore, he did not have his full force. More importantly, McClellan's intelligence gatherers, including the Pinkerton Detective Agency, greatly inflated the actual numbers of rebel defenders. For a month the two armies faced each other with little action taken by either side. Behind the lines, however, it was a different story. Johnston used the time to bring additional units from western Virginia to reinforce his defense of Richmond.

By May 3, Johnston was satisfied with the defenses nearer to Richmond and ordered Magruder and other forward elements to withdraw. A rear guard action took place at Williamsburg on May 5, but it only delayed McClellan from pushing on toward the Confederate capital. The Federal navy accompanied McClellan's advance by sailing up the James River. Confederate artillery batteries finally halted the fleet at Drewry's Bluff on May 15, about the same time the rebel land defenses stopped the Union army.

Although McClellan was within seven miles of Richmond, he once again was stopped by Confederate defenses. The Union force was also in a position vulnerable to counterattack, a situation of which Johnston quickly took advantage. On May 31, Johnston attacked at Seven Pines and Fair Oaks. His well-conceived plan should have dealt McClellan a crippling defeat, but Johnston's subordinate units did not execute it well and the Federals fought better than expected.

After the battle, Lee moved from consultant to commander and replaced Johnston, who had been wounded in the fight. Both sides received reinforcements and strengthened their positions. The ever-reluctant McClellan, still believing in exaggerated rebel army size, stalled his attack. Lee, seeing that McClellan was not going to advance, went on the offensive. He dispatched J. E. B. Stuart's (23) cavalry on a reconnaissance that rode completely around the Union army on June 12–15.

On June 25, Lee began a series of attacks known as the Seven Days' Battles that pushed back the Union forces at Oak Grove, Mechanicsville, Gaines's Mill, Garnett's and Golding's Farms, Savage's Station, White Oak Swamp, and Malvern Hill. Superior artillery and greater numbers allowed the Union army to withdraw rather than be defeated. McClellan, aware of weaknesses in his rear areas from Stuart's ride around his army, had wisely relocated his base from the York to the James River. McClellan consolidated his force at Harrison's Landing, where his request to move against Petersburg was turned down and he was ordered to return to Washington.

The failure of the Union's Peninsular Campaign raised the morale and confidence of the South. It also displayed the difficulties of controlling multiple divisions and caused Lee to institute subordinate corps to increase his control over his army. The campaign also influenced Lee to resume offensive actions and move against the Union transportation and supply center that had been reestablished at Manassas Junction.

The Peninsular Campaign could—and likely should—have been the war's most influential battle. If McClellan had not stopped at the Warwick River, his superior numbers would have likely taken him into Richmond and ended the war. Instead, he resisted, the rebels reinforced, and Lee took command, setting the stage for three more years of warfare. McClellan's reluctance lost the campaign and extended the war, thus, the influence of the Peninsular Campaign ranks nearer the middle than the top of this list.

33

EDMUND KIRBY SMITH

Confederate General

1824–1893

Edmund Kirby Smith served first in the eastern theater before transferring to the West in early 1863 to take command of the Trans-Mississippi Department. After the Union army took control of the Mississippi River in the summer of 1863 and cut off communication from Richmond, Smith commanded his department with almost total independence until the end of the war. Smith's army was the last significant Confederate force to surrender.

Born on May 16, 1824, in St. Augustine, Florida, to parents from New England, Smith joined the Class of 1845 at the U.S. Military Academy. Known at West Point as "Seminole" because of his Florida origins, Smith graduated number nineteen in a class of thirty-seven cadets. He then fought as an artillery officer in the Mexican War, where he earned two brevet promotions for gallantry.

From 1849 to 1852, Smith served as a professor of mathematics at West Point before joining the Indian Campaigns on the Texas frontier. Wounded in a battle with Native Americans in 1859, Smith recovered to be promoted to major in command of Fort Colorado, Texas, in 1861. Several weeks before the firing on Fort Sumter, Smith refused to surrender his fort to Southern sympathizers. When news reached him of Florida's secession, he resigned his commission on April 6, 1861, and traveled to Virginia.

As a lieutenant colonel in the Confederate army, Smith joined Joseph E. Johnston (17) in the Shenandoah Valley. Promoted to brigadier general, Smith led a brigade at First Bull Run (10), where he was severely wounded. Upon recovery, he commanded a division as major general in October 1861. After additional operations in Virginia under P. G. T. Beauregard (43), Smith took command of the Department of East Tennessee at Knoxville.

In late summer of 1862, Smith joined Braxton Bragg's (60) invasion of Kentucky, where his troops defeated the Federals at Richmond on August 30. Smith served under Bragg in their unsuccessful fight for Perryville that turned back the Confederate invasion of Kentucky in October.

The Confederate government recognized Smith with an official "Thanks of Congress" and a promotion to lieutenant general for his service in Kentucky. Smith, disgusted with Bragg's leadership, traveled to Virginia and requested a separate command. In January 1863 his wishes were granted, and he assumed the leadership of all Confederate troops west of the Mississippi River.

For the remainder of the war Smith led the huge Trans-Mississippi Department. After the fall of Port Hudson and Vicksburg (7) gave the Union control of the Mississippi River, Smith acted almost independently from Richmond. In recognition of the size and independence of his command, President Jefferson Davis (9), in one of his few directives to Texas, promoted Smith to full general on February 19, 1864.

With no support from the East, Smith arranged for the acquisition of supplies and arms from the local countryside, across the river from Mexico, and by blockade runners (25) at Galveston. He also ordered cotton destroyed rather than allow it to fall in the hands of Union troops. He controlled local civilian governments as well as his own command. Although he had no authorization from Richmond to do so, Smith promoted officers to the rank of general. His virtual control of the Trans-Mississippi River gained the region the nickname of "Kirby Smithdom" to both his supporters and to detractors.

Smith soundly defeated Nathaniel Banks's (92) Red River Campaign (81) in the spring of 1864. He then attempted to send reinforcements to the eastern theater, but this proved impractical because the Union continued to control the Mississippi River. In the fall of 1864, Smith dispatched the majority of his cavalry forces under the command of

Sterling Price into Missouri. After initial successes, the column was forced to retreat back to Arkansas with heavy losses.

For the remainder of the war, Smith was able to mount only small operations and guerrilla activities. Despite his lack of support from Richmond and the large area of his responsibility, Smith was the last Confederate general to surrender his command. Still in control of much of Kirby Smithdom, the general did not agree to meet with Union officials at Galveston until June 2, 1865—more than seven weeks after Robert E. Lee had surrendered at Appomattox.

Shortly after his surrender, Smith heard rumors that several Confederate commanders had been detained in Virginia for their participation in the rebellion. As a result, he fled to Mexico and then to Cuba before returning to the United States in November 1865 after being informed he would not be arrested. Following an unsuccessful business venture, he became the president of the University of Nashville. In 1875 he joined the faculty of the University of the South at Sewanee, Tennessee, where he taught mathematics for the next fifteen years. Smith died at Sewanee on March 28, 1893, and is buried in the city cemetery.

Everything about Smith was controversial, including his name. Both he and his older brother Ephraim, who was killed in the Mexican War, had their mother's maiden name of Kirby as middle names. Ted to his family, he began signing his name E. Kirby Smith at the beginning of the war to distinguish himself from the many other Smiths. As his fame grew, both he and his family became known as the Kirby Smiths—sometimes printed with a hyphen—but Edmund never considered his surname to be anything other than Smith.

Also controversial was the way Smith handled his command. Even though he kept the Trans-Mississippi in the hands of the Confederates, the government in Richmond was not totally pleased with him. Davis disapproved of Smith's unauthorized promotion of subordinates to general ranks. The president finally officially approved some of the direct promotions; he simply ignored others.

Smith's very location during the war was polarized, too. Because he was located far from Richmond, he received little support from the Confederate government. Yet, this distance was also an advantage because he was mostly left alone, by friend and foe alike, to govern Kirby Smithdom as he saw fit. From all indicators, he performed this difficult job well. However, his influence on the war, despite his almost absolute control over the Trans-Mississippi, was not pronounced. Once the Union controlled the Mississippi River, the war's outcome rested with actions in the East and Deep South. Kirby Smithdom and the Confederacy itself were Lost Causes long before the final surrender.

34

TRANSPORTATION AND COMMUNICATIONS

1861–1865

To fight effectively, any army must have the capability to transport its soldiers, arms, and supplies where needed and to communicate among units in the field. Transportation and communications in the Civil War reached previously unmatched proficiency and established means and standards that were readily adopted by other armies around the world.

In the mid-nineteenth century the primary means of transporting armies was little changed from the beginnings of organized warfare. The vast majority of soldiers walked into battle while horses or mules pulled their artillery and supply wagons. "Footpower" continued to be the primary transportation of soldiers during this war, too, but the number of mounted cavalry animals available increased throughout its duration. According to the 1860 census, the U.S. horse population totaled 6,115,458, of which 1,698,328 were located in the seceding states. Conversely, the South had the advantage in the number of mules with 800,663 as opposed to only 328,890 in the North. Working oxen totaled a little more than two million, with about half that number on each side. With the average service of a cavalry mount lasting only four months and draft animals a little longer, replacement livestock was a priority in the North and the South alike.

Other means of transportation were also employed in the war. Although railroads had seen limited use in the Crimean War of 1853–1856, transportation by rail made its first significant impact on warfare in the Civil War. At the outbreak of the conflict, the U.S. rail network extended more than thirty thousand miles, with a little less than a third of that amount in the Confederacy.

In addition to the larger number of rail miles, the Union also had the advantage of more standardization of rail size and better rail line management. The railroads in the South were almost exclusively oriented north and south with little capability for east-west movement. The major difference in the rail lines between the North and South was their location. Because the war was fought mostly in the South, the invading Union armies constantly captured, destroyed, or interrupted rail usage. Conversely, the Union rail lines were generally beyond the reach of the Confederates.

Both sides effectively used railways to transport troops and supplies. The most notable use came in September 1863 when the Confederates defeated a Union force at Chickamauga (74). In response, the U.S. War Department dispatched an entire army of twenty-three thousand men, ten artillery batteries, and food and supplies by rail from Bristoe Station, Virginia, to Louisville, to Nashville, to Chattanooga—a distance of 1,233 miles—in only eleven days. The reinforcements contributed to the victory at Chattanooga (12) in November, opening the way for the Union advance on Atlanta (20).

The Union also exploited the use of steam vessels to move troops at sea, on rivers, and on other inland waterways. Sail- and oar-driven vessels had long been used to transport soldiers, but wind and manpower were neither reliable nor practical. The invention of the steam engine allowed ships of all sizes to quickly and efficiently move men and supplies. Many of the war's early battles were initiated by the North to secure waterways in Virginia as well as the Tennessee and Mississippi Rivers in the West. In the Peninsular Campaign (32) of 1862, the Union employed more than 400 ships to move 121,500 men; 14,500 animals; and all the needed food, ammunition,

and other supplies from the North to the Virginia shore.

Communications also evolved and improved during the conflict. For centuries armies had been limited to verbal messengers and written notes to dispatch information and orders. The Civil War produced great advances in signaling techniques, including the use of flags (semaphores), lights, and reflecting devices. By 1861 telegraph lines linked the major and many of the smaller towns all across the United States.

Like the railroads, the telegraph had seen its first war service in the Crimea, but its first widespread use and significant impact came in the Civil War. During the conflict, the U.S. Military Telegraph extended its wires more than fifteen thousand miles. The Union army added the Beardslee Telegraph, a system that increased mobility by replacing heavy batteries with a hand-turned magneto, to this fixed-line system to provide even greater communications for units directly on the battlefield. Confederate commanders relied on the telegraph to maintain contact among their units and with Richmond. Telegraph lines erected by both sides often changed hands with the ebb and flow of battle lines. Both sides tapped into the lines of the opposition in search of intelligence, causing the invention of various codes and ciphers to secure messages.

Presidents Abraham Lincoln (2) and Jefferson Davis (9) and their staffs depended on the telegraph for much of their information from the battlefronts. The White House had no telegraph room of its own, but Lincoln made daily visits to the War Department telegraph office. He frequently remained there for much of the day, waiting for news while also taking advantage of the privacy to work on other matters.

By the time U. S. Grant (3) took command of all Union troops in the spring of 1864, the Union telegraph network permitted him to have daily contact with commands in Virginia, West Virginia, and Georgia. His daily outgoing orders and incoming reports aided his coordination of the final offensives that defeated the rebellion. William Sherman (6) credited the wire message system with shortening the war, stating, "The value of the telegram cannot be exaggerated, as illustrated by the perfect accord of action of the armies of Virginia and Georgia."

The telegraph, as well as other technological advances, also kept civilians on both sides informed about the war's progress. Newspaper reporters and sketch artists accompanied armies in the field, and by horse messenger and the telegraph they were able to have war news on the front pages of newspapers in the North and South within days of a battle. Mathew Brady (41) and other photographers recorded battle results that brought visual images of death and destruction displayed in public expositions.

Advances in transportation and communications impressed observers from foreign countries who accompanied armies on both sides. Five years after Appomattox, Prussian officers employed telegraphic technologies from the American Civil War to mobilize their units quickly in their war against France. They also transported their army to the front by railroad to defeat and occupy France in the Franco-Prussian War.

The Union had the advantage in transportation and communications innovations in the Civil War as they did in practically every other resource. Southern leaders used innovations in transport and communications when possible, but they never could match the Union resources in either area. These advantages certainly contributed to the ultimate Union victory, but the real influence in the improvements were in their adaptation by other armies around the world. Footpower of the infantry would still dominate the battlefield, but over the next half century horses would be replaced by mechanized vehicles, supplies would move rapidly by rail, water, and eventually by air, and communications would go through the airwaves rather than by messenger or wire.

35

FORT DONELSON

February 11–16, 1862

The capture of Fort Donelson by the Federal army accomplished several objectives. It insured that Kentucky would remain in the Union, it opened the way for the invasion and occupation of Tennessee, it secured the Tennessee and Cumberland Rivers for Union army transportation, and it led to the eventual control of the Mississippi. The battle also displayed the talents and potential of U. S. Grant (3) and Nathan Bedford Forrest (21).

With the early Confederate victories in the East at Fort Sumter (50) and First Bull Run (10) and in the West at Wilson's Creek (70), the prospects for defeating the rebellion had looked bleak. Even as President Lincoln (2) and his generals had planned the Peninsular Campaign (32) against Richmond, they had also realized they had to take action in the West to maintain the neutrality of the border states and to implement the provisions of the Anaconda Plan to control the Mississippi River.

By early 1862 the Confederate army occupied Fort Henry on the Tennessee River and Fort Donelson on the Cumberland, gaining them control of Western Kentucky and the primary water routes from the Ohio River into Tennessee. In February, General Henry Halleck (63) authorized Grant and fifteen thousand men to neutralize the forts.

Both positions had artillery focused on the river and infantry to guard land approaches. Grant teamed with Commodore Andrew Foote of the U.S. Navy to launch a joint water and land assault on Fort Henry. Grant landed his infantry four miles from the fort to prepare an assault, while Foote maneuvered his boats to attack from the river. Fort Henry was still under construction and unprepared when Foote opened fire on the breastworks with his gunboats. The rebels briefly returned fire before surrendering on February 6. Neither Union nor Confederate casualties totaled more than two dozen.

By the time Grant arrived at Fort Henry the battle was already over. He then began the twelve-mile march to Fort Donelson while Foote retraced his route down the Tennessee River to the Ohio and then up the Cumberland River toward the Confederate defenses. On February 14, the Union army and navy were in position when Foote opened the battle with cannon fire from the river. The Donelson gunners, better prepared than those at Henry, returned fire, wounding Foote and forcing the Union gunboats to withdraw.

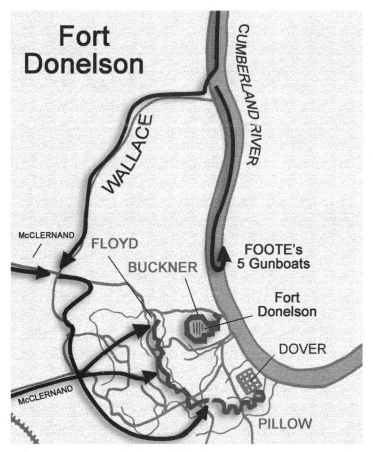

Except for the gun positions, Fort Donelson was little more than crude huts and trench lines. Snow and mud covered much of the ground and the Southern soldiers were low on food and other supplies. The Confederate commanders, Generals Gideon Pillow, John Floyd (28), and Simon Buckner, mindful of these conditions, decided that with the river blocked by the Union navy and Grant's force now numbering about twenty-five thousand—and gaining reinforcements daily—that they could not defend the fort despite having nearly twenty-one thousand soldiers. At daybreak on February 15, the Confederates struck out across snow-covered ground against Grant's right flank with hopes of opening an escape route to the south. Pillow was initially successful, but Floyd decided the resistance was too heavy and retreated back to Donelson. This forced Pillow and Buckner to also return to the fort's trenches. Grant immediately counterattacked, sealing the Confederate lines and even occupying some of the Confederate's trenches.

During the night, Floyd, a former secretary of war in President Buchanan's administration from 1857 to 1860, turned his troops over to Pillow, explaining that he feared execution as a traitor if captured. Pillow immediately turned his command over to Buckner. Pillow, Floyd, and about two thousand men fled across the Cumberland to Nashville. Nathan Bedford Forrest (21) refused to surrender his cavalry and escaped under the cover of darkness with his regiment and an unknown number of infantrymen. The following morning Buckner approached Grant at a hotel in nearby Dover asking for surrender terms. Grant responded, "No terms except unconditional and immediate surrender can be accepted. I propose to move immediately upon your works."

Buckner, a prewar friend of Grant, reluctantly replied, "The distribution of forces and the overwhelming force under your command compel me to accept the ungenerous and unchivalrous terms which you propose." With two thousand men already dead or wounded, Buckner and more than eleven thousand of his men laid down their arms. Union casualties totaled about five hundred dead and two thousand wounded.

News of the victory in the West swept across the country, providing joy in the North where good news had been sparse. The same news met with grief and doubt in the South. Although Lincoln would go through several more generals as he sought someone who could defeat Lee, he took notice of the previously unknown general now known as "Unconditional Surrender" Grant.

In addition to affecting the morale in both the North and the South, the fall of Fort Donelson also had significant strategic influence. The control of the Cumberland and Tennessee Rivers maintained the neutrality of Kentucky and opened the way for a land invasion of Tennessee, Mississippi, and Georgia. With these waterways secured, the Union now could use the protected Ohio River to stage an offensive down the Mississippi to eventually split the Confederacy.

The Union victory at Fort Henry would have been mostly meaningless by itself. The Union had to capture both forts to meet its objectives. On the other hand, Confederate control of either fort was as good as controlling both. While the two battles were small in relation to the huge fights looming in the East, they were influential in many ways. In addition to opening the way into the Deep South and the Mississippi River, the battles showcased the abilities of Grant and brought him to the attention of Lincoln. They also displayed Grant's abilities to integrate land and water forces that would prove successful in capturing Vicksburg (7) in July 1863. All these reasons combine to elevate the ranking of Fort Donelson into to the top half of this list.

36

THOMAS JONATHAN "STONEWALL" JACKSON

Confederate General

1824–1863

Thomas Jonathan "Stonewall" Jackson is second only to Robert E. Lee (5) as the most revered Confederate commander. He earned this honor for his skills in independent command and for his abilities to move his troops rapidly by foot and rail to change the course of battles. While Jackson was not without his faults, he was a superior combat commander whose long-lasting reputation is as much the result of his early death as his battlefield accomplishments.

Born on January 21, 1824, in Clarksburg, Virginia (now West Virginia), Jackson was orphaned at an early age and reared by a series of relatives. Despite growing up in poverty and receiving only a basic education, he obtained an appointment to West Point as a member of the Class of 1846. Jackson struggled with the Academy's academics in his early years but began to excel the longer he stayed. By graduation he ranked number seventeen of fifty-nine cadets.

Commissioned in the artillery, Jackson's first assignment was with Winfield Scott's army in Mexico, where he fought in the war's final battles and earned brevets to the rank of major. He then served for several years in Florida and New York before resigning his commission to become a professor of artillery tactics and natural philosophy at the Virginia Military Institute (VMI) in Lexington.

While in Mexico, Jackson had "found religion" and joined the Presbyterian Church. During his decade at VMI he became involved with the church to the point that the cadets called him "Tom Fool Jackson." During his summers Jackson traveled from VMI throughout the North and across Europe. These visits did not focus on military matters or history but rather on culture and the arts. His only association with politics during this period was to escort a company of cadets to observe the hanging of John Brown (54) in 1859.

Except to a few of his classmates and fellow veterans of the Mexican War, Jackson was unknown to the military or the civilian population at the outbreak of the Civil War. Jackson strongly supported the secessionists. In March 1861 he voiced his feelings when

he spoke to the VMI cadets, telling them, "The time may come for when your state may need your services; and if that time does come, then draw your swords, and throw away the scabbards."

When Virginia joined the Confederacy, Jackson did indeed draw his saber. After briefly training new recruits at Richmond, he organized a brigade and led them to Manassas where he and his unit earned the name of "Stonewall" in the Battle of First Bull Run (10) the following July.

Jackson went from unknown to celebrity in a single day's battle and advanced to the rank of brigadier general. By October he was a major general in charge of Confederate forces in the Shenandoah Valley. During his first major campaign that winter, he failed to exhibit the leadership that would mark his later successes, and this failure brought to light Jackson's inability to always get along with his peers as well as his subordinates. This trait almost brought an end to his career.

First, Jackson failed to defeat the Union army at Romney, Virginia, in January 1862, and then he ordered General William Loring to take the strategically important village. Loring appealed the order to the Confederate secretary of war, who rescinded Jackson's instructions and ordered Loring back to Winchester. Jackson reacted with a message to the secretary, as well as to the governor of Virginia, stating he could not tolerate such interference with his command and offering his resignation. Need for good commanders won out over politics. Loring was transferred and Jackson returned to operations in the Valley.

Again, Jackson was not successful. At Kernstown on March 23, he attacked what he thought was an inferior force. He miscalculated the strength of the Union defenses and had to retreat, nearly losing his supply and medical wagons. Jackson blamed his loss on faulty intelligence and violation of the Sabbath.

After Kernstown, Jackson joined Lee in halting Union's Peninsular Campaign (32). Although Lee proved successful, Jackson made few contributions, as he was defeated along the Chickahominy at Mechanicsburg, Gaines's Mill, Savage's Station, Glendale, and Malvern Hill. In later years he would be known as the heroic "Jackson of the Valley," but in the spring of 1862 he was known negatively as "Jackson of the Chickahominy."

At West Point, Jackson had earned the reputation as a slow learner but one who eventually got it right. Following his initial success at First Bull Run, Jackson went through a period of learning and adjustment. By the time he returned to the Shenandoah from the Peninsula, he had learned his lessons and learned them well.

His lightning envelopment of the Union northern flank at Second Bull Run (40) in August 1862 was the battle's turning point. His rapid march from Harpers Ferry to reinforce Lee at Antietam (1) the next month probably saved the Southern army from total defeat. In October he advanced to the rank of lieutenant general in command of the reorganized II Corps and took responsibility for holding the right side of the line at Fredericksburg (53) in December 1862.

Jackson, who had gained his first fame in the defense of First Bull Run, was aware of his offensive failures on the Peninsula. He was happy to once again be in the position of defender. To a subordinate he said, "Major, my men have sometimes failed to take a position, but to defend one, never! I am glad the Yankees are coming."

At Fredericksburg, Jackson significantly influenced the Confederate victory and Lee now looked upon him as his most trusted subordinate. His ability to plan rail transportation in order to rapidly move his army greatly increased their mobility. When rail transportation was either not available or impractical, Jackson's motivated army could march so fast that they became known as "foot cavalry." On May 2, 1863, Jackson showed the merits of his foot cavalry by rapidly moving his men more than sixteen miles to strike an exposed Union flank at Chancellorsville (31).

It was Jackson's finest hour but also nearly his last. Following the victory he rode forward of his lines to reconnoiter the Union positions. In the advancing darkness, Confederate pickets mistook the returning general and his party for the enemy. A musket ball to the left arm seriously wounded Jackson. He was evacuated by wagon to Guinea Station south of Frederickburg, where doctors amputated his limb. Lee wrote to him, "You are better off than I am, for while you have lost your left, I have lost my right arm."

Lee had indeed lost his right arm. Jackson, weakened from loss of blood and from pneumonia, died on May 10. His body was honored in Richmond before being buried in Lexington.

"Old Jack" to his soldiers and "Stonewall" to his adoring public, he had stood six feet tall and weighed about 175 pounds. He possessed blue eyes and a beard described as "rusty." Religious to the point of piety, he lived, some said, by the New Testament but fought by the Old. His personal bravery, ability to motivate his troops, skills in preparing defenses, and aptitude for rapidly maneuvering to gain the advantage on the battlefield were as good as any commander of either side. Had he lived, the outcome at Gettysburg—and perhaps the war as well—might have been different.

Jackson's ranking, however, rests on reality rather than potential. His poor performance on the Peninsula has been largely overlooked because Southerners exalted him to almost deity status along with Lee and the Lost Cause. However, by the time of Fredericksburg, Jackson had more than "earned his spurs" as a superior battlefield leader and most likely would have favorably influenced future battles had he lived. Death not only ended what he might have accomplished, but also it added to his status of celebrity and hero of the Confederacy. That he did not live to remain Lee's right arm and because his efforts were for the losing side, his ranking in the top half of this list is more for his lasting fame than a result of his actual performance.

37

APPOMATTOX CAMPAIGN

March 29–April 9, 1865

The Appomattox Campaign stands as one of the most successful pursuits and blocking operations in military history. U. S. Grant (3) cut off every avenue of retreat for the Army of Northern Virginia, forcing Robert E. Lee (5) to surrender on April 9 at Appomattox Court House in south-central Virginia. Other Confederate armies in the South and West followed. The American Civil War was over.

After Grant assumed command of the Union army in the spring of 1864, he began the Overland Campaign to defeat Lee and capture Richmond. By June he had the Confederate capital surrounded and Lee besieged at Petersburg (46). For ten months Lee held the line at Petersburg, but he realized that he could not continue his defense when William Sherman (6) marched his army from the Carolinas to join with Grant. Lee feared for the survival of his army and the Confederacy if the two Union forces combined.

On February 8, 1865, Lee wrote to the newly appointed Confederate secretary of war John Breckinridge (84), "You must not be surprised if calamity befalls us."

Lee knew that for his army and the rebellion to endure he had to break out of Petersburg and join up with Joseph Johnston's (17) army, which was opposing Sherman in North Carolina. Only by regaining the offensive could Lee avoid defeat. Lee was also aware that his army was short of food and supplies and that his horses and draft animals were in poor condition. This, along with muddy roads and winter conditions, also forced him to postpone his breakout until early spring.

On March 25, 1865, Lee attempted to break through the Union lines east of Petersburg at Fort Steadman. The Federals easily beat back the assault, but Grant was not willing to simply continue the siege. Instead, he took the initiative by sending Phillip Sheridan (8) to the southwest of the Confederate defenses to capture the important road junction at Five Forks. On April 1, Sheridan drove the Confederate defenders, commanded by George Pickett (93), from Five Forks.

With the last of his supply lines cut and the threat of Sherman joining Grant, Lee had no choice but to abandon Petersburg and Richmond. On April 2 and 3, Lee's army left their trenches and either avoided Union troops or fought their way through.

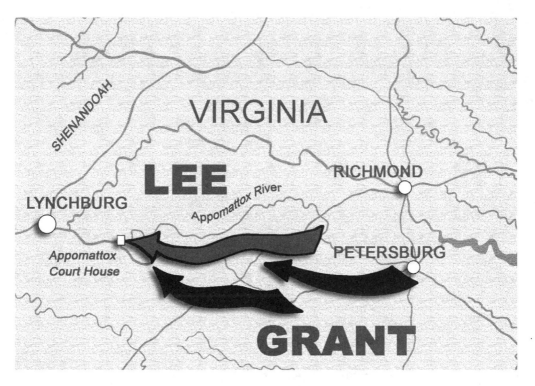

Lee planned to consolidate his army at Amelia Court House, where they would receive much needed rations sent from Richmond. They would then march down the Richmond and Danville Railroad Line, unite with Johnston, who was advancing from the south, and resume offensive operations.

Lee arrived at Amelia Court House on April 4 only to discover the rations from Richmond had been delayed by bad weather. With his army hungry, Lee postponed his march and sent wagons into the countryside to gather food from the locals. Farms and villages in the region had little to contribute, and Lee was forced to move on with his soldiers still hungry.

Grant knew he had the advantage and pushed his subordinates to aggressively pursue and block the Confederate retreat. Lee's delay at Amelia Court House allowed Sheridan time to cut the Richmond and Danville Railroad to the south at Jetersville on April 5. Lee now had to turn westward toward Lynchburg and march his army night and day to keep ahead of the Federals. Both men and animals began to drop by the wayside of hunger and fatigue.

On April 6, the Union pursuers caught up with the Confederate rear at Saylor's Creek and attacked. In a brief battle, the rebels lost seven thousand men captured, including six generals, as well as most of their few remaining supply wagons. Meanwhile, Grant dispatched Sheridan's cavalry to ride around the retreating army and block its path westward.

On April 7, Grant sent a message to Lee asking for his surrender. Lee read the letter and, still hoping to escape to the west, turned to James Longstreet (13) and said, "Not yet."

Lee continued his march and by the next night could hear Union artillery fire to his front and see thousands of campfires of soldiers blocking his way near Appomattox Court House. At dawn on April 9, Lee's army made one last assault on the Union lines at Appomattox Station. By 8:30 a.m. the Confederate corps commanded by James B. Gordon were repulsed. When Gordon sent a message to Lee that he could no longer go forward, the Confederate commander replied, "There is nothing left for me to do but to go and see General Grant, and I would rather die a thousand deaths."

At 4:00 p.m. that afternoon, Lee surrendered to Grant in the parlor of Wilmer McLean's home in Appomattox Court House. McLean had previously lived near Manassas, Virginia, where his house had been damaged in the Battle of First Bull Run (10). He had moved to Appomattox, Virginia, to avoid the war, only to have it end in his living room.

Lee's army formally marched past silent lines of Union troops on April 12 to turn over their arms and colors. News of the surrender soon reached the remaining rebels in the field. Johnston surrendered on April 18, and E. Kirby Smith (33) gave up in the West on May 26. The war was finally over.

The Union army in the Appomattox Campaign numbered more than 120,000, as opposed to only about 50,000 Confederates. Union casualties in the campaign totaled about ten thousand, while Lee lost half his army to death, wounds, capture, or desertion. When they surrendered at Appomattox Court House, the Army of Northern Virginia had only 26,765 survivors in its ranks.

Even if Lee had been successful in escaping and in uniting with Johnston, it is unlikely he could have done little more than prolong the war a few weeks. Some Confederate leaders wanted Lee to break up his army into guerrilla bands and flee to the mountains of western Virginia and North Carolina to continue resistance. Lee knew that this would only antagonize U.S. officials and add to the South's punishment for the rebellion. Lee, like Grant, understood that it was time for healing and reuniting rather than continuing the carnage.

The importance of the Appomattox Campaign is primarily because it was the last. Lee and the Confederacy had been on the decline since Antietam (1) and defeated since Gettysburg (3) and Vicksburg (7). It was just a matter of time, and that time came at Appomattox Court House in Virginia on April 9, 1865.

38

BLACK SOLDIERS AND SAILORS

1861–1865

The end of slavery for African Americans was the most important legacy of the Civil War. Black soldiers and sailors, despite discrimination in equipment and pay, significantly contributed to the conflict by fighting for their freedom and the preservation of the Union. Even though forced to serve exclusively under white officers, black soldiers showed the dedication and proficiency for them to have a place in the postwar U.S. military and established that black and white military history would be inseparable from that point forward.

Abraham Lincoln (2) declared at the beginning of the Civil War that its purpose was to preserve the Union; freeing of the slaves was secondary at the time. Most Union officials foresaw the war as being short, and only a few proposed the use of black soldiers and sailors to fight the rebellion. While many Northerners supported abolition, few accepted blacks on an equal basis in their society or their armed forces. Some military commanders feared that their white soldiers would refuse to fight if blacks were included in their ranks. Lincoln also recognized the fact that the border states, where slavery was legal, might bolt to the Confederacy if he solicited black soldiers.

This exclusion of blacks from military service was not new. Similar policies had been followed in the beginning of the American Revolution and the War of 1812, but as these wars continued in duration, the need for manpower presented opportunity for black enlistment. More than five thousand blacks served in the Revolutionary War, contributing to the independence of the United States that also kept their brothers in bondage on the arrival of peace.

Once again, in the Civil War, the need for soldiers and sailors provided the opportunity for blacks to don the uniform of their country. By early 1862, with the obvious conclusion that the war would not be of a short duration, battle casualties and disease had dramatically reduced the Union army numbers. Northern military commanders, as well as newspapers, called for the enlistment of African Americans. Several commanders took matters in their own hands and formed black units even before Secretary of War Edwin Stanton issued orders in August 1862 authorizing General Rufus Saxton to "recruit, arm, and equip" a regiment of five thousand black soldiers at Port Royal,

South Carolina. While Stanton promised that each volunteer soldier and his family would be declared "forever free," he held the officer slots for whites only.

Saxton formed his black regiment, but the First South Carolina Colored Volunteers was not officially called to active duty until January 31, 1863, because Lincoln delayed most actions concerning blacks and slavery. He wanted the Union army finally to achieve a victory, like the turning back of Robert E. Lee's (5) invasion of the North at Antietam (1) in September 1862, before he proceeded. Lincoln then used the victory to announce his Emancipation Proclamation (22) that, for the first time, made ending slavery a key objective of the war. With this purpose finally declared, the way opened for black units to fill the manpower need.

Black manpower was welcomed into the Union army, but many white soldiers and commanders expressed doubts about the blacks' fighting abilities. The performance of the black units in direct combat quelled these concerns. Black regiments from Louisiana, composed of freemen as well as former slaves, repeatedly assaulted Confederate positions at Port Hudson on May 27, 1863, earning them the respect of their fellow U.S. soldiers and praise from their commanders.

General Nathaniel P. Banks (92), who expressed reservations about black soldiers before the Battle of Port Hudson, declared, "Whatever any doubts may have existed heretofore as to the efficiency of Negro regiments, the history of this day proves conclusively to those who were in condition to observe the conduct of these regiments that the government will find in this class of troops effective supporters and defenders. The severe test to which they were subjected, and the determined manner in which they encountered the enemy, leaves upon my mind no doubt of their ultimate success."

Any further concerns were sated when the 54th Massachusetts Colored Regiment, commanded by Colonel Robert G. Shaw, assaulted Fort Wagner, South Carolina, the following July. Although the attack failed and Shaw and many of his regiment were killed, the battle provided even more proof that black soldiers could and would fight—even in the most severe combat conditions.

The performance of black regiments at Port Hudson and Fort Wagner verified their fighting abilities, and Union officials quickly began tapping into this large pool of recruits. In addition to soliciting freemen in the North, the black regiments accepted escaped slaves from the South, each of whom further depleted Southern resources by removing another worker.

During the last two years of the war, more than 180,000 African Americans served in the U.S. Army in one hundred twenty infantry regiments, twelve artillery regiments, seven cavalry regiments, and five regiments of engineers. This total represents more than 10 percent of the entire Union force. At least twenty-seven hundred blacks died as a result of direct battle with the Confederate army. Many more perished of accidents and disease.

Blacks also served as sailors in the Union cause. Exact numbers are elusive but at least 8 percent of the U.S. Navy in the Civil War was African American. Filling crews of any seagoing vessel had always been difficult, and ship captains had welcomed black sailors on board even before the American Revolution. Although they were generally restricted to the lower ranks, blacks fought side-by-side with their white shipmates. Joachim Peace, a cannon loader aboard the USS *Kearsarge,* earned the Medal of Honor for his bravery in the battle against the Confederate raider *Alabama* (90) off the French coast on June 19, 1864.

It is noteworthy that even the Confederates recognized the advantages of recruiting blacks into their ranks. General Pat Cleburne recommended enlisting black soldiers in exchange for their freedom as early as January 1864, but President Jefferson Davis (9) refused to act on the idea. A month before the war ended, Davis, on the recommendation of Lee, was reconsidering the proposal but the conflict concluded before any significant action took place.

Throughout their service to the army and navy of the Union, black soldiers and sailors faced discrimination in the quality of equipment they received and the amount of compensation paid. Besides racism from their fellow soldiers, they faced the hatred of their Confederate opponents who threatened to execute or re-enslave captured African Americans. None of the internal or external slights and threats, however, stopped blacks from proving their value as soldiers and sailors and in participating in the fight for their freedom.

The North would have won the war without placing blacks in uniform, but the service of African Americans certainly aided the Union victory. Although more than eighty years would pass before blacks were totally integrated into the U.S. armed forces, from the Civil War onward they remained on active, albeit segregated, duty. In the decades following the war, regiments of black infantrymen and cavalrymen fought in the Indian Wars on the western frontier and participated in every U.S. conflict before their integration into regular units after World War II.

The history of the black soldier and sailor is much more honorable than is the treatment they received from their country and commanders. However, their performance in the Civil War was influential not only for their contributions but also for their establishing themselves as a lasting and integral part of the U.S. military.

39

JOHN SEDGWICK

Union General

1813–1864

John Sedgwick was the most beloved senior officer in the Union army and proved himself both brave and dependable in battle. He earned the reputation as one of the most outstanding corps commanders, and only his death in battle a year before the end of the war prevented him from assuming even higher command.

Born in Cornwall Hollow, Connecticut, on September 13, 1813, Sedgwick lived there as a boy, and after graduation from high school, remained in the village to teach for the next two years. At age twenty he entered the U.S. Military Academy where he graduated twenty-fourth of fifty in the Class of 1837. Among his classmates were future Union general Joe Hooker (48) and Confederate generals Braxton Bragg (60) and Jubal Early (19).

Over the next twenty-four years he served as an artillery officer in the Seminole War, in the Mexican War, and on the western frontier against the Indians. In 1855 he transferred to the mounted army, where he became a major in the 2nd Cavalry, a unit commanded by Robert E. Lee (5), at the outbreak of the Civil War. When Lee resigned his U.S. commission to join his home state of Virginia's forces, Sedgwick advanced to colonel and took command of the regiment.

By August 1861, Sedgwick commanded a division in the Peninsular Campaign (32) and fought at Yorktown and Seven Pines. He was seriously wounded June 30, 1862, during the Seven Days' battle at Frayser's Farm. Although not fully recovered, he returned to the field and earned commendations for his leadership and valor at Antietam (1) the following September. During the fight near Sharpsburg, the general suffered two additional wounds—the second leaving him unconscious on the field—that kept him out of the Battle of Fredericksburg (53) the following December.

Sedgwick returned to the Army of the Potomac as a corps commander in time to participate in the Battle of Chancellorsville (31). His corps initially covered Joe Hooker's army's advance against Chancellorsville by protecting the Union flank near Fredericksburg. When Stonewall Jackson (36) flanked Hooker, Sedgwick stormed

and overran the Confederate defenses at Marye's Heights that had repelled the Union attack in the previous Fredericksburg battle.

Sedgwick then turned his corps to reinforce Hooker at Chancellorsville, but on May 4, 1863, at Salem Church he found he was all but surrounded by Lee's army. When some of his subordinates suggested they give up rather than be annihilated, Sedgwick replied simply, "There will be no surrendering." He then led a breakout and retreat that saved most of his command.

The following July at Gettysburg (4), Sedgwick's corps remained in reserve for much of the battle. Four months later, however, Sedgwick—now in command of two corps at the battle of Rappahannock Bridge—captured seventeen hundred rebel prisoners, eight battle flags, and four pieces of artillery.

In early May 1864, Sedgwick again led his corps with distinction at the Wilderness (62). On May 9 he maneuvered his command into position at Spotsylvania Court House (65). In his usual manner of leading from the front, he personally rode to the forward lines to select the best positions for his artillery.

Sedgwick's aides and several of the artillerymen warned the general to take cover from sniper fire coming from enemy positions in a tree line about eight hundred meters distant. After a bullet went over their heads, several of the men hit the ground. Sedgwick continued to walk around and admonished, "I'm ashamed of you dodging that way. They couldn't hit an elephant at this distance."

The next round, likely fired from an English precision-manufactured Whitworth sniper rifle, struck Sedgwick under the left eye, killing him instantly. His body was returned to his place of birth for interment in the Cornwall Hollow cemetery.

Sedgwick left behind the reputation of being a strong but fair disciplinarian who was genuinely liked by his subordinates, peers, and superiors alike. Called "Uncle John" by his men, he never married and his only vice appears to have been an addiction to various card games of solitaire.

Monuments to Sedgwick were erected after the war at Gettysburg, the site where he was killed, and at his burial place. Surviving classmates from the Class of 1837 dedicated a monument to the general in 1868 at West Point, supposedly cast from cannons captured by Sedgwick's commands during the war. This monument itself has provided influence, inspiration, and perhaps hope to every cadet at the Military Academy since. According to tradition, if a cadet is deficient in academics, he should go to the monument the night before his end-term examination in full dress uniform, under arms, and spin the rowels on the monument's spurs. The luck provided is supposed to help the cadet pass his tests.

Sedgwick proved time and time again that he was one of the Union's most influential corps commanders. Because of his death in action, he never had the opportunity to command at even higher levels and possibly earn a higher placement on this list. The simple fact that he was an extremely efficient commander who maintained the respect, if not love, of all who knew him moves him up in the rankings. While not as influential as the Union big three—Grant (3), Sherman (6), and Sheridan (8)—or as several Confederate leaders, Sedgwick is well deserving of the honors he received, the monuments dedicated to him, and his ranking on the list.

40

SECOND BULL RUN

August 29–30, 1862

When John Pope (86) assumed command of the Union army in the summer of 1862, he bragged to his new units that, in his previous command in the West, his men had seen only the backs of the enemy. At Second Bull Run, he and his army got a full-front view of the rebels as Robert E. Lee's (5) better-organized army soundly defeated the Union force. Like the battle on the same ground a year before, the Confederates sent Yankees in retreat back to Washington. The victory gave Lee control of Northern Virginia and opened the way for his first invasion of the North into Maryland and Antietam (1).

As the indecisive but bloody Peninsular Campaign (32) came to an end in July 1862, President Lincoln (2) and his staff decided to unite the three separate Union armies in the East under the command of Pope. Pope's mission was to continue to guard Washington, to protect the Shenandoah Valley, and to move toward Charlottesville to draw Lee away from defending Richmond. Lee recognized that it was imperative to fight the individual armies before they could unite into one large force.

The Confederate commander responded on August 24 by dividing his own army and dispatching Stonewall Jackson (36) to circle Pope's troops deployed along the Orange and Alexandria Railroad south of Manassas. Lee sent the other half of his army, under James Longstreet (13), about thirty miles west near the small town of Orleans.

On August 27, Jackson's swift-marching infantry captured the primary Union supply depot at Manassas, took what they needed, and destroyed the rest. Jackson then defeated a small Northern force at Union Mills, destroyed its railroad bridge, and prepared defenses along an incomplete railroad cut at Stoney Ridge near Sudley Springs. The defensive line covered much of the same ground where First Bull Run (10) had been fought a year earlier.

Pope hurried his command toward Manassas, but in the movement his divisions became scattered over an area too large to control. On the morning of August 29, Pope ordered his army of sixty-two thousand to destroy Jackson's twenty thousand soldiers. Instead of a united attack, the unorganized, confused Union army advanced

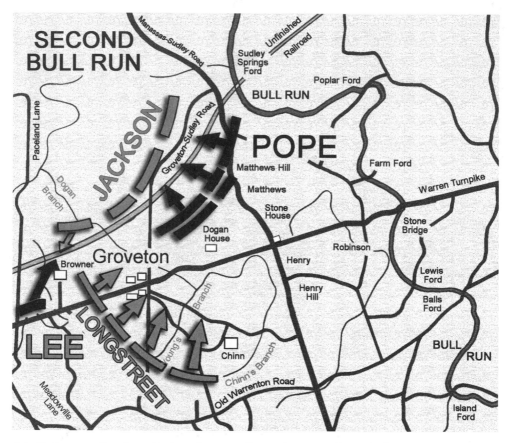

with little coordination. Jackson's men, from their excellent defenses along the railroad cut, easily pushed back the piecemeal, frontal attack. James Longstreet's (13) corps arrived on Jackson's right flank about noon.

Pope, unaware of Longstreet's approach, once again attacked Jackson on the morning of August 30. Longstreet later wrote of the Union attack, "Evidently Pope supposed that I was gone, as he was ignoring me entirely. His whole army seemed to surge up against Jackson as if to crush him."

Pope failed to "crush" Jackson and then learned the whereabouts of Longstreet fully when Lee ordered him to envelop the Union left flank. Defeated and nearly surrounded, Pope ordered a retreat back toward Washington. Only a stubborn fight by a Union delaying force at Henry House Hill allowed Pope's survivors to escape.

Lee pursued the retreating Federals along their west flank and inflicted more casualties on a Union rear guard force near Chantilly on September 1. Pope and the remainder of his army withdrew to positions around Washington. Lee, aware that the defenses around the Federal capital were too strong to successfully attack, consolidated his army and began plans to invade the North.

The battle was costly to both sides. Of the seventy-five thousand Union troops ultimately committed to the battle, sixteen thousand, or 21 percent, became casualties. Southern losses totaled nine thousand, or 19 percent, of the forty-eight thousand combatants. These numbers reflected the Confederate victory but they also were an indicator of the future. The South could ill afford such losses. Its manpower base nowhere equaled that of the North. Replacements in blue uniforms easily filled those lost to death, wounds, or capture, while replacements for those in gray were becoming more difficult to find.

The Union army arrived outside Washington defeated and demoralized. Pope blamed the loss on his subordinates and even sought the court martial of one of his generals. However, Pope no longer had, or never had gained, the confidence of his army and the president. Lincoln relieved him and reinstated George McClellan (51) in command.

Second Bull Run left the Union army in shambles with doubts about their own leaders and their abilities to defeat the rebellion. Lee emerged from the fight with the growing reputation as a superior tactical leader and a motivator of his soldiers. With Richmond and Northern Virginia now secure, Lee looked to take the war into the United States to gain more substantial victories in order to force the North to recognize the independence of the South.

By the beginning of September 1862, the war was in its second year and Lee and the Confederacy had progressed from defending the capital of Richmond to gaining control of all of Virginia. The Confederate army was now better led and trained than its opponent and possessed a much higher morale. Many Southerners believed that victory and independence were in sight, but the war still had many years to pass and many more battles to be fought before its end. The rebels would win additional battles in the future, but the Union would dominate the key fights because of its vast resources in war materials and men. More importantly, the Union found emerging leaders who could match and defeat Lee. Other battles would gain the monikers of "high tide" and "zenith" of the Confederacy, but it may very well be that Lee and the South were more in control after Second Bull Run than at any other period in the long war.

For this reason, Second Bull Run deserves a high ranking on this list. It was pivotal in securing the defenses of the early Confederacy, but the confidence it provided encouraged Lee to advance toward his first major defeat, and the war's turning point, at Antietam (1) only weeks after the second victory at Manassas. For that reason it ranks below Antietam as well as the decisive battles at Gettysburg (4), Vicksburg (7), and Atlanta (20).

41

MATHEW B. BRADY

Photographer

1823–1896

Mathew B. Brady became the most famous and popular photographer of his time. President Abraham Lincoln (2) credited Brady's photograph with helping him win the election of 1860. Brady's later photographs were the first to thoroughly document a war and it leaders. His images remain today as the best, and, in most cases the only, actual pictorial record of the Civil War.

Much about Brady's early life is unknown other than he was born sometime in 1823 in Warren County, New York. As a teenager he worked in Saratoga as a graphic artist before moving to New York City in the early 1840s to manufacture jewel cases. Soon after his arrival he met the inventor Samuel F. B. Morse, who taught Brady the daguerreotype method of photography that had been developed in 1837.

Brady opened a portrait studio in 1843 and quickly became the city's most popular photographer for the famous as well as ordinary citizens. Using his jewel case skills, he designed and made cases for his photographs, which he exhibited in his own gallery. Brady, clearly a leader in the early days of photography, soon gained accolades and fortunes. In 1851 he toured Europe with his exhibit of photographs, adding more awards and more fame to his reputation as the leading pioneer in a new medium.

Brady's poor eyesight, a problem since his youth, further deteriorated during his tour, and he realized that he needed assistants to continue and expand his work. By the mid-1850s Brady had a host of helpers working in all aspects of his photography business. His principal assistant, Alexander Gardner, introduced Brady to the collodion, or wet plate process, that made the development and reprinting of pictures faster and cheaper. Brady's gallery quickly became a leader in the production of Carte-de-Visite, business-card-size photographs that allowed pictures to be freely distributed and collected.

In 1858, Brady established a second gallery in Washington, D.C., with Gardner in charge. Over the next two years the two studios photographed nearly every famous elected official, entertainer, and other public person on the East Coast.

On February 27, 1860, a little-known Republican candidate for president visited Brady's New York studio on the afternoon before a scheduled speech at the Cooper Union Hall. Copies of Brady's picture of the rugged but distinguished face of Abraham Lincoln soon circulated throughout the country as additions to private collections as well as reproductions in newspapers and periodicals. Lincoln later said, "Brady and Cooper Union made me president."

At the outbreak of the Civil War, Brady was the most famous and wealthy photographer in the United States. He could have easily maintained his fame and fortune by continuing his portrait business, but he felt drawn to recording the events of the war. Brady was at his Washington studio when the Union army moved toward Manassas in July 1861 in what many thought would bring a quick end to the rebellion. Brady loaded his equipment on a wagon and joined the Washington sightseers on their way to observe the fight.

Brady did not arrive at First Bull Run (10) in time to see the battle, and some of his equipment was damaged in the wild Union retreat back to Washington. While he did not get photos of Bull Run, he did record some of the retreat, and his observations significantly influenced his career and the future of combat photography.

On his return to Washington, Brady equipped teams of his assistants with cameras and wagons and dispatched them to the front. When later asked why he left a profitable practice to travel with his staff to the field, he simply responded, "A spirit in my feet said 'Go' and I went."

Before the American Civil War, pioneer photographers had taken a few images on European battlefields, but until Brady no one had successfully recorded extensive images of battles and those who fought and died in them. Focused mostly on leaders and activities in rear areas, Brady's early photographs were best described in a *New York World* article in July 1862, which read, "They have threaded the weary stadia of every march; have hung on the skirts of every battle scene; have caught the compassion of the hospital; the romance of the bivouac, the pomp and panoply of the field review."

Brady's first detailed photographic record of a battle took place at Antietam (1) in September 1862. The smoke had barely cleared the battlefield before Brady's images, mostly actually taken by Alexander Gardner, his assistant, were shown in New York in an exhibit titled "The Dead of Antietam."

The exhibit opened to mixed reviews. Many visitors were shocked by the pictures, but all who saw them better understood the destruction and death on the battlefield. After visiting the exhibit, writer Oliver Wendell Holmes proclaimed, "Let him who wishes to know what war is look at this series of illustrations. It is so nearly like visiting the battlefield to look over these views that all the emotions excited by the actual sight of the stained and sordid scene come back to us, and we buried them in the recesses of our cabinet as we would have buried the mutilated remains of the dead they too vividly represent."

On October 20, 1862, the *New York Times* stated, "Mr. Brady has done something to bring home to us the terrible reality and earnestness of war. If he has not brought bodies and laid them on our dooryard and along the streets, he has done something very like it. It seems somewhat singular that the same sun that looked down on the faces of the slain, blistering them, blotting out from the bodies all the semblance to humanity, and hastening corruption, should have thus caught their features upon canvas, and given them perpetuity forever."

For the remainder of the war Brady or his assistants followed the Union army, recording the soldiers in camp, in battle, and during the aftermath of campaigns. He invested more than $100,000 of his own money to obtain about ten thousand prints. Because of his failing eyesight, Brady had to rely mostly on his assistants for the actual photography work, but the resulting pictures were almost exclusively credited to Brady and his studio.

By the end of the war, Brady had spent all of his personal fortune and was deeply in debt. He presumed, or at least hoped, that the U.S. government would buy his photographs as a historical record. Brady discovered that neither the government nor the American public wanted further reminders of the war. Once peace arrived, no one would buy or pay admission to see photographs of the war and its dead. Brady was forced to sell his New York studio and go into bankruptcy.

Brady fell into despair and alcoholism. Congress finally granted him $25,000 in 1875 for his photographic archive, but he remained in debt. He continued to drink, and worked for other photographers, but accomplished little over his remaining years. On January 15, 1896, Brady, blind and broke, died in the charity ward of New York's Presbyterian Hospital. Friends and admirers arranged for his burial in the Congressional Cemetery in Washington, D.C.

Shortly before his death, Brady said, "No one will ever know what I went through to secure those negatives. The world can never appreciate it. It changed the whole course of my life."

Ironically, Brady died only a few weeks before an exhibit of his photographs opened in New York. The war was far enough in the past for Brady's images to once again be appreciated. Since that time, practically no book, magazine article, television show, or other medium story on the Civil War has not included one or more of Brady's images.

Before Brady, only veterans or immediate visitors to battlefields had any idea of the death, blood, and carnage of war. After Brady, anyone around the world with access to periodicals or traveling exhibits could observe and gain an understanding of the horrors of combat. Photography and the recording of warfare would never be the same.

Brady's influence on the Civil War is at best difficult to evaluate and impossible to compare to that of leaders and battles. However, Brady is well deserving of a ranking in at least the upper half for bringing the war to the masses and in recording lasting images of the conflict that provided an awareness and understanding absent in written accounts.

42

ANDERSONVILLE PRISON

February 1864–April 1865

The Confederate prisoner of war camp at Andersonville, Georgia—officially named Camp Sumter—was the most notorious and deadly prison camp of the Civil War. Its open-air construction without shelters, poor sanitation, limited rations, and ruthless guards led to its label as the "hell camp." More than twelve thousand died there in only fourteen months. When the South finally surrendered, the only rebel hung as a war criminal was Henry Wirz, the prison commandant.

During the first year of the Civil War, the skirmishes and minor battles that marked the period produced few prisoners. Prisoner exchanges, common in other conflicts, were not conducted because the United States refused to recognize the Confederacy as a lawful nation. When the scale and intensity of the conflict increased in early 1862, officials in both the North and South realized that something had to be done with the increasing number of captured soldiers. In July 1862, Union and Confederate officials came to an agreement for an exchange of prisoners based on rank—one general for sixty privates, one colonel for fifteen, one lieutenant for four, and one sergeant for two.

Exchanges, however, decreased in 1863 for several reasons. As more and more black soldiers (38) joined the Union ranks, Confederate officials refused to exchange them and threatened to return them to slavery. At the same time, Northern officials objected to the exchange system because freed Confederate prisoners were often back in the front lines within days of their release.

U. S. Grant (3) particularly opposed the exchange system because he believed it provided much-needed manpower to the rebels while the Union population was sufficient to muster recruits without the help of exchanged prisoners. Other generals and officials agreed and by the time Grant took command of the Union army in early 1864, prisoner exchange had ended.

Prisoner exchange had already significantly slowed by this time. More than one hundred fifty military prisons in the North and South overflowed with prisoners, resulting from the increased intensity of the war. Most of these confinement areas were composed of former fortifications, penitentiaries, and abandoned factories. A few were constructed with tents surrounded by walls and guard towers.

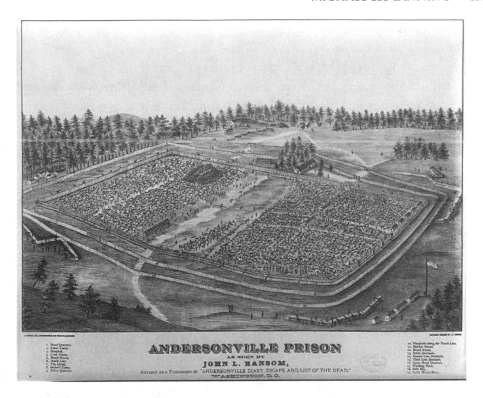

ANDERSONVILLE PRISON
AS SEEN BY
JOHN L. RANSOM,
AUTHOR AND PUBLISHER OF "ANDERSONVILLE DIARY, ESCAPE AND LIST OF THE DEAD."
WASHINGTON, D. C.

None of the prisons on either side were pleasant places to reside, but generally those in the North provided minimal levels of satisfactory shelter and food. In the South, where even the army was poorly clothed and fed, the conditions were not so good. The best facilities for Union prisoners were in large buildings, mostly former tobacco drying and storage areas. These provided adequate shelter, but food was always in short supply.

In late 1863, Confederate officials ordered the construction of a sixteen-and-a-half-acre prison northeast of Americus, Georgia, outside of Andersonville, officially designated Camp Sumter. The camp layout, increased to twenty-six acres, was a rectangular log stockade with a stream running through it to both provide water and wash away waste. The sparse camp had no tents or any other kind of shelter.

The first group of six hundred Union prisoners arrived at Andersonville on February 24, 1864. Originally designed to hold only ten thousand prisoners, the camp had its numbers increase to more than forty-five thousand over the following months. Food consisted of limited amounts of often rotting cornmeal, peas, and beans. Medical care was limited, and the stream running through the compound did not provide adequate sanitation. Dysentery, scurvy, and malaria swept the compound.

Poor nutrition, disease, and constant exposure to the elements killed inmates at a rate that quickly rose to one hundred per day.

Confederate general J. H. Winder was in overall command of Andersonville when it opened. In April 1864, Winder appointed Captain Henry Wirz as the camp's commander. Wirz, born in Switzerland in 1822 and educated as a medical doctor, had immigrated to the United States in 1849. Living in Louisiana at the outbreak of the Civil War, Wirz volunteered for the Confederate army. Wounds at Fair Oaks in May 1862 cost Wirz his right arm and removed him from active combat duty. Upon recovery he joined Winder, who at the time was responsible for prisoner of war camps in Richmond. Wirz served on a brief mission back to his native Europe, seeking aid for the Confederacy, before assuming command of the Georgia prison.

Many prisoners were transferred from Andersonville to Charleston when William Sherman's (6) army approached in September 1864. Sufficient numbers remained, however, to continue to fill the camp's cemetery, where there were so many burials that bodies were placed in trenches with their arms overlapping to save space. By the time the Union army finally liberated the prison in May 1865, the buried officially totaled 12,912.

Photographers and sketch artists accompanied the liberators and their illustrations of the barbarity of Andersonville soon filled the Northern newspapers. Survivors told stories of harsh treatment, including stories of Wirz threatening to "starve every damn Yankee" if anyone attempted to escape. Demands for justice for the Andersonville prisoners swept across the victorious Union.

Recommendations were soon made to charge Confederate secretary of war James Seddon, Robert E. Lee (5), and several other rebel military officers and officials with "conspiring to injure the health and destroy the lives of United States soldiers held as prisoners by the Confederate States." Cooler heads, especially those seeking to reunite the North and South, soon prevailed. In August 1865, President Andrew Johnson (83) ordered that all charges against Confederate officers and officials be dropped. Aware that many still demanded vengeance for the Andersonville dead, Jackson called for Wirz to be tried for "wanton cruelty." James Winder would have likely been included in the charges, but he had died of illness the previous February.

Wirz appeared before a military commission that began on August 21, 1865. He presented evidence that he had made several requests for additional food for his prisoners and that he had had to deal with guards who were too young or too old to fight in the regular army. His defense, however, was far overshadowed by a series of former prisoners who testified about the harsh conditions and treatment in the camp.

On November 6 the commission found Wirz guilty and sentenced him to death. Justice was swift; his execution was scheduled for only four days later. On November

10, Wirz mounted the gallows in the same Washington, D.C., yard where those involved in the Lincoln assassination had been executed. The officer in charge read the death warrant and turned to Wirz, telling him that he "deplored this duty." Wirz replied, "I know what orders are, major. And I am being hanged for obeying them."

A black hood was placed over Wirz's head, the noose adjusted around his neck, and the trap door sprung. The fall failed to break Wirz's neck, and it took several minutes for him to strangle to death. All the while the Union soldiers surrounding the gallows chanted, "Wirz, remember Andersonville."

Wirz was the only Confederate executed for "war crimes." He and Andersonville remain today as symbols of the harshness and barbarity of the war—particularly to those in the North. Many Southerners refute the excesses of Wirz and the camp, pointing to the poor conditions for regular Confederate soldiers of the same period. Postwar Confederate groups even erected a monument to Wirz and declared him a hero rather than a war criminal. Andersonville remains today a major, unresolved event of the Civil War that still separates North and South.

Wirz's execution may not have been necessary, or even justified, in the absence of others being punished, but the nearly thirteen thousand graves at Andersonville called for justice, however delivered. Today many in the South still condemn the hanging of Wirz, but Andersonville remains a serious blot on the claims of chivalry of the Confederacy.

No other events of the Civil War can compare to Andersonville and the hanging of Wirz. Nevertheless, Andersonville Prison and the people on both sides of the log enclosure played an important role in the war and its aftermath.

43

PIERRE GUSTAVE TOUTANT BEAUREGARD

Confederate General

1818–1893

The South hailed Pierre G. T. Beauregard as the first Confederate hero for his performance at Fort Sumter (50) and First Bull Run (10). Although his talents were not used to their fullest during the remainder of the war because of his differences with President Jefferson Davis (9), the name Beauregard continues to convey esteem in the South as a symbol of the officers who led the Lost Cause.

Born on May 28, 1818, in Saint Bernard Parish near New Orleans, Louisiana, Beauregard attended West Point, where he graduated second of forty-five cadets in the Class of 1838. As an engineer officer, Beauregard served in the Mexican War where he was wounded twice and brevetted for bravery on two additional occasions. After the war he supervised several construction and drainage projects along the Mississippi River and Gulf Coast.

In January 1861, Beauregard transferred to West Point to become the superintendent of the Military Academy. His is the shortest tenure in the Academy's history. Never one to repress his thoughts and beliefs, Beauregard, soon after his arrival, announced he would follow his native state if it seceded from the Union. His remarks brought his immediate dismissal.

Beauregard stayed true to his word and resigned his commission in February to accept the rank of brigadier general in the newly formed Confederate army. Because of his engineering background, he was dispatched to Charleston to take command of the siege of Fort Sumter. It was Beauregard who ordered the first shot fired against the fort's Union garrison, and it was he who accepted its surrender. The relatively bloodless fight in Charleston Harbor provided the spark that set off the firestorm of four years of war between the states. It also elevated Beauregard to status of hero and living legend as the representative of the gallant, gentleman officer of the Confederacy.

Beauregard did not shy away from his newfound fame. The Confederate capital at Richmond welcomed the well-mannered general in his impeccably tailored uniform as a conqueror. Some Southerners, however, disdained his posturing and superiority,

considering him an ambitious martinet; they even referred to the diminutive officer as "Little Napoleon."

President Davis appreciated Beauregard's performance at Fort Sumter and recognized his potential for leadership. However, Davis also shared the conclusions of those who believed the general was more show than substance. From their first meetings, Davis and Beauregard simply did not get along; theirs was a personality conflict that would spill over into the future.

Despite his personal objections to Beauregard, Davis ordered him to northern Virginia as second in command to Joseph E. Johnston (17). Beauregard took charge of the rebel army assembling around the rail junction at Manassas and constructed defenses along Bull Run Creek. Johnston, meanwhile, was gathering and training additional troops in the Shenandoah Valley.

Beauregard displayed his zeal for the war in a proclamation issued to the people of Virginia on June 1, 1861. He wrote, "A reckless and unprincipled tyrant has invaded your soil. Abraham Lincoln, regardless of all moral, legal, and constitutional restraints, has thrown his abolitionist hosts among you, who are murdering and imprisoning your citizens, confiscating and destroying your property, and committing other acts of violence and outrage too shocking and revolting to humanity to be enumerated."

When Irwin McDowell (80) moved toward Manassas in July 1861, Johnston joined Beauregard in what would become the war's first great battle. Johnston remained nominally in command of the combined Confederate force, but deferred to his subordinate's advice for the deployment and preparation of defenses because of Beauregard's familiarity with the area. On July 20, the day before the battle, Beauregard rallied his troops, telling them, "We fight for our homes, our firesides, and for the independence of our country."

Neither the Union nor the Confederate forces were trained or prepared for the lethality of cannons and rifled muskets that dominated the ensuing battle. Confusion reigned, but the Southern forces had the advantage of defense and soon the Union army was in a wild retreat. After the battle ended, Beauregard claimed that, if Richmond had dispatched adequate resupplies to their army, he would have been able to pursue the Union army all the way to Washington. These remarks only added to Davis's animosity toward the general.

Despite Davis's personal feelings, he was aware that Beauregard's status as a hero of the rebellion had only become larger. He promoted him to full general, and by the spring of 1862 Beauregard was second in command to Albert S. Johnston (85) in the Army of Tennessee. Beauregard drafted the plan for the attack at Shiloh (18) and then assumed command when Johnston was mortally wounded. His failure to exploit an early advantage in the battle and his decision to retreat toward Corinth the following day still inspires debate over whether his judgment was correct or flawed.

In late May 1862, the Union army forced Beauregard to withdraw from Corinth. Because of illness, Beauregard turned over his command to Braxton Bragg (60) in June and went on sick leave. President Davis used the incident as an excuse to relieve Beauregard from command on the pretext that he had gone on sick leave without permission.

When he regained his health, Beauregard assumed the responsibility for the defense of the South Carolina and Georgia coasts. He performed ably in these tasks and kept a low enough profile to avoid further wrath from President Davis. In May 1864, he joined Lee in Virginia and significantly contributed to the defense of Richmond with his leadership at Drewry's Bluff. Despite differences with Lee on the deployment of his army, Beauregard fought well at Petersburg (46). He then joined Johnston in his final campaign in the Carolinas.

After the war, Beauregard returned to New Orleans where he served as a railroad president, worked with Jubal Early (19) on the Louisiana lottery, and stood as his state's adjutant general. His reputation and fame had extended beyond the Confederacy, and the countries of Egypt and Romania both approached him with offers to have him lead their armies. Beauregard turned down the offers and continued to serve his state and to write numerous articles and books until his death on

February 20, 1893. He is buried in the Metairie Cemetery in New Orleans.

Beauregard remained a hero of the South even after his death. His victories on the battlefield, his Creole style, and his old New Orleans grace made him a symbol of the South and of the Confederacy. His reputation was further enhanced by his design of the Confederate flag. Although it was not the official flag of the Confederacy, this is the flag—a red cloth with a blue Saint Andrews cross—that, after First Bull Run, became the lasting symbol of the Lost Cause.

Despite Beauregard's disfavor in Richmond, he led the Confederacy at many of its most important battles and performed well in combat. As one of the South's premier generals, he defeated many of his Union opponents, including George McClellan (51) and Benjamin Butler (71) on the battlefield. His influence exceeds that of most of his peers in gray, earning him a place in the middle of these rankings.

44

PEA RIDGE

March 6–8, 1862

The Battle of Pea Ridge in far northern Arkansas in March 1862 provided the Union its first significant victory of the war. It also left Missouri and northern Arkansas in the hands of the Federals.

After their success at the Battle of Wilson's Creek in August 1861, some of the victorious Confederates under Sterling Price wintered in Springfield, Missouri. Others, under the command of Ben McCulloch, withdrew to northern Arkansas. Despite their joint success at Wilson's Creek, Price and McCulloch continued their personal feud over who was the senior commander. Aware of the difficulties between the two generals, President Jefferson Davis (9) dispatched Earl Van Dorn to assume command and unite the two forces into the Military District of the Trans-Mississippi.

The Union force defeated at Wilson's Creek also faced leadership problems. With Nathaniel Lyon dead of wounds and John Fremont out of favor in Washington, President Abraham Lincoln (2) placed General Samuel Curtis in command of the Federal Army of the Southwest in Missouri. Curtis immediately initiated plans to push Confederate forces out of Missouri, and in February he moved against Price at Springfield. Price offered little resistance and withdrew his force into the Boston Mountains of northwestern Arkansas.

In Arkansas, Price joined McCulloch and other Confederate forces, including about eight hundred Native Americans led by Cherokee Stand Watie, under the overall command of Van Dorn. With his army consolidated, Van Dorn maneuvered to counter Curtis, who had followed Price from Missouri. With an army that now totaled seventeen thousand, Van Dorn marched north to meet Curtis and his eleven thousand Federals.

Union scouts, who included, according to some claims, the future legendary Western lawman "Wild Bill" Hickock, informed Curtis of Van Dorn's movement. Curtis, a member of the West Point Class of 1831 and a Mexican War veteran, took up defensive positions near Pea Ridge facing south overlooking Little Sugar Creek. When Van Dorn, a West Point graduate in 1842 and also a Mexican War veteran, approached the Union defenses from the south, he decided a frontal attack would be too costly. Instead he decided to make a night march around the Union positions and attack them

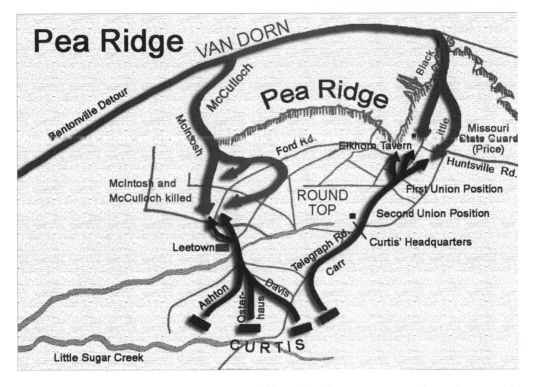

from the north. Once in position, he would launch a diversionary attack on the enemy's western flank and a main assault on the Union eastern flank at Elkhorn Tavern.

Van Dorn's plan was adequate, except that he failed to consider that his command was exhausted from their long march, hungry from lack of supplies, and suffering from cold weather that included snow. Van Dorn himself was ill from the long march and had to direct the battle from an ambulance wagon rather than horseback.

On March 7, Van Dorn, together with McCulloch, launched the Confederate attack against the western flank, and Price charged into the eastern flank at Elkhorn Tavern. Curtis, having learned of Van Dorn's maneuver, reoriented his army to the north and marched to meet the Confederate attack. On the western flank McCulloch, supported by the Native Americans, forced the Federals back. In the fight McCulloch was fatally wounded, as was his replacement James McIntosh. The Union force then counterattacked, forcing the rebels on the western side of the battlefield to withdraw back toward Pea Ridge.

Early in the war, the Confederacy had promised the Native American tribes in Oklahoma that they would only have to defend their own territory if they joined the South. Many of the tribes held the United States responsible for their removal from their homelands to the Indian Territory and readily joined the Confederacy. When

Van Dorn had offered payment in advance for their service in Arkansas, the Indians had readily joined his force. From all accounts, the Native American soldiers performed adequately as cavalry and infantry in McCulloch's initial attack. However, when the Union counterattacked with an artillery barrage, most of the Indians, who had never encountered cannon fire, fled the battlefield. Their reputation was further diminished when Union troops later claimed to have discovered that thirty of their soldiers had been mutilated and scalped by the Indian warriors.

On the eastern flank, Van Dorn also experienced early success before being halted by the Union defenders. Late in the day Van Dorn ordered a small detachment to hold the west flank while the rest joined him to prepare for another attack in the east. Van Dorn was determined to renew the attack on the morning of March 8, but Curtis took action first. The Union commander ordered Franz Sigel (67), with two divisions, to drive the Confederates from their positions in the west on Pea Ridge. With that accomplished, Curtis united his entire force in an attack against Van Dorn.

A Union officer later wrote of the attack, "That beautiful charge I shall never forget. With banners streaming, with drums beating, and our long line of blue coats advancing upon the double quick, with their deadly bayonets gleaming in the sunlight, and every man and officer yelling at the top of his lungs. The rebel yell was nowhere in comparison."

By noon the Confederates were in a disorganized retreat to the northeast. Although outnumbered, Curtis had won the first great Union victory of the war. It had not come cheaply; about 13 percent of the Federal force was dead, wounded, or missing. Van Dorn never revealed Confederate casualties, but they were likely about the same as that of the Union.

Curtis remained in command in Missouri and the West for the remainder of the war but never achieved the fame warranted by his victory at Pea Ridge. There is no evidence that this particularly bothered the Union general, who was saddened by the dead and wounded of both sides. In a letter to his brother shortly after the battle he wrote, "The scene is silent and sad—the vulture and the wolf now have the dominion and the dead friends and foes sleep in the same lonely graves."

Van Dorn's retreat left Missouri and northern Arkansas under Union control. The Confederates not only retreated from Pea Ridge, but also completely abandoned the theater. Van Dorn and his survivors were ordered eastward to assist in the defense of the Mississippi River. The governor of Arkansas, Henry M. Rector, was so distraught that he threatened to secede from the Confederacy.

The Battle of Shiloh (18), fought the next month, overtook much of the news of Pea Ridge. While Shiloh and Vicksburg (7) the next year exceeded the influence of Pea Ridge, the battle around Elkhorn Tavern opened the way for Union control of the West.

45

JOHN BELL HOOD

Confederate General

1831–1879

John Bell Hood appeared to enjoy combat and love fighting. As a brigade and division commander, he led from the front, earning himself the respect and affection of his men. Ultimately, however, he was promoted beyond his talents and failed to successfully master the complexities of administration and planning at the corps and army levels.

Born in Owingsville, Kentucky, on June 1, 1831, Hood ignored his father's desire to have his son join him as a country doctor so that he could accept an appointment to West Point as a member of the Class of 1853. As a cadet, Hood was disciplined so many times that he had to complete his entire senior year without any demerits in order to graduate number forty-four in his class of fifty-two.

Hood served for two years before joining the 2nd U.S. Cavalry in Texas, led by future Confederate generals Albert S. Johnston (85) and Robert E. Lee (5). At Devil's River on July 20, 1857, Hood received his first battle wound when a Comanche arrow penetrated his left hand. Hood remained in Texas until April 16, 1861, when he resigned his commission and traveled to Montgomery, Alabama, to enter the Confederate army.

As a lieutenant, Hood joined the Army of Northern Virginia where he quickly rose thorough the ranks as reward for his combat leadership. In March 1862 he took command of the Texas Brigade as a brigadier general. The Texans were reluctant to accept an "outsider" even though they were aware of Hood's service in their state before the war as well as his reputation as a fighter against the Union's Peninsular Campaign (32). Hood led the Texas Brigade with distinction at Gaines's Mill and Second Bull Run (40) and saved the Confederate left flank from being turned at Antietam (1). By this time the unit was proudly known as Hood's Texas Brigade, a title it would maintain for the rest of the war.

Hood left the brigade in October 1862 to accept promotion to major general and command of a division in James Longstreet's (13) corps. He stood with his division at Fredericksburg (53) and then fought at Gettysburg (4), where on the second day of the battle he suffered a wound that permanently crippled his left arm.

The general recovered sufficiently to rejoin his division in September 1863 at the Battle of Chickamauga (74) where he broke the Union line and forced William Rosecran's army to retreat. During the battle Hood was once again wounded, this time forcing the amputation of his right leg. After the battle, Longstreet recommended Hood for another promotion, stating, "General Hood handled his troops with the coolness and ability that I have rarely known by any officer, on any field."

During his recovery in Richmond, Hood became a close friend of fellow Kentuckian Jefferson Davis (9). When Hood sufficiently recovered, he accepted the president's request to report to northern Georgia to assume command of a corps under Johnston. With his crippled arm tucked in his shirt and an empty trouser leg pinned to his thigh, Hood joined his corps for the Battle of Atlanta (20). Even though Atlanta was key to the survival of the Confederacy, the rebel army could not hold the city against the larger and better-supplied Union army.

When it became evident that Johnston would not be able to successfully defend Atlanta, Davis relieved him of command and placed Hood as a full general in command of the Army of Tennessee. "The Gallant Hood," as the newspapers now called him, was no more successful than his predecessor. On September 1, Hood evacuated Atlanta rather than continue to risk his army in its defense.

In November, Hood decided that he must regain the offensive and led his army into Tennessee. The Union army withdrew at first and then made a stand, shattering Hood's army at Franklin (15) on November 30. Despite his losses, Hood continued his offensive against Nashville (87) where he was again defeated on December 16.

Hood retreated from Tennessee into northern Mississippi, where he departed his command at his own request on January 23, 1865, and reverted back to the rank of lieutenant general. Hood was on his way west on orders from Davis to recruit another army in Texas when he learned of Lee's surrender. On May 31, 1865, he surrendered to Federal authorities in Natchez, Mississippi.

After the war Hood worked as a cotton broker and insurance agent in New Orleans. He married in 1868 and over the next ten years fathered eleven children, including three sets of twins. Hood lost his modest fortune during the yellow fever epidemic of the winter of 1878–79. On August 30, 1879, he died of the fever within days of losing his wife and a child to the illness. His surviving ten children, now destitute, were adopted by seven different families in Louisiana, Mississippi, Georgia, Kentucky, and New York. Hood is buried in the Metairie Cemetery in New Orleans.

Without a doubt, the six foot, two inch blond Hood was one of the bravest generals on either side during the war. He led from the front, inspired his men, and indeed enchanted the entire South. The image of "the Gallant Hood"—missing a leg and fighting with a crippled arm, while strapped to his saddle in the midst of battle—was one that did much to enhance the glory and glamour of the Lost Cause that endures today.

Unfortunately for Hood and the South, the gallant general's bravery and personal leadership abilities far exceeded his talent in commanding above the division level. Quite simply, Hood's courage extended beyond his intelligence. When he could lead, he succeeded; when he had to plan and organize, he failed.

If Hood had retired after his leg wound at Chickamauga, his reputation as one of the war's best generals would have remained intact. However, his failure at Atlanta and his poorly planned and executed offensive into Tennessee, along with his tendency to blame his subordinates for his own inadequacies, severely blemished his reputation and thus, his position on this ranking.

Hood never achieved the lasting influence of Lee, Longstreet, and other Confederate leaders or that of the successful Union commanders like Grant (3), Sherman (6), Thomas (11), and their like. In the long run, he is much more in the class of the Union commanders such as McClellan (51), Burnside (57), and Hooker (48), who rose in rank and responsibility to exceed their capabilities.

46

PETERSBURG CAMPAIGN

June 15, 1864–March 29, 1865

The Petersburg Campaign in Virginia demonstrated the defensive talents of Robert E. Lee (5) and the tactical skills of U. S. Grant (3). While Petersburg set the stage for the end of the Civil War, it also introduced the type of trench warfare that would mark the First World War of the next century.

After Grant assumed command of the Union army in the spring of 1864, he went on the offensive to defeat Lee's Army of Northern Virginia and to capture Richmond. His tactics proved sound as he gained victories at the Wilderness (62) and Spotsylvania Court House (65) in May. Grant, however, had to change his direct march toward Richmond when Lee repelled the repeated Union attacks at Cold Harbor (59) in June.

In a brilliant maneuver, Grant withdrew from Cold Harbor and marched the Army of the Potomac, commanded by George Meade (24), to the east of Richmond and across the James River to the rail center of Petersburg twenty-three miles south of the Confederate capital. Although the plan and maneuver were executed almost flawlessly, the advance Union units slowed and moved cautiously when they reached the outskirts of Petersburg on June 15. As a result, only three thousand Confederate defenders led by Pierre G. T. Beauregard (43) prevented the Union forces from entering and occupying the city.

Over the next few days both Lee and Grant rushed additional units to the area. The outnumbered Confederates took advantage of hastily dug trenches and other barriers to turn back attacks over the next three days. By June 18, Lee had a line of defenses on the eastern side of the city that repulsed several attacks. Grant's hopes of a quick victory faded as Lee continued to improve his defenses.

Over the next month the Petersburg Campaign became the Petersburg Siege as skirmishes and sniper fire replaced large scale direct attacks. Abraham Lincoln (2) advised Grant, "Hold on with a bulldog grip and chew and choke as much as possible."

Grant believed that he could either defeat Lee at Petersburg or force him to withdraw from the city and be beaten in the field. The Union general, however, did not remain idle but rather followed the president's advice to "chew and choke." Grant approved a plan by Lieutenant Colonel Henry Pleasants to form a special unit of former coal miners to

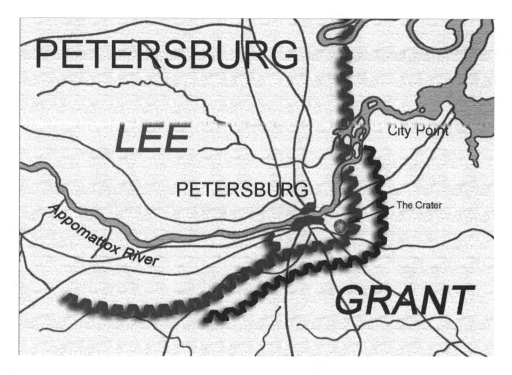

dig under the Confederate lines. At the end of a 511-foot-long tunnel the miners placed eight thousand pounds of gunpowder.

At 4:40 a.m. on July 30 the miners exploded the charge, creating a crater sixty to eighty feet wide and thirty feet deep that produced a fifty-yard gap in the Confederate lines. The attack to exploit the gap was poorly led and the Confederates, again commanded by Beauregard, counterattacked to regain the line. Confederate losses at the Battle of the Crater totaled about fifteen hundred, while Union casualties numbered nearly four thousand.

In August, Grant tested the Confederate defenses of Richmond north of the James River and extended his siege lines south and southwest of Petersburg. Grant continued to tighten his grip on the city in the fall. The Confederates successfully defended their supply route at Ream's Station on August 25, but the Union forces gained an advantage at Chaffin's Farm and New Market Heights on September 28 to 30 and then again at Peeble's Farm on October 2. The approach of winter and heavy rainfall then brought an end to further significant action as both sides remained in their trenches.

The Confederate army was not faring well in other theaters either during the Petersburg siege. Phil Sheridan (8) was neutralizing the rebel army in the Shenandoah

Valley Campaign (29), and John Bell Hood's (45) army was met with crushing defeat at Franklin, Tennessee (15). Johnston's army was retreating northward into the Carolinas just one step ahead of William Sherman (6). Lee knew that the only chance for the survival of the Confederacy was to break out of Petersburg and join Johnston in North Carolina.

When spring arrived and the roads began to dry, Lee made his move. On March 25 he attacked the north end of the Union trenches at Fort Steadman only to be beaten back with heavy losses. On April 1, Union cavalry drove the rebel defenders from the important road junction of Five Forks. During the night of April 2 to 3, Lee withdrew his remaining thirty thousand men to the west. On April 3, Union troops swept into Petersburg and then occupied Richmond. The Petersburg Campaign was over and the Confederate retreat and eventual surrender at Appomattox Court House (37) had begun.

Grant would have preferred to have defeated Lee either before or at Petersburg, but the casualties he suffered at Cold Harbor (59) discouraged him from repeated frontal attacks. He was willing to besiege Petersburg and add to the attrition of Lee's army with small battles and skirmishes during the summer and fall and then let hunger and disease further reduce Lee's ranks during the long winter. The campaign ultimately proved costly for both sides with forty-two thousand Union and twenty-eight thousand Confederate casualties.

Petersburg marked the last days of Lee's army as its numbers and strength dwindled, leading directly to surrender at Appomattox Court House. Both Lee and Grant performed well during the campaign, enhancing their reputations as America's premier commanders of the Civil War and the century. In addition to leading to the end of the war, Petersburg also displayed the complexities of trench warfare and provided information on this type of combat for European observers and students as well as American forces deployed to France in World War I.

Ultimately, Grant fought the Petersburg Campaign with more restraint and caution that his previous operations. Cold Harbor influenced the general so that he was more willing to engage in a protracted siege. As for Lee, he followed his only available option. His defensive innovations and skills extended the siege through the winter and on to the spring of 1865. In doing so, he gave the Confederacy a few additional months of existence, but the Southern cause was already lost. Petersburg just gave it a few more breaths and added to the list of dead and wounded on both sides.

Petersburg was certainly a turning point that led to Appomattox and the final surrender. However, even if the long siege had not occurred, Lee and the South were doomed and the next-to-last campaign would have taken place elsewhere. For this reason, its relevance falls in the middle rather than near the top of these rankings.

47

WEAPONS TECHNOLOGY

1861–1865

Technological advances in weapons before and during the Civil War contributed to its being the bloodiest conflict up to that time. Throughout the war, both sides armed themselves with similar weapons that far exceeded the range and accuracy of those used in previous battles. The use of these modern weapons in conjunction with antiquated tactics appropriate for a bygone era filled the hospitals and the burial grounds of both the North and the South.

The United States military of the mid-nineteenth century was led almost exclusively by graduates of West Point who studied the military tactics of French military expert Antoine Henri Jomini—tactics based on the Napoleonic wars of the early part of the century, tactics designed for soldiers armed with short-range, smooth-bore muskets fighting on open plains. Civil War commanders on both sides went into battle using Jomini's teachings that called for massing infantry into shoulder-to-shoulder ranks and closing to within fifty to one hundred yards of the enemy before firing.

From the end of the Napoleonic wars until the beginning of the Civil War, technology rapidly made the essence of these tactics nearly obsolete. Percussion caps, introduced in 1807, replaced flintlocks, producing a much more reliable means of firing muskets. In 1848, French Captain Claude E. Minie created a cylindrical lead bullet with a conical head and an iron cupped base to replace the round shot that had been used for the first five hundred years of firearms. The Minie ball was easy to load in rifled muskets. It expanded into the barrel groves when fired, greatly increasing its accuracy.

The first rifled musket in the U.S. was the Model 1855, produced in the year of its name. Several improvements were made before the Model 1861 became the standard rifled musket of Union soldiers.

More than a quarter million of the Model 1861s were produced by Union arsenals in the first three years of the war. Slight modifications evolved to make the manufacturing process easier, and another quarter-million of the resulting Model 1863s were fielded during the next two years.

The Model 1863 was the last muzzle-loading rifle issued to American soldiers. In 1860, Christopher Spencer introduced a breech-loading, repeating rifle that by 1864 had become the standard weapon of the Union cavalry. The U.S. government purchased more than 77,000 of the seven-shot rifles during the war, and their rapid rate of fire provided Union cavalrymen a marked advantage. Confederates captured some of the rifles but never had a reliable source for their ammunition.

Early in the war the Confederates augmented their supply of Model 1855s with all kinds of muskets, hunting rifles, shotguns, and anything that would shoot. They also confiscated thousands of the Model 1861s warehoused in the South under the direction of U.S. secretary of war John B. Floyd (28) before he resigned his position to join the Confederacy.

As the war progressed, the Confederates added captured Model 1861s to their armaments and manufactured some of their own that duplicated the Union rifle musket. By the middle of the war, nearly all infantrymen on both sides were armed with the fifty-six-inch long, nine-and-three-quarters pound, .58-caliber Model 1861 or its copy. It could be fired up to six times per minute with a maximum range of one thousand yards.

Soldiers of both sides also used pistols varying widely in manufacturer and caliber. The Model 1851 and Model 1860 revolvers, mostly manufactured by the Colt Arms Company, were the most popular pistols of the war. Union forces ordered more than three hundred thousand of these revolvers during the conflict, many of which ultimately ended up in the hands of their enemies.

The basic artillery piece for both the North and South was the muzzle-loading, smooth-bore, twelve-pounder gun known as the Napoleon. A three-inch rifled gun called the Ordnance Gun was the secondary cannon. Other guns and mortars of differing calibers also were used but the Napoleon and Ordnance Guns, with their range of fifteen hundred and twenty-five hundred yards, respectively, inflicted the vast majority of artillery casualties.

At the beginning of the war, the Union army had about 4,100 pieces of artillery of various caliber and age. During the conflict they added nearly eight thousand more cannons, mostly Napoleons and Ordnance Guns. The Confederates had little capacity to produce cannons and relied mostly on captured weapons. They did employ 129 six-inch guns purchased from England and brought in through the Union blockade.

Both sides manufactured their own gunpowder during the war. Much of the Union powder came from the Dupont factory near Wilmington, Delaware. The Confederates began the war with a shortage of powder and with little manufacturing capability. They quickly amassed a production base of small factories that ultimately produced a quality powder in ample amounts to support the rebellion.

Despite shortages and a limited industrial base, the South never lost a battle because of a lack of firearms or gunpowder. Both sides were sufficiently armed, and the high number of casualties reflects proficiency of use. As the war progressed, tactics adapted to the lethal destruction caused by the weapons, but there was never any shortage of work for the medical officers and grave diggers.

Edged weapons were also a regular part of the armament of both sides. Rifles came with an eighteen-inch long triangular bayonet. Although the bayonets looked deadly, soldiers used them more often for appearances or cooking on a campfire than in actual combat. On only two occasions during the entire

war did commanders call for organized bayonet assaults, once by a Wisconsin regiment at Corinth, Mississippi, in 1862, and, a second time by a another Wisconsin regiment and a Maine unit at Kelley's Ford the following year.

Officers carried swords as symbols of their rank; the cavalries of both the North and South carried them as weapons. Union horsemen began the war armed with forty-two-inch-long scimitars that quickly became known as "wrist breakers" because of their length and weight. Even when these swords were soon reduced to thirty-six inches, they were still unwieldy, as evidenced by Union cavalry horses, which were often missing an ear from a misguided sword swing by their riders. Southern soldiers again armed themselves with captured Union swords or any other blade they could secure. It was rare, however, for either side to use a saber in combat. Rifles and pistols at a long range were much preferred to direct saber fights.

Bayonet charges and cavalry charges complete with waving swords are popular in the lore of the Civil War, but edged weapons actually played an extremely minor role in inflicting wounds or in killing the enemy. Of the approximately 250,000 wounded treated in Union hospitals during the war, nearly all were the victims of rifle and artillery fire. A mere 922 wounded were hospitalized from saber or bayonet wounds, and many of these were the result of private quarrels within the ranks or from accidents.

Weapons technology during the war took place at sea as well as on land. The Battle of Hampton Roads (72) introduced ironclads to modern naval warfare, and the CSS *Hunley* demonstrated at Charleston Harbor (97) the future of submarines.

Weapons, of course, were extremely influential during the Civil War, but they, like a carpenter's tools or an artist's brushes, are useless without men to operate them.

Collectors today still fondle weapons of the period and argue the gram weights of powder or effects of certain calibers, but no bullet or weapon ever killed anyone without a soldier loading, aiming, and pulling the trigger. For that reason, weapons technology ranks in the middle of this list rather than near its top.

JOSEPH HOOKER

Union General

1814–1879

Joseph Hooker became commander of the Army of the Potomac, only to find that his quarrelsome behavior and inability to get along with both superiors and subordinates would be his downfall. Like most of the Union senior commanders before him, Hooker was promoted to a rank and position that exceeded his capabilities.

Born on November 13, 1814, in Hadley, Massachusetts, as the grandson of a Revolutionary War captain, Hooker graduated from West Point in the middle—twenty-nine of fifty—of his Class of 1837 as an artilleryman. He served with distinction as a junior officer in the Seminole War, on the frontier, and as a staff officer at West Point before fighting in the Mexican War. In Mexico he earned brevet promotions for his bravery on three occasions.

After the war, Hooker joined the Division of the Pacific in California. Hooker, who did not particularly enjoy the peacetime army, often disagreed with his superiors. After two years, he requested a leave of absence and then on February 21, 1853, he resigned his commission. Hooker remained in California to farm near the town of Sonoma, where he joined a local militia. He found little success as a civilian or a militiaman. In 1858 he requested to return to active duty. These efforts were turned down by military officials who had no desire to see him back in uniform.

The Civil War was already a month old before the secretary of war finally relented and restored Hooker to active duty. He assumed command of a brigade in defense of Washington and quickly advanced to lead a division in the Union's early offensive into the South led by George B. McClellan (51). During late 1861 and into the spring of 1862, Hooker came to the attention of war correspondents covering the battles. One press release led with the banner, "Fighting—Joe Hooker." The Northern public, anxious and desperate for heroes, dropped the dash and "Fighting Joe Hooker" was born. Hooker never cared for the name or the correspondents who gave him the label.

By September 1862, McClellan had promoted Hooker to command the I Corps of the Army of the Potomac. His corps performed well on the northern flank at the

Battle of Antietam (1) despite his suffering a slight wound. Hooker was a leading candidate to replace McClellan when President Lincoln relieved the general of command. Opposition from other generals and leaders in the War Department, who reacted more against Hooker's personality than his leadership abilities, ensured the position for Ambrose Burnside (57), instead.

Under Burnside's reorganization of the Army of the Potomac, Hooker took command of the Center Grand Division composed of the III and V Corps. Hooker opposed Burnside's strategy for engaging Robert E. Lee's (5) army at Fredericksburg (53) but followed orders to attack into the Confederate strength.

The defeat and huge casualties at Fredericksburg resulted in Burnside's removal from command. Hooker took over the Army of the Potomac on January 26, 1863. Many officers who opposed Hooker made negative public statements about their new commander, but President Lincoln was still seeking a general who would fight. Besides, Hooker looked good in uniform, and more importantly, had no political ambitions. Nevertheless, Lincoln sent a letter to Hooker praising his past performance while also expressing reservations.

Hooker accepted the command and the reservations held by his president. His reorganization of the army proved to be Hooker's high point of command. He abolished Burnside's "Grand Division" plan and returned to the previous corps organization. Hooker also combined the various separate and independent cavalry units into an independent single corps. In a change that endures through to today's army, Hooker approved distinctive corps and division insignia.

Once satisfied with his changes, Hooker moved his army against Lee. The Union and Confederate armies met at Chancellorsville (31) in May 1863, where Hooker seemed to lose his confidence as he assumed the defensive rather than remain on the attack. Lee, assisted by a brilliant flanking movement that rolled up the Union right flank, soon had the Army of the Potomac in retreat.

Hooker, however, moved to block Lee's possible advance against Washington while also anticipating that the rebel leader might instead march into Pennsylvania to "take the war to the North." For this move to keep the U.S. capital secure, Hooker received a "Thanks of Congress," one of only fifteen awarded during the entire war, on January 28, 1864.

By the time Hooker had positioned his troops, he was furious about not receiving requested reinforcements. Sure that he had lost the confidence of his subordinates and leaders in Washington, he requested that he be relieved from command, and Lincoln obliged him and appointed George Meade (24) as his replacement on June 28.

Hooker returned to corps command, serving in the western theater. He performed well in several battles and regained national recognition for his actions at Lookout Mountain on November 24, 1863, through a song and story called "The Battle Above the Clouds." U. S. Grant (3), overall commander in the battle, later remarked that it was not much of a fight, implying that he was not impressed with Hooker.

Over the next seven months Hooker continued to lead his corps in the advance against Atlanta. When he was passed over for command of the Army of the Tennessee on July 24, 1864, he asked to be relieved from command in "an army in which rank and service are ignored." Hooker was tired as well as angry. Theodore Lyman, a staff officer at the time, wrote to his wife in 1864 about Hooker, saying that he was "very disappointed with his appearance…red faced with a lackluster eye and an uncertainty of gait and carriage that suggests a used-up man."

For the reminder of the war Hooker commanded various minor noncombat departments in the North. After the conflict he remained on active duty in subsequent minor positions until retiring in 1868 after suffering a paralytic stroke. He died in Garden City, New York, on October 31, 1879, and is buried in his wife's hometown of Cincinnati, Ohio.

Hooker's primary influence was his organizational abilities, followed by his abilities in commanding at the corps level. Some erroneously associate "Fighting Joe Hooker" with the term "hooker" for prostitutes because the general did little to discourage the women from following his command and even visiting his headquarters.

However, the term predates the war and appeared in print as early as 1845, long before Hooker became a prominent figure.

One lasting influence that was Hooker's, besides his design of unit insignia, was his imprint on journalism. Prior to 1863, journalists published without byline or credit except occasionally "Our correspondent." A few famous writers signed with their initials but generally a reader had no idea who had written a story. After the "Fighting Joe" story, Hooker required all journalists to sign their dispatches so proper credit—or blame—could be given.

Hooker's overall accomplishments in the war gain him higher ranking of influence than his rival Burnside but far below Grant, Sherman, and other leaders who ultimately defeated the rebellion. As with many of his contemporaries, Hooker was ultimately a man promoted beyond his capabilities.

49

UNCLE TOM'S CABIN

1851

U*ncle Tom's Cabin* by Harriet Beecher Stowe is credited by many as one of the most—if not the single most—influential books in American history. While its literary merits are certainly debatable, it is fact that the novel was the most important force in uniting the North against slavery. As the first American international bestseller, the book rallied abolition support for the Union around the world.

When the book became famous, Stowe modestly claimed, "God wrote it." However, her real inspiration came from the U.S. Congress passing the Fugitive Slave Act of 1850, an act that provided measures to punish anyone who aided runaway slaves and to further diminish the limited rights of both free blacks and those still held in bondage. Stowe took up her pen to expose what she thought was the world's number one evil and the institution that corrupted all aspects of American life.

Born into the religious Beecher family of Connecticut on June 14, 1811, the author had never actually lived in a slave state but, while she resided in Cincinnati, Ohio, she had observed slaves' desire for freedom as they escaped along the Underground Railroad. In 1836 she married Calvin Stowe and eventually had seven children. Few employment opportunities were available to women during these times, but she was able to add to her family's financial support by writing for local and religious periodicals.

Uncle Tom's Cabin was Stowe's first full-length novel. The Washington, D.C.-based antislavery weekly *National Era* published the first installment of the book on June 5, 1851, and continued the saga over the next eleven months. Various adaptations of the book for the stage soon were performed all across the Northern states, opening the eyes of many to the harsh realities of slavery.

The basic plot of the book revolves around the Shelby family, forced by hard times to sell their slaves. George Shelby promises his former slaves that he will eventually buy them back. Eliza, a young mulatto girl, fears her new owner and flees across a frozen river with her child. The book then opens on Uncle Tom, a Christian slave who is taken aboard a steamship for transport to a New Orleans auction block by a slave trader. Along the way he rescues Eva, the daughter of Augustine St. Clair. Eva convinces her father to purchase Tom and make him their plantation's head coachman.

Tom spends much of his time with the angelic Eva, who teaches him and other slaves, including a girl named Topsy, about love and forgiveness. Eva falls ill and from her deathbed gives a lock of her hair to each slave and tells them that they must become Christians so they can all meet again in Heaven. She also convinces her father to free Tom, but St. Clair and his daughter die before any of the slaves are emancipated.

Simon Legree, an evil plantation owner, acquires Tom but soon begins to fear the slave's growing spirit of independence. When Tom refuses to give information on the whereabouts of two escaped slaves, Legree beats him to death. George Shelby arrives too late to save Tom; he is so upset and saddened that he declares that he will dedicate the remainder of his life to abolition.

After its serialization in the *National Era, Uncle Tom's Cabin* appeared in book form in the United States and around the world, selling hundreds of thousands of copies. Stowe became an international celebrity as she traveled, giving lectures and writing to support abolition.

Stowe's book brought the inhumanity of slavery to Americans in the North and to Europeans across the Atlantic Ocean who had never witnessed the practice. Images of the brave Eliza, the brutal Legree, and the kindly Uncle Tom put faces on slavery and provided stereotypes that still survive today. Despite the sympathetic Eva and reform experienced by George Shelby, slave owners and other Southerners condemned the book as unfair and inaccurate. They noted that Beecher Stowe had never set foot on a Southern plantation and branded her "a vile wench in petticoats."

By the time of the outbreak of the Civil War in 1861, *Uncle Tom's Cabin* had sold more than a million copies and was the most widely read book, other than the Bible, in the Northern states. Nearly every young man of military age had read it as a boy, had seen it portrayed on stage, or at least had heard it discussed. No other single factor had informed more people of the ills of slavery and had united them in opposition to the practice. The book's impact was so great that when President Abraham Lincoln (2) was introduced to Beecher Stowe in 1862, he is alleged to have declared, "So you're the little woman who wrote the book that made this great war."

Stowe wrote nine additional books—none of which ever achieved any prominence—before her death at age eighty-five. At the time, as today, Harriet Beecher Stowe was and is one of the most famous American women authors. She is buried in Hartford, Connecticut.

Today *Uncle Tom's Cabin* remains one of the best-known, but little-read, books in American history. Its simplification of difficult issues into Christian sensibilities is much more romantic than a portrait of reality, but it remains a symbol of America's ultimate realization of the inhumanity of slavery. It also provides archetype characters that endure today. Even the many who have never read the book are well aware of the evil of Simon Legree. Oddly, Uncle Tom, who is the book's strongest character and its basic hero, has become associated with African Americans who sell themselves out to whites instead of standing up for their rights.

Uncle Tom's Cabin remains in print today under the aegis of several publishers. Because the copyright is long expired, it can also be downloaded completely on the Internet at no cost. Although it is rarely performed on stage, audio versions of the book are available.

The many issues that eventually led to the American Civil War are complex. *Uncle Tom's Cabin* is one of the few events that can specifically and concretely be credited with making a difference. The book directly united the antislavery factions and increased the drive for separation from those who supported the practice. The book by no means caused the war, as Lincoln may have jokingly said, but it did much to fan the spark that soon ignited incensed Northerners. Although the war would have been fought without Stowe's writings, the book ranks as one of the most influential events leading up to open warfare.

50

FORT SUMTER

April 12–14, 1861

Every major event must begin somewhere and on some date. For America's Civil War that place was Fort Sumter, South Carolina, and the date was April 12, 1861.

From the beginnings of the American colonization in the seventeenth century, the peoples of the North and South differed widely in social, economic, and political practices. The colonies united to gain their independence from Great Britain in the eighteenth century, but their differences continued to divide the regions over the following decades. By the mid-nineteenth century, the issues between the North and South had been distilled into the interpretation of states' rights versus federal authority and slavery versus abolition. After the election of Abraham Lincoln (2), the Southern states began seceding from the United States.

Not all Northerners opposed the separation. General Winfield Scott (30), hero of the Mexican War and commander of the U.S. Army, spoke for many when he declared, "Wayward sisters, depart in peace."

When South Carolina passed its Ordinance of Secession on December 20, 1860, six states quickly followed and formed the Confederate States of America. The militias of the seceding states seized U.S. arsenals and other government property. By the time of Lincoln's inauguration on March 4, 1861, only two installations in the newly formed Confederate states still flew the Stars and Stripes—Fort Pickens in Florida and Fort Sumter in South Carolina.

Six days after South Carolina seceded, Major Robert Anderson moved from Fort Moultrie and consolidated his detachment of seventy-six U.S. troops at Fort Sumter in Charleston Harbor. The pentagonal fort—three hundred feet by three hundred fifty feet across, forty feet high, with twelve-foot-thick walls—was still incomplete even though it had been begun in 1829. The fort was a formidable structure.

South Carolina officials consolidated artillery batteries on the nearby mainland about two thousand yards away and demanded that Anderson turn over the fort to state authorities. Anderson refused. He was awaiting orders from Washington, where President Lincoln knew that if he sent reinforcements, the South Carolinians would block them and thus preclude any peaceful methods of reuniting the country.

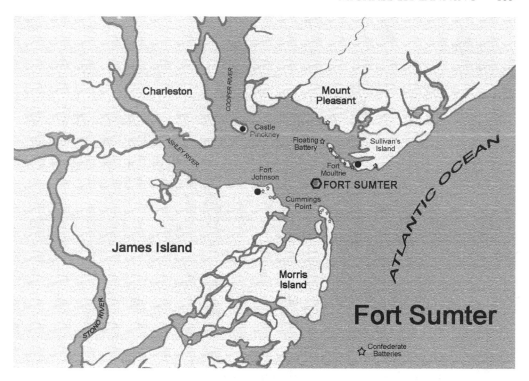

Lincoln attempted a middle-of-the-road approach by informing South Carolina that an expedition would be dispatched to provision the federal garrison but that no reinforcements would be landed. Confederate officials—led by General P. G. T. Beauregard (43) who assumed authority of South Carolina—announced that they would not allow Sumter to be reprovisioned, and on April 11 they again demanded Anderson surrender. Anderson again refused. He did say he would evacuate the fort on the fifteenth unless he was attacked, received supplies, or received other instructions from Washington.

Beauregard answered that this response was unsatisfactory and that he would bombard the fort on the morning of April 12. At 4:30 a.m. on April 12, the attack began. Just who fired the first shot for the Confederacy is not clear; several claimed the "honor." Generally accepted as fact is that the first shot was a signal for the other batteries to commence firing. This honor was offered to Roger A. Pryor of Virginia, who deferred to Captain George S. James. James's signal shot initiated fire from the forty-seven artillery guns and mortars around the harbor. Edmund Ruffin, a sixty-five-year-old ardent secessionist and member of the Palmetto Guard of South Carolina received credit for firing the first actual shot against the fort. Others, including cadets from the Citadel, also later claimed to have fired the first shot of the first battle of the war.

Three hours after the Confederate barrage began, Captain Abner Doubleday, who would achieve more lasting fame as the man responsible for the early proliferation of baseball, fired the initial answering shot. Anderson had forty-eight guns but only twenty-one of these were in a position to safely return the rebel's fire. Due to a lack of ammunition and powder, only six Union guns were still in action by the early afternoon.

The bombardment lasted thirty-four hours. With his own supplies nearly exhausted, Anderson finally agreed to terms of surrender. At noon on April 14 he lowered the U.S. flag and evacuated the fort. No casualties on either side had been inflicted in the battle, but an exploding cannon killed one Union artilleryman and wounded three others shortly before the evacuation.

The little bloodshed at Fort Sumter was not an accurate preview of what was to come. The encounter opened the door to the most deadly carnage and destruction in American history. Northerners who previously condoned the South leaving the Union or who had hoped for a peaceful settlement were incensed that the rebels had fired on the U.S. flag. Lincoln promptly called for an enlistment of seventy-five thousand militiamen, and so many volunteers came forward that many had to be turned away.

Southern states that had not yet joined the Confederacy saw Lincoln's reaction to Fort Sumter as a prelude to war and invasion of their territory. A united Confederacy with its capital in Richmond prepared to defend its independence.

Fort Sumter remained in Confederate control throughout the war despite several Union efforts to retake the island. On April 14, 1865, Robert Anderson, now a brevet major general, returned to Fort Sumter after Robert E. Lee (5) surrendered at Appomattox (37). He brought with him the original flag that he had lowered in defeat four years earlier and once again hoisted it above the fort's ramparts.

The Battle of Fort Sumter is far more symbolic than significant. In itself it determined little, but with those first shots came the ultimate division of a nation. Fort Sumter was the threshold to battle after battle, row after row of cemetery mounds covering soldiers in blue and gray, and family after family destroyed by the loss of loved ones.

Fort Sumter gains its ranking by being "first." It would be even higher on this list except for the simple fact that war between the North and South was inevitable. If it had not begun in Charleston Harbor, it would have begun elsewhere in a matter of days or weeks. Sumter simply provided the location and date for the beginning of the Civil War.

51

GEORGE BRINTON MCCLELLAN

Union General

1826–1885

In addition to being a brilliant organizer and administrator, George Brinton McClellan possessed strong personal magnetism that earned him the love and respect of his subordinates. Although short in stature, he perhaps looked the part of a general more than any of the war's other leaders. Unfortunately for the Union, McClellan was a reluctant commander who lacked the ability to successfully lead a large army.

Born to privilege in a Philadelphia family headed by a surgeon on December 3, 1826, McClellan entered West Point at the youthful age of fifteen as a part of the Class of 1846. In the class of fifty-nine cadets, twenty of whom would achieve the rank of general in either the Union or Confederate armies, McClellan ranked second.

McClellan served as an engineer in the Mexican War, where he received two brevet promotions for his bravery and for his abilities in constructing roads along the route of advance. After the war, McClellan returned to West Point as an instructor and translated a French manual on the use of the bayonet into English. He then worked on survey expeditions to determine possible routes for a transcontinental railroad before sailing for Europe in 1856 as an observer of the Crimean War. His report on his return included recommendations for the use of a cavalry saddle like the one he had observed used by the Hungarian army. The army adopted his idea and the "McClellan saddle" remained in use until mechanized forces replaced the horse cavalry in the 1940s.

In 1857 McClellan, frustrated with the slow promotions in the peacetime army, resigned his commission as a captain to become the chief engineer of the Illinois Central Railroad. He found promotions in the civilian world much more rapid and by the time of the outbreak of the Civil War, he was president of the Ohio & Mississippi Railroad headquartered in Cincinnati.

McClellan rejoined the army by accepting an appointment as a major general of volunteers from the governor of Ohio. His immediate organizational abilities and overall zeal came to the attention of President Abraham Lincoln (2) who appointed McClellan a major general in the Regular Army. The former captain was now second in rank only to Winfield Scott (30), the general in chief of the Union Armies.

As commander of the Army of the Ohio, McClellan achieved several minor victories in mid-July 1861 that gave the Union control over the land and railways that would one day become West Virginia. This accomplishment, combined with the Union disaster at First Bull Run (10) at the end of July, led to McClellan's appointment to command the Division of the Potomac that was responsible for the defense of Washington.

McClellan began to reorganize and train the tattered army that had been so completely defeated at Bull Run. He also lobbied Lincoln and other government officials to retire the aging Scott and appoint him as the replacement. His organizational skills as well as his political savvy brought McClellan the title of "Young Napoleon."

In November 1861, McClellan replaced Scott. Not only did McClellan now hold the rank he desired, but also he encountered the expectations Lincoln held for his top general. Lincoln and his cabinet demanded that McClellan take the offensive and invade the rebel states with a march on Richmond. McClellan, displaying both the arrogance that became his trademark and the reluctance to fight that foretold his future actions, demanded more men and supplies. He did not share his plans for the attack on Richmond with Lincoln, and on one occasion even refused to meet with the president. McClellan's delays grew while he was bedridden much of December 1861 with typhoid.

In March 1862, McClellan finally began his march into Virginia. His plan was to land at Fort Monroe and then advance to Richmond in what became known as the

Peninsular Campaign (32). Despite vastly superior numbers, several factors caused his plan to fail. First, Robert E. Lee (5), a brilliant defensive planner, had assumed command of the rebel army forces in the area. Second, McClellan, always hesitant, believed the Confederate force to be much larger than it actually was because his intelligence chief, Allen Pinkerton—who later ran a civilian detective agency—was an abysmal failure in gathering and analyzing battlefield information.

McClellan's plodding advance allowed Lee to bring in reinforcements. The Confederate commander then defeated McClellan in several battles, forcing the Union army to withdraw from the Peninsula in August. Lincoln lost confidence in McClellan during the long, unsuccessful campaign and replaced him as chief of the army. Lincoln ordered McClellan, who was now hostile toward the president, to return to Washington. McClellan continued to blame Lincoln for not sending sufficient reinforcements—accusations he shared with newspaper correspondents who followed his headquarters.

Still affectionately called "Little Mac" by his men, McClellan garnered other labels from the Washington politicians and members of the press. These included "Mac the Unready" and the "Corporal of Unsought Fields."

In a letter from Gaines's Mill, Virginia, on June 28, 1862, to the secretary of war, McClellan expressed his frustrations as well as his general hostility toward his civilian superiors. He wrote, "If I save the army now, I tell you plainly that I owe no thanks to any other person in the Washington. You have done your best to sacrifice this army."

Yet, when the rebels defeated the Union army at Second Bull Run (40) in late August 1862, Lincoln once again called upon the general to reorganize and restore the morale of the army. One more time McClellan proved a superior organizer and administrator.

Just two weeks later, McClellan moved to block Lee's advance into western Maryland. The two armies met at Antietam (1) in mid-September with the Union having every advantage. They outnumbered the Confederates nearly two to one, and they even possessed Lee's entire battle plan gleaned from a document found near the battlefield. But true to form, McClellan was indecisive. Instead of a combined attack, his advance occurred piecemeal at three different times at three separate locations. Despite these errors, McClellan's larger force gained the upper hand, only to have the reluctant general fail to pursue the retreating rebel army.

Once again, McClellan blamed Washington for his failure and demanded more men and equipment before resuming the offensive. An unhappy Lincoln finally relieved him of command for the second time and ordered him to go home to await further orders. Lincoln reportedly said, "Sending reinforcements to McClellan is like shoveling flies across a barn."

"Further orders" were never issued to McClellan. His war as a soldier was over, but the Democratic Party nominated him to run against Lincoln in the election of 1864. McClellan denounced his own party's platform of "peace at any cost" and stated he was for the rigorous pursuit of a military ending to the rebellion. He resigned his commission on Election Day and then returned to civilian life when Lincoln took the victory at the polls.

After a three-year visit to Europe, McClellan accepted the position of chief of docks for New York City in 1868. In 1878 he reentered politics and served as the governor of New Jersey from 1878 to 1881. He died on October 29, 1885, in Orange, New Jersey, and is buried in Trenton's Riverside Cemetery.

McClellan is but one of several Union generals who was promoted beyond his capabilities. Although smarter than many of his contemporaries, McClellan's ego far exceeded his actual performance. His overall influence results from his failures rather than his successes. It is even possible, if not reasonable, to say that McClellan's reluctance cost the Union early victories on the Peninsula that might have led to the taking of Richmond and the early conclusion to the war. Only his partial victory at Antietam prevents his even lower ranking on the list.

52

GEORGE ARMSTRONG CUSTER

Union General

1839–1876

When the first shots of the Civil War sounded at Fort Sumter (50) in April 1861, George Armstrong Custer was still a cadet at West Point. Four years later, Custer was a major general, a veteran of nearly every major battle, and one of the Union's boldest, most successful commanders. He would go on to become the most controversial character in American military history.

Custer was born on December 5, 1839, in New Rumley, Ohio, but he lived most of his childhood with his half-sister and brother-in-law in Monroe, Michigan. After a brief time of teaching high school, he received an appointment to West Point as a member of the Class of 1861. Some stories credit his appointment to a local father who desperately wanted Custer out of the state and away from his young daughter.

Throughout his time at West Point, Custer lived on the verge of expulsion. Excessive demerits, poor performance in the classroom, and discipline problems contributed to his graduating in last place in his class of thirty-four cadets. Indeed, he was still serving a detention at the time of his graduation. While at the academy, he excelled only in horsemanship.

The Civil War was already two months old when the newly commissioned second lieutenant reported to Washington. On the eve of First Bull Run (10), Winfield Scott (30) detailed Custer as a messenger to carry dispatches to Irwin McDowell (80), who was in route to Manassas, Virginia. Custer joined McDowell staff's and then remained as a staff officer with the Union army through a succession of commanders. He served as George McClellan's (51) aide-de-camp and then performed the same duties for Alfred Pleasonton. Both generals were so impressed with Custer's enthusiasm and bravery that they advanced him to captain.

Union commanders were desperately in need of officers who could and would fight. In a conflict that defied the past "rules" of warfare and introduced a degree of firepower previously unknown, commanders focused on finding subordinates with desire and skill rather than promoting by age and experience. Custer displayed all these desired characteristics in the Battle of Brandy Station and in the Rappahannock

Campaign. At age twenty-three and with only two years on active duty, Custer went from captain to brigadier general on June 29, 1863, when Pleasonton placed him in command of the 3rd Cavalry Division's Michigan Brigade.

A week later, Custer's brigade was instrumental in preventing J. E. B. Stuart (23) from turning the Union flank at Gettysburg (4). On October 2, 1864, Custer assumed command of the entire 3rd Cavalry and, as a part of Phil Sheridan's (8) army, led his horseman at Yellow Tavern, Winchester, Five Forks, and Appomattox (37). During the war's final campaign, Custer, promoted to major general in April 1865, was instrumental in the pursuit of Lee's retreat and eventually blocking the Confederate avenue of escape. His command received the first flag of truce sent forward by Lee's army.

Custer was a classic hero. He had eleven horses killed out from under him during the war but received only one wound himself. In addition to brevet promotions, he earned the praise of the Union leadership. Sheridan so respected Custer that he purchased the table on which Grant and Lee signed their surrender documents and later presented it to the young general's wife.

The "boy-general" summed up his contributions to the war's final campaign in a message to his troops on April 9, 1865, from Appomattox Court House. He wrote, "During the past six months, though in most instances confronted by superior numbers, you have captured from the enemy in open battle 111 pieces of field artillery, 65 battle flags, and upward of 10,000 prisoners of war, including seven general officers. Within the past ten days, and included in the above you have captured 46 field-pieces of artillery, and 37 battle flags. You have never lost a gun, never lost a color, and never been defeated; and not withstanding the numerous engagements in which you have borne a prominent part, including those memorable battles in the Shenandoah, you have captured every piece of artillery which the enemy has dared to open upon you."

Custer's success, élan, and youth caught the attention of the entire Union. His friends called him Armstrong or Audie; his troops called him Curly because of his long hair; his West Point classmates called him Fanny; the Union called him Hero. Nearly six feet in height and of strong build, Custer looked and played the role of cavalry commander.

Union staff officer Theodore Lyman wrote that the young general "looks like a circus rider gone mad! He wears a hussar jacket and tight trousers of faded black velvet trimmed with tarnished lace." Lyman continued, writing that Custer wore his hair in "short, dry, flaxen ringlets" and that "he has a very merry blue eye, and a devil-may-care style."

Custer remained in the army as a major general of volunteers after the war and, following a brief assignment with the Reconstruction forces in Texas, returned to Washington to head the army's cavalry branch. In March 1866 the U.S. Army did away with its huge ranks of volunteers and returned to its Regular Army organization. In the reorganization, Custer resigned his volunteer rank of major general and reverted to his regular rank of captain. The following July he gained promotion to lieutenant colonel and joined the 7th Cavalry.

On the Western Plains, Custer added to his fame as well as to the controversy that seemed to follow his path. In 1867 he led his horse soldiers in campaigns against the Sioux and Cheyenne but was court-martialed and suspended for leaving the front for an unauthorized visit to his wife. A year later his old friend Phil Sheridan (9) restored him to active duty and, in November 1868, Custer led the assault that destroyed a Cheyenne village on the Washita. Some praised Custer for conducting an offensive in the winter and for eliminating a large number of Indians. Others called the attack a massacre.

During the next eight years, Custer served mostly on the western frontier. His fame and popularity among the American people even had talk of his becoming a presidential candidate before he met his fate at the Battle of the Little Big Horn in Montana on June 25, 1876, when a much larger number of Sioux warriors defeated a portion of the 7th Cavalry Regiment.

Over the succeeding years debate has waged over the reasons for Custer's dividing his command into three columns and for his overzealous attack against a much larger force. Many people malign him as a practitioner of genocide against the Native Americans while others use him as an example of the biased, foolish leadership they credit to the army in general.

In reality, Custer at Little Big Horn was the victim of an intelligence failure that did not warn him about the larger number of his opponents and the fact that they had secured repeating rifles superior to the single-shot weapons carried by his own men. Custer, accustomed to Indians running instead of fighting, made the decision to charge, a tactic that has gained him rank and accolades in the Civil War. At Little Big Horn it gained him a grave and lasting fame.

Custer and his men were buried where they fell. A year later Custer's remains, or at least those thought to be his, were removed to West Point for final interment. His wife, Elizabeth, survived him by fifty-seven years and her writings and speeches did much to create and maintain the fame of her husband.

Custer is much better known for his death at Little Big Horn than for his accomplishments in the Civil War. However, he is most deserving of his placement on this list for his actions during the conflict. Custer was present on nearly every major battlefield in the East, and his direct leadership and overall bravery achieved needed victories. His flamboyant style and bravery in battle raised the morale of his command as well as the people of the North. While the reasons for his fame may well be far overblown, his fighting abilities were all but unequaled. He best summarized his own influence on the conflict in his report from Appomattox at the end of the war, detailing the guns, flags, and men captured.

53

FREDERICKSBURG

December 13, 1862

The terrible carnage of the Battle of Fredericksburg in December 1862 was matched only by its futility. Once again a new Union commander, this time Ambrose Burnside (57), proved inept in battle against Robert E. Lee (5) and his Army of Northern Virginia.

For more than a month after the Battle of Antietam (1) concluded in September 1862, President Abraham Lincoln (2) waited for General George McClellan (51) to pursue the Confederates as they withdrew back to Virginia. Frustrated with McClellan's lack of initiative and exaggerated caution, Lincoln replaced McClellan with Burnside on November 7.

After his retreat from Antietam, Lee correctly anticipated McClellan's reluctance to pursue and divided his army of seventy-four thousand into two elements. He dispatched the first under Stonewall Jackson (36) to the Shenandoah Valley while he sent the second under James Longstreet (13) to block the Union approach at Culpepper. This division of forces went against most tactical doctrine, but against the "slow" McClellan it proved the correct tactic.

When Burnside took command of the 115,000-man Union army camped around Warrenton, he ordered the troops to move toward Fredericksburg, about halfway between Washington and Richmond. Lee had to take immediate action to secure the town and block the Union approach to the Confederate capital. When Burnside's lead units arrived along the Rappahannock River to the north and northeast of the town, Lee had relocated only a few thousand troops to defend Fredericksburg. Unfortunately for Burnside, his infantry had outdistanced his engineers, and he was forced to wait for pontoons to arrive to bridge the four-hundred-foot-wide river.

Even after his bridging arrived, Burnside delayed his attack for several more weeks while he planned and reorganized his giant force. Meanwhile, Lee consolidated his army around Fredericksburg. Longstreet arrived first on November 19 and took up positions directly behind Fredericksburg on a line of hills that included Marye's Heights. Jackson arrived a week later and took up positions facing the river southeast of the town and Longstreet.

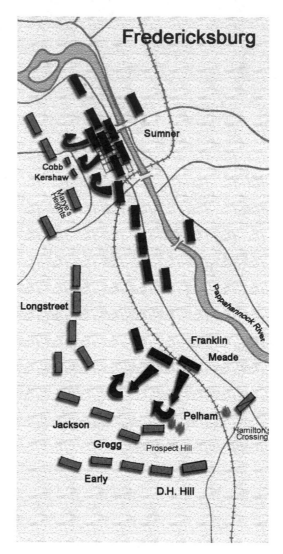

Lee, unsure where Burnside would concentrate his main attack, and fearful of getting his army surrounded within the buildings and streets of Fredericksburg, established his defenses on the hills behind the town. He hoped that by not directly defending Fredericksburg, he could spare the town. The flaw in this plan was that Lee spread his army over a twenty-mile front that did not allow Longstreet and Jackson to be mutually supporting.

Burnside had difficulties in determining just where to attack and found no agreement among his corps and division commanders. Finally, on December 11, he erected bridges at three locations and attacked both Longstreet and Jackson.

The plan had problems from its beginning. When his engineers assembled pontoons on the river directly across from Fredericksburg, a Mississippi brigade slipped into the town and began a withering sniper fire against those engineers. Nine times they attempted to build the bridges only to be driven from the river by the Mississippi riflemen.

To neutralize the rifle fire, Burnside ordered his 150 pieces of artillery to shell the city. After a barrage of eight thousand rounds, the engineers once again approached the bridges only to once again be beaten back by rifle fire. Burnside finally gathered a group of volunteer units and ferried them across the river upstream from the town. They then assembled, attacked and—after a pitched battle—drove the rebel snipers from the buildings.

The engineers finished erecting their bridges, and during the night the Union army crossed the Rappahannock. Instead of attacking on the morning of the December 12, however, the Union army stopped to loot and to destroy what remained of Fredericksburg.

Finally, on the morning of December 13, the Union's left flank attacked Jackson's defenses. Jackson did not have the advantage of the hills that protected Longstreet's sector, but he had an open area of about five hundred yards in front of his position. The Union failed to coordinate its attack and sent divisions forward piecemeal instead of unified in one attack. Confederate artillery ripped through the Union ranks. With their infantry pinned down, the Union artillery dueled with the Confederate gunners. So many of Jackson's horses that pulled his artillery were killed that gunners referred to this position as "Dead Horse Hill."

When a Union artillery shell struck and exploded a Confederate ammunition wagon, the Federal commander ordered the infantry to resume the attack. Mostly by luck they struck a six-hundred-yard gap in Jackson's lines and quickly penetrated the rebel rear area. Jackson ordered a counterattack that finally forced the Union soldiers back to the river after ferocious and deadly fighting.

Burnside had planned for his forces to defeat Jackson and then turn to flank Longstreet in tandem with a direct attack against Marye's Heights from Fredericksburg. When the attack against Jackson failed, he nevertheless ordered the attack against Longstreet. The results were some of the bloodiest and most catastrophic of the war. Over the afternoon, fourteen attacks by brigade-sized forces charged the Confederates protected by both a sunken road and a stone fence at Marye's Heights. Not a single Union soldier breached the Confederate defenses. By dark, the fields at Marye's Heights were so full of dead and wounded that bodies literally carpeted the ground.

Lee observed Jackson's counterattack and the almost casual destruction of the Union advance at Marye's Heights from nearby Telegraph Hill. Astounded and over-joyed by the success, he turned to Longstreet and remarked, "It is well that war is so terrible—we would grow too fond of it."

The next morning Burnside wanted to personally lead another attack, but he found his subordinate leaders reluctant to the point of mutiny. Late on December 15 he withdrew his army across the Rappahannock and dismantled his bridges behind him. Union casualties totaled more than 12,500 killed, wounded, or missing—about two-thirds of this number having fallen at Marye's Heights. Confederate casualties were about half this number.

Burnside accepted the blame for Fredericksburg. Lincoln, still looking for a gen-eral who could defeat the Army of Northern Virginia, relieved him from command and placed Joseph Hooker (48) in charge.

Fredericksburg stands as one of the most clear-cut victories by the Confederates in the war. In addition to inflicting massive casualties on the enemy, the rebels stopped another Union advance toward Richmond. The victory, however, was costly. Unlike the Union army, the Confederates faced a dwindling number of available replace-ments. Even worse, the Confederate victory at Fredericksburg, coupled with their win at Chancellorsville (31) the following May, set the stage for Lee's second and disas-trous invasion of the North at Gettysburg (3) in July.

Fredericksburg further depleted the sinking morale of the Union army, but their ability to replace casualties meant they would maintain superior numbers over the rebels. The murderous battle at Marye's Heights did provide the Union soldiers a bat-tle cry at Gettysburg where they shouted, "Fredericksburg, Fredericksburg," as they mowed down Pickett's Charge.

Despite all these factors, Fredericksburg was but one of the many battles that delayed the war's conclusion and ended the command of yet another Union general. Its influence is far overshadowed by the earlier Antietam and the later Gettysburg and Vicksburg (7) battles. Its ranking comes more from the blood shed by its participants and the mistakes by Burnside than in any real effect on the war.

54

JOHN BROWN

Abolitionist

1800–1859

Fanatic, traitor, patriot, and martyr—these are but a few of the words used to describe the abolitionist John Brown, and each is correct. Brown's raid on Harpers Ferry in 1859 convinced many in the South that there was a movement to violently end their practice of slavery. At the same time, the North gained a martyr to glorify their efforts to end human bondage and save the Union.

For the first half-century of his life, John Brown exerted little influence beyond his own family and managed to fail at every business and profession he pursued. Born on May 9, 1800, in Torrington, Connecticut, Brown moved with his family five years later to Ohio, where his father worked as a tanner. He claimed to have briefly herded cattle for the U.S. Army during the War of 1812, but he spent more of his time becoming an opponent of government authority and a student of the Bible.

As an adult, Brown married twice and fathered twenty children. He briefly studied for the ministry but left school to join his father in the tanning business. He later worked as a land surveyor, wool merchant, and farmer, but he failed in all these vocations. On at least one occasion he was accused of supporting his family by stealing horses. By 1849, Brown was active in the Underground Railroad, assisting runaway slaves in reaching freedom. He lived for two years in a community of free blacks in North Elba, New York, where his antislavery zeal increased.

In 1855, Brown and five of his sons moved to Osawatomie, Kansas, to support that state's position against slavery. Brown worked part-time as a surveyor but spent most of his hours organizing the village's militia. When pro-slavery forces raided Lawrence in 1856, Brown declared that he was an "instrument of God" with instructions to avenge the attack. On May 23, 1856, Brown, accompanied by four of his sons and two other men, went to homes of pro-slavery families along Osawatomie Creek. Brown and his band dragged five unarmed men from their homes and hacked them to death with swords.

Brown's savage attacks gained him the praise and support of eastern abolitionists. Pro-slavery factions were appalled at the murders and attempted to bring Brown to

justice over the summer. They managed to burn his home and kill one of his sons, but Brown escaped to Virginia where he, with the support of New England backers, established a refuge for runaway slaves.

Over the next two years Brown developed a plan to free all the slaves in the South. His plan was simple—but also unrealistic. On the night of October 16, 1859, Brown led a band of twenty-one men, including several of his sons and five black men, into Harpers Ferry in western Virginia. His plan was to seize the town's government armory and gun-manufacturing plant so he could arm runaway slaves who joined his fight. In an ever-expanding web of armed former slaves, he intended to spread his men across the South, bringing freedom to all.

The first casualty of the raid on Harpers Ferry was a free black man named Hayward Shepherd, a railway baggage handler who was shot by Brown's men for no apparent reason. Four more residents of the town died before the locals reacted and surrounded Brown and his men in a firehouse. Telegraph messages called for federal assistance, and officials in Washington dispatched a U.S. Marine company to Harpers Ferry. At the head of the detachment was an army officer named Robert E. Lee (5).

The Marines stormed the firehouse on October 18, capturing Brown and killing seven of his men, including two of his sons. Lee protected Brown from the town's angry folks and secured him for trial. Over the next few weeks the abolitionist was interviewed by government officials as well as the press.

A reporter for the *New York Herald* was one of the first to talk with Brown. In an article that appeared on October 21, he wrote, "Brown is fifty-five years of age, rather small-sized, with keen and restless gray eyes, and a grizzly beard and hair. He is a wiry, active man…his hair is matted and tangled, and his face, hands, and clothes are smutched and smeared with blood."

Brown's trial drew media attention from across the country. "Old Brown," as he was now called, had ample opportunity to proclaim his antislavery stance, to posture himself as a self-proclaimed man of faith, and to stand as a hero of the people. Brown would neither reveal who had funded his operation nor would he make any significant defense. His supporters provided seventeen affidavits that claimed Brown was not of sound mind. They noted that thirteen of his close relatives, including his mother and grandmother, had been certified as insane. To no surprise, the jury found Brown guilty of treason and sentenced him to hang. At Charlestown on December 2, Brown climbed the gallows in what witness and future Confederate general Stonewall Jackson (36) later described as "unflinching firmness." Six of Brown's raiders followed him to the gallows.

Even before the trap door dropped Brown to eternity, Southerners were already proclaiming his raid an example of the North's desires to end slavery at any costs. Southern newspapers carried articles about "murderous abolitionists" who were financing a black rebellion.

Some Northerners condemned Brown for the raid as well as for his bloody past. Most people, however, considered him a righteous reformer whom they elevated to a martyr for the cause of ending slavery. Writer Henry David Thoreau called the raid "a brave and humane deed" while his fellow New Englander and poet Ralph Waldo Emerson compared Brown to Jesus Christ.

Soon after his capture, Brown himself provided the best prospective on his raid when he said, "You had better, all you people of the South, prepare yourselves for a settlement of this question. It must come up for settlement sooner than you are prepared for it, and the sooner you commence that preparation, the better for you. You may dispose of me very easily; I am nearly disposed of now; but this question is still to be settled—the Negro question, I mean."

By the time Union soldiers marched off to fight their Confederate brothers, "John Brown's Body" was the tune they sang to remind themselves that while the old man's body might "lie a-mould'ing in his grave," "his soul is marching on." Soon they were changing lyrics as the North's most popular tune of the war became "Battle Hymn of the Republic," adapted from "John Brown's Body" by Julia Ward Howe in February 1862.

John Brown's raid and execution provided a defining moment in the stalemate between pro- and antislavery factions. Doubtlessly, the war would have begun without the help of Brown, but his actions further divided a nation already coming apart at the seams. In hindsight, Confederates saw that the State of Virginia would have been much wiser to commit Brown to a lunatic asylum rather than grant him martyrdom at the end of a rope.

55

WINFIELD SCOTT HANCOCK

Union General

1824–1886

Winfield Scott Hancock earned the praise of his superiors as the finest corps commander in the Union army and won the respect of his subordinates for his organizational skills and overall leadership abilities. Hancock was at the center of most of the pivotal battles in the East, including Gettysburg (4), where he defeated the Confederate flanking attack on July 2, 1863, and then held the line against Pickett's Charge the following day.

Born on February 14, 1824, in Montgomery Square, Pennsylvania, Hancock joined the West Point Class of 1844, where he graduated number eighteen of twenty-five cadets. As an infantry officer, he briefly served on the Western frontier before joining the American forces in the Mexican War. There he fought under his namesake General Winfield Scott (30) and earned a brevet promotion for bravery. After the war he served mostly in quartermaster corps positions, including duty in the Kansas border disputes and Indian conflicts on the frontier.

At the outbreak of the Civil War, Hancock was the chief quartermaster of the military depot in Los Angeles. Always the gentleman, Hancock hosted a dinner for his officer friends who were departing California to join the Confederate army. After Hancock helped secure Los Angeles from Californians who favored the South, he, too, traveled east. As a captain, he expected to continue as a quartermaster, but upon his arrival in Washington, George McClellan (51) appointed Hancock a brigadier general of infantry volunteers on September 23, 1861.

Hancock joined the army in the field and for the remainder of the war seemed to be at every future critical fight and juncture in the eastern theater. In his first major action in the Peninsular Campaign (32) in the spring of 1862, Hancock's brigade was instrumental in the successful flanking attack at Williamsburg. By the end of the campaign, his organizational abilities and his tactical execution had earned him the nickname of "Hancock the Superb" from officers and enlisted men alike.

At the Battle of Antietam (1) in September 1862, Hancock advanced to command

a division and again performed well. Hancock's men were in the thickest of the fighting at Fredericksburg (53), where they participated in the murderous assault on Marye's Heights on December 13. The following spring, Hancock's division skillfully covered the Union withdrawal from Chancellorsville (31).

In the spring of 1863, Hancock, now a major general, assumed command of II Corps of the Army of the Potomac. Although junior to other corps commanders, it was Hancock whom George Meade (24) dispatched to Gettysburg in July to determine if that is where they should fight the Confederate invasion of Pennsylvania. It was Hancock who selected Cemetery Ridge as the center of the Union positions.

On the second day of the Battle of Gettysburg, Hancock took command of the entire Union left to turn back James Longstreet's (13) assault at Little Round Top. The next day Hancock's corps absorbed and defeated the brunt of Pickett's Charge into the Union center. During the fight Hancock suffered a severe wound when a bullet struck the pommel of his saddle and drove a nail and bits of wood into his thigh. Despite the wound, Hancock refused evacuation until the battle concluded. Among the Confederate dead in front of his position were Generals Lewis Armistead and Richard Garrett, both of whom had attended Hancock's departure dinner in Los Angeles two years earlier.

Hancock spent the remainder of 1863 convalescing from his wound. He rejoined the Army of the Potomac at the Wilderness (62) in May 1864 and led the attack against the Bloody Angle at Spotsylvania Court House (65) later in the month. At

Cold Harbor (59) in June, Hancock's corps sustained significant losses in the continued assaults into the Confederate defenses that U. S. Grant (3) ordered.

During the Petersburg Campaign (46), Hancock's corps suffered major casualties in a fight at Reams's Station on August 25, 1864. In November, distraught from this reversal, concerned that Grant's war of attrition was creating unreasonable Union casualties, and still suffering from the Gettysburg wound that had never healed properly, Hancock departed his corps to convalesce in Washington. There he led a recruiting effort and then served in the Middle Military Division until the end of the war.

Hancock remained in uniform after the South surrendered. After a series of positions in the West and South, he took command of the Department of the East at Governor's Island in New York in 1877. During this period Grant and other U.S. officials criticized Hancock for his support of leniency toward the defeated Confederates. However, as early as 1868 the Democratic Party considered Hancock as their presidential candidate and finally made him so in 1877. He lost by a narrow margin to fellow Civil War veteran James A. Garfield (83).

In the nineteenth century, military officers could engage in politics without resigning their commissions. Throughout the campaign Hancock remained in command of Governor's Island and was still there on active duty when he died on February 9, 1886. He is buried in Montgomery Cemetery in Norristown, Pennsylvania.

Hancock was a tall man who most described as "soldierly" and "impressive." His fellow officers noted that he always had clean white shirts, and no one knew just where he got them. A member of his staff, Captain Henry H. Bingham, later explained the way the men reacted to their commander when he said, "One felt safe when near him."

Although Hancock disagreed with Grant over attrition warfare and postwar treatment of the South, the Union commander praised his subordinate. Grant wrote in his memoirs: "Hancock stands the most conspicuous figure of all the general officers who did not exercise a separate command. He commanded a corps longer than any other one, and his name was never mentioned as having committed a battle blunder for which he was responsible. He was a man of very conspicuous personal appearance. Tall, well-formed, and, at the time of which I now write, young and fresh-looking, he presented an appearance that would attract the attention of an army as he passed. His genial disposition made him friends, and his personal courage and his presence with his command in the thickest of the fight won for him the confidence of troops serving under him. No matter how hard the fight, the II Corps always felt their commander was looking after them."

Such praise verifies Hancock's importance and influence. Not only was he the finest Union corps commander of the war, but he also was the kind of officer with who any soldier would like to serve.

56

MOBILE BAY

August 2–23, 1864

By August 1864, actions by the Union army on land and its naval blockade at sea had reduced the number of Southern ports open to Confederate blockade runners to two. The first, Galveston, Texas, was too far from the main battle area to be of great significance. Mobile Bay, Alabama, remained the most important open port in the Confederacy and had to be neutralized for the North to control the Deep South.

The successful Union offensives in eastern Tennessee in the fall of 1863 and their occupation of Atlanta in July 1864 had earned the Federal forces the upper hand in the Gulf States of the Confederacy. In August a combined U.S. army and naval force moved against the heavily fortified port of Mobile Bay.

Never large or influential, the Confederate navy nonetheless had a defensive flotilla of three wooden gunboats and the ironclad *Tennessee* under the command of Admiral Franklin Buchanan at anchor in the bay. Buchanan's fleet was not capable of successfully engaging the much larger Union navy at sea, but with its large field of floating torpedoes—as mines were then known—to aid the defense, Confederate ships could defend the harbor. More importantly, Buchanan's vessels, and Mobile itself, were also defended by three strong-walled garrisons that protected the opening of the bay. Southern artillery gunners manned 104 large-caliber artillery pieces at Forts Gaines, Morgan, and Powell that had the capability of sinking any ship that attempted to enter the harbor.

The Union plan called for destruction of the Confederate fleet and the capture of the three forts. General Gordon Granger and his 5,500 soldiers of the XIII Corps landed on the western end of Dauphine Island at the opening of Mobile Bay on August 3 and moved against Fort Gaines. While the Union army continued its attack on the fort, a U.S. Navy flotilla of four ironclads and fourteen wooden ships commanded by Admiral David Farragut (14) sailed into the bay on August 5. Farragut, aboard his flagship the USS *Hartford,* climbed up into the ship's rigging so he could better observe the battle and maneuver his force. To prevent his falling from his perch if he were wounded, Farragut had a crew member tie him to the mast.

The Union's lead vessel, the USS *Tecumseh,* entered the harbor about 7:00 a.m. and immediately came under fire from Fort Morgan. Three-quarters of an hour later

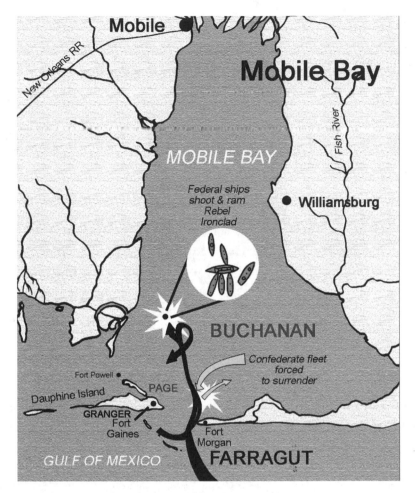

the *Tecumseh* turned to attack the *Tennessee* and struck a mine. The ironclad started to sink quickly. The Union crew evacuated the ship under the supervision of Commander Tunis A. M. Craven. With the vessel about to capsize, Craven turned to crew member John Collins and said, "After you, pilot." Having yielded his slot to another, Craven and 90 of his crew of 114 then went to bottom with their ship.

Observing the artillery fire from the forts, the explosion, the sinking *Tecumseh*, and the dozens of floating torpedoes to his front, the commander of the next ship in line gave the order to back away. Farragut saw the hesitancy and reportedly ordered, "Damn the torpedoes, full speed ahead."

The Union fleet obeyed and pushed into the bay. Several struck torpedoes, but the water-logged mines failed to explode. For the next hour the Union and Confederate ships rammed each other and fired their cannons at point blank range. The three smaller Confederate wooden ships were quickly sunk or run aground, leaving the *Tennessee* alone to combat the Union fleet. Finally, at 10:00 a.m., with its steering mechanism destroyed and Buchanan struck down with a leg wound, the *Tennessee* surrendered.

Of the 470 Confederate sailors involved in the fight, 312 were killed or captured. Federal dead and wounded totaled 319 of the 3,000 sailors engaged.

Farragut turned his fleet to support Granger's continued attack on the forts around the bay. The last of these was finally neutralized by the Union on August 23, yielding nearly fifteen hundred prisoners. With the port entrance in their control, the combined Union army and navy maintained an occupation force that prevented further arrival of blockade runners. The city of Mobile, still heavily fortified, was no longer significant and left uncaptured, but isolated, until the end of the war.

Union naval officials, rarely receiving credit or accolades for fighting the rebellion, took most of the credit for the victory at Mobile Bay. Secretary of the Navy Gideon Welles sent congratulations to Farragut, stating, "In the success which has attended your operations you have illustrated the efficiency and irresistible power of a naval force led by a bold and vigorous mind, and insufficiency of any batteries to prevent the passage of a fleet thus led and commanded."

Farragut accepted the praise and his elevation to the war's best-known and most famous naval commander. His order of "Damn the torpedoes…" added to his reputation and fame but, in fact, there is some doubt that he ever uttered the oft-quoted words. Even if he had done so, it is difficult to imagine how it could have been communicated to the other ships from his post in his vessel's riggings. However, if he did not say it, he should have, and as far as history remembers, he did so.

The Battle of Mobile Bay blocked the last major harbor through which the South could move and receive goods. It was a strong point that the Union had to neutralize to ensure the total defeat of the rebellion. It is likely that the same objective could have been accomplished by a larger sea blockade, but the U.S. Navy was available and spoiling for a fight to prove their merit and future as an important part of the U.S. defense team. Mobile Bay provided a more than sufficient victory for the navy and fame for its leader.

As for its ranking, Mobile Bay belongs in the middle of this list because of Farragut and his famous quote more than for the importance of the actual battle. Still, it is one of the few naval conflicts of consequence in the war, and it also helped secure Farragut's ranking, which exceeds that of the battle itself.

57

AMBROSE EVERETT BURNSIDE

Union General

1824–1881

Ambrose Everett Burnside showed such great promise as a commander when he led a Union brigade that everyone was sure he would excel equally well when Abraham Lincoln (2) promoted him to be commander of the Army of the Potomac just before the Battle of Fredericksburg. However, by war's end, Burnside was without command of any kind, but not before he dramatically impacted the tides of the war. A leader of limited abilities who was well aware of his shortcomings, Burnside proved to be one of the most inept of the Union leaders. His negative influence resulted from the number of Union troops he sacrificed and the number of battles he lost that prolonged the war. Burnside was his own worst enemy under fire.

Born on May 23, 1824, in Liberty, Indiana, to a father who had freed his slaves when he moved from South Carolina, Burnside apprenticed to a tailor after completing his primary education. At age nineteen his politically connected father secured him an appointment to West Point where he graduated as an artillery lieutenant, ranked number eighteen of thirty-eight graduates of the Class of 1847.

Burnside served briefly at the end of the Mexican War and then performed garrison duty in the southwestern United States during the Indian Wars. He saw little combat in either of the assignments but was slightly wounded in a skirmish with the Apaches. In 1853 he resigned his commission and settled in Bristol, Rhode Island, where he manufactured breech-loading rifles he had designed while in the army. The venture failed and in 1857 Burnside was forced into bankruptcy. An old friend from West Point and service in Mexico, George B. McClellan (51), found him a job with the Illinois Central Railroad, where he worked as a treasurer.

Upon learning of the firing on Fort Sumter (50), Burnside returned to Rhode Island, where he had previously been active in the militia, and recruited the 1st R.I. Volunteers. He served satisfactorily as a colonel in the Union defeat at First Bull Run (10) on July 21, 1861, gaining promotion to brigadier general. In 1862 he led a seaborne expeditionary force against rebel forces on the North Carolina coast where he captured Roanoke Island on February 7 and New Bern on March 14.

His performance in North Carolina brought Burnside to the attention of President Abraham Lincoln (2), who was desperately seeking an aggressive commander for the Army of the Potomac. Burnside, more knowledgeable than the president on his abilities to command large units, twice turned down Lincoln's offer. At the Battle of Antietam (1) in September 1862, Burnside commanded the IX Corps under the overall command of his old friend McClellan. Burnside's slow response to orders, confusion among his subordinate commanders, and insistence on crossing a small bridge on Antietam Creek rather than fording the shallow waterway allowed Robert E. Lee's (5) Confederate army to escape what might have been capture or annihilation.

Upset at the failure of his army to achieve complete victory at Antietam and their slow pursuit of Lee's force, Lincoln relieved McClellan from command and once again offered the Army of the Potomac to Burnside. This time Lincoln made it clear that a refusal would not be accepted. Burnside's fellow generals also encouraged him to take the command because they feared that Joseph Hooker (48), whom they did not like, would be the other likely candidate.

Proving that many leaders are promoted beyond their capabilities, Burnside assumed command and reorganized the Army of the Potomac into an unwieldy organization of Left, Center, and Right. Despite the advice of Lincoln and his subordinate generals, Burnside ordered a winter offensive into Virginia. After moving in bad weather in what his own troops called the "Mud March," the Army of the Potomac met Lee's Army of Northern Virginia at Fredericksburg (53) on December 13, 1862. Although the Union troops outnumbered the rebels, Burnside's attack against the Confederate strength on Marye's Heights resulted in a clear rebel victory. Burnside suffered more than thirteen thousand casualties compared to only five thousand on the rebel side.

The Union general was aware the defeat was primarily his fault. He resigned command and offered to resign his commission as well. Lincoln accepted the former but believed Burnside could still contribute to the Union cause. The president transferred Burnside to command the Department and Army of the Ohio. Despite difficulties with local political leaders who objected to Lincoln's government, he once again proved he could adequately lead smaller units. In July 1863, he blocked John Hunt Morgan's (88) cavalry raid into Ohio and then moved into Tennessee where he held Knoxville against the attack by James Longstreet (13) the following November.

In January 1864, Burnside reassumed command of the IX Corps and participated in the battles of the Wilderness (62), Spotsylvania Court House (65), and numerous smaller fights before he joined the siege of Petersburg (46). In July 1864, Union miners detonated a large explosion under the rebel lines, but Burnside, in his usual indecisiveness, failed to exploit the resulting wide gap in the Confederate lines. He was relieved of command and remained on leave until the end of the war. Burnside finally resigned his commission on April 15, 1865.

Burnside briefly returned to work with the railroad before his election as governor of Rhode Island in 1866 and was then twice reelected. In 1870 he went to Europe as a mediator to end the Franco-Prussian War. On his return home he won the election for Rhode Island senator in 1874 and served in the U.S. Senate until his death at Bristol on September 13, 1881. Burnside rests in the Swan Point Cemetery in Providence.

Despite his failures in command, including the disastrous attack at Fredericksburg, Burnside remained popular with both civilians and veterans alike. In the same year he gained election to the Senate, he was also selected as the National Commander of the Grand Army of the Republic.

At six feet in height, Burnside was an impressive, handsome man whose particular style of whiskers eventually provided the name "sideburns." Lincoln should have heeded Burnside's knowledge of his personal command limitations. He could have spared many men's lives, and perhaps shortened the war without Burnside.

Burnside's ranking on this list comes much more from his failures that influenced the war rather than any successes. The best description of Burnside comes from U. S. Grant (3). In his memoirs, Grant wrote that Burnside was "an officer who was generally liked and respected. He was not, however, fitted to command an army. No one knew this better than himself."

58

DRED SCOTT DECISION

March 6, 1857

The U.S. Supreme Court's *Dred Scott* decision declared that a black slave was not a citizen, that he had no right to sue for his freedom, and that previous legislation limiting slavery in certain territories was unconstitutional. Overall, the decision widened the political and social gap between the North and South and pushed the country nearer to civil war.

Born in about 1800 in Virginia, Dred Scott traveled west with his master Peter Blow to Alabama and then to St. Louis in 1830. Blow died two years later and Dr. John Emerson, an army surgeon, purchased Scott from the estate. Emerson took Scott along when he was transferred to the state of Illinois and on to the Wisconsin Territory in 1836. While in Wisconsin, Scott met and married Harriet Robinson, whom Emerson purchased. Apparently Scott was unaware that he was technically free while in Illinois and Wisconsin, where slavery was illegal.

In 1838 the army transferred Emerson back to St. Louis and then to Louisiana. Emerson traveled alone, and once established, sent for his slaves, who traveled on their own from free territory back to where slavery was legal.

In 1843 Emerson died, leaving his slaves to his wife. Scott attempted to buy his freedom from Mrs. Emerson, but she turned down his offer. Although Scott was illiterate, he was intelligent—and desired to be free. Encouraged, and monetarily supported by local abolitionists, Scott sued in the local courts to gain his freedom, claiming his extended stay in free territory had legally released him from bondage.

Scott's case finally went to trial in June 1847, but he lost on the technicality that he could not prove Mrs. Emerson actually owned him. The following year the Missouri Supreme Court ruled that the case should be retried, and in 1850 a state circuit court declared that Scott should be freed. However, he remained in bondage during the appeals. Two years later, the Missouri Supreme Court reversed the circuit decision. Scott's lawyers then appealed to the U.S. Circuit Court that upheld the Missouri Supreme Court decision.

The last source for justice now lay with the U.S. Supreme Court, which heard Scott's appeal in early 1857. The Court was not without its biases. Seven of the justices had been appointed by pro-slavery presidents and five were from slave-owning families. The Supreme Court proceeded to take a simple question of jurisdiction and whether Scott was indeed a citizen and make it a much more complex, far-reaching issue. Legally, the Court could have followed the standing law and dismissed the case on the grounds that Scott, as a Negro slave, was not a citizen and therefore had no right to sue. Instead, the Court, led by Chief Justice Robert B. Taney—a staunch supporter of slavery from Maryland—decided to use the case to make a sweeping ruling.

On March 6, 1857, the Court, in a vote of seven to two, announced its judgment. According to the decision, Scott as a slave was private property and could be taken to and removed from states or territories regardless of their slavery laws. The Court also declared that the Missouri Compromise of 1820 (78) that prohibited slavery north of the parallel 38 degrees 30 minutes to be unconstitutional. It justified this latter decision by citing the Fifth Amendment to the U.S. Constitution that prohibits Congress from depriving persons of their property without due process of law.

The decision was well-received by Southerners, who believed that slavery could no longer be barred in the territories. Northerners were angry because they had seen barring slavery in the territories to be a step to abolishing the practice. They recognized the composition of the Court and saw the *Dred Scott* case as more of a political than legal decision. Abraham Lincoln (2) reacted to the decision with disgust and spoke out against the ruling as he became more involved in the political process that eventually would lead to his presidency.

The most immediate impact of the decision was upon Dred Scott, who himself remained in bondage. Throughout the legal process, the sons of his original owner Peter Blow, who had been childhood friends of Scott's, had joined other abolitionists in providing funds. When the Supreme Court failed to free Scott, the Blow sons purchased Scott and his wife and set them free. Nine months later Scott died—a free man.

Fort Sumter (50) is generally considered the spark that set off the Civil War. While those cannons at Charleston Harbor might have been the first gunfire, the paper trail of the long court case of Dred Scott provided the tender that later led to the blaze of war. Differences over regional and social issues between North and South had threatened to divide the country since the colonies had won their independence. Slavery widened these differences, and the *Dred Scott* decision helped extend this gap from disagreement and argument to war and bloodshed.

While the *Dred Scott* decision influenced the political career of Lincoln, his election, and the eventual break between North and South, it was but one of many causes of the Civil War. The South would have declared its independence at some future point, and the North would have fought to maintain the Union, regardless of what happened to a simple Missouri slave and a Supreme Court decision. The *Dred Scott* decision did, however, probably hasten the outbreak of the war and is certainly more influential than the Missouri Compromise (78) that it superseded.

59

COLD HARBOR

May 31–June 12, 1864

The Battle of Cold Harbor in the summer of 1864 provided Robert E. Lee (5) his last victory of the Civil War and delayed the capture of Richmond for another ten months. It also changed the tactics of the conflict from maneuver to entrenchment and siege.

The Confederate loss at Gettysburg (4) in July 1863 drove the rebels back into Virginia and forced Lee to once more defend Richmond to insure the continuation of the Confederacy. George Meade (24) remained in command of the Army of the Potomac after his victory in Pennsylvania, but his failure to pursue and destroy the retreating rebel army displeased Abraham Lincoln (2). As a result, the president promoted U. S. Grant (3) to "General in Chief of the Armies" on March 12 to assume command of the Union forces, including Meade's and other Union armies. Grant co-located his headquarters with Meade and began a campaign of attrition to defeat Lee and to end the rebellion.

Grant's offensive advanced southeast toward Richmond, engaging Lee's army at the Wilderness (62) on May 5–7, at Spotsylvania Court House (65) on May 8–21, and at North Anna on May 23–27. While these were tactical victories for the Confederates in that they stalled the Union advance, in each Lee and his army had to withdraw farther south.

From North Anna, Grant once again attempted to outflank Lee and move into Richmond itself. After skirmishing along Totopotomoy Creek, Grant ordered Phil Sheridan (8) and his cavalry to occupy the crossroads of Old Cold Harbor only ten miles northeast of Richmond, a settlement with a far inland hotel that provided shelter but no hot meals—thus a "cold harbor."

Sheridan's cavalry and the Confederate cavalry commanded by Fitz Lee arrived about the same time at Cold Harbor, but the Union horsemen with their repeating Spencer rifles pushed the rebels back about a half-mile. Both Robert E. Lee and Grant poured additional units into the fight until they faced each other along a line seven miles in length. Early on June 1, Confederate infantry attacked the Union positions but were repulsed. Late in the day Grant ordered his own attack but that, too, failed.

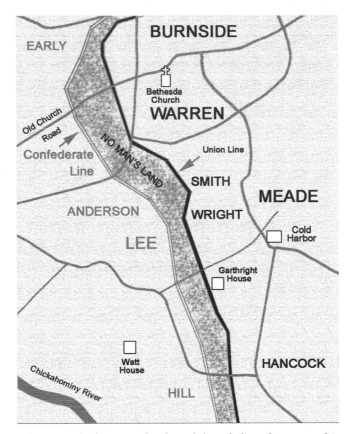

Grant wanted to attack the next day but delayed the advance so his exhausted men could rest and refit before the fight. The Confederates took advantage of the delay to dig defensive trenches reinforced with logs. By the end of June 2 the Union army totaled more than 105,000 men compared to about 59,000 on the Confederate side. Despite the numerical advantages, Grant's army contained many raw recruits and inexperienced units who had been defending Washington. Lee, while outnumbered, had pulled veterans from other theaters to enlarge his force.

By the time the Union army moved forward on the morning of June 3, the Confederates were well protected and ready. The Confederates met the Union advance with concentrated rifle and cannon fire in a battle that was so one-sided even a Southern soldier later described it as "simply murder." Again and again the Union troops withdrew, reorganized and reinforced, and charged the Confederate defenses—each time with the same bloody result. Grant's soldiers understood the futility of the attacks—one even wrote a final diary entry just before his unit's advances that was later found on the battlefield: "June 3, 1864, Cold Harbor. I was killed"—but they answered the call and charged ahead. Midday, Grant finally called off the attacks.

From June 4 to 12, the Union and Confederate armies occupied their trenches only a hundred yards apart. They continued cannon and sniper fire but neither side risked an advance. Between the trenches many of those wounded on June 3 bled to death or died of exposure as Grant and Lee could not come to terms for a truce to recover the dead and injured.

On June 13, Grant realized that direct attacks against Lee's forces protecting Richmond would prove too costly. He proceeded to move southward to cross the James River, circling east of the Confederate capital to attack the rail center at Petersburg. Lee managed to beat Grant to his objective and prepared to defend the city. Except for his eventual retreat during the last week of the war, Lee would spend the remainder of the conflict in the defense of Petersburg.

Other than a brief victory at the Petersburg's Battle of the Crater, Lee's Army of Virginia did not win another fight, but Cold Harbor had gained the Confederacy another ten months of existence. The price had been high for both sides. Northern casualties numbered more than seven thousand dead and wounded to fifteen hundred on the Southern side. Total casualties over the past four months' battles totaled fifty thousand for the Union and thirty thousand for the Confederates.

The number of Union casualties at Cold Harbor, combined with those in the previous battles over the past months, brought Grant harsh criticism from the Northern press. References to him as a "butcher" appeared in the newspapers. In his memoirs, Grant later wrote, "I have always regretted that last assault at Cold Harbor was ever made."

Despite the misgivings of both Grant and the press, Cold Harbor forced Lee into the defense for the remainder of the war. Unable to maneuver, he could only hold out for another winter while Grant tightened the siege at Petersburg. Gettysburg may have marked the high tide of the Confederacy, but Cold Harbor represents its last great splash before falling beneath the waves of the Union army.

The Wilderness and Spotsylvania battles led up to Cold Harbor, but they failed to change the war from maneuver to entrenchment warfare and ultimately bring the war to an end; therefore, they have a lower ranking. Cold Harbor would rank even higher on this list except for one primary factor—the better supplied and manned Union army was already well on its way to victory. Cold Harbor was a bloody stop along the way, but the South's eventual doom was already a certainty.

60

BRAXTON BRAGG

Confederate General

1817–1876

Braxton Bragg was one of the most controversial Confederate generals. Known for his high moral character and strict following of regulations and discipline, Bragg achieved both success and failure in the western theater. Although he consistently failed to get along with his fellow commanders, Bragg remained a favorite of President Jefferson Davis (9) throughout the conflict.

Born on March 22, 1817, in Warrenton, North Carolina, Bragg graduated fifth of the fifty cadets in the West Point Class of 1837. Commissioned in the artillery, he served in the Seminole War until 1841 and then earned three brevets in the Mexican War. Bragg resigned his commission in 1856 to run his plantation in Louisiana and to design the state's levee and drainage system.

Bragg accepted a commission in the Louisiana militia in early 1861 and quickly advanced to the rank of major general of volunteers. Appointed a brigadier general in the Confederate army in March 1861, Bragg assumed command of defenses between Mobile and Pensacola along the Gulf Coast. His quick reorganization, training, and provisioning of the force earned him promotion to major general the following September.

After joining Albert S. Johnston (85) in Kentucky, Bragg took command of a corps and led the Confederate right wing at the Battle of Shiloh (18) in April. When Johnston was killed, Bragg took command with the rank of full general. Two months later Davis put him in command of the Army of Tennessee, replacing P. G. T. Beauregard (43). Part of the reason for this change was Beauregard's ill health, but Davis also based his decision on the fact that he did not get along well with Beauregard and Bragg had been a friend since the Mexican War.

Bragg's organizational and planning skills once again proved successful as he moved more than thirty thousand men by rail from Tupelo, Mississippi, around the Union force at Corinth to occupy Tennessee and then push into Kentucky. The march northward was stopped at Perryville on October 8 and, although the battle ended in a draw and Confederate casualties were fewer than those of the Union,

Bragg decided to retreat—leaving his dead and wounded behind.

By the time Bragg established his defenses in eastern Tennessee, he had lost much of the confidence and support of his subordinate commanders. At the end of December, Bragg fought another indecisive battle at Stone's River and again withdrew to the southeast, giving up most of the ground he had taken in his fall offensive. In order to block a Union advance against Chattanooga, Bragg established defenses at Tullahoma in south-central Tennessee.

The Union army pushed Bragg out of Tullahoma in June 1863, forcing the Confederate army to fall back toward Chattanooga. Bragg fought a delaying action for the next six weeks before he launched a counterattack along Chickamauga Creek (74) on September 19. By day two of the battle, the Confederates gained the advantage and forced the Union army to retreat toward Chattanooga. Bragg further alienated his subordinate generals—including D. H. Hill, Leonidas Polk, James Longstreet (13), and Nathan Forrest (21)—when he refused to exploit the advantage and pursue the escaping army.

Back in Richmond, Davis knew that Bragg was not getting along well with his subordinates. He may or may not have also been aware that Bragg had difficulty riding horseback because of skin boils and that he was also frequently disabled by severe migraine headaches. In October the Confederate president visited Bragg's headquarters to discuss his concerns. Davis listened, and then expressed his support for his old friend Bragg and transferred his subordinates Hill and Polk to other commands.

In November, Bragg attacked Chattanooga (12) only to be soundly defeated. Bragg withdrew to Dalton, Georgia, where on February 24, 1864, he requested Davis remove him from command. Davis did so but brought Bragg to Richmond where he became the president's military advisor. Although this position was supposedly superior to the Confederate generals in the field, Bragg had little authority and accomplished little over the next year. In January 1865 he returned to action to command the Department of North Carolina.

After Lee's surrender at the Appomattox Court House (37), Bragg returned to Richmond to aid the escape of President Davis. A loyal friend to the end, he was captured along with the Confederate president on May 9, 1865.

Upon receiving his parole, Bragg accepted a civil engineering position in Alabama since his Louisiana plantations had been destroyed in the war. He later moved to Texas where he died in Galveston on September 27, 1876. He is buried in Mobile, Alabama.

Tall, bearded, enthusiastic, and intelligent, Bragg was far from handsome. During the final retreat from Richmond, a Georgia schoolgirl observed and described President Davis's party. In her diary she wrote, "Bragg might be called the ugliest. He looks like an old porcupine."

While most agreed on Bragg's physical appearance, his effectiveness as a leader was much debated at the time and continues to be so today. He had his supporters—most importantly President Davis—but most of his subordinate generals had no faith in his leadership and many disliked him personally. His demand for strict discipline was both positive and negative, depending on the one's stance. Bragg's success on his initial invasion of Tennessee and Kentucky proved masterful, and his victory at Chickamauga was one of the South's greatest victories of the war. However, his failure to hold ground in Kentucky, his reluctance to take advantage when able, and his final defeat at Chattanooga relegate him to a low ranking as to his overall influence on the war.

Commanders can succeed despite their inability to gain the confidence of their subordinates. Conversely, just because a commander is liked, or even beloved, does not guarantee success. Whatever the commander's personality, victory goes to those with the most assets, the best plans, and the superior leadership. Bragg's physical difficulties bear part of the blame for his failures, which further alienated his subordinates. Most importantly, Bragg's leadership and planning skills never exceeded his inability to get along with nearly everyone he encountered. In the end, Bragg was sometimes victorious, sometimes indecisive, and always unpopular.

61

WAR CORRESPONDENTS

1861–1865

The American Civil War was the first conflict in military history that journalists and sketch artists thoroughly documented as eyewitnesses. Correspondents, both American and foreign, accompanied the armies of the North and the South, covering every major battle. Their reports, along with editorials about the war and its leaders, helped form the opinions of Americans on both sides of the conflict.

Newspapers had existed in the United States since before the country gained its independence. These periodicals, however, little resembled the newspapers of today or those that evolved during the War Between the States. Until the middle of the nineteenth century, newspapers consisted mostly of editorials that supported one political group or another. Newspaper producers and their readers looked upon the printed sheets as a means of shaping or reinforcing opinions rather than as a medium for information about current events.

War correspondents were almost nonexistent in the first half of the nineteenth century. Several newsmen accompanied the United States' invasion of Mexico in 1846, but distance and technology prevented their dispatch of war news. It was not until the Crimean War of 1853 to 1856 between Russia and Turkey that English correspondents filed a few reports from the battlefront.

Despite this lack of "hard news," newspapers in the North and South played an important role even before the Civil War began. Editorials supporting and opposing the election of Lincoln filled broadsheets in the North while editors in the South expressed their opinions on secession.

At the outbreak of the Civil War in 1861, there were twenty-five hundred newspapers in the United States. Many advances had taken place during the three decades before the war that made reporting easier and faster for these papers. Shorthand had made note-taking more reliable; the telegraph had opened the way for the rapid transmission of information. The Associated Press had been formed to report, exchange, and distribute news stories for its member papers. Emerging technology allowed sketches to be published in weeklies like *Harper's* and *Frank Leslie's,* enabling the public to see as well as read about events.

The American public was desperate for news during the war. With soldiers and readers on both sides sharing the same language and much of the same culture, the

same issues—the future of the Union, states' rights, and slavery—were of great interest to everyone. Families and friends of the men fighting in the bloodiest war in American history clamored for news from the front about battles and, more importantly, casualties.

Correspondents accompanied the armies of the North and South from the beginning of the war. After First Bull Run (10) newsmen—or "specials," as they were better known—raced back to Washington with the news of the Union defeat. Before many of the soldiers returned to the city, newspapers reporting about the battle were on the street.

Over the next four years about three hundred fifty correspondents covered the Union and about one hundred fifty covered the South. Foreign correspondents, particularly from England, arrived to report on one or the other side, or on occasion to cross the lines to cover both armies.

As the war progressed, newspapers added battle maps and chronologies showing how a fight progressed. Following each story, usually in a smaller typeface, was the list of dead, wounded, and missing.

At the beginning of the war there was no such thing as a "war correspondent" on either side. Newspapers dispatched experienced reporters when they could. At other times they sent anyone willing to accept the hardship of the camps and battlefields. The quality of their reports was mixed. Dispatches were usually published with the writer identified only as "Our Correspondent" or "Special Correspondent" because bylines had not yet become routine.

This lack of experience and identification, combined with the general confusion on the battlefield, hampered accuracy. Some reporters wrote stories without checking details or considering the effect of their words on their readers. On May 27, 1861, the *Baltimore Sun* published an editorial about the problem, stating, "Every hour gives to the most extravagant reports. The press North and South seems to have entered upon a war of crimination and recrimination, and instead of calming the excitement and allaying unfounded prejudices, to rejoin in adding to the excitement of the moment."

Northern newspapers both informed and promoted public opinion. The most common rallying cry of the Union in the war, "On to Richmond," originated from the pen of a correspondent of the New York *Tribune*. However, unlike the South, where newspapers generally favored the rebellion, many Northern newspapers openly opposed Lincoln and the war.

Union field commanders also had mixed feeling about the newsmen who casually referred to themselves as the Bohemian Brigade because of their travel and living conditions. In several instances, generals claimed that newspapers were the best source of intelligence for Confederate commanders. Southern leaders likewise complained about newspapers identifying their units and locations. It is a fact that the opposing sides read each others' newspapers, often within hours of publication.

Some generals restricted reporters but rarely were successful in totally limiting their access. William Sherman (6) was no fan of correspondents but recognized that they could get their stories regardless of the conditions. When informed that an exploding shell had killed three correspondents, Sherman replied, "Good! Now we shall have news from hell before breakfast."

Although newspapers made mostly the same contributions, as well as mistakes, on both sides during the war, the coverage of the war in the South was not as extensive as that in the North. The reasons for these differences were simple—supply, personnel, and circumstance. At the beginning of the war only about 5 percent of American paper mills were located in Confederate States and quality ink was already in short supply. By war's end, several Southern newspapers produced limited editions on wrapping paper or wallpaper because of the shortage of regular newsprint.

In addition to the shortage of paper, the South was always desperate for manpower. Qualified printers were given muskets and placed on the front lines as infantrymen, leaving the presses vacant or manned by inexperienced boys. Furthermore, the vast majority of the war was fought in the South. Newspaper offices in conquered or contested territory were destroyed, shut down, or limited by their occupiers in what they could publish.

Despite the problems, Civil War journalism informed the public on both sides in a manner much superior to any previous conflict. In addition to information gathered in the midst or immediately following battles, correspondents provided a written and visual history of the war that was unmatched to that time. War correspondents informed and influenced the American public, both North and South, as well as its combatants and commanders. In turn, the conflict influenced the profession of war correspondents. Since the Appomattox Campaign (37), reporters have accompanied every army and covered every conflict around the world.

62

WILDERNESS

May 5–7, 1864

The Battle of the Wilderness in May 1864 provided the first combat meeting of U. S. Grant (3) and Robert E. Lee (5). Fought in dense woods, the battle was one of the most confusing of the war. Although it ended in a draw, Grant did not retreat as had his predecessors, making the Wilderness an important first step in the long march to Richmond and victory.

With the second and final Confederate invasion of the North stopped at Gettysburg (4), the Union marched against Richmond to end the war. After a long search for a general who could, and would, defeat the rebellion, President Abraham Lincoln (2) elevated Grant to be the commander of all Federal land forces on March 9, 1864. Grant immediately plotted his offensive and announced that he would "hammer continuously against the armed forces of the enemy and his resources until by mere attrition, if by nothing else, there should be nothing left for him but an equal submission with the loyal section of our common country to the Constitution and the laws."

To accomplish his objective, Grant directed William Sherman (6) to move toward Atlanta in the South while he himself joined George Meade's (24) Army of the Potomac in an advance toward the Confederate capital. Despite their losses in 1863, the Confederates were still confident, spirited, and well-led. Their numbers, however, were decreasing as available replacements dwindled. The Union army remained larger as well as better fed and equipped.

Grant crossed the Rapidan River about halfway between Washington and Richmond on May 4, 1864, in what he called the Overland Campaign. Lee, always looking for an advantage in terrain, moved to counter the Union advance and marched toward the Wilderness near Chancellorsville (31), where he had defeated Joseph Hooker (48) a year earlier.

The two armies met in the thick forest and dense underbrush of the Wilderness on the morning of May 5. Heavy fighting, in that neither could gain the advantage, forced both sides to build log and earthen defenses as darkness approached. On the morning of May 6, Grant chose to leave his defenses and move his 119,000 men against Lee's 64,000 soldiers.

Using his numerical advantage, Grant attacked the Confederate right and left flanks. The Confederates on the left flank held but gave way on the right. As the Union soldiers pursued the fleeing enemy, it appeared the entire Confederate line would retreat, but James Longstreet (13) arrived with reinforcements and reestablished the defensive line. By late morning both sides were so exhausted that combat mostly ceased.

Longstreet exploited the lull in fighting by dispatching four brigades to flank the Union left. The attack was in position to turn the Union flank when Longstreet ordered a supplemental attack against the front. In the thick woods, now covered in smoke from the morning's battle, Longstreet was accidentally wounded by his own men. Longstreet's absence and the time it took Lee to replace him halted the Confederate advance. At the end of the day both sides were back in their defensive breastworks.

Little action took place the next day. The agonized screams of the wounded, some of whom were burned alive by a fire that swept the woods, could be heard by Union and Confederate alike. Soldiers of both sides later wrote about the horrors of the fire as well as finding skeletal remains from the fight a year earlier still lying unburied on the battlefield.

For all intents and purposes, the Wilderness portion of the Overland Campaign was over. During the night Grant moved his army around the Confederate defenses to the southeast toward Richmond. Lee countered by maneuvering to block the Union advance at the important road intersection at Spotsylvania Court House (65).

Despite the lack of a clear victor, the Battle of the Wilderness was important to Grant's campaign against Richmond. He had proven his army could stand against Lee and, if not defeat him, at least force him to withdraw. Some in the North spoke of Grant's being "bogged down" in the Wilderness, but the battle fit in with his plans of attrition.

The Battle of the Wilderness was so confused and disorderly that neither side could accurately account for their casualties. Best estimates place Union losses at more than seventeen thousand with about twenty-two hundred dead. The Confederates suffered about half those numbers. Both sides lost senior officers. Two Union generals were killed, two wounded, and another pair captured. Lee lost three generals killed and four, including Longstreet, wounded.

The number of generals lost on both sides was significant but, with the exception of Longstreet, not particularly influential. Colonels who had years of combat experience were more than qualified to advance to star rank. Longstreet, Lee's primary lieutenant and best subordinate tactical leader, would be out of action for about six months. By the time he returned, Lee and his army were besieged at Petersburg (46) and the Confederacy was well on its way to becoming a Lost Cause.

Although the Wilderness was a tactical draw, it acted as the first step in Grant's strategy to end the rebellion. It was a proving ground for his new command from which he launched the long offensive that led to the fall of Richmond and the end of the Confederacy.

63

HENRY WAGER HALLECK

Union General

1815–1872

As one of the most senior officers in the U.S. Army, Henry Wager Halleck was an excellent organizer and procurer of men and supplies, but he proved totally inept on the field of combat. In Washington, as commander in chief of the army and later as chief of staff, Halleck generated criticism from the president, the cabinet, and his fellow officers. Despite his reputation as "the most hated man in Washington," Halleck possessed extraordinary administrative abilities. His demands for order and discipline greatly contributed to the final Union victory.

Born on January 16, 1815, Halleck ran away from home as a boy because of his dislike of farming. Raised by his maternal grandfather, Halleck attended several schools before gaining an appointment to the West Point Class of 1839. Graduating number three of thirty-one cadets, Halleck remained at the Military Academy as an assistant professor for two years. Known as "Old Brains" by his fellow cadets, Halleck both wrote and translated books on military matters that were later studied and used by Civil War leaders on both sides.

During the Mexican War, Halleck served in California, where he took part in several skirmishes and acted in various capacities in the area's military government. At the conclusion of the war, Halleck, now a captain in the corps of engineers, remained on the West Coast to oversee construction of lighthouses and fortifications.

Halleck resigned his commission in 1854 and joined the leading law firm in California. He helped write the state constitution while also serving on the boards of several mining companies. He turned down a position on the state supreme court and a seat in the U.S. Senate. Halleck instead acquired land and managed a thirty thousand-acre ranch in Marin County while he also maintained his involvement in the military. He rose to the rank of major general in the state militia.

At the outbreak of the Civil War, Winfield Scott recommended Halleck for appointment to major general in the Regular Army. When the rank was approved on August 19, 1861, Halleck became the fourth highest ranking officer in the U.S.

Army. Halleck soon showed his administrative abilities by establishing order in the previously chaotic Department of the Missouri. As the senior commander, he shone in the reflected glory of victories won by his subordinate generals at Fort Donelson (35), Pea Ridge (44), and Shiloh (18) in the winter and spring of 1862.

After the Union victory at Shiloh, Halleck assumed his first field command and pursued the retreating rebels toward Corinth, Mississippi. His advance was so careful and deliberate, often moving forward only a mile a day, that the Confederates had ample time to escape.

Back in Washington, President Abraham Lincoln (2) was unhappy with how the war was progressing in the East. Impressed with the victories achieved by Halleck's subordinates in the West, he ordered the general to Washington on July 1, 1862, and promoted him to general in chief of all the Union armies. Critics noted that Halleck had been rewarded for his poor leadership of one army by being given command of all the armies.

Halleck's administrative abilities in raising volunteers, in securing arms and supplies, and in enforcing discipline and order at all levels quickly made a contribution. However, his poor tactical advice, his failure to keep his officers informed, and his tendency to blame others for his own mistakes brought more resentment than respect from his subordinate commanders.

When Grant assumed command of all of the Union armies in March 1864, Halleck's role was reduced to army chief of staff. This position, almost entirely administrative, was much more suited to his abilities, but Halleck still managed to add to his unpopularity with his surly disposition and open disdain for politicians.

Halleck remained in uniform after the war ended and briefly commanded a military district in Virginia before returning to California to command the Pacific region. In 1869 he assumed command of the Division of the South in Louisville, Kentucky, where he died on January 8, 1872. He is buried in Greenwood Cemetery in Brooklyn, New York.

There are probably many more negative remarks on the record about Halleck than any officer of the Civil War. His physical appearance—his pop-eyes, flabbiness, and surliness—only added to his reputation. President Lincoln, for whom Halleck served as a pallbearer, referred to him as "little more than a first-rate clerk" while Secretary of War Edwin M. Stanton characterized Halleck as "probably the greatest scoundrel and most barefaced villain in America."

Secretary of the Navy Gideon Wells went even further when he wrote in his diary that Halleck "originates nothing, anticipates nothing…takes no responsibility, plans nothing, suggests nothing, is good for nothing."

Comments such as these are certainly damning, but they must also be put in the context in which politicians voiced them. Halleck's military subordinates certainly had no great affection or respect for their chief of staff, but none criticized his abilities to fill their ranks with men and to place weapons in their arms and food in their haversacks. Regardless of his own lack of field leadership abilities, Halleck does get credit for the early Union victories in the West, while his fellow commanders in the East experienced defeat after defeat.

If one only looks at the negatives connected to Halleck, he would rank near the end of this list, or not in this ranking at all, and his influence would be for its negative rather than positive value. Looking beyond the negatives though, is the fact that Halleck labored under the close supervision of Lincoln and his cabinet in a war where much of the action took place within fifty miles of the Union capital. In a most difficult and extremely complex war, Halleck likely did as well as anyone could have in his position. Henry Halleck may not have been a general one would want to follow into battle, but he was the kind of administrator who insured that the men and supplies were available to win the war.

64

JAMES HARRISON WILSON

Union General

1837–1925

James Harrison Wilson was one of the most distinguished "boy generals" of the Civil War. He participated in battles in all of the war's theaters and advanced to command William T. Sherman's (6) horse soldiers in the final offensive in the Department of the Mississippi which resulted in the conflict's most successful cavalry raid. His innovations in cavalry operations included arming his men with repeating Spencer rifles. In one of the last actions of the long war, it was Wilson's men who captured the fleeing Confederate president Jefferson Davis (9).

Born on September 2, 1837, near Shawneetown, Illinois, to a pioneer family from Virginia, Wilson attended McKendree College before securing an appointment to the U.S. Military Academy. Wilson graduated number six of forty-one cadets in the Class of 1860 and was posted to Fort Vancouver, Washington, as a topographical engineer. At the outbreak of the Civil War, he returned east in time to participate in the battles for Port Royal, South Carolina, in November 1861 and Fort Pulaski, Georgia, the following April.

In the fall of 1862, Wilson became George McClellan's (51) aide-de-camp and served in that capacity at South Mountain and Antietam (1). A month after Sharpsburg, Wilson joined U. S. Grant's (3) staff as a lieutenant colonel and fought in the battles leading up to the surrender of Vicksburg (7) in July 1863. Wilson became a favorite of Grant as well as Sherman, with whom he served during the Chattanooga (12) campaign of November 1863 and the relief of Knoxville the following month.

When officials in Washington sought Grant's advice for someone to head the newly formed Cavalry Bureau, the general recommended Wilson. Wilson took charge of the bureau on February 17, 1864, as a brigadier general. Wilson quickly displayed the talents for leadership and organization in the Bureau that had earned him the praise of Grant and Sherman on the battlefield in the West. The young general's most important contribution was to add to the firepower of the Union cavalry by acquiring Spencer repeating rifles for his horse soldiers.

Wilson left the Bureau in April to assume command of a cavalry division under Philip Sheridan (8), and fought in the Shenandoah Valley. His division led the Union advance from the Rapidan through the Wilderness. In April he once again rode west to join Sherman as his chief of cavalry—a position equal to that held by Sheridan in the East. Wilson's performance in the East had so impressed Grant that the general sent a message to Sherman stating, "I believe Wilson will add 50 percent to the effectiveness of your cavalry."

With a corps of seventeen thousand cavalrymen, Wilson played an important role in the defeat of John Bell Hood at Franklin (15) in November and the victory at Nashville (87) in December. By the following spring the Confederacy was weakening on all fronts. On March 22, 1865, Wilson led his cavalry corps from its camps in the northwest corner of Alabama to raid the armories, gun manufacturing plant, and warehouses in Selma, located in the center of the state.

During the twenty-eight-day-long raid, Wilson consistently outmaneuvered and outfought the Confederate cavalry of Nathan Bedford Forrest (21) in one of the Union's most successful operations. Wilson captured Selma on April 2, and after a brief rest rode east to capture Montgomery on April 12 and Columbus, Georgia, on April 16. On April 20, Wilson took Macon, where he learned of Lee's surrender in Virginia. In less than a month Wilson had captured five fortified Confederate cities, twenty-three stands of colors, 288 pieces of artillery, and nearly seven thousand prisoners.

Hostilities were mostly concluded, but Wilson's cavalry continued to patrol the Georgia roads and woods. On May 10, 1865, one of Wilson's units captured the fleeing Jefferson Davis and members of his party at Irwinsville.

Wilson, now a brigadier general in the Regular Army and a major general of volunteers, remained on active duty after the war until accepting discharge at his own request in 1870. For the next thirteen years he engaged in business in the Mississippi Valley and in New England before settling in Wilmington to write about the war. When the hostilities against Spain broke out in 1898, he immediately volunteered to return to uniform to serve in Puerto Rico and Cuba. He also took part in the Boxer Rebellion in China where he was second-in-command of the Peking Relief Expedition of 1900.

A year later, Wilson retired from the army and the following year served as President Theodore Roosevelt's official representative to the coronation of Edward VII in England. Wilson then returned to Wilmington where he continued to write until his death at eighty-seven on February 23, 1925. He is buried in Wilmington's Old Swedes Churchyard. Wilson was the last living member of his West Point class and was survived by only three of the 583 Union officers who achieved the rank of general in the Civil War.

At about five feet ten inches in height, Wilson's military bearing made him appear taller and older. As a "boy general" who was still only in his late twenties when the war ended, Wilson well earned the distinction of one of the Union's finest cavalry leaders. Sheridan exceeded Wilson's influence by a longer term in command and his performance in the critical Virginia theater. George Custer (52), younger than Wilson by more than a year, ranks higher more as a result of his fame during the war and his death at Little Big Horn. In reality, Wilson commanded more troops in the war and performed equally or even better than his fellow West Pointer, Custer.

65

SPOTSYLVANIA COURT HOUSE

May 8–21, 1864

At Spotsylvania Court House in May 1864, U. S. Grant (3) failed to defeat the Confederate army on his march toward Richmond, but he accomplished his objective of continuing attrition of the rebels. In turn, Robert E. Lee (5) failed to hold the defensive line along the Rapidan River, but sufficiently delayed Grant so other Southern units in the Shenandoah Valley and around Richmond could reinforce their defenses.

When Grant had assumed command of the Union army in March 1864, he had announced that he intended to "hammer continuously" against the enemy until attrition forced them into submission. Grant ordered William Sherman (6) to capture Atlanta while he himself joined George Meade (24) in the Overland Campaign toward Richmond. Capturing the Confederate capital was the ultimate objective, but, as Grant stated, he would be satisfied with reducing the Confederate army to the point of surrender.

When asked by his engineers how many pontoons he wanted available to bridge the Rapidan River in case they had to retreat, Grant responded, "If I beat General Lee I sha'n't want any pontoons, and if General Lee beats me I can take all the men I intend to take back across the river on a log." Grant knew that a war of attrition would be costly to the Union army, but he was also aware that the much larger population of the North, supported by units being formed of former slaves, could replace any losses he sustained. Lee and the Confederacy were not so fortunate. At this stage of the war, when a rebel soldier fell, no replacement was available to take his place.

Grant began his offensive in early May and had his first encounter with Lee about halfway between Washington and Richmond at the Wilderness (62). The confused, bloody battle ended in a stalemate, but Confederate casualties numbered more than eight thousand. When Grant determined that the difficult terrain of the Wilderness would no longer support his attack, he decided to maneuver around Lee and continue his advance toward Richmond.

Early on the morning of May 7, 1864, Grant issued an order to George Meade (24), "General: Make all preparations during the day for a night march to take position at Spotsylvania Court House." Grant knew that it was critical for Union forces

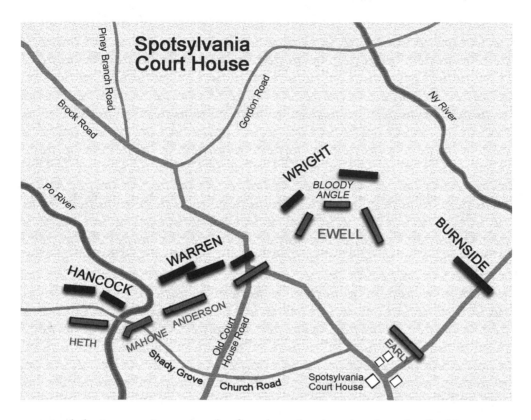

to control the intersecting network of roads at that location in order for his army to advance. He hoped occupying Spotsylvania would allow him to again engage Lee, and again, if not defeat the Army of Northern Virginia, then at least continue its attrition.

Lee anticipated Grant's move toward Spotsylvania and also understood the importance of the town's road intersections. He dispatched a corps under Richard Anderson, who had replaced James Longstreet (13) when he was wounded at the Wilderness, to hurry to Spotsylvania. Anderson won the race to the Spotsylvania crossroads and blocked Meade's advance on the afternoon of May 8. The rest of Lee's army of 56,000 and Grant's of 101,000 arrived over the next few hours.

By darkness on May 9, the Army of Northern Virginia occupied a U-shaped defense oriented to the north with Spotsylvania and its road intersections within its lines. On May 10, Grant attacked Lee's flank on the west but was beaten back. Undiscouraged, Grant prepared for a sustained battle. To his superiors in Washington, Grant telegraphed that losses on both sides were heavy but concluded, "I propose to fight it out on this line if it takes all summer."

On May 12 Grant struck the apex of the Confederate horseshoe with a corps of about twenty thousand men. The Union troops broke through the rebel defenses only to be driven back by a counterattack. All day and into the night the battle raged, often hand-to-hand for a piece of ground that became known as the Bloody Angle. About 2:00 a.m. on May 13 troops on both sides were startled when an eighteen to twenty-inch-oak tree toppled to the ground on the western edge of the salient. Its trunk had been completely blown in two by repeated strikes from musket balls.

By dawn on May 13, the lines had stabilized near their original positions of the day before. During the next five days Grant probed first the enemy's right flank and then the left but found the Confederates well entrenched. Lee ordered an attack against the Union right flank on May 19 but the Confederates, too, found the defenses strong.

Again, as they had at the Wilderness, Grant and Lee found themselves stalemated. Grant decided not to spend the rest of the summer on the line at Spotsylvania and shifted his army to the south and east toward Richmond. Again, Lee maneuvered to block the advance against the Confederate capital, setting the stage for the two armies to clash again at North Anna and Cold Harbor (59) in early June.

In less than two weeks the Union army suffered nearly eighteen thousand casualties, including one of their better corps commanders, John Sedgwick (39), who was killed by a sharpshooter. The Confederates, fighting mostly from a defensive position, totaled about nine thousand dead, wounded, and captured.

Spotsylvania Court House, like the Wilderness, proved neither a victory nor a defeat for either side. Grant accomplished his stated purpose of continuing the attrition of the Army of Northern Virginia and of moving closer to Richmond. However, the time Lee gained at Spotsylvania allowed other units to strengthen the defenses of the Confederate capital. Grant would soon be able to encircle Lee at Petersburg (46), but it would be nearly another year before he captured Richmond and forced Lee out of Petersburg and finally to surrender.

The Battle of Spotsylvania Court House was not nearly as decisive as Gettysburg (4) or Vicksburg (7) or as influential as Antietam (1). Other battles at the same time were more important, but Spotsylvania, like the Wilderness, was a crucial step in Grant's march to Richmond and the destruction of the Confederate army. Both the Wilderness and Spotsylvania were indecisive but bloody. Spotsylvania ranks slightly behind the Wilderness primarily because the Wilderness battle was fought first, and it introduced Grant's attrition warfare and proved that the Union army could stand against Lee on his home territory.

66

GETTYSBURG ADDRESS

November 19, 1863

On November 19, 1863, Abraham Lincoln (2) spoke at the dedication of Soldiers Cemetery, where the Union dead from the Battle of Gettysburg (4) were interred. The president's brief remarks only four months after the conclusion of the battle rank among history's greatest orations. More importantly, Lincoln's Gettysburg Address articulated the importance of the war and the dedication of the people for the preservation of the Union and the principle of equality.

Popular belief is that Lincoln quickly composed the address while on a train from Washington to Gettysburg. Actually, the president wrote the first draft in the executive mansion earlier in the month and revised it several times before departing for the ceremonies. He made minor adjustments to the speech on the train and again the night before its delivery at the home of David Wills, his host in Gettysburg.

Lincoln was not the principal speaker for the cemetery's dedication. That honor went to Edward Everett—a leading orator, clergyman, former governor and senator from Massachusetts, and the current president of Harvard University—who spoke for almost two hours before relinquishing the platform to Lincoln.

In his short but eloquent remarks, Lincoln took the day. At least five written versions of his speech exist, but his second draft, now preserved at the U.S. Library of Congress, is the one generally accepted as the speech he delivered at the battlefield cemetery.

> *Four score and seven years ago, our fathers brought forth upon this continent a new nation, conceived in liberty and dedicated to the proposition that all men are created equal.*
>
> *Now we are engaged in a great civil war, testing whether that nation or any nation so conceived and so dedicated can long endure. We are met here on a great battlefield of that war. We have come to dedicate a portion of it, as a final resting place for those who here gave their lives that that nation might live. It is altogether fitting and proper that we should do this.*
>
> *But in a larger sense, we cannot dedicate—we cannot consecrate—we cannot hallow—this ground. The brave men, living and dead, who struggled here, have*

consecrated it, far above our poor power to add or detract. The world will little note, nor long remember, what we say here, but can never forget what they did here. It is for us the living, rather, to be dedicated here to the unfinished work which they who fought here have thus far so nobly carried on. It is rather for us to be here dedicated to the great task remaining before us—that from these honored dead we take increased devotion to that cause for which they here gave the last full measure of devotion—that we here highly resolve that these dead shall not have died in vain—that this nation, shall have a new birth of freedom—and that government of the people, by the people, for the people, shall not perish from the earth.

Neither the crowd nor the news media were overly impressed by the president's words. Several newspapers, especially those that opposed Lincoln, criticized the speech as nonsense and inappropriate because of its briefness. The London *Times* went so far as to call it "ludicrous."

Lincoln himself was not impressed with his own effort. To a friend he remarked, "It is a flat failure."

But not all agreed. Everett wrote to the president the next day stating, "I should be glad, if I came as near to the central idea of the occasion, in two hours, as you did in two minutes."

Lincoln's response emphasized his belief in the greater good of the Union over the rights of individual states. He wrote to Everett, "I am pleased to know that, in your judgment, the little I did say was not entirely a failure…. The point made against the theory of the general government being only an agency, whose principals are the states, was new to me, and, I think, is one of the best arguments for the national supremacy."

The orations of Everett and Lincoln were made only eighteen weeks after the Battle of Gettysburg. Bodies were still being buried or reburied in the new cemetery. The smell of gunsmoke had hardly cleared; the stench of the dead probably still lingered. Gettysburg had marked the "high tide" of the Confederacy and, although many battles were yet to be fought, the South was doomed. Lincoln's words not only paid homage to the dead but also prophesied a unified country of the future where equality would reign.

Today the Soldiers Cemetery in Gettysburg is a National Cemetery where, alongside the thirty-five hundred Union dead of the 1863 battle, lie American veterans of every war since. Lincoln's oration is chiseled in stone on the wall of his memorial on the Mall in Washington, and is printed in every child's schoolbook. The president's unmatched economy of language lives on as the best-known oration in American history.

If this were a ranking of great American speeches or even a listing of the great orations of all times, it would be at the top. This ranking, however, is of influential leaders, battles, and events of the Civil War, and, therefore, Lincoln's Gettysburg Address does not rate so high. Few Northerners at the time appreciated his remarks as only a small number had the opportunity to read them in the newspapers. In the South, where Lincoln was largely credited with being the primary cause of the war and was generally despised, few were aware of the address and even fewer cared.

Still, despite Lincoln's own words that the world would "little note, nor long remember" his speech, it has stood the test of time as words for the ages. His promise of a government of, by, and for the people lives on as an American creed and as a hope and guide for freedom-loving people everywhere.

67

FRANZ SIGEL

Union General

1824–1902

Franz Sigel understood modern warfare as well as anyone at the outbreak of the Civil War, and he had more experience in combat than most Americans at the time. Although he ultimately proved inept in battle, he significantly contributed to his adopted country by encouraging German immigrants to support the Union cause.

Born on November 18, 1824, in the village of Sinsheim in Germany's Grand Duchy of Baden, Sigel graduated from the military academy at Karlsruhe in 1843 and entered the German army as a lieutenant. In 1847 he resigned his commission after killing a fellow officer in a duel fought over political differences. When a revolt broke out against the Baden royal regime in 1848, Sigel organized a brigade of four thousand rebels to support the cause.

The Royal troops twice defeated Sigel, forcing him to flee to Switzerland. He returned at the head of another army in 1849 but was again defeated. Swiss authorities deported him to England in 1851, and he sailed from there to America the following year. In the United States, Sigel taught school in New York City and joined the militia, where he rose to the rank of major. In 1857 he moved to St. Louis to become the director of the city's public schools.

Sigel was an outspoken critic of slavery, and when war erupted he accepted a commission as colonel in command of the 2nd Missouri Brigade. The citizens of Missouri were torn between supporting the North and following the South. Thanks to Sigel, the large German communities in St. Louis and the state rallied behind the Union. Sigel soon became a hero to German Americans and the leader of their support for the United States.

After several successful skirmishes against pro-South factions around St. Louis, Sigel fought in the first major battle in the West at Wilson's Creek (70) on August 10, 1861. Although his performance was not distinguished, he advanced to the rank of brigadier general in command of two divisions at the battle of Pea Ridge (44) in Arkansas the following March. Pea Ridge proved to be Sigel's best battle performance, as his actions helped win the confrontation and begin the Union's series of victories west of the Mississippi.

The battle also earned Sigel promotion to major general of volunteers and orders to join the Army of the Potomac in the East. He arrived early enough to lead a corps at Second Bull Run (40) in August. From September 1862 to February 1863, Sigel commanded the IX Corps, known as the German Corps because many of its soldiers were originally from Germany. This corps, however, remained mostly in reserve or in support roles until Sigel gave up his command because of poor health.

Sigel recovered sufficiently to take the leadership of the Department of West Virginia in March 1864 to conduct operations in the Shenandoah Valley. On May 15, Sigel encountered a Confederate army led by John Breckenridge (84) at New Market, Virginia, that soundly defeated him. In July, Sigel successfully delayed a raid toward Washington by Jubal Early (19), only to be relieved from command for what his superiors stated was "a lack of aggression."

For the remainder of the war Sigel remained mostly in seclusion to "recover his health" and resigned his commission on May 4, 1865. For two years he edited a German-language newspaper in Baltimore before moving to New York where he worked as a pension agent, a revenue collector, and again as a newspaper editor before his death on August 21, 1902. He is buried in New York's Woodlawn Cemetery.

Sigel's primary influence on the war was his status as leader of German immigrants. German Americans, both in and outside his command, proudly proclaimed, "I fights mit Sigel." Considering the fact that many German immigrated to the U.S.

to escape war-torn Europe or to ensure that their sons would not be drafted into the army, Sigel's part in drawing them to support the Union cause was significant and provided a large source of manpower. Regardless of his performance on the battlefield, he was a hero in every aspect to German Americans.

Sigel's fellow officers and commanders were not so laudatory. General John Pope (86), who commanded Sigel at Second Bull Run, called him "the goddamnest coward I ever knew."

When Sigel retreated from New Market, General Henry Halleck (63) wrote to U. S. Grant (3), "Sigel is in full retreat. He will do nothing but run; never did anything else."

Sigel was not the coward that Pope and Halleck proclaimed, but he was indeed a reluctant commander. His lack of aggression was probably caused by fear of seeing his own men killed and maimed, but his attitude did nothing to win battles and end the war. Although he had slightly superior numbers at New Market, and some of the rebel army soldiers were hastily activated cadets from the nearby Virginia Military Institute, Sigel was slow to advance. Finally he declared, "We may as well fight them today as any other day. We will advance."

Like many generals on both sides of the conflict, Sigel attained more rank and responsibility than he was capable of managing. Despite his shortcomings, he did not suffer the casualties of Ambrose Burnside (57) or Joe Hooker (48). Overall his key role was off the battlefield where he was very successful in uniting German Americans in the North in their support of the Union.

68

MUSIC

1861–1865

Music was a part of every activity for both sides during the Civil War—from the drums that kept the troops in step on the drill fields to the bands that inspired patriotism in the midst of battle, from the lone bugler to the sentimental songs sung around the campfires. In 1864 Robert E. Lee (5) wrote, "I don't think we could have an army without music."

Bugles awoke soldiers in the morning, called them to meals and work stations, and reminded them when it was time for "lights out" to end the day. Fifes and drums kept companies in line during battle and helped them maintain their organization. Bands marched with soldiers into battle and continued to play near the front lines in the midst of mayhem and murderous combat. After the fight, the bands often adjourned to rear-area hospitals to lift the morale of suffering soldiers. Whatever the event—be it battle, parade, funeral, or even execution—military musicians were present.

Bands played formal roles in the armies of both the North and South, but music also was a part of the day-to-day life of Yankee and rebel soldiers alike. With books and reading materials in short supply, soldiers had little to occupy their time, and they frequently sang to pass the lonely, and often dangerous, hours. Many of these songs were also sung back home by those who anxiously awaited news of husbands, fathers, and sons from the battlefields.

Music had been part of organized warfare long before the Civil War, but the lengthy conflict between North and South produced the largest numbers of musicians in uniform in American military history. By the end of 1861 the U.S. Army had 618 bands composed of 28,000 musicians—or one bandsman for every 41 soldiers. Confederate records are not as complete, but estimates suggest that they also had about this ratio.

On July 22, 1861, the Union army issued regulations that authorized two musicians for each infantry, artillery, and cavalry company and an additional twenty-four men to form a band for each regiment. As the war progressed and resources for both money and men became scarce, the army reduced its number of regular bands to sixty, but many additional musicians remained in uniform as part of militia organizations and unofficial groups. "Drummer boys" as young as twelve years of age often provided a unit's music in order to free older men to jobs in the infantry and artillery.

Commanders used the bands in a variety of ways. Other than musical duties, the band members provided security for regimental headquarters, served as stretcher bearers during and after battles, and assisted surgeons in field hospitals. Some commanders believed the bands should be deployed as far forward as possible to raise and maintain morale. General Philip Sheridan (8) graced his cavalry bands with special uniforms and the best mounts available. In return he placed them with his troops on the front lines. On March 31, 1865, at Dinwiddie Court House during the Battle of Five Forks, Sheridan ordered his bands forward with the order to "play the gayest tunes…play them loud and keep playing them and never mind if a bullet goes through a trombone, or even a trombonist, now and then."

One of the general's subordinates, Horace Porter, later recalled that at a crossroads during the battle he "encountered one of Sheridan's bands, under heavy fire, playing 'Nelly Bly' as cheerily as if it were furnishing music for a country picnic."

Following the battle Sheridan paid tribute to his bandsmen, saying, "Music has done its share, and more than its share, in winning this war."

Not all of Sheridan's fellow Union generals shared his appreciation for military bands, yet they did recognize their value. At the Battle of Williamsburg in May 1862, III Corps Commander Samuel P. Heintzelman discovered his ranks broken and about to be overrun. Finding several regimental bands cowering in the rear he ordered them forward and shouted, "Play! Play! It's all you're good for. Play, damn it! Play some marching tune! Play 'Yankee Doodle,' or any other doodle you can think of, only play something."

The band played, the Union force rallied, and the Confederates withdrew. One of the Union soldiers later wrote that the music was worth "a thousand men" and that it "saved the battle."

Confederate generals also used their bands to encourage their troops. When Lee's army began its attack on the third day of the Battle of Gettysburg (4), regimental bands played martial and patriotic music. A survivor of George Pickett's (93) disastrous attack later recalled that his regimental band played "Nearer My God to Thee" as the survivors streamed back to friendly lines.

However, not all Confederate generals believed that music was more important than muskets. When Division Commander Daniel H. Hill received a request from an infantryman wanting to transfer to a band in February 1862, the rebel general responded,

"Respectfully forwarded, disapproved. Shooters are more needed than tooters."

Both sides had songs they claimed for "their own" while many, especially the sentimental verses about home and family, were shared by all. The North and the South used many of the same tunes; only the lyrics differed to reflect their opposing causes.

The "Battle Hymn of the Republic" became the Union's favorite. William Steffe wrote the music in 1852, and the adopted lyrics became "John Brown's Body Lies A-Moulderin' in His Grave" and "We'll Hang Old Jeff Davis from a Sour Apple Tree." In the fall of 1861, abolitionist Julia Ward Howe visited the Fifth Vermont Regiment outside Washington, D.C., where she heard the soldiers singing the various lyrics. That evening she wrote new words that became the "Battle Hymn of the Republic." First published in the *Atlantic Monthly* in February 1862, the new rendition soon became the most popular tune throughout the North. Its phrases, such as "He hath loosed the fateful lightning of his terrible swift sword" and "let us die to make men free" provided promises of might and right.

The Confederates adopted as their favorite song one that was a popular name for the South. Louisiana had long been known as Dix's Land because of the French word for ten on its currency and the land survey that established the Mason-Dixon Line that divided North and South. Dix and Dixon had evolved into Dixie by the mid-nineteenth century. Minstrel performer Daniel D. Emmett wrote a song about taking a stand and living and dying in Dixie that he first performed on stage in New York in 1859. By the time the Southern states seceded, it had become favored enough to be played at Jefferson Davis's (9) inauguration on February 18, 1861.

In camp and on the march, Union soldiers sang the "Battle Cry of Freedom" and their version of "My Maryland." The rebels also had their version of "My Maryland" and sadly sang of loves left behind, "A hundred months have passed, Lorena, since last I held that hand in mine."

From the time of enlistment until triumph or defeat, music accompanied Union and Confederate soldiers. Its importance is difficult to evaluate but it certainly was more influential to the overall conduct of the war than many individuals and some small battles.

A day after Lee surrendered at Appomattox Court House, President Abraham Lincoln paid homage to music. At the White House on April 10, 1865, reporters asked him for a statement. He responded, "I have always thought that 'Dixie' was one of the best tunes I ever heard. I insisted yesterday that we had fairly captured it."

69

WADE HAMPTON

Confederate General

1818–1902

Wade Hampton reluctantly entered the Civil War at the head of a brigade he armed and uniformed at his own expense. By the end of the conflict he was the senior cavalry commander in the Confederate army. Wounded multiple times, Hampton was known for his bravery, his gentlemanly conduct, and his skills as one of the South's finest horsemen.

The Hamptons of South Carolina predated the American Revolution. Wade Hampton's grandfather served in the Revolutionary War, and his father was a general in the War of 1812. When Wade was born on March 28, 1818, in Charleston, South Carolina, his family was reputed to be the largest land owners in the South with three thousand slaves working cotton, corn, rice, and sugar plantations in their home state as well as in Mississippi and Louisiana.

Hampton graduated from South Carolina College in 1836 and returned home to manage his family assets, which he inherited on the death of his father in 1858. During this time he also found time to serve in the South Carolina legislature from 1852 to 1861. While in public office, Hampton expressed the belief that South Carolina had the right to leave the Union, but that he personally opposed secession.

When South Carolina seceded in 1861, Hampton put aside his opposition and with his own money raised "Hampton's Legion" of six hundred men. Despite no prior military training, Hampton quickly had his force ready for action and participated in First Bull Run (10), where he was slightly wounded. He performed so well in the battle that his senior commanders personally praised his efforts. The modest Hampton later said to a friend, "I have not ventured to write their remarks, even to my wife, lest I appear vain."

Hampton then led his brigade throughout the Union's Peninsular Campaign (32) and was again wounded at Seven Pines on May 31, 1862, shortly after his promotion to brigadier general. Upon his recovery, Hampton assumed command of a cavalry brigade and on September 2 became J. E. B. Stuart's (23) second in command of the

cavalry corps of the Army of Northern Virginia. In that capacity he fought at Antietam (1) and in the Gettysburg campaign (4).

At Gettysburg, Hampton once again displayed his bravery as well as his shooting ability and chivalry. When the cavalry general ventured too close to a Michigan infantry unit, he came under fire from a young Union rifleman. The two exchanged several shots to no avail. When the Union soldier had trouble reloading his rifle, he raised a hand to Hampton asking for a brief "time out." The gentleman Hampton complied, but when the soldier completed his loading and raised his rifle, the Confederate general put a round through his opponent's wrist.

Before the battle concluded, Hampton was once again wounded and once again recovered to be promoted to major general and fight in the Shenandoah Valley Campaign (29). When a Union soldier killed Stuart in May 1864, Hampton assumed command of the cavalry corps. Hampton faced serious shortages in supplies, arms, and horses for the remainder of the war. Unable to mount any serious offensives, Hampton fought small battles and skirmishes as he raided Union rear areas to secure supplies and to disrupt their operations. When he joined Robert E. Lee's (5) Petersburg Campaign (46), he was forced to train his cavalrymen to fight on foot because of the shortage of horses.

In January 1865, Hampton rode to South Carolina to obtain additional mounts and to assist Joseph E. Johnston's (17) defense of the Carolinas. On February 15, 1865, he advanced in rank to lieutenant general and was assigned to cover Johnston's retreat. When Lee surrendered at Appomattox Court House in April, Hampton contacted

President Jefferson Davis (9) and offered to escort him to Texas to continue the war. When the plan failed, Hampton surrendered and returned to South Carolina.

On his arrival, he found his home destroyed, his slaves free, and his plantations ruined or confiscated. Hampton did not dwell on his losses, saying he claimed nothing further from South Carolina other than "a grave in yonder churchyard."

Hampton then began concentrated efforts to reclaim his native state from the carpetbaggers and Reconstruction. He unsuccessfully lobbied for the vote for blacks and worked for reconciliation of the North and South. When Reconstruction finally ended in 1876, Hampton was elected governor and in 1879 won a seat in the U.S. Senate, where he served until 1891. From 1893 to 1897 Hampton acted as the U.S. commissioner of Pacific Railways before he finally retired to Columbia, South Carolina, where he died on April 11, 1902. On his deathbed he talked about his old battles. As the end approached he called to his son, who had been killed before his eyes at Petersburg, and with his last breath said, "God bless all my people, black and white." He is buried in the Columbia city cemetery.

Hampton's service throughout the war was exemplary, especially considering his total lack of prior military experience. From the beginning to the end, Hampton led his cavalry in the major campaigns and battles in the East. Few matched his personal courage, as he earned the reputation as one of the war's finest cavalry leaders. Hampton's superior service on the battlefield, coupled with his postwar efforts to assist South Carolina and to reunite the United States, earn him this ranking among the war's most influential personalities.

70

WILSON'S CREEK

August 10, 1861

Less than a month after First Bull Run (10) in Virginia, the Battle of Wilson's Creek in southwestern Missouri in August 1861 demonstrated that the war would be fought in the West as well as the East and that a quick peace was unattainable. The Battle of Wilson's Creek, while relatively small, made up for its lack of scale in bloodshed with more than a quarter of the Union force becoming casualties—including General Nathaniel Lyons, the first Union general killed in the war.

Although it was a slave state, Missouri did not join the secession of Southern states that formed the Confederacy. As a border state, it declared its neutrality, but both pro-Northern and pro-Southern factions immediately tried to take political and military control of the region.

Unionists gained the early advantage in the state government. They expelled pro-Confederate factions and replaced them with their own officials. They also secured Jefferson City and St. Louis with the help of U.S. Army captain Nathaniel Lyon, who they promoted to general in command of Missouri Volunteers.

Those who favored the Confederacy were led by the former governor of Missouri and its militia commander, Sterling "Pap" Price. When Price realized that Unionists had gained control, he fled to southwestern Missouri with a small force and recruited additional troops from his own state as well as from Arkansas and Louisiana. Officially, Price's rank as commander came from his previous Missouri militia experience; he did not officially become a major general in the Confederate army until March 1862. While his rank may not have been official, Price and his soldiers thoroughly understood they were fighting for Missouri and the Confederacy.

In early August, Price assembled more than eleven thousand men, but many of these were Arkansas troops commanded by Ben McCulloch, a former Texas Ranger who had been commissioned brigadier general in the Confederate army the previous May. The fiery Texan refused to place his soldiers under Price's control and, after a heated discussion, the Missourian agreed to place himself and his command subordinate to McCulloch. The combined army marched northward and made camp along Wilson's Creek about ten miles southwest of Springfield. Selection of the site was simple; the creek provided water and a nearby cornfield with ripening ears would feed the troops.

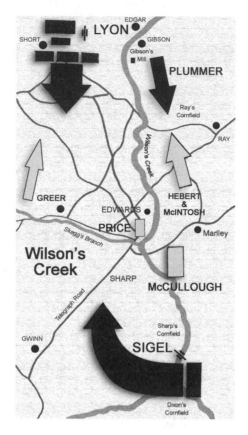

Lyon, even though he had only about fifty-four hundred soldiers, decided that he must attack the rebels to secure Missouri from the Confederacy. He believed that he could counter the odds of being outnumbered by a surprise attack with his main force from the north while Franz Sigel (67) circled the enemy force to strike its right flank and rear. During the late evening of August 9, Lyon and Sigel began their maneuver. Aided by a rainstorm that covered their movement, Lyon's force neared the enemy on a 150-foot rise above the creek's west side while another column proceeded down the east side of the waterway.

At dawn the Confederate pickets detected the enemy's approach and the battle began. McCulloch's infantry stopped the Union advance on the eastern edge of the battlefield and the action shifted to Lyon's advance on the west. When Sigel heard the initial fire from the battle, he launched his own attack against the Confederate rear. The rebels rallied to turn him back and were assisted when Sigel mistook one of the Confederate regiments for his own. Another Confederate counterattack sent Sigel into retreat and out of the battle. McCulloch now could concentrate all of his troops to again attack Lyon.

By noon the Confederates had assaulted the Union line three times and on each occasion had been beaten back. Both sides faced heavy musket and cannon fire as Lyon, despite head and leg wounds from a bursting shell, continued to rally his men. Mounting a horse, Lyon waved his sword as he shouted encouragement to his soldiers. Near the end of the battle, a rifle bullet struck Lyon in the chest. The general turned to his orderly and calmly said, "I am killed," and fell dead.

At the time Lyon was struck down, the battle had already raged for nearly five hours. Both sides were exhausted and low on ammunition. The highest ranking officer on the Union side, Major Samuel D. Sturgis, assumed command and ensured that the last Confederate attack was turned back. Sturgis then ordered a withdrawal back toward Springfield. The Confederates, too tired and disorganized to pursue, declared victory and reoccupied their original camp.

Appalling casualties from both sides littered the small primary battle area that measured only 520 yards long by 175 yards wide. Union losses totaled more than 1,300 with 258 dead. The Confederate casualties numbered about the same with 281 killed.

Although Wilson's Creek was a tactical victory for the Confederates, Lyon and his pro-Union army succeeded in their purpose of holding the Southern forces in the southwestern part of the state. However, Missouri would remain a contested area for much of the remainder of the war. Lyon, one of the better Union leaders available at the beginning of the war and the first general to be killed in combat, was hailed as a hero in the North. His loss, however, opened the way for U. S. Grant (3) and William T. Sherman (6), who earned their reputations in the West and eventually won the war with their actions in the East and Deep South.

When news of Wilson's Creek reached the East, it became clear to those in the North that preserving the Union would require a long and costly war. In addition to this bloody warning, Wilson's Creek altered the future of Missouri and maintained its status as a border state. Except for the battles of Pea Ridge (44) and Shiloh (18) the next year and Vicksburg (7) in 1863, Wilson's Creek was the most influential battle in the West. If it had been fought in Virginia rather than Missouri, it would have shared the fame of First Bull Run as the war's most significant early battle.

71

BENJAMIN FRANKLIN BUTLER

Union General

1818–1893

Hailed as a hero in the North early in the war and damned as a beast and bandit in the South later, Benjamin Franklin Butler created controversy wherever and whenever he served. His lasting influences were his early battle successes, his assistance to runaway slaves, and his encouragement of black regiments in the Union army.

Born on November 5, 1818, in Deerfield, New Hampshire, Butler graduated from Waterville (now Colby) College in Maine. In 1838 he opened a successful criminal law practice in Lowell, Massachusetts, and participated in that state's politics. As a Democrat he served two terms in the state legislature, earning a reputation as a supporter of the poor and disenfranchised. In the 1860 Democratic National Convention, he supported Jefferson Davis (9) and then John Breckenridge (84) for his party's nomination for U.S. president.

Despite his Democratic Party activities, he immediately expressed his support for President Abraham Lincoln (2) and the Union at the outbreak of the Civil War. Butler, now a brigadier general in the Massachusetts militia, rushed his unit to protect approaches to Washington. In one of the war's first actions, Butler ousted the rebels from Baltimore and secured the city for the Union on May 13, 1861. Lincoln was so impressed that he promoted Butler to major general and placed him in command of Fort Monroe, Virginia, leaving him in that position even after Butler was defeated in the war's first large land battle on June 10 at Big Bethel.

Shortly thereafter, runaway slaves began to seek protection and freedom at the fort. Despite demands from Virginians that their property be returned—a demand supported by some in the North—Butler refused to acquiesce. Instead he termed the runaways "contraband of war," a term that became common for the remainder of the conflict.

In August, Butler led an offensive against the North Carolina coast and captured Forts Hatteras and Clark. He then returned to Massachusetts to recruit a new unit to operate against rebel installations on the Gulf Coast. After Admiral David Farragut's (14) naval forces had neutralized the city's defenses, Butler occupied New Orleans on May 1, 1862.

Butler assumed the position of the city's military governor, maintaining order and increasing sanitation. His relationship with the city's residents and representatives, however, was less than satisfactory. Before Butler had entered the city, a Union flag had been raised above the U.S. Mint building, but a local gambler named William B. Mumford had pulled down the colors. When Butler learned of the incident, he had Mumford arrested, tried, and—against pleas of local citizens—hanged at the scene of his crime on June 7.

This harsh enforcement of the occupation extended to any citizen who opposed his own rules, including the arrest of journalists and women. On May 15, 1862, he issued General Order Number 28 that stated, "As officers and soldiers of the United States have been subjected to repeated insults from the women (calling themselves ladies) of New Orleans…it is ordered that hereafter any female shall, by word, gesture, or movement, insult or show of contempt for any officer or soldier of the United States, she shall be regarded and held liable to be treated as a woman of the town plying her avocation."

Butler's implication that the women of New Orleans were common prostitutes inflamed the contempt directed at him. To add further injury to his insults, Butler confiscated $80,000 from the Dutch consul that he claimed was rebel money earmarked to buy war supplies.

Butler's actions in New Orleans enraged the entire South. Jefferson Davis declared him a bandit and authorized his execution in event of capture. Louisiana residents called Butler "the Beast" for his harsh rule and "Spoons" for his looting of the silverware from the homes he occupied.

Largely because of the controversy, Butler was removed from command of New Orleans in December 1862 and spent nearly a year on inactive status. In late 1863 he returned to field command in charge of the Department of the James. During this period he was one of the strongest advocates of forming freemen from the North and escaped slaves from the South into all-black regiments. His actual performance on the battlefield, however, was less than satisfactory and U. S. Grant (3) removed him from command.

Although condemned in the South and unpopular with senior Union military commanders, Butler remained a hero in the North and a favorite of Lincoln's and his cabinet. In October 1864 the secretary of war transferred Butler to New York to ensure the Draft Riot (76) that had plagued the city during the summer of 1863 would not resume and disrupt the pending national elections.

Again, Butler performed well and Lincoln, seeking support from Northern Democrats, asked him to be his vice-presidential running mate. Butler turned down the offer. Grant, however, was not happy with Butler's battlefield leadership and in January 1865 sent Butler home to await further orders. Orders never came and with the war finally over, Butler resigned his commission effective November 30, 1865.

Butler returned to Massachusetts politics to be elected to the U.S. Congress as a Republican in 1866. He argued for the reassignment of property in the South to freed slaves, encouraged the strong enforcement of Reconstruction policies, and strongly opposed the rise of the Ku Klux Klan. In 1867 he even made accusations that President Andrew Johnson (83) had been involved in the assassination of Lincoln; he then actively supported the president's impeachment.

These actions made Butler many enemies within both parties, but he was still able to successfully run for governor of Massachusetts in 1883. He ran unsuccessfully as a third party candidate for the presidency the following year. Butler published his memoirs in 1892 and died the following year on January 11 in Washington. He is buried in his wife's family plot in Lowell.

Butler remains a reviled figure in the South, ranking only behind William Sherman (6) in a hatred that lingers today. While he never excelled as a battlefield commander, his early successes were good for the Union morale. His administrations in New Orleans and New York, despite controversy, were more successful than not. His efforts to maintain the freedom of "contrabands" and his support of arming black soldiers were important.

72

HAMPTON ROADS

March 8–9, 1862

The battle between the ironclads USS *Monitor* and CSS *Virginia* on the waters off Hampton Roads, Virginia, in March 1862 concluded in a military draw, giving neither the United States nor the Confederacy a clear victory. Ultimately, the battle was not so much about rebellion or blockade as it was about the future of naval combat.

Wood had dominated the construction of military and commercial vessels from the beginning of naval history because of its availability, buoyancy, and flexibility. Even when small, oar-driven galleys gave way to large, sailing man-of-wars with multiple gun decks, wood remained the material of choice for shipbuilding. However, steel shot and iron shells easily penetrated wooden ships, either sinking them or setting them afire. Shipbuilders and sea captains attempted to make their vessels less vulnerable by using the hardest of woods in multiple layers and placing barriers— cloth, raw cotton, or metal sheeting—around the most vulnerable areas. While these efforts somewhat "hardened" the sides of their ships, these additions also affected their maneuverability and stability.

Yi Sun-Shin, a Korean sailor, was the first to reinforce his boats with iron. In 1592, Yi covered several of his hundred-foot-long vessels with metal studs intended to reinforce their effectiveness as rams. Yi sank several Japanese vessels in the Yellow Sea with his "turtle ships" before being killed. Even though Yi became a Korean national hero, his concept of iron-studded boats was soon forgotten. Other experiments over the following years proved that it was impractical to cover sailing ships with iron plating because of the loss of buoyancy and speed.

The invention of the steam engine early in the nineteenth century provided a more reliable means of propulsion for water vessels and, ultimately, was an innovation in naval warfare. Initially, while steam-powered vessels were excellent for commercial use, their huge side or stern wheels were far too vulnerable for military employment. A single well-aimed shot into these wooden paddle wheels could disable the entire ship. The major event that eventually opened the way for the influence of steam engines in naval warfare was the invention of internal drives and propellers that were below the waterline and protected from enemy fire.

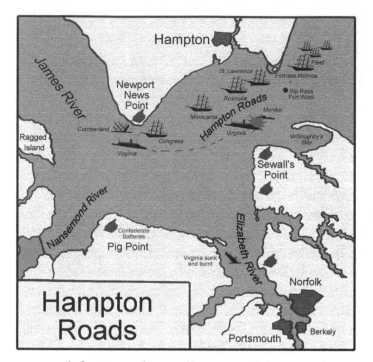

The first great need for internal propeller, steam-driven vessels came when the Southern states seceded to form the Confederacy. At the beginning of the Civil War in the spring of 1861, early Confederate victories forced the U.S. Navy to abandon the Norfolk Naval Yard in Virginia. Several ships in the yard waiting for maintenance were set afire rather than be left intact to fall in rebel hands. These included the USS *Merrimack,* a wooden steamer commissioned in 1856. The ship burned to the water-line, but the Confederates raised the wreck, reworked the steam engines, and added four inches of wrought iron bars to its wooden deck and sides. Decks slanted upward from the waterline, high enough only for the casement of six nine-inch smoothbore cannons and four six- or seven-inch rifled guns. When launched, the 263-foot Confederate iron-clad had a draught of twenty-two feet and a four-foot cast iron ramming prowl. Its two aged six-hundred-horsepower steam engines could propel the vessel at a top speed of only four knots (about four and a half miles per hour), and it took the heavy ship, which resembled "a floating barn roof," a full half-hour to turn completely around.

During its reconstruction, the old *Merrimack* became known as the *Merrimac.* However, on its launch date of March 5, 1862, its official name became the CSS *Virginia.*

Union intelligence learned of the construction of a Confederate ironclad early in its makeover. A key part of the Anaconda Plan (27) to defeat the rebellion was a

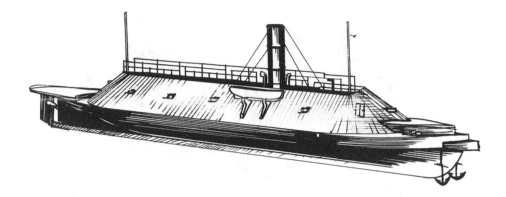

CSS Virginia/Ex-Merrimack (Hampton Roads-2)

blockade to stop exports and imports from and to the South. The Confederate navy was much too small to break the blockade, but a single ironclad might sink a sufficient number of wooden Union ships to allow shipping to resume in the South. Some Union leaders even feared that a Confederate ironclad might sail up the Atlantic coast and shell major Northern cities.

Aware that only an iron ship could defeat another iron ship, the Union navy drew up plans for its own ironclad. Instead of converting a wooden ship, the much more industrialized Union decided to build a totally new iron ship. It adopted a design by Swedish inventor John Ericsson for a 172-foot, flat decked iron vessel with a 140-ton revolving turret containing two eleven-inch smoothbore cannons—a design that earned the description, "a cheese box on a raft."

The keel of the USS *Monitor* was laid on October 25, 1861, and it was launched in an amazingly short period of just under a hundred days on January 30, 1862. Despite its strange appearance, the ship, with its eight inches of iron plates on the turret and four and a half inches on its sides and decks, was fast and maneuverable. Although it had only two guns, the independent turret allowed the crew to reorient quickly without turning the boat itself.

On the morning of March 8, the CSS *Virginia* sailed into the Hampton Roads waterway and attacked the Union wooden fleet blockade. The rebel ironclad rammed and sank the thirty-gun USS *Cumberland* and then forced the fifty-gun USS *Congress* aground. The *Virginia* next ran the USS *Minnesota* aground before being forced by the outgoing tide to withdraw to deeper waters.

At dawn on the morning of March 9, the *Virginia* again moved against the

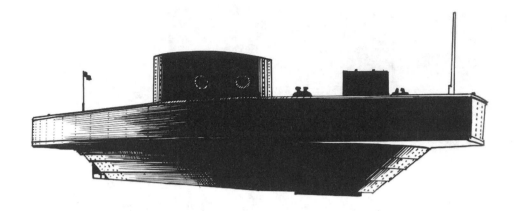

USS Monitor

Minnesota to complete its destruction. However, when the rebel ironclad neared the Union wooden vessel, the Confederate sailors found the *Monitor,* which had arrived from New York during the night, blocking their way. At 9:00 a.m. the two ironclads opened fire. During the following battle, the *Monitor* proved much more maneuverable, but neither side could significantly damage the other, as cannonballs bounced harmlessly off steel plates.

After two hours, the Union boat briefly withdrew to replenish its ammunition. When it returned to the fight at 11:30 a.m., the *Virginia* concentrated its fire on the *Monitor*'s small pilot house near its bow, wounding the Union Captain Lieutenant John L. Worden with a shot that exploded thorough his observation slot. The blinded Worden withdrew his ship, and a short time later the *Virginia* returned to its Norfolk port.

More than four hundred Union and twenty Confederate seamen were killed or wounded during the two-day battle at Hampton Roads, but not a single sailor died in the direct clash between the *Virginia* and the *Monitor.* While the battle between the two ironclads had been indecisive, the *Virginia* had been unable to break the Union blockade. The Confederate ironclad remained in port until May 9, when advancing Union ground forces captured Norfolk during the Peninsular Campaign (32). The crew of the *Virginia* scuttled their boat rather than let it fall in Union hands. The *Monitor* also sank a few months later when it encountered a gale off Cape Hatteras, North Carolina, on December 31, 1862.

Even if the *Virginia* had defeated the *Monitor,* or if the Union had not built its own ironclad, it is doubtful if the battle off Hampton Roads would have seriously influenced the outcome of the Civil War. The Confederacy lacked the industrial base to launch additional ironclads, and the top-heavy, slow-moving *Virginia* would have been ineffective outside the protected inland waterways.

The real influence of the Battle of Hampton Roads lay not in the fight itself or in its impact on the Civil War overall, but in its effect on the future of ship design. Even though the Union navy had already been successfully placing light armor on the sides of its small steamers on the Mississippi River, and England and France were experimenting with similar armament, it was not until the Battle of Hampton Roads that the world realized the full potential of ironclads. Three-quarters of a century later, British leader and historian Winston Churchill noted, "The combat of the *Merrimac* and the *Monitor* made the greatest change in sea-fighting since cannon fired by gunpowder had been mounted on ships."

The success of the *Virginia* against the *Cumberland* and *Congress* on March 8 forever established that wood could not endure against iron. The battle on the following day between the *Virginia* and the *Monitor* proved that only steel could stand against steel.

Within weeks of the battle, every navy of note in the world began to consider a transformation to ironclads. Soon sails flew only above wooden pleasure boats and isolated commercial vessels because steam-power steel-hulled ships ruled future sea battles.

Few incidents in warfare provide such a distinct mark in weapons and combat development as did the battle between the "floating barn roof" and the "cheese box on a raft." If this ranking was of lasting influence on naval warfare rather than the Civil War, it would rank much higher.

73

THOMAS LAFAYETTE ROSSER

Confederate General

1836–1910

Thomas Lafayette Rosser left West Point two weeks before graduation to join the Confederate army. Over the next four years he served in the artillery and cavalry as he rose from lieutenant to major general while participating in nearly every major action in the eastern theater. Rosser is representative of the many young men totally dedicated to the cause of the South, but who, after the war, worked to reunite the country.

Born on October 5, 1836, in Campbell Country, Virginia, Rosser moved to the Sabine River country of Texas with his family at age thirteen. In 1856 he earned an appointment to West Point as a member of the Class of 1861. A friend and one-time roommate of his at the Military Academy was George A. Custer (52).

Only days before graduation, Rosser left West Point to enlist in the newly formed Confederate army. In Virginia he accepted a lieutenant's commission in the artillery and fought at First Bull Run (10). Early in the Union's Peninsular Campaign (32) he earned the honor of being the first commander in American history to shoot down an observation balloon. In these early battles, Rosser impressed his superiors, including J. E. B. Stuart (23) for the disciplined, accurate fire of his guns as well as his personal bravery under fire.

Rosser was wounded at Mechanicsville in June 1862 and upon recovery—on the recommendation of Stuart—was promoted to colonel in command of the 5th Virginia Cavalry. His regiment accompanied Stuart on the raid against Catlett's Station in August that captured General John Pope's Union headquarters. Rosser then led his cavalry regiment in the battles of Second Bull Run (40) and South Mountain.

During the subsequent advance toward Pennsylvania, Rosser and his regiment found themselves nearly surrounded at Aldie, Virginia, on June 17, 1863. Rosser ordered his regiment to draw sabers and he then led a charge that broke the Union line. In a later report to his commander, Rosser explained, "The enemy greatly outnumbered us, appearing in force everywhere, and it became apparent that victory was the only means of escape."

On September 28, 1863, Rosser pinned on the rank of a brigadier general and assumed command of a cavalry brigade. Three weeks later the young general had his first encounter with his old West Point roommate when his cavalry routed those commanded by George Custer in a brief skirmish at Buckland Mills, Virginia.

Buckland Mills was only the first in a series of fights between the two old friends over the next year as they struggled for control over the Shenandoah Valley. Rosser executed several raids for horses and supplies into West Virginia but did not fare as well in his future fights with Custer, who defeated him at Cedar Creek and Woodstock. However, in their final battle in the Valley three days before Christmas 1864 at Chester Gap, Rosser drove Custer from the field and captured forty of his cavalrymen.

During the Union's Valley Campaign (29), Rosser constantly stood against larger forces and remained one the most successful Confederate commanders in the Shenandoah. Southern newspapers even went so far as to label him "the Savior of the Valley."

In early 1865, Rosser joined the Confederate army consolidating around Petersburg (46). On April 1, 1865, Rosser's cavalry fought in the Battle of Five Oaks and then held open the Southside Railroad for the evacuation of the Confederate army. Rosser was with the army near Appomattox Court House (37) on April 9. He refused to surrender his command and led a charge through Union lines. His freedom was brief as he was forced to surrender on May 2 near Hanover Court House.

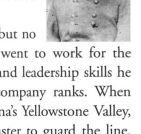

There was some initial talk of trying Rosser for his escape, but no charges followed. He was paroled a few weeks later. Rosser went to work for the Northern Pacific Railroad and, using the same organizational and leadership skills he found successful during the war, quickly advanced up the company ranks. When Indians threatened the railroad workers laying track in Montana's Yellowstone Valley, the U.S. Army dispatched cavalry commanded by George Custer to guard the line. Rosser and his fellow West Point cadet put aside their differences over the war and resumed their friendship.

Rosser would outlive Custer, who died at the Little Big Horn in 1876, by nearly thirty-five years. By the 1890s Rosser had amassed a substantial fortune in rail and other speculations and settled into the life of a gentleman farmer near Charlottesville, Virginia. During the decades after the end of the war Rosser made friends with many of his former battlefield enemies, but hard feelings between the North and South still lingered. At the outbreak of the Spanish American War in 1898, President William McKinley saw the conflict as an opportunity to reunite the country as well as gain freedom for Cuba.

McKinley commissioned Rosser a brigadier general of U.S. volunteers. The old rebel donned the blue uniform that he had fought against so well three and a half decades earlier. Rosser did not make it to Cuba but spent the war training volunteers at a camp located on the old battlefield at Chickamauga (74)—one of the few battlegrounds where the aged general had not fought.

After the war Rosser returned to Charlottesville, where he died on March 29, 1910. He is buried it the city's Riverview Cemetery.

Rosser is one of those characters of the Civil War who fought in many of the most important battles, earned the respect of the best generals, and demonstrated leadership and bravery superior to most, yet he remains mostly unknown and uncelebrated. Perhaps if the South had won the war he would have had the "boy general" reputation that went to Custer, but Rosser was not a great self-promoter and, of course, he fought on the losing side.

Still, Rosser's influence was significant, particularly in the Union's Valley Campaign, and he is well-deserving of inclusion on this list. Had he been a bit older and more experienced at the beginning of the war, he might have very easily reached the level of Lee (5), Jackson (36), Longstreet (13), and others. He is also worthy for rejoining the U.S. Army and wearing the uniform of his former enemy to fight new wars for the saved Union.

74

CHICKAMAUGA

September 19–20, 1863

The Battle of Chickamauga in the fall of 1863 temporarily blocked the Union advance against Atlanta. Although it was a Confederate victory, the battle maneuvers left Chattanooga in the hands of the Federal army. The confused, poorly coordinated fight ended the career of several generals, solidified the reputations of several more, and introduced still others as the leaders of the future.

During the summer of 1863, the Union army defeated what would be the last invasion of its home territory at Gettysburg (4) and secured the Mississippi River with its capture of Vicksburg (7). Union General William Rosecrans had also conducted an offensive at about the same time that secured eastern Tennessee for the Union, pushing the Confederates into defensive positions at Chattanooga in the far southeastern part of the state on the Georgia border.

In early September Rosecrans gathered Federal units from throughout Tennessee and marched toward Chattanooga. When Rosecrans maneuvered around the western side of the city on September 8, the Confederate commander Braxton Bragg (60), fearful of having his supply lines from Atlanta cut, withdrew twenty-two miles south to the vicinity of Lafayette, Georgia. Bragg believed that the mountains and thick forest to his north would force the Union army to split into smaller elements that he could easily defeat. Then he could reoccupy Chattanooga.

Both armies maneuvered over the difficult terrain during the next ten days, seldom knowing the enemy's positions or even the location of their own forces. By September 18, Bragg had his three corps positioned north of Chickamauga Creek, from where he planned to attack and turn the Federal left flank commanded by General Thomas Crittenden. On the 19th Bragg attacked, only to discover that a corps led by General George Thomas (11) had arrived to support Crittenden. After a day of confused fighting, Bragg withdrew; neither side had gained the advantage.

The next morning Bragg ordered General James Longstreet (13), who had just arrived with his corps from the eastern theater, to assault the Union right flank. Early in the battle Rosecrans was erroneously informed that he had a gap in his lines. When he maneuvered to fill the nonexistent gap, he actually formed one instead. Longstreet,

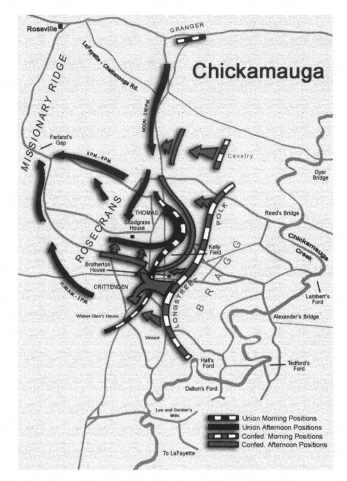

by skill or by luck, as some later claimed, promptly exploited the opening and pushed into the Union rear. Almost immediately, fully a third of the Union army, including Rosecrans, were in wild retreat back toward Chattanooga.

Not everyone agreed with the withdrawal orders. Rosecran's own chief of staff, General James A. Garfield (83), accompanied his boss back to Chattanooga. Once he was sure Rosecrans was secure, Garfield, who would be elected president of the United States seventeen years later, returned to the fight.

Upon arrival in the city, Rosecrans sent two telegrams. First to his Washington superiors he reported, "We have met with a serious disaster…we have no certainty of holding our position here." His second message to Thomas ordered his subordinate to also withdraw to Chattanooga.

Thomas, the hero of the previous day's fighting, had to first ensure his army's survival before considering a retreat. He took charge of the Union left and consolidated a defense. Longstreet turned his corps northeastward to join the remainder of Bragg's attack against Thomas. Despite being outnumbered, the Union army held off several attacks. Just when it appeared they would be defeated, General Gordon Granger, commander of the reserve corps, marched to support Thomas. Granger, despite no orders to do so and only on his own initiative, stopped the Confederate advance.

After dark, Thomas and Granger withdrew their forces back to Chattanooga to reunite with Rosecrans. Bragg slowly pursued and took up siege positions around the city he had given up without a fight only weeks earlier.

Losses were extensive on both sides. Of the sixty-six thousand Confederates in the battle, more than twenty-three hundred lay dead. Another fifteen thousand were wounded or missing. Of the fifty-eight thousand Union participants, more than sixteen hundred were killed and another fourteen thousand wounded or missing. Total casualties for both sides were about 28 percent of their committed forces.

Within a month of the battle's conclusion, Rosecrans was relieved of command. He never occupied a significant position for the remainder of the war. Thomas, now known as the "Rock of Chickamauga," and Granger were hailed as heroes. On the Confederate side, Longstreet was recognized for his exploitation of the gap in the Union lines and for his usual steady battlefield leadership. Bragg, who had won the battle but given up the key communications center of Chattanooga, remained in charge. He was later relieved of command when the Union army began its advance southeast in its Atlanta Campaign (20).

Whether Bragg might have been more successful had he defended Chattanooga rather than attempt to defeat the Union army in the field, will, of course, never be known. Bragg's proposal to destroy the enemy piecemeal in the mountains and forests was a good plan; unfortunately, the difficult terrain adversely effected his own observations and maneuvers as much as that of the enemy's.

Ultimately, Chickamauga only served as a lead-in to the more influential Battle of Chattanooga (12) two months later. By the next spring the Union army would be well on its way to Atlanta and then beginning its March to the Sea (16).

75

JOHN WILKES BOOTH

Actor and Assassin

1838–1865

John Wilkes Booth became the most infamous of American assassins when he fired a bullet into the back of the head of Abraham Lincoln (2) on April 14, 1865. The president's death the next morning from his wound transformed Lincoln from a leader both loved and hated by his fellow countrymen to the greatest martyr-hero of the United States.

Born on May 10, 1838, on a farm near Bel Air, Maryland, about twenty-five miles northeast of Baltimore, Booth entered a family headed by his father Janius, one of the most famous actors on the American stage. The family farm included several slaves and, as a young boy, Booth expressed support for states' rights and the superiority of the white race. Booth dropped out of school when his father died in 1852 and worked on the family farm for several years. Farm work was, however, not to his liking, and he often said what he really wanted was to be more famous than his father.

Booth made his acting debut at age seventeen in Richmond and remained in the city performing in plays for the next four years. The young actor, who stood five foot eight and had jet black hair and ivory skin, became a local celebrity and many called him the "handsomest man in America." In addition to gaining acting skills, Booth experienced a growing appreciation for the South during his residence in Virginia.

Booth left the Richmond Theater Company to enlist in the Richmond Grays militia unit on November 20, 1859. He had no real desire to serve in the military, but the Grays were on orders to provide security for the hanging of John Brown (54) at Charleston on December 2. His brief, and only, time in uniform provided him a free trip and access to Brown's execution. Shortly after the hanging, Booth returned to Richmond and was discharged from the militia.

Returning to the stage, Booth performed in plays in cities throughout the country from New York to New Orleans. By the end of 1860 he was earning more than $20,000 a year, a huge sum for the time. At the outbreak of the Civil War, Booth settled in Washington, D.C., and began making appearances at Ford Theater. Booth

told friends he supported the Confederacy but claimed he had promised his mother he would not enlist in the rebel army.

During the early years of the war Booth operated as a spy for the Confederacy in an extremely limited manner. Although he traveled throughout the North performing on stage, there is no conclusive evidence that he provided any significant information to Richmond. It is known, however, that he did participate in a limited smuggling operation to transfer medical supplies to the Southern states.

Booth lived a comfortable life during this period and even found time to invest in oil exploration in western Pennsylvania. He courted several women and earned the reputation as a real "ladies' man." Back in Washington, Ford Theater became his second home as he received mail there while appearing on stage. On November 9, 1863, President Lincoln and a party of dignitaries attended a Booth performance.

In 1864 Booth had traveled to Montreal, where he met with several Confederate officials. Just what transpired is unknown other than Booth returned to Washington with letters of introduction to other Confederate supporters in the area. It was at this time the actor made plans to kidnap the president. Booth wanted to abduct Lincoln and hurry to Richmond with the help of his new supporters. Lincoln would then be exchanged for all the Confederate prisoners held in the North. These freed men would provide an "instant army" to the Confederacy that was in great need of manpower to continue the rebellion. There is also evidence that Booth considered blowing up the executive mansion with a homemade bomb, but the plot never advanced beyond the planning stage.

Booth decided to take advantage of Lincoln's fatalistic attitude about personal security. Lincoln believed that no number of guards could protect him from a dedicated assassin. For months Booth planned to abduct Lincoln during one of his rides in the city or visits to nearby hospitals and military units. It was not until March 17, 1865, that Booth finally decided conditions were satisfactory to grab the president during a visit to a hospital outside Washington. The plot was thwarted when at the last minute Lincoln changed his plans to attend a luncheon—ironically at the same hotel where Booth resided.

Two weeks later the Union army marched into Richmond and Robert E. Lee (5) surrendered his army on April 9. Other Confederate forces were still operating in the western theater but the war was as good as over. With the option of kidnapping Lincoln to save the South now impractical, Booth sought revenge for the Lost Cause while also gaining lasting fame for himself.

On April 11 the president gave a speech at the White House, commenting on future rights for blacks. Included were suggestions for conferring voting rights "on the very intelligent, and on those who serve our cause as soldiers." Booth, who was in the crowd, was enraged. To a friend he promised, "That is the last speech he will ever make."

Booth assembled fellow conspirators to plot the murder of Lincoln as well as Vice President Andrew Johnson (83) and Secretary of State William Seward. Shortly before 10:00 p.m. on April 14, Booth entered Ford Theater, where the president and Mrs. Lincoln were attending a performance of *Our American Cousin*. Booth, familiar with the play, waited for about twenty-five minutes until a line was delivered that he knew would bring laughter. When the crowd erupted, Booth entered Lincoln's booth and shot him in the head with a small pistol.

Booth leaped to the stage to make his way to an exit where he had a horse for his escape. In his jump one of his spurs caught in a flag hanging from the booth, causing the assassin to fall and break his leg. Despite the injury, Booth made his way to the alley and rode south.

There are several accounts of what Booth shouted as he jumped to the stage to make his final exit. Some accounts say he declared *"Sic semper tyrannis!"*—"Thus ever be to tyrants." Others said he said, "The South is avenged." Still others claim he made both statements.

Booth's comrades managed to wound Seward but made no attempt on Johnson. All conspirators were quickly arrested and imprisoned at Fort Monroe. Booth, with some help from Confederate agents, made it about twenty miles southeast of Fredericksburg to Bowling Green before Union soldiers surrounded him in a barn on

April 26. The barn was set afire and orders given to capture Booth alive. Instead, Sergeant Boston Corbett shot Booth, who in his last breaths looked at his own hands and uttered, "Useless, useless." After a military trial, Booth's four fellow conspirators were hung on July 7, 1865.

Other than revenge for the South and fame for himself, it is unclear just why Booth carried out his assassination plan. He did leave behind a letter but it reveals more about Booth's personal motivation than his overall purpose. In the note Booth stated, "For years I have devoted my time, my energies, and every dollar I possess to the furtherance of an object. I have been baffled and disappointed. The hour has come when I must change my plan. Many, I know—the vulgar herd—will blame me for what I am about to do, but posterity, I am sure, will justify me. Right or wrong, God judge me, not man…. This country was formed for the white, not for the black man. And looking upon African slavery from the same standpoint as the noble framers of our Constitution, I, for one, have ever considered it one of the greatest blessings, both for themselves and us, that God ever bestowed upon a favored nation."

By the time Booth died, almost the entire Confederacy had surrendered and the final shots were only a few weeks away. The war was lost and Booth's killing of Lincoln had no influence on its outcome. Booth's own words of "Useless, useless" provide the best summary of the assassination itself. Still there was long-term impact. The absence of Lincoln led to a harsher Reconstruction than that perceived by the president. Resentment, and downright hatred, of the South by many Northerners increased with the news of the murder.

The assassination of Abraham Lincoln was a major event in American history. If it had occurred earlier in the war, its influence might have easily gained it a higher ranking on this list. However, because it took place in the war's last days, it merits a much lower rank.

76

DRAFT RIOTS

Summer 1863

When sufficient numbers of volunteers no longer came forward to fill the ranks of the Union army, President Abraham Lincoln (2) called for a draft to begin in the summer of 1863. Across the North, particularly in areas controlled by Democrats, riots broke out in protest. Government buildings were attacked and burned. Rioters, mostly recent Irish immigrants, also beat and lynched African Americans, whom they blamed for the continuation of the war.

The Civil War had begun with a great patriotic movement in both the North and South; men, young and old, flocked to recruitment centers. With no awareness of the brutality of the modern battlefield and assurance that the war would be over in a matter of months, volunteers hurried to don the uniform of the blue or the gray so that they could defend their cause and share in the glory. Two years later, they had learned that glory was often accompanied with a grave.

However, a sense of patriotism still rallied those uninitiated in the realities of combat to voluntarily enlist. Those who remained reluctant to risk their lives and to sacrifice civilian comforts faced strong social pressure from their communities to join the fight. These patriotic and social forces provided about 90 percent of the Union army needs, but officials had to look elsewhere for the additional 10 percent.

As early as August 1862, Lincoln called upon state governors to enlist three hundred thousand militiamen for a period of nine months. He included instructions that if sufficient numbers of volunteers did not come forward, the governors should draft the remainder of the quota. Protests broke out in Indiana, Wisconsin, and Pennsylvania, forcing the president to postpone his orders for a draft.

Although the South was generally more supportive of the war than the North, it had a smaller population to call upon for volunteers. President Jefferson Davis (9) initiated a draft in April 1862 to fill units short of personnel. The draft was not popular but there were no riots in protest. The Confederacy met its quota, except for a few isolated areas, particularly in the Appalachian Mountains populated by pro-Northern families or those who just wanted to be left alone.

The North and South shared in their dislike for the unfairness of involuntary conscription. Regulations on both sides provided provisions for a person who was drafted to hire a substitute for as little as $300. Additional exemptions were granted in the South for owners or overseers of twenty or more slaves in order to prevent possible uprisings from unsupervised blacks. These exemptions, particularly the hiring of substitutes, caused complaints about "a rich man's war, but a poor man's fight." This awareness of class, the harshness of military discipline, and especially the realities of the bloody battlefield created the largest number of deserters in American military history.

After Lincoln's failed initial attempt to institute a draft, the Union army began a system of bounties of as much as $1,000 to encourage volunteers. The bounty system did help fill the ranks but it also added to the list of deserters when volunteers accepted a bounty, deserted, and then enlisted under another name to collect another bounty.

By the spring of 1863 neither patriotism nor bounties were sufficient to fill the Union ranks. With Lincoln's support, the Congress passed the Enrollment Act on March 3, 1863. There were verbal protests, especially from New York Democratic governor Horatio Seymour, but little other conflict took place until the initial draftees were announced the following July.

The first draftees were drawn in New York City on July 11, and their names were published in the local newspapers the next day. Crowds gathered to protest the draft, but political and racial factors were as much the cause as any negative feeling toward the military. Most of the protesters, who soon became rioters, were recent Irish immigrants who wanted to work and establish new lives rather than accept the risks on a battlefield for a cause they did not completely understand or support.

Initially the Irish protesters gathered outside government and military buildings and threw a few rocks, rotten vegetables, and words of protest. As the crowd grew to about fifty thousand and New York authorities took little or ineffectual action, the protesters became rioters. They also turned their wrath away from the government and focused on the city's black population. Many of the Irish blamed the blacks for the war in general and disliked them in particular because they had to compete with them for the available low-paying jobs.

From July 13 to 15, 1863, the mob terrorized the East Side of New York as they looted stores, beat blacks on the streets, and lynched several from the lampposts. They also burned a black church and an African American orphanage.

The rioting ended only with the arrival of regular troops from the U.S. Army—many of whom marched directly from the battlefield at Gettysburg (4) to New York City. Estimates of the total killed in the riots, nearly all black, ranged from thirty to one hundred; more than $1.5 million (about $200 million in today's dollars) in damages occurred.

Other, less destructive, riots occurred about the same time in Boston, Massachusetts; Portsmouth, New Hampshire; Rutland, Vermont; Troy, New York; and Wooster, Ohio. None were particularly destructive, especially compared to New York, and after their conclusion these cities, and the rest of the North, peacefully accepted the draft.

The draft riots diverted troops from the battlefront but only temporarily. Their long-term influence on the war was minimal; today they symbolize that racism was not limited to the South and that everyone in the North did not support the efforts to preserve the Union and end slavery. The special exemptions for the wealthy and well-connected also established a trend that continues today in that the United States still expects and allows its lower socioeconomic classes to man its military and fight its wars.

77

JOSEPH WHEELER

Confederate General

1836–1906

Joseph Wheeler earned the rank of major general and command of the cavalry of the Army of the Mississippi at the age of only twenty-six and fought in every major campaign in the western theater. He was particularly successful in leading raids behind enemy lines to capture supplies and to interrupt Union lines of communications. His support of reuniting the South with the North after the war resulted in his appointment as a major general in the U.S. Army during the Spanish American War of 1898.

Born near Augusta, Georgia, on September 10, 1836, Wheeler joined the Class of 1859 at West Point where he graduated number nineteen of twenty-two cadets. As a dragoon officer, Wheeler fought in Indian campaigns in Kansas and New Mexico before resigning his commission at the outbreak of the Civil War. Wheeler began the war as an artillery lieutenant, but his organizational abilities and leadership quickly earned him promotion to a colonel in the infantry. His first significant combat was at Shiloh (18) in April 1862 as a brigade commander where he covered the Confederate retreat on the battle's second day.

In July, Wheeler took command of Braxton Bragg's (60) cavalry in the Army of Mississippi and remained in the field in almost constant operations until the end of the war. During Bragg's campaign into Tennessee and Kentucky in August and September, Wheeler's cavalry led the advance and fought well at Perryville in October before again covering the Confederate retreat. Promoted to brigadier general, Wheeler fought at Stones River at the end of the year and earned another advance to major general the following month.

Wheeler's cavalry played an important role in September 1863 in the Battle of Chickamauga (74) and then helped stop the Union advance at Chattanooga. With the Union offensive blocked, Wheeler led his cavalry into the Union rear in central Tennessee, and destroyed more than five hundred supply wagons and one thousand mules. Wheeler also cut the rail line that provided the primary supply link to the forward Union forces before returning to Confederate lines.

In November 1863, Wheeler joined James Longstreet (13) in the defense of Knoxville, Tennessee, and again covered the Confederate withdrawal at the end of the month. Early in 1864, Wheeler's cavalry opposed William Sherman's (6) advance toward Atlanta (20) and engaged in several skirmishes with the Union cavalry commanded by George Stoneman (89). On August 10, Wheeler led a month-long raid behind Union lines between Atlanta and Nashville and again destroyed the rail supply line.

After the fall of Atlanta, Wheeler's far-outnumbered cavalrymen fell back slowly before Sherman's March to the Sea (16). While they could not stop the Union offensive, they were able to somewhat limit foragers and looters to reduce the destruction to as narrow a front as possible.

In February 1865, Wheeler, now a lieutenant general, joined Joseph Johnston (17) in the final operations in the Carolinas. After Johnston surrendered to Sherman in late April, Wheeler continued operations for two more weeks before he, too, was captured.

Wheeler settled in New Orleans after the war and became a businessman. He moved to Wheeler, Alabama, a town named in his honor, in 1868 to practice law and raise cotton. He entered politics in 1881 and won his first of eight terms in the U.S. Congress. As a congressman he chaired the House ways and means committee and became respected and popular with his comrades on both sides of the aisle, regardless of their home state. He used his fame from the Civil War and his popularity as a congressman to become an early proponent of healing old wounds and for the reunification of North and South.

When the Spanish American War broke out in 1898, Wheeler offered his services to President William McKinley. Although there was a more than an ample number of officers available who had not fought against the United States as a part of the rebel Confederacy, McKinley saw the offer as an excellent opportunity to gain the support of the South for the war and to put aside old differences.

As a major general, Wheeler commanded the cavalry division, including the Leonard Wood's and Theodore Roosevelt's Rough Riders, in Cuba at the Battle of San Juan Hill. Except for occasionally in the heat of battle referring to the enemy as "Yankees" rather than Spaniards, Wheeler performed well. After Cuba was secured, Wheeler served in the Philippines before returning to the U.S. to command the Department of the Lakes. During this time he resigned his volunteer commission as a major general and accepted an appointment as a brigadier general in the regular army. He retired at this rank in September 1900.

Wheeler died at the home of his sister in Brooklyn, New York, on January 25, 1906. He is buried in Arlington National Cemetery—one of only two former Confederate generals (the second was Marcus J. Wright who died in 1922) to be interred there.

Wheeler was known his entire military career for his aggressiveness and hard-hitting tactics. His bravery under fire was spectacular as he suffered three wounds and had sixteen horses shot from under him. Wheeler always rode into the heaviest action, a practice that resulted in thirty-six of his staff officers who accompanied him becoming battle casualties.

Called "Fighting Joe" by his men and the Confederate press, Wheeler was one of the "boy generals" who brought spirit and dedication to the war. Exceeded in influence as a cavalryman only by Nathan B. Forrest (21), J. E. B. Stuart (23), and Wade Hampton (69) in the South, Wheeler earned his ranking through long-term operations on the battlefield. If his side had succeeded in its revolution, he might have ranked above Phil Sheridan (8) and George Custer (52). His ranking is reinforced by his postwar service to the U.S. Army and his efforts to reunite the country.

78

MISSOURI COMPROMISE

1820

The Missouri Compromise of 1820 was part of a continued effort on the part of the U.S. Congress to ease tensions between the North and South over the issue of slavery in emerging new states and territories. Although it satisfied few, the Missouri Compromise helped maintain the Union for another four decades.

From the time of independence, the issue of slavery divided the United States. The first session of the U.S. Congress in 1787 compromised on the slavery issue by declaring the practice legal in territories south of the Ohio River and illegal on the north side. The U.S. honored this Northwest Ordinance of 1787, as it was known, over the next few decades as territories entered the Union as either slave state or free state, as defined by the provision.

When the ordinance was passed, the population and wealth of the United States was distributed fairly equally. With the passage of years, however, the assets and the number of citizens of the North steadily exceeded that of the South. In addition to better lifestyles, this more importantly meant that the North controlled the U.S. Congress since seats were based on population. The South accepted the Northern advantage in the House as long as the number of slave states equaled free states, which meant neither side had an advantage in the Senate where each state has two votes regardless of population.

In 1818 the Territory of Missouri reached a sufficient population to request statehood. Most of the settlers of the territory had migrated there from the South and expected Missouri to be admitted to the Union as a slave state. At the time, the twenty-two states of the United States were equally divided between free and slave. Admitting another slave state would disrupt the balance in the Senate; many Northerners, including those in the House of Representatives, opposed that change.

When the Missouri statehood bill appeared before the House in 1819, James Tallmadge of New York proposed an amendment that would forbid further importation of slaves into Missouri and provided measures to free those currently held in the state. The House, with its dominance of Northern congressmen, passed the bill in February 1819, but the balanced Senate deleted the restrictions on slavery before approving the bill. Debate spread across the country, inflaming passions, exacerbating sectional differences, and spilling repressed bitterness.

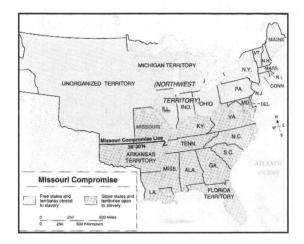

When Congress went back into session in 1820, representatives and senators on both sides continued their arguments. The situation became even more critical with the admission of a bill in the House to admit Maine, formally a part of Massachusetts, to the Union as a free state. Diplomacy finally trumped hostility when the two sides agreed to a compromise that at least appeased the majority.

Henry Clay, as Speaker of the House, did much to secure the passage of the agreement, but Senator Jesse B. Thomas of Illinois was far more responsible for its wording and guiding it through the legislative process. The Missouri Compromise, or Thomas Proviso as it was known to many at the time, admitted Missouri as a slave state while approving the admission of Maine as free. Furthermore, the compromise included provisions that banned slavery in the remainder of lands included in the Louisiana Purchase north of the southern boundary of Missouri. Even this reasonably fair compromise almost failed a final vote because Missouri officials wanted to bar the immigration of free blacks into their state. Only when Missouri withdrew this provision did the compromise finally pass.

Groups in both the North and South condemned the Missouri Compromise as appeasement but, in reality, it was an example of statesmanship that preserved the Union for another forty years. Questions, however, had been raised or expanded about the role of slavery in the future of the United States and whether this and other decisions should rest within the state or be decided at the federal level.

Provisions of the Missouri Compromise maintained a perilous balance until the Supreme Court overruled parts of it in the *Dred Scott* decision (58) of 1857 on the basis that it deprived individuals of private property without due process of law. The last provisions of the Missouri Compromise that established the boundary line above which slavery was outlawed were repealed by the Kansas-Nebraska Act of 1854.

The Kansas-Nebraska Act opened territories to all migrant groups and left the issue of slavery up to popular sovereignty. Local choice erupted into open warfare between free and slave factions and soon turned the territory into what became known as Bleeding Kansas.

The next five years brought even more need for another compromise all across the United States, especially in Kansas. Unfortunately, by 1861 it was impossible for any leader to find middle ground between the North and the South. A civil war, seemingly destined from the time of the original U.S. Constitution, swept the former Union.

The Missouri Compromise secures its ranking in this list for at least postponing the Civil War. It showed that widely separate factions could and did reach a compromise for the general good. If it had lasted until slavery and other regional issues could have been peacefully settled, it might very well have been one of the most important documents in American history. But it did not, and in all reality could not, prevent the war and, as a result, rests near the end of this list.

79

JOSHUA LAWRENCE CHAMBERLAIN

Union General

1828–1914

Joshua Lawrence Chamberlain fought in twenty-four battles and suffered six wounds while proving to be one of the most influential regimental commanders in the Union army. His leadership at Gettysburg (4) prevented the rebels from turning the Union left flank at Little Round Top and perhaps winning the battle. His sustained performance and bravery earned him a direct promotion to brigadier general by U. S. Grant (3) and the privilege of receiving the formal surrender of the Army of Northern Virginia at Appomattox Court House (37).

Born on September 8, 1828, in Brewer, Maine, Chamberlain graduated from Bowdoin College in 1852 and from Bangor Theological Seminary in 1855. Upon graduation from the seminary, he turned down opportunities to become a missionary and minister, choosing instead to return to Bowdoin as an English professor. Bowdoin did not want to lose Chamberlain to the army when the Civil War began and offered to finance his further education in Europe so he could study languages. Chamberlain refused the offer and accepted a commission as a lieutenant colonel in the 20th Maine Infantry in August 1862.

Despite his only experience in uniform being a brief stay as a teenager at a military school, Chamberlain quickly learned the art of military science. Along with his tactical instincts, he constantly exposed himself to rally his men at the battles of Antietam (1), Fredericksburg (53), and Chancellorsville (31), as well as many skirmishes in between. At Gettysburg on July 2, 1863, the 20th Maine occupied Little Round Top at the far western edge of the Union defenses. His regiment held the ground against repeated Confederate attacks, preventing the flank from being turned and forcing Robert E. Lee (5) to make his disastrous charge into the Union center the next day. More than two decades later, the U.S. Congress finally recognized Chamberlain's performance at Gettysburg with a belated Medal of Honor (one of about twelve hundred awarded for Civil War gallantry).

Chamberlain, promoted to full colonel, left his regiment in the fall of 1863 to heal from wounds suffered at Little Round Top and a case of malaria. He rejoined his regiment in May 1864 at Petersburg (46) and advanced to brigade command the following month. On June 18 he was again seriously wounded while leading his brigade. Grant promoted him to brigadier general on the spot. Chamberlain again recovered to lead his brigade in the final days of the siege of Petersburg only to be again wounded at Five Forks.

Despite the wound, Chamberlain, now a brevet major general on orders from Grant, remained in command and in the westward pursuit of the Army of Northern Virginia. When Lee's army formally surrendered their colors and arms at Appomattox Court House, Grant placed Chamberlain in charge of the proceedings. When the defeated Confederates marched past their conquerors, Chamberlain ordered his men to attention and saluted the defeated rebels. In doing so, the always chivalrous Chamberlain made the first significant effort toward peace and the reunification of the country, as Grant wished.

Chamberlain left the army in June 1866 and returned to academic duties at Bowdoin

College. His time in the classroom was brief, as the citizens of Maine elected the war hero to governor. Chamberlain led his state until 1871, when he returned to become the president of Bowdoin, where he also taught and lectured.

In 1883, Chamberlain, still suffering from effects of the 1864 wound at Petersburg where a minie ball pierced both hip bones, left Bowdoin to further recover. He was not idle long, soon becoming involved in real estate speculation in Florida. Over the next three decades he remained active in business and wrote and lectured about his Civil War experiences. Unlike Grant, William Sherman (6), and other leaders of the war who believed that "war is hell" and a very grim business, Chamberlain professed a much more idealized concept where courage, compassion, and steadfastness were tested by battle and an individual's fate was entirely given to Providence.

Chamberlain died in Portland, Maine, on February 24, 1914, and is buried in the Pine Grove Cemetery at Brunswick. While famous and well-respected in Maine, Chamberlain's reputation did not extend beyond his native state until the early part of the twentieth century when his books were published. The focus of several television documentaries on the Civil War and on Gettysburg about Chamberlain in the 1990s elevated him to one of the war's greatest heroes.

This recent attention has raised Chamberlain to a status more lofty than deserved. Although he fought well and bravely, his performance was equaled if not exceeded by many of his fellow regimental and brigade commanders. Still, Chamberlain did influence the outcome at Gettysburg and earned Grant's respect. Chamberlain's salute to the defeated rebels at Appomattox also served as a beginning point of the new United States.

80

IRWIN MCDOWELL

Union General

1818–1885

Irwin McDowell became the first Union commander of the war to obtain his rank solely through political connections instead of military experience or skills. His lack of qualifications enabled the South to win the war's first major battle at Bull Run (10), setting the stage for the long, bloody conflict.

Born on October 15, 1818, in Columbus, Ohio, McDowell received his early education in France before returning home to accept an appointment to West Point as a member of the Class of 1838. Graduating twenty-third in his class of forty-five, McDowell became an artillery officer on the Canadian border and then returned to the Military Academy as a tactics instructor in 1841.

In October 1845 he became the aide-de-camp to General John E. Wool for the duration of the Mexican War. For his service to the general at Buena Vista in February 1847, he earned a brevet promotion to captain though he never commanded any troops.

At the end of the Mexican War, McDowell transferred to the office of the adjutant general, where he performed staff duties from 1848 until 1861. During this period McDowell developed a close relationship with General Winfield Scott (20), Secretary of Treasury Salmon P. Chase, and other high-ranking Washington officials. These connections served McDowell well, for at the outbreak of the war these mentors convinced President Abraham Lincoln (2) to make him commander of the Union army assembled around Washington. Lincoln did so on May 14, 1861.

Because most people in Washington believed the war would be short and end decisively in favor of the Union, no one was concerned that the leader of the U.S. Army was a staff officer who had never so as much led a squad in the field. McDowell, though, faced a difficult situation. On the one hand, he was more comfortable behind a desk in Washington than in the saddle leading an army into combat. On the other, he was under tremendous pressure to move against the rebel army in Northern Virginia.

Despite his lack of command experience, McDowell did develop a good plan to flank and envelop the Confederate army under P. G. T. Beauregard (43) near

Manassas, Virginia. Marching out of Washington with bands playing and troops shouting "On to Richmond," the Union army looked forward to a quick victory and a short war. Unfortunately for McDowell and the Union, the battle did not go as planned. The Union army was inexperienced and poorly led at every level. McDowell moved slowly and acted indecisively, compounding the problem.

When the two armies finally fully met along Bull Run Creek on July 21, 1861, the Confederates quickly gained the advantage and the Union troops retreated back toward Washington. The retreat then turned into a rout. First Bull Run would later be described as the "best planned and worst fought" battle of the war. It made the North realize that the war would not be ended quickly and it gave the South the confidence that it would be able to successfully defend its newly declared independence.

McDowell's own description of the battle portrayed its destruction and offered a look at what both sides could anticipate. In a letter, McDowell wrote, "The scene of carnage was beyond description. Here a pile of dead and dying men; there struggling, crippled horses, and over the...hitherto peaceful fields, the surging angry waves of battle still adding its victims to the long list."

Bull Run also showed Lincoln and his cabinet that a staff officer was not the appropriate military leader to save the Union. Shortly after McDowell returned with the survivors of his army to Washington, George McClellan (51) replaced him. McDowell took command of a division under the new Union commander but remained a part of the defense of Washington rather than join McClellan's Peninsular Campaign (32).

McDowell saw little combat but advanced to lead a corps at Cedar Mountain and Second Bull Run (40) under John Pope (86) the following August. Second Bull Run proved no better for the Union or for McDowell. The Union army once again moved and reacted slowly, and their leaders' indecision led to another Confederate victory. Both Pope and McDowell blamed the debacle on subordinates, but Lincoln relieved both of them of their commands.

McDowell demanded a court of inquiry to clear his name. Although there was ample evidence of his failures at Bull Run, the court exonerated him. Some credited McDowell's political connections for the court's decisions. Others noted it might be a reward for his testimony against Fitz-John Porter, who ultimately became the battle's scapegoat when he was court-martialed for his failure to obey orders to attack Stonewall Jackson's (36) army.

Despite the court's exoneration of McDowell, leaders in Washington now fully recognized his inadequacies as a field commander. He served on various boards and commissions in Washington for the next two years before finally securing the command of the Union forces that composed the Department of the Pacific in California on July 1, 1864.

After the war, by virtue of the Regular Army seniority system rather than performance in the conflict, McDowell commanded the Department of the East and then the Division of the South during Reconstruction before returning to California in 1876. For the next six years he once again headed the Department of the Pacific, where one of his few accomplishments was improvements to the Presidio of San Francisco.

McDowell retired in October 1882 and died on May 4, 1885, in San Francisco. He is buried in the cemetery of the Presidio.

Accounts describe McDowell as a powerfully built man, frank, and agreeable. He was clearly affable with his superiors, which led to their personal interest in his career. This mentorship, however, served neither McDowell nor the Union well. McDowell, while a superior staff officer, proved to be a poor combat leader.

McDowell belongs on this list only because his ineptitude influenced the length of the war and encouraged the South to believe it could prevail. If this were a list of "great leaders" rather than influential ones, McDowell would not have been remotely considered—even as a footnote. He is the classic example of an officer who excelled in peace, and in an office environment, but failed miserably in combat.

81

RED RIVER CAMPAIGN

March 10–May 22, 1864

The Union offensive up the Red River in Louisiana during the spring of 1864 was designed to capture the state's temporary capital of Shreveport, a major supply depot and gateway to Texas. According to the plan, occupation of the area would provide great quantities of captured cotton for Northern mills while also establishing a Federal "show of force" to the French who had recently occupied Mexico.

With the tightening of the sea blockade (25), the fall of Vicksburg (7), and the Union victory at Gettysburg (4), the North had all the parts of its Anaconda Plan (27) in place for final offensives to capture Atlanta (20) and Richmond and end the war. Although the original plan did not call for an offensive west of the Mississippi after the river was under total Union control, President Abraham Lincoln (2) and his cabinet determined that it was imperative that the Union gain complete control of Louisiana and establish a presence in Texas. The reasons behind this thinking were twofold. First, Northern mills stood idle and, despite the need for manpower in the military, many civilians remained unemployed. Capturing the cotton warehouses and fertile fields of western Louisiana and eastern Texas could provide the raw materials to resume profitable manufacturing in New England.

Furthermore, there was a political need to at least establish a U.S. presence in Texas. When the Civil War began, Union units—as well as volunteers for the Confederate army—left the area of the Mexico-Texas border. With all its energies totally involved in trying to preserve the Union, the United States had no resources to enforce its Monroe Doctrine to keep outsiders out of the western hemisphere. On the pretext of collecting unpaid debts from Mexico and ending the internal unrest in the country, forces from France and Austria landed at Vera Cruz in 1863 and quickly took control. By 1864, French cavalry patrolled along the Rio Grande border with Texas. Lincoln and others feared that the French might cross the river in an attempt to occupy Texas or to ally with the Confederate army.

To gain control of the cotton and to discourage French expansion, Lincoln ordered General Nathaniel Banks (92), accompanied by a flotilla commanded by Admiral David Porter, to advance up the Red River from near Baton Rouge to capture Alexandria and then push on to occupy Shreveport. From there cotton could be

transported down the Red River to the Mississippi and then on north by sea. Further land expeditions could then push into Texas.

Banks had failed miserably in the Shenandoah Valley Campaign two years earlier and wasted much of his army in repeated charges against Port Hudson after his arrival in Louisiana. Still, he claimed victory and glory when Port Hudson finally surrendered to his siege with the news that Vicksburg had fallen. On March 10, Banks began his march toward Alexandria with seventeen thousand men. Another ten thousand soldiers commanded by Andrew J. Smith from the Vicksburg battle were to meet him there along with fifteen thousand marching south from Arkansas under General Frederick Steele.

The initial objective of the offensive was Fort De Russy, a post that guarded the Red River about twenty miles south of Alexandria. Smith's column and Porter's gunboats captured the fort on March 14. Other portions of Smith's force occupied Alexandria on the eighteenth with little resistance. Banks finally arrived on March 4, but then Steele's army from Arkansas was delayed and never participated in the campaign.

Meanwhile, General Edmund Kirby Smith (33), the Confederate commander of the region, consolidated his army around Shreveport. While preparing his defenses, he also dispatched small patrols to disrupt the Union march.

Banks slowly continued his advance while low water levels and rapids prevented Porter from getting all but his smaller boats past Alexandria. The Union army reached Natchitoches, about seventy-five miles southeast of Shreveport, on April 2. Banks delayed until April 6, and then continued his advance. Cavalry patrols skirmished with the Union column but no significant action occurred until a consolidated Confederate force of cavalry, infantry, and artillery numbering about eight thousand blocked the way near Mansfield at Sabine Cross Roads on April 8.

The Union army neared Mansfield spread out for miles along the road. Confederate general Richard Taylor saw the advantage and ordered his army to attack. Taylor quickly routed Banks's army, sending them in an unorganized retreat that abandoned the wounded, deserted supply wagons, and left artillery pieces. Banks finally reorganized his army about ten miles south at Pleasant Hill and repulsed another attack by Taylor on April 9.

Banks then ordered a retreat back down the Red River Valley, finally reaching the safety of Donaldsonville, south of Baton Rouge, on May 26. Kirby Smith and Taylor argued about whether to pursue the fleeing Union army, but, other than ordering a few harassing cavalry attacks, allowed them to escape. The Union columns, especially the one commanded by Andrew Smith, burned and looted along the way, including razing Alexandria.

Northern Louisiana remained in control of the Confederates as did Texas. Lincoln relieved Banks from command and the general never again led Union soldiers in combat. Cotton speculators who had bought up available cotton to sell to the Northern victors went broke. They would not have likely profited anyway. Early in the campaign, Kirby Smith ordered stores of cotton burned so it would not fall into Union hands. On March 14 an estimated 150,000 bales of cotton valued at more than $60 million (more than $650 million in today's dollars) went up in smoke.

By the time the dust and smoke had cleared along the Red River, the Confederates could claim complete victory. They, however, had missed the opportunity to exploit their advantage by possibly destroying Banks's army and Porter's navy to recapture New Orleans and control of the Mississippi River. With that accomplished, General William Sherman (6) would have had to retake Louisiana rather than marching to Atlanta and on through Georgia to final victory.

None of this occurred, however, and the Red River Campaign did little to preserve the Confederacy or to end the rebellion. While it provided the South one of its last great battlefield victories, its overall influence on the war was minimal, and it remains one of the least-known campaigns of the long war.

82

WILLIAM MAHONE

Confederate General

1826–1895

William Mahone earned recognition from Robert E. Lee (5) as one of the most outstanding brigade and division commanders of the Civil War. Mahone participated in every major campaign that the Army of Northern Virginia fought in, from blocking the Union's Peninsular Campaign (32) to Appomattox (37). His commands garnered reputations for their fighting abilities and esprit de corps.

Born on December 1, 1826, at Monroe, Southampton County, Virginia, Mahone joined a family in which both of his grandfathers were veterans of the War of 1812. Mahone's father, however, was a saloon keeper of limited means, and Mahone later claimed that he had financed his own education at the Virginia Military Institute with winnings from a card game. After graduating from VMI in 1847, Mahone taught for several years before joining the Norfolk and Petersburg Railroad as a civil engineer. During the next ten years he advanced to become the company's superintendent.

When Virginia seceded from the Union, Mahone volunteered for the state's militia, assuming command of the 6th Virginia Infantry Regiment as a colonel. His first action was the capture of the Norfolk Navy Yard. Promoted to brigadier general in November 1861, Mahone joined the Army of Northern Virginia in its efforts to thwart the Union's Peninsular Campaign advance and fought at Seven Pines and Malvern Hill as a part of James Longstreet's (13) corps. Mahone led his brigade in the Confederate victory at Second Bull Run (40) in August 1862, where he was severely wounded. His injury prevented his direct participation in the Antietam (1) campaign, but his brigade distinguished itself in battles for the South Mountain passes leading to Sharpsburg.

Mahone, affectionately called "Little Billy" by his troops because of his small stature, returned to lead his brigade at Fredericksburg (53), Chancellorsville (31), and Gettysburg (4). During the Battle of the Wilderness (62) in May 1864, Mahone advanced in command when his division commander replaced the wounded Longstreet. Mahone promptly led his division on a successful flanking attack.

Mahone remained in division command through the Battle of Spotsylvania Court House (65) a few weeks later and then through the battles that led to Lee's army's

encirclement at Petersburg (46). When Union engineers exploded a large charge under the Confederate Petersburg lines on July 30, 1864, it initially appeared that the Federals would pour through the gap into the Confederate rear. When ordered to retake the gap formed by the blast crater, Mahone responded, "If we don't carry it by the first attack, we will renew the assault as long as a man of us is left, or until the work is ours."

When Mahone stopped the Union advance, he had trapped enemy soldiers in the blast crater, many unable to advance or retreat. Mahone ordered his men to fire into the crater shouting, "Give 'em hell, boys."

Colonel W. H. Stuart of the 61st Virginia observed the battle and later wrote of the general, "The whole movement was under the immediate and personal direction of Mahone, and to him, above all, save the brave men who bore the muskets, belong the honor and credit of recapturing the Confederate lines."

Colonel Stuart was not alone in his recognition and praise for Mahone. Lee rewarded the general with an immediate promotion to major general. Mahone remained in command of his division for the remainder of the Petersburg Campaign and until the surrender at Appomattox (37). During the war's final months, many of the Confederate units were greatly reduced in manpower and spirit, yet Mahone's division remained unified and combat-ready to the very end.

After the war, Mahone stayed in Virginia, returning to his old job with the railroad where he expanded the company into the Norfolk and Western. He also entered politics and, following several unsuccessful campaigns, won a U.S. Senate seat in 1880. After one term he ran unsuccessfully for governor of Virginia. Mahone died in Washington, D.C., on October 8, 1895, and is buried in Blandford Cemetery at Petersburg, near the crater where he fought his greatest battle.

Mahone, with a voice described as "thin and piping," wore a long beard, slouch hat, and peg-top trousers for the entire war. His military appearance may not have been remarkable, but his performance was meritorious in every aspect. His fellow surviving officers later noted that Mahone seemed to just get better and better as a commander as the war progressed. Lee remarked that Mahone made the largest contribution of any brigade or division leader to the organization and command of the Army of Northern Virginia.

Units of both sides of the Civil War held reunions for years after the conflict ended until old age and infirmities finally brought their meetings to an end. The reunions of Mahone's commands were the best attended and most enthusiastic of all.

If this were a ranking of the "best" or "most efficient" commanders of the war, then "Little Billy" Mahone would appear near the top. Since it is a list of influential rather than best, however, his ranking is near the end. Other corps and army commanders, major battles, and events had greater influence on the war's outcome. Mahone is included not only because he was a proficient combat leader, but also because he represented the group of the brigade and division leaders who led from the front and served as the real heroes of the war. While senior commanders determined the outcomes of most battles and the war, Mahone was the type of leader for whom men wanted to serve.

83

PRESIDENTS OF THE FUTURE

1865–1901

Every president of the United States from 1865 to 1901, with a single exception, was a veteran of the American Civil War. The service of these seven men ranged from field grade officer to commander of the entire Union army. While their impact on the war varied, the conflict influenced them all and their experiences played a role in their future administrations.

Andrew Johnson (1808–1875) became the first war veteran to assume the presidency upon the assassination of Abraham Lincoln (2) in April 1865. Born into poverty in North Carolina, Johnson moved as a teenager to Tennessee, where he apprenticed to a tailor. Johnson did not learn to read and write until he married. His political career began a short time later and over the years he moved up from local to state politics as a Democrat to become governor in 1853 and U.S. senator in 1857.

At the outbreak of the Civil War, Johnson was one of only two senators from the thirteen states that seceded to form the Confederacy who refused to resign his Senate seat. He declared his loyalty to the Union. In March 1862, Lincoln rewarded Johnson by appointing him the military governor of Tennessee with a commission as a brigadier general of volunteers.

In 1864, in order to attract Democrats and border state voters, Lincoln selected Johnson as his vice president. Johnson was intoxicated at his inauguration and made little impact in his brief time as vice president. When he replaced Lincoln, Johnson promised to follow the dead president's reconstruction plan without bitterness or malice. This clashed with the desires of radical Republicans to punish the South and eventually led to a resolution of impeachment against Johnson that failed by a single vote.

Johnson served out his term but his accomplishments were few. His most influential contribution consisted of an amnesty made to all ranks and classes of former Confederates. In 1875, Johnson became the only ex-president to be reelected to the U.S. Senate, but he died shortly after taking his seat.

Johnson was an honest but unpopular president. His military career was even less remarkable. During the war he remained at his civil-military headquarters in Nashville and saw no combat. Johnson did restore the Tennessee government to federal control that later allowed the state to avoid much of the harshness of Reconstruction.

Andrew Johnson

Rutherford B. Hayes

U. S. Grant (3) replaced Johnson in the White House in 1868 and was reelected in 1872. Grant proved to be a far better military commander than a political leader, and his administration earned the reputation as being one of the most corrupt in American history. In all fairness, most of these difficulties were the result of actions on the part of his subordinates, rather than any dishonestly on the part of Grant himself.

Rutherford B. Hayes (1822–1893) became the nineteenth president of the United States upon his election in 1876. Born in Ohio, Hayes graduated from Harvard Law School and worked as an attorney and local politician upon his return home in 1850. In June 1861, Hayes accepted a commission as a major in the Ohio volunteers and fought in the Shenandoah Valley before being wounded at South Mountain in September 1862. Hayes participated in the capture of Confederate cavalryman John Hunt Morgan (88) during the latter's raid into Ohio in July 1863. By October 1864, Hayes had advanced in rank to brigadier general and joined Phil Sheridan (8) in the Shenandoah Valley Campaign (29). During the final battle of the Petersburg (46), Hayes earned a brevet promotion to major general "for gallant and distinguished service."

Hayes resigned his commission when the war ended and returned to politics in Ohio. His campaign for governor in 1875 gained him national recognition and the Republican nomination for president. In a disputed election, Hayes was finally declared the winner when he placated his Democratic opposition by promising to end Reconstruction in the South. Within sixty days of taking office he did so, gaining him the wrath of his own party.

In 1881, Hayes kept another promise he had made, that of only serving one term. He went back to Ohio, where he engaged in humanitarian causes and made a few

James Garfield

Chester Arthur

speeches before his death in 1893. Hayes's Civil War service was marked by gallantry and overall competence, but he did not distinguish himself above his fellow officers. He did his job well and from all evidence did not hold any grudges against his former enemies when he became president.

James Abram Garfield (1831–1881), another Ohio native, worked his way out of poverty to graduate from Williams College in 1856. He became a schoolteacher and local politician before he accepted a commission as a lieutenant colonel when the Civil War began. He served in Kentucky and fought at the Battle of Shiloh (18) in April 1862. Garfield joined William Rosecrans as a brigadier general and chief of staff of the Army of the Cumberland in January 1863. Garfield was one of the few Union generals to perform well at the Battle of Chickamauga (74) the following September, earning him promotion to major general.

In December 1863, Ohio voters elected Garfield to the U.S. Congress. He resigned his commission and served in the Congress and then the Senate until his election as the twentieth president in 1880. Only four months after taking office, Garfield was shot and killed by a mentally unbalanced office seeker named Charles J. Guiteau.

Garfield's military service was distinguished, and he might have gone on to even higher commands if not selected for Congress. As president he had little time to make an impression before his untimely death.

When Garfield died of his wound on September 19, 1881, his vice president Chester Alan Arthur (1829–1886) assumed the presidency. Arthur, a Vermont native and former school administrator and lawyer, briefly served as the quartermaster general of the New York militia when the Civil War began. All of his service was administrative

Benjamin Harrison

William McKinley

and, although he contributed to the reorganization of the state militia, he did not join them on the battlefield.

In 1862, Arthur left the militia and returned to his law practice. He served in several appointed positions before joining Garfield as his vice president. Arthur's presidency was unremarkable, and he retired to New York after his administration ended.

Grover Cleveland, the first and only non-veteran and Democrat to be elected president after the Civil War until the twentieth century, took office in 1884. The New Jersey native had hired a substitute to take his place in uniform during the war and explained that he did so because he was the sole supporter of his family.

In 1888 the American voters resumed electing veterans of the Civil War. Benjamin Harrison of Indiana, the grandson of President William H. Harrison, was known for his oratory skills and his abilities as an attorney. At the outbreak of the Civil War he remained in his law practice before accepting a commission as a second lieutenant in the Indiana volunteers in July 1862. That fall he fought against Braxton Bragg (60) in Kentucky and joined William Sherman (6) in his Atlanta Campaign (20) in 1864. Harrison then briefly returned to Indiana to assist in Lincoln's reelection effort before rejoining his unit for the final campaigns of 1865 in North Carolina.

During the war, Harrison steadily advanced in rank to colonel and received a brevet to brigadier general. He performed well but was generally unpopular with his commands because of his demands for discipline.

Harrison resumed his law practice in Indiana after the war, before his election to the U.S. Senate and then to the presidency. As president, Harrison supported programs for Civil War veterans and secured funding to enlarge the military, particularly the navy. Cleveland, the only president ever reelected after defeat, replaced Harrison in the election of 1892. The Civil War veteran returned home to Indiana, where he died in 1901.

In 1896 the last Civil War veteran to become president of the United States took office. William McKinley (1843–1901) volunteered as a mere teenager to become an infantry private in the Ohio volunteers when the war began. He fought in several skirmishes in western Virginia before participating as a commissary sergeant in the Battle of Antietam (1) in September 1862. At the height of the battle, Sergeant McKinley drove a mule-pulled wagon full of food and fresh coffee to soldiers on the front lines. His bravery earned him a promotion to lieutenant.

The remainder of McKinley's war service was unremarkable, and by its end he was a brevet major for his service in the Shenandoah Valley Campaign (29). He then returned to Ohio, earned a law degree, and entered politics. The most significant event of McKinley's presidency was the Spanish American War of 1898. In addition to adding valuable territory to the United States, McKinley also used the war to soothe lingering hostilities and divisions from the Civil War by appointing former Confederate officers, including Joe Wheeler (77) and Thomas Rosser (73) to positions in the U.S. Army.

In September 1901, McKinley died of an assassin's wounds in Buffalo, New York. His vice president and replacement, Theodore Roosevelt, born in 1858, had been too young to fight in the Civil War.

Of all the Civil War veterans to advance to the highest office in the United States, Grant was the only professional soldier. The others were citizens who joined to preserve the Union and then returned to civilian life after the war. With the single exception of Grant, who had a great impact on the outcome, the Civil War more heavily influenced the future presidents than did the future presidents influence the war.

84

JOHN CABELL BRECKINRIDGE

Confederate General and Secretary of War

1821–1875

John Cabell Breckinridge, a former vice president of the United States, joined the Confederacy and served as a division commander during campaigns in both the eastern and western theater campaigns. During the final months of the war, he became a member of the cabinet of President Jefferson Davis (9) as secretary of war, and he was instrumental in ensuring that much of the records of the Confederacy were not destroyed at the end of the war.

Born near Lexington, Kentucky, on January 16, 1821, Breckinridge graduated from Centre College in Danville in 1839 and attended the College of New Jersey (now Princeton University) before returning home to study law at Transylvania. Upon admission to the bar, he practiced in Iowa before returning to Lexington, where he joined the Third Kentucky Volunteers during the Mexican War.

Breckinridge began a political career in 1849 that took him to the Kentucky House of Representatives and then to the U.S. Congress for two terms in 1851. In 1856 at age thirty-five, he became the youngest vice president in U.S. history when he was elected on the ticket with James Buchanan. Breckinridge ran unsuccessfully for president in 1860, coming in second to Abraham Lincoln (2) in a four-man field. Elected to the Senate from his home state, Breckinridge worked to prevent the secession of the Southern states. After the war began, he expressed his support for the Confederacy and was formally expelled from the Senate on December 4, 1861.

Breckinridge was not present for his expulsion. He had departed Washington in October to accept a commission as a brigadier general in the Confederate army. In April 1862, the former vice president commanded the reserves at Shiloh (18), where he was wounded. Promoted to major general, he participated in the attack against Port Hudson, Louisiana, in March 1863; served as a division commander in the Vicksburg (7) campaign the following summer; and again led a division at Chickamauga (74) in September.

Breckinridge then transferred to the eastern theater, and in May 1864 he participated in the Battle of New Market, where he incorporated the cadets of the nearby Virginia Military Academy into his unit. Reluctant to use the young teens as soldiers, he finally was forced by manpower shortages to commit them to the battle. As he did so, he sadly stated, "Put the boys in...and may God forgive me for the order."

Breckinridge then fought with Robert E. Lee (5) at Cold Harbor (59) in June 1864 and rode with Jubal Early (19) on his raid toward Washington in July.

In September 1864, Breckinridge assumed command of the Department of Southwest Virginia, where he participated in several small battles before joining the major fight at Nashville (87) in December. On February 4, 1865, President Davis called Breckinridge to Richmond to assume the duties of secretary of war. With U. S. Grant (3) threatening the Confederate capital and losses mounting throughout the South, Breckinridge realized the war was nearing an end. He urged efforts for an honorable surrender, but Davis overruled his secretary of war, vowing to fight to the bitter end.

As Union troops neared Richmond in early April, Breckinridge made his most significant contribution to the war's history. Many in the Confederate government wanted to destroy its records rather than let them fall into enemy hands. Breckinridge, realizing that the South would once again be part of the Union, arranged for many of the records—both civilian and military—to be captured intact rather than be destroyed. These documents remain today as critical elements in the official history of the Confederate States of America.

Although Breckinridge saw to the preservation of the Confederate records, he doubted his own safety if captured by the Union army. Fearing that he would be tried as a traitor, he fled Richmond with Davis. In the confusion of the journey, Breckinridge became separated from the Confederate president, thus avoiding capture with Davis and his party.

Breckinridge and a small group made their way down the Florida coast and then escaped from the Keys to Cuba in a small boat. From Havana he sailed to England and later to Canada before again returning to England. In 1869 the United States granted amnesty to its former vice president. Breckinridge returned to Lexington, where townspeople greeted him as a hero and where he practiced law before accepting a position with the Elizabethtown, Lexington, and Big Sandy Railroad Company. Although encouraged to return to politics, he turned down all offers. The nearest he came to the political arena again was to actively speak out against the activities of the Ku Klux Klan. Breckinridge died on May 17, 1875, in Lexington. He is buried in the city cemetery.

Breckinridge was a great politician who did his best to prevent the war between the states. Once the conflict began, he proved himself a more than adequate division commander who understood that politics were insurmountable to war. In the Shenandoah Valley in March 1864, he stated, "The time for speeches has passed…the hour for action has arrived."

Breckinridge would likely have earned a ranking nearer the end of this list, or perhaps not all, if his influence were solely based on his battlefield performance. While his combat leadership was satisfactory, it was little different than that of a host of leaders in both gray and blue uniforms. Instead, Breckinridge earns his ranking for his actions in Richmond in the war's final days when he saw to it that the Confederate archives would be preserved for the ages rather than go up in smoke. This is even more remarkable when it is considered that portions of these records confirmed what many in the North thought was treason on the part of Breckinridge.

85

ALBERT SIDNEY JOHNSTON

Confederate General

1803–1862

At the outbreak of the Civil War, Americans in both the North and the South believed that Albert Sidney Johnston was the finest officer in uniform. When offered high rank in both armies, Johnston chose the Confederacy, only to face defeat in his early battles and death in his only significant victory.

Born on February 2, 1803, in Washington, Kentucky, as the youngest son of a country physician and native of Connecticut, Johnston graduated eighth of forty-one in the West Point Class of 1826. For the next eight years he served as an infantry officer and saw his first combat in the Black Hawk War. He resigned his commission in 1834 to care for his terminally ill wife. Upon her death in 1835, he briefly farmed near St. Louis, Missouri, before moving to Texas, where he joined that newly declared independent country's army as a private.

Within a year he rose to the rank of the army's senior general and survived a serious wound suffered in a duel with a rival officer. After Texas successfully defended its independence from Mexico, Johnston served as the republic's secretary of war. When Texas joined the United States, he accepted a commission as a colonel in the Texas militia and fought in the Mexican War under General Zachary Taylor. Taylor later remarked that Johnston was "the best soldier he ever commanded."

Johnston returned to his farm in Texas after the Mexican War but had little success tilling the soil. In 1849 he requested reinstatement in the army and his old admirer Taylor, now the president of the United States, secured him a commission as a major. In 1855, Johnston took command of the 2nd U.S. Cavalry as a colonel and led the arduous Mormon Expedition in 1857 to maintain Utah as a U.S. territory. For two years he remained in Utah as a brigadier general before transferring to the Department of the Pacific.

After the firing on Fort Sumter (50), the federal government offered Johnston the position of second in command of the entire U.S. Army. He turned down the offer and on May 3, 1861, Johnston submitted his resignation to the U.S. War Department. Out of a sense of duty and a lingering loyalty to the Union, he remained in command until a proper replacement arrived to look after American interests.

Despite his misgivings about secession, Johnston had no reservations about joining the Confederacy and the war. En route to Richmond he wrote to his wife from New Mexico Territory on July 1, 1861, "Never before have I had so many probabilities of success and better grounds for the belief that my star will continue to be in ascendant."

As a result of his waiting in California, Johnston did not arrive back east until the following August 1861. Upon his arrival, President Jefferson Davis (9) appointed him general and assigned him command of the Western Department that included the states west of those on the Atlantic and north of those on the Gulf of Mexico.

Johnston was immediately faced by enemy forces that outnumbered him two to one. His situation was compounded by a lack of supplies and replacement personnel. His situation became more precarious when subordinate commands were defeated at Forts Henry and Donelson (35) in February 1862. Forced out of Kentucky and Tennessee, Johnston consolidated his command at Corinth, Mississippi.

In April, Johnston moved his army against Union concentrations commanded by U. S. Grant (3) at Shiloh (18), Tennessee. When informed by his subordinates on April 5 that they were outnumbered by the Union forces, Johnston, who understood the importance of the pending fight, replied, "We must this day conquer or perish." He then added, "I would fight them if they were a million."

On the morning of April 6, Johnston personally led an attack that took the Union army defending Shiloh by surprise. By afternoon the Federal forces were in retreat back toward Pittsburg Landing on the Tennessee River. Johnston continued to lead the attack before being struck by a rifle bullet in the thigh at about 2:30 in the afternoon. The general thought the wound to be minor and continued in command after refusing medical treatment. A short time later he bled to death. Lacking Johnston's leadership and facing reinforcements rallying to Grant's side, the Confederate army withdrew from the battlefield.

Johnston's body was taken to New Orleans for burial. After the war his remains were moved to the State Cemetery in Austin, Texas. General Phil Sheridan (8) forbade any public ceremony for the reburial but did not attempt to stop the large crowd that silently followed the body through the streets.

President Jefferson Davis declared that Johnston was "the greatest man, civil or military, Confederate or Federal." Conjecture suggests that had Johnston lived, his accomplishments would have exceeded those of Robert E. Lee (5). Johnston might have even changed the outcome of the war.

It is difficult to evaluate the potential of a general who spent the last three years of the war in the grave rather than on the battlefield. It is doubtful that he could have lived up to the expectations, for several reasons. The Western front never received the attention or support from Richmond that Lee's Army of Northern Virginia did. Also, Johnston had to face two of the war's best generals in Grant and William Sherman (6). It is equally noteworthy that Johnston was already nearly sixty years of age when he was killed. No one knows if he would have been able to physically sustain many more years of battle.

In his memoirs, Grant differed with Davis and others about Johnston, writing that while the general was bold, he was also overrated. Grant concluded that Johnston was "vacillating and undecided in his actions."

An evaluation of Johnston must rest on his performance and on his influence, not on his potential. For that reason he stands near the end of this list.

86

JOHN POPE

Union General

1822–1892

As one of the Civil War's most controversial generals, John Pope won several important victories in the West early in the conflict. However, his success and his political connections elevated him to a level of command far beyond his capabilities. Ultimately, Pope alienated his own officers and soldiers and became one of the most hated Union commanders in both the North and the South.

Pope was born on March 16, 1822, in Louisville, Kentucky, to an influential family that included senators and judges who claimed George Washington in the family lineage. He graduated from West Point ranking number seventeen of fifty-six in the Class of 1842. As an engineer officer, Pope conducted survey work in Florida and the Northeast before joining Zachary Taylor's army in Mexico, where he earned two brevet promotions.

After the Mexican War, Pope continued survey and other engineer operations in the Northwest and Far West. In 1861 he commanded Abraham Lincoln's (2) honor guard at the president's first inauguration—a position Pope probably gained from his relation by marriage to Mary Todd Lincoln. This connection also was influential in his advance in rank from captain to brigadier general at the outbreak of the Civil War.

Even though his promotion resulted from political connections, Pope initially proved to be more than worthy of the rank. Assigned to the Western front, Pope led operations in March and April 1862 that captured the Confederate positions of New Madrid and Island Number 10 in Missouri, thus opening the way for Union dominance of the Mississippi River. Promoted to major general, he then commanded the Union left wing in the advance against Corinth, Mississippi, the following May.

Desperate for a commander who could defeat Robert E. Lee (5) in Virginia, President Lincoln called Pope to Washington in June. George McClellan (51) was to remain in command on the Peninsula, but Pope would assume responsibility for the rest of the Union army in Virginia and the defense of the capital. Pope's personal connections with Lincoln likely influenced the decision, but his performance in the war's first year definitely merited the promotion.

Unfortunately for Pope and the Union, the general's assumption of command did not go well. Soon after arriving in the East, he announced he would be an active, frontline commander with his "headquarters in the saddle." Critics who opposed his promotion sarcastically responded that "Pope's headquarters would be in his hindquarters."

Pope's promotion jumped him over several officers who had previously been senior to him. Pope soon alienated them—and others—when he compared them unfavorably to the soldiers he had commanded in the West. He then angered the enlisted men of his new command when he issued a general order on July 14, 1862, that criticized their past performance.

On this path of generating hostility, Pope included the South when he offered his ideas about how occupied areas of the South should be treated and about how ultimately the defeated rebels should be punished. The Southern press widely published his comments, and even the gentlemanly Robert E. Lee (5) expressed anger about Pope's ideas.

So before firing his first shot or directing his first artillery barrage in Virginia, Pope managed to earn the disfavor and even the hatred of his own army as well as that of his enemy. Pope soon proved to be no better in direct command of a large army in battle than he was in his personal relations with his subordinates and opponents.

Stonewall Jackson (36) defeated part of Pope's army at Cedar Mountain, Virginia, on August 9, allowing Lee to encircle Pope's main force. On August 27 the

Confederates captured the primary Union supply depot at Manassas, providing needed food and ammunition. The next day Lee attacked and soundly defeated Pope's main force in what became known as the Battle of Second Bull Run (40). Once again the Union army retreated in disarray back to Washington in a manner similar to that of their first defeat in the same area a year earlier.

Pope immediately placed the blame for the debacle on his subordinates. He accused many of his officers of failing to cooperate or to follow his orders. He relieved Major General Fitz-John Porter, commander of the Union V Corps, for disobedience, disloyalty, and misconduct in the face of the army and had him dismissed from the army, despite the fact that Porter's orders were considered impossible to carry out.

Neither casting blame elsewhere nor his continued political connections were enough to preserve Pope's command. Lincoln relieved him on September 2 and returned what was left of Pope's army to McClellan. A few weeks later Pope took command of the Department of the Northwest—a thousand miles from the front lines with the rebels. He remained there for the rest of the war and served well, including putting down an uprising of Sioux Indians in Minnesota.

Pope's seniority and continuing political connections allowed him to remain on active duty after the war ended. His assignments ranged from the Southeast to the Far West and included his establishing Fort Hayes, Kansas, and commanding the Department of California. Pope retired in 1886 and died in Sandusky, Ohio, on September 23, 1892. He is buried in Bellefontaine Cemetery in St. Louis, Missouri.

Contemporaries of Pope described him as a good horseman, soldierly, and even dashing and handsome. No one, however, expressed any particular respect or affection for the outspoken general.

Pope performed well in command of small units in the West. However, he never recovered from the statements he made on assumption of command, and he proved inept in command of a large army. Pope, of course, was not alone in his failure to lead the Union army to victory and was but one of a long line of unsuccessful generals like McClellan (51), Burnside (57), and Hooker (48). All of these leaders rank above Pope, however, because not only did Pope encounter defeat on the battlefield, but also he generated the contempt of his own officers and men while his ineptness gave the Confederacy victories and hope.

87

NASHVILLE

December 15–16, 1864

The Union army severely wounded the Army of Tennessee led by John Bell Hood (45) at the Battle of Franklin (15) on November 30, 1864. Despite his losses, Hood continued to advance in hopes of drawing William Sherman (6) away from Atlanta, but, when confronted by a large army at Nashville, he had to take defensive positions. On December 15, the Union forces commanded by George Thomas (11) left Nashville and attacked Hood. After a two-day battle, what was left of the Army of Tennessee was in retreat and was never again an effective fighting force.

When Sherman captured Atlanta (20) in September 1864, Confederate leaders feared that the Union army would push on toward the Atlantic and then turn northward to join U. S. Grant (3) in capturing Richmond. In a campaign to divert Sherman back toward Tennessee, Hood moved around Atlanta and through Alabama to cut the Union supply lines from Chattanooga. He then headed on to Nashville. Sherman followed for a while, but then returned to Atlanta to prepare for his March to the Sea (16). He left a force under John Schofield to block Hood and to join Thomas if necessary to defend Nashville.

The armies of Hood, Schofield, and Thomas each had about thirty thousand men. The Confederate commander knew his best option was to defeat the Union force following him from Atlanta before it could join the army at Nashville. Hood almost cut off Schofield at Spring Hill on November 29, but the Federals safely moved to Franklin, about eighteen miles south of Nashville. Hood attacked on November 30 and drove Schofield from Franklin, but the victory was costly in the loss of men and leaders.

Hood, always a driven, aggressive commander, pushed on toward Nashville despite his losses. When he neared Nashville, however, he saw that he was not only outnumbered about two to one, but also that Union engineers had well fortified the city. On December 2, Hood placed his army on a line of hills paralleling Union defenses on Nashville's southern side. There he prepared his own fortifications. Too weak to attack, Hood hoped for reinforcements from Texas, or at least to be able to weaken the Union force if they assaulted his defenses.

Thomas began a deliberate plan to do just what Hood desired. To his superiors back east who were frustrated with their own siege of Petersburg (46), it seemed that

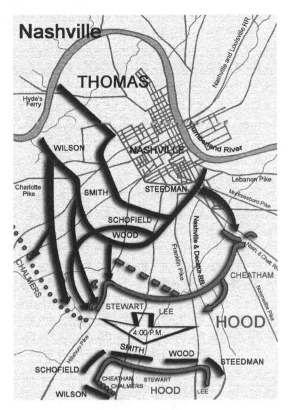

Thomas, who had the well-deserved reputation as one of the better Union generals, was too deliberate. On December 9, Grant sent Thomas a message, "I have as much confidence in your conducting a battle rightly as I have in any other officer, but it has seemed to me that you have been slow, and I have no explanation of affairs to convince me otherwise."

Thomas responded, "I could not concentrate my troops and get their transportation in order in shorter time than it has been done."

At daylight on December 15, Union infantry struck Hood's right flank. About noon, more Union troops struck the Confederate left flank. With both flanks threatened—and finally realizing that he was occupying a line too long for his number of troops—Hood withdrew during the night. On a ridgeline about two miles south of his original positions, Hood again prepared defenses. The Union forces followed and threw up their defensive works about 250 yards from the rebels.

At 3:30 p.m. the next day, the Confederate right flank stopped a furious attack. However, Hood's left flank gave way under a charge about the same time. Federal troops penetrated into Hood's rear, collapsing his entire line. Only a heavy rain and the approach of darkness allowed the surviving Confederates to escape the battlefield.

For the next ten days Thomas pursued Hood as the Confederates fled south. Not until the rebels crossed the Tennessee River into Mississippi did the Union army turn back toward Nashville. From his headquarters in Tupelo, Hood requested, and was granted, relief of command. Neither he nor the Army of Tennessee would play significant roles for the remainder of the war.

Casualties at the Battle of Nashville were fairly low considering the number of participants and the importance of the fight. Hood lost about forty-four hundred of his army of thirty-one thousand while Thomas's losses numbered about twenty-two hundred of forty-nine thousand Union participants.

The Battle of Nashville was the last gasp of the Confederacy in the Tennessee-Georgia-Deep South region. Sherman was already nearing Savannah when Hood began his retreat. Only Lee in Virginia, Joseph Johnston (17) in the Carolinas, and Kirby Smith (33) in Texas kept the Confederacy from toppling.

The battle outside Nashville ended the career of Hood as well as the Army of Tennessee. It, however, was actually the final act in a bloody drama where the climax had already occurred at Franklin a few weeks earlier. The Battle of Franklin severely wounded Hood's army and is, therefore, more influential and higher ranked. Nashville provided the coup de grace.

Hood, who earned his rank and reputation as commander of the Texas Brigade, had adopted "The Yellow Rose of Texas" as one of his marching songs. This continued in the Army of Tennessee, but as his soldiers retreated from Nashville they knew their glory days were far behind them. Instead of singing about the girl they left behind, they sang of their defeat and longing for the return of their previous commander, Joe Johnston.

As the rebels withdrew southward in the icy winter, they sang, "And now I'm going southward, for my heart is full of woe / I'm going back to Georgia, to find my Uncle Joe / You may sing about your dearest maid, and sing of Rosalie / But the gallant Hood of Texas, played hell in Tennessee."

88

JOHN HUNT MORGAN

Confederate General

1825–1864

John Hunt Morgan, one of the most influential Confederate raiders, harassed Union rear areas and captured or destroyed arms and supplies. His Ohio raid in the summer of 1863 penetrated farther into U.S. territory than any other Confederate operation.

Born in Huntsville, Alabama, on June 1, 1825, Morgan moved at age six to Lexington, Kentucky, where he was reared by his maternal grandparents. He attended Transylvania College but dropped out after participating in a duel. He enlisted in the army for the Mexican War. After combat service in Mexico, he left the army in 1847 and returned to Lexington, where he became a merchant and owner of a hemp factory.

In 1857, Morgan organized a local militia unit known as the Lexington Rifles that had sympathies with the growing independence movement in the South. Kentucky remained neutral when the Civil War began, but Morgan hoisted a Confederate flag above his factory. He also transferred his militia's arms to the South, and when Union authorities arrived to confiscate them, they found only empty crates. The federal authorities issued an arrest warrant for Morgan and confiscated his factory.

When Morgan's first wife died in July 1861, he followed his rifles south and offered his services to the newly declared Confederate States. He then led a squadron as a captain in mostly guerrilla-type operations in Kentucky and participated in the Battle of Shiloh (18) in April 1862 as a colonel in command of regular cavalry.

In July 1862, Morgan began a series of raids behind Union lines that brought him to the front pages of newspapers in the South as well as the North. Raiding across Tennessee and into Kentucky, Morgan and his eight hundred horsemen, along with another column led by Nathan Bedford Forrest (21), slowed and demoralized the Union advance toward Chattanooga (12). In twenty-four days, Morgan's raiders rode more than a thousand miles and captured and paroled twelve hundred prisoners.

By October 1862, Morgan commanded a cavalry brigade of the Army of Tennessee and covered the retreat from his hometown of Lexington. Using his detailed knowledge of the surrounding countryside, Morgan led eighteen hundred horsemen on a raid that reentered Lexington and then continued operations along Union supply and communications lines to slow their pursuit of the retreating Confederates.

Morgan returned to Confederate lines near Carthage, Tennessee, only long enough to rest and refit his horses and men. On December 21, Morgan, now a brigadier general, led his third operation—his famous "Christmas Raid"—north to cut the Louisville & Nashville Railroad, which provided the primary supply lines to the Union army led by General William S. Rosecrans. Morgan successfully destroyed the rail line north of Munfordville. By the time he returned to friendly lines on January 1, 1863, he had captured more than eighteen hundred Union soldiers and destroyed $2 million in supplies at the loss of only two killed and twenty-four wounded in his own command.

Morgan's three successful raids directly damaged the Union army by capturing its men and destroying its supplies. More importantly, each of the raids had diverted thousands of Union soldiers from their advance against the regular Confederate lines, providing the South additional time for preparation of defenses. Morgan's name was now well-known in the North, where he was cursed at best as a guerrilla and at worst as a bandit. Southerners, however, hailed him as a hero, and he received an official thanks from the Confederate Congress for his accomplishments.

When Morgan was not raiding behind enemy lines, he performed as regular cavalry, usually in a reconnaissance role. His performance in this conventional cavalry mode was rather routine and unmarked by significant accomplishments. Morgan and his superiors knew that his greatest contributions were as a raider, and it was not long before he once again struck out to raise havoc in the Union rear.

In early June 1863, General Braxton Bragg (60) ordered Morgan to return to Kentucky to slow Rosecran's newest offensive toward Chattanooga. Morgan asked permission to extend his operation into Ohio, but Bragg ordered him to limit his operations to Kentucky. On July 2, Morgan crossed into Union territory at the head of twenty-five hundred cavalrymen. Over the next week Morgan burned and captured Union stores as he advanced northward.

Morgan's advance guard captured several steamboats when they reached the Ohio River. Using the vessels, Morgan ignored his orders from Bragg and crossed the river into Indiana. Morgan defied his orders for several other reasons. He firmly believed that a deep penetration into Union territory would disrupt the Federal offensive on both the Western and Eastern fronts. Morgan did not think of the raid as a suicide mission, but rather believed he could raid north and eastward to eventually link up with Robert E. Lee (5), whom he knew was advancing toward Gettysburg (4) in Pennsylvania. He also thought it would provide a most-needed morale boost to the Confederacy and, of course, he was not opposed to adding to his personal glory.

Opposed only by home guards, Corydon, Indiana, was easy prey for Morgan when he arrived there on July 9. He then turned east toward Cincinnati, Ohio, where the very rumor of Morgan set the entire town in a panic. Morgan bypassed the city and struck out northeast. Initially, the Confederate raider faced only poorly trained and poorly armed home guards, but over the next two weeks thousands of regular Union soldiers came in pursuit. Morgan reached the Ohio River on the border with Pennsylvania only to find it flooded by recent rains and patrolled by Union gunboats. Unable to cross, he continued northward where most of his command was captured at Buffington Island in Meigs County on July 19.

Morgan and about three hundred of his cavalrymen managed to escape but were still unable to cross into Pennsylvania. On July 26 they finally surrendered at Salineville after advancing to ninety miles south of Lake Erie.

The raiders were confined at a civilian prison in Columbus, Ohio, but on November 26, Morgan and several of his men tunneled out of their cells and escaped. Confederate newspapers once again hailed Morgan as a hero, but his commanders were not happy with his failure to follow orders. However, his skills as a raider were still needed, and in April 1864 he was back in command of a cavalry brigade raiding into occupied Kentucky.

This operation did not match Morgan's previous successes and his reputation suffered. Some critics believe he was too careful because of his recent remarriage. More realistic observers credit the increase in Union soldiers throughout the region. Accusations that his soldiers looted from civilians as well as the enemy also plagued Morgan.

In the summer of 1864, Morgan was accused of robbing a bank in Mt. Sterling, Kentucky. While it was a fact that some of his men had committed the crime, there was no evidence that Morgan knew about it or condoned the action. Nevertheless, he stayed at the home of a friend in Greeneville, Tennessee, while he tried to clear his name. A Union cavalry raid struck the town on September 4, 1864. When Morgan attempted to escape, he was shot and killed. He was eventually buried in Lexington.

The South mourned Morgan as one of its great heroes. Along with J. E. B. Stuart (23), who had been killed the previous May, he was widely praised among Southern civilians as one of the greatest cavalry leaders of the war. Confederate military leaders, while saddened by the loss, were aware that by the time of his death his current operations were accomplishing little. Because he had failed to follow orders, they doubted his reliability.

Doubtless, Morgan was an outstanding leader of cavalry, but there is more than enough evidence that he was as interested in personal fame as in the rebellion. His raids did influence campaigns but did not stop or defeat any Union operation. At best, Morgan was a nuisance to the regular Union army. His lasting legacy was his raid across the Ohio River. Yet while it thoroughly terrorized the people of Indiana and Ohio, it had little lasting effect.

Morgan's deeds were good for the newspapers and morale, but his fame exceeded his actual impact. His significance in the war was far overshadowed by that of Stuart and Forrest on his own side, as well as by Phil Sheridan (8) in the North. His overall contributions to the war were not even in the same category as the principal leaders like Lee, Jackson, Grant, and Sherman.

89

GEORGE STONEMAN

Union General

1822–1894

George Stoneman experienced great successes and extreme failures in his service as a Union cavalry leader and corps commander. Several of his horse-mounted raids in Confederate-held territory greatly disrupted rebel lines of communications and boosted the morale of Union soldiers and civilians. Unfortunately for Stoneman, another raid ended disastrously, resulting in Stoneman's being the highest-ranking Union officer captured in the war.

Born on August 22, 1822, on his family's farm in western New York near the village of Busti, Stoneman earned an appointment to the Military Academy as a member of the Class of 1846. Stonewall Jackson (36) was his roommate and George McClellan (51) a classmate. After graduating thirty-third of fifty-nine cadets, he joined the Mormon Battalion in its celebrated, grueling march from Fort Leavenworth, Kansas, to San Diego, California, as a part of the Mexican War.

For the next fifteen years Stoneman served in the Southwest where he fought against the Indians and assisted in the survey of California's Sierra Nevada range. At the outbreak of the Civil War, he was in command of Fort Brown, Texas, on the Rio Grande. When Confederate officials, including his former commander, General David Twigs, demanded that he surrender his garrison, Stoneman refused and escaped with most of his men to Union lines.

When his old classmate McClellan assumed command of the Army of the Potomac in August 1861, he promoted his former fellow classmate. Stoneman then became brigadier general in charge of the cavalry. McClellan, however, did not unify his cavalry command, and as a result, Stoneman's appointment was more symbolic that real. One of the many factors that led to McClellan's failures and relief from command was his decision to parcel out his horsemen in small detachments to subordinate units rather than leave them under Stoneman. The consequence was that Stoneman's rebel counterpart, J. E. B. Stuart (23) was able to literally ride circles around the Union army.

In September 1862, Stoneman took command of a division and fought well enough to gain command of a corps at Fredericksburg (53) the following

December. His corps performed well in the battle, and when Joe Hooker (48) assumed command of the Army of the Potomac after the fight, he called upon Stoneman to command the army's cavalry once more. Hooker, unlike McClellan, understood the importance of a united cavalry unit and placed most of his horse-mounted units under Stoneman's command.

Part of Hooker's plan for the Chancellorsville (31) campaign was for his cavalry to raid behind rebel lines in Virginia to divert Robert E. Lee's (5) own cavalry and to disrupt Confederate lines of communications. "Stoneman's Raid" did cause consternation in Richmond, which rejuvenated the morale of Northern soldiers and civilians alike who were still reeling from their defeat at Fredericksburg. However, moral victory was all the raid actually accomplished. It deprived Lee of neither his cavalry nor supplies and left Hooker without a greatly needed reconnaissance asset prior to and during the battle at Chancellorsville.

When Hooker failed to achieve victory at Chancellorsville, he looked for a scapegoat and quickly placed blame on Stoneman. Hooker replaced the cavalry leader, transferring him to Washington on what he claimed were medical grounds. Stoneman's only medical problem was an extreme case of hemorrhoids, an uncomfortable condition for a cavalry leader but not one that should have cost him his command.

Blaming his cavalry commander did not save Hooker his job, but doing so did remove Stoneman from the battlefield. From July 1863 through January 1864, Stoneman headed the Cavalry Bureau, an administrative position in Washington in charge of procuring horses and training new cavalrymen.

Stoneman still had many friends and admirers in the army and in February 1864 he gained the command of the cavalry of the Army of the Ohio in William Sherman's (6) advance against Atlanta. During the campaign Sherman ordered Stoneman to conduct another raid behind enemy lines to cut the rail line at Macon. Stoneman requested and received permission to extend his raid to the notorious rebel prisoner of war camp at nearby Andersonville (42).

The raid destroyed some rebel supplies, but the Confederate cavalry and local militias reacted quickly to the invasion. Outside of Macon the rebels surrounded Stoneman's force. Stoneman managed to fight a rearguard action that allowed the majority of his force to break out and escape, but he and seven hundred of his men were captured. As a major general, Stoneman gained the unenviable title of the Union's highest-ranking prisoner of the war.

Sherman accepted the blame for the capture of the cavalry commander and within a few months arranged for his exchange and freedom. Stoneman rejoined Sherman in the final offensive into Virginia. In late December 1864, Stoneman assisted in driving the Confederates out of eastern Tennessee and then led still another cavalry raid behind enemy lines and destroyed critical saltworks and lead mines in western Virginia. During the final month of the war, Stoneman conducted his last cavalry raid when he cut several Confederate railroad lines and began closing in on President Jefferson Davis's (9) escape column before another Union cavalry unit captured the rebel leader.

After the war, Stoneman administered occupied Memphis where a riot broke out on May 1, 1865, between black soldiers and black civilians on one side and Irish immigrants on the other. A congressional investigation report later commended Stoneman for how he handled the incident, but, in a manner typical of his up-and-down career, it also rebuked him for not taking action sooner. In 1866 Stoneman headed Reconstruction efforts in Petersburg, Virginia, where he developed the reputation as a fair, and even easy, administrator to the defeated rebels.

Stoneman mustered out of his position as a major general of volunteers and reverted to his rank of lieutenant colonel in the Regular Army in September 1866. By 1870 he had advanced to the rank of full colonel in command of U.S. troops in Arizona. In September of the following year he retired, again amid some controversy about his failure to quell several Indian uprisings. He moved his family to the San Gabriel Valley in California.

Stoneman served as his adopted state's railroad commissioner from 1876 to 1878 and was elected governor in 1882. Once again, after a great success, he experienced failure. After four years he lost the support of his party and was not nominated to run for a second term. About this same time his home burned and, without insurance, Stoneman was impoverished.

As a result, Stoneman was forced to return to western New York to live with family members. He died of a stroke on September 5, 1894, and is buried in Bentley Cemetery in Lakewood, near his birthplace. His simple headstone provides a brief history of his military service, but appropriate to the ups and downs of his career, it contains a misspelling of Potomac.

At six feet, four inches in height, Stoneman was a quiet, serious man who preferred to think rather than talk. When he was at his best, he was rivaled in the North only by Sheridan as a leader of cavalry. Unfortunately, fate seemed often to turn against Stoneman despite his best efforts. Thus his ranking on this list is rather low, but Stoneman remains one of those generals who rarely had difficulty finding a command or soldiers to ride with him.

90

USS *KEARSARGE* VS. CSS *ALABAMA*

June 19, 1864

The victory by the USS *Kearsarge* over the CSS *Alabama* off the coast of France on June 19, 1864, sent the Confederate's most famous and successful sea raider to the bottom of the sea. Although the sinking of the *Alabama* did not significantly contribute to the outcome of the Civil War, it did further lower the already deteriorating morale of the Confederate States. It also served as an example of the difficulties in enforcing neutrality laws with European countries and set the stage for legal claims by the United States against the British for their support of the Confederate navy.

The blockade of the South that the Union conducted under its Anaconda Plan (27) steadily reduced the commercial shipping in and out of the rebel states to a trickle. Other than the unsuccessful effort by the ironclad *Virginia* to break the blockade off Hampton Roads (72) in 1862, the Confederate navy was limited in its offensive actions against the United States on the high seas. To "show the flag," harass U.S. commercial shipping, and capture merchant vessels as "prizes," the Confederacy purchased and commissioned several ships from the English. These ships sailed in seas around the world as they captured or sank merchant vessels while generally avoiding the U.S. Navy.

The most successful and best known of these Confederate raiders was the *Alabama.* James D. Bullock, the Confederate naval agent in Europe, contracted for a 1,050 ton ship powered by both steam engines and sails early in 1862. It would be built by funds from the Confederate States as well as those contributed by English supporters of the rebellion. Charles F. Adams, the U.S. minister in London, learned of the contract and protested that the ship's construction violated Britain's 1861 declaration of neutrality. The Confederate agent and the English shipbuilders solved the problem by christening the ship as the *Enrica* and launching the vessel without armament on July 29, 1862. Captain Raphael Semmes and crew of the Confederate navy met the ship at sea, renamed it the *Alabama,* and took on cannons and other war supplies near the Azores.

Semmes, a native of Maryland, had served in the U.S. Navy for thirty-five years before resigning his commission to join the Confederacy. In the early days of the war he exploited the greed of some Union merchants and purchased much-needed fuses and ammunition to transport to the South. He then took command of the cruiser *Sumter* and, during a six-month cruise, captured eighteen prizes. Early in 1862 the Union navy blockaded the *Sumter* in the neutral harbor of Gibraltar, forcing Semmes to abandon the vessel and make his way to England and eventually to the *Alabama.*

Over the next twenty-one months the *Alabama* sailed more than seventy-five thousand miles as it captured, sank, or burned sixty-nine Union ships. Except for a brief visit to Galveston, Texas, after running the blockade, the *Alabama* never entered a Confederate port. Instead, it visited ports in Brazil, South Africa, Singapore, and France to refit and rearm, and to land prisoners.

On June 11, 1864, the Confederate raider anchored in the French harbor of Cherbourg with intentions of conducting much-needed maintenance. Semmes planned to stay in port for several months but the French, prodded by the U.S. representative, informed the rebel captain that the neutrality laws would limit his stay. Meanwhile, the USS *Kearsarge,* which had been looking for the raider, arrived off shore. The *Kearsarge,* named for a New Hampshire mountain, had joined the U.S. fleet upon its launch in 1861. Powered by steam and sails, the 1,031-ton vessel, captained by Charles W. Pickering, had participated in the blockade of the *Sumter* in 1862.

Semmes, lacking protection from the French but not wanting to lose the *Alabama* to a blockade as he had the *Sumter,* decided to fight. He had little choice, but he also relished the opportunity to attack a ship flying the flag that had chased him around the world. He announced to one of his lieutenants, "Although the Confederate government has ordered me to avoid engagement with the enemy cruisers, I am tired of running from that flaunting flag."

On the morning of June 19 the *Alabama* sailed out of Cherbourg. More than fifteen thousand civilians, sailors, and government officials lined the high points of the town, gathered on the breakwater, and even scaled the rigging of ships in port to observe the pending battle. At 10:57 a.m. the 150-man crew of the Confederate raider opened fire with its seven guns. The eight guns manned by the 162-man crew of the Union vessel returned fire. For the next hour the two ships exchanged fire at ranges of a quarter- to a half-mile. The *Alabama,* in poor condition from its long term at sea without maintenance, began to sink under the fire from the Union ship. In addition to its better condition, the *Kearsarge* also had the advantage of iron sheet chains that protected its most vulnerable parts.

Semmes attempted to sail his stricken vessel to beach it on the French coast, but the *Alabama* slipped beneath the waves near the battle area. The Confederate captain and forty of his crew were rescued by the *Deerhound,* a British yacht that had sailed nearby

to observe the battle. Nine of the *Alabama* crew died in the battle; another twenty-one were wounded. Casualties aboard the *Kearsarge* totaled only one dead and two wounded.

Semmes made his way from England back to the Confederate States where he was welcomed as a hero and placed in command of war ships on the James River defending Richmond. He was briefly imprisoned after the war and, when released, practiced law and wrote. In his reports on the loss of the *Alabama,* he reported, "I must say that on my vessel every officer and man did his duty, bravely and worthily, and I may add 'All is lost save honor.'" Still hailed as the South's greatest sea captain, he died at Point Clear, Alabama, in 1877. In 1984, French divers discovered the remains of the *Alabama* in about 195 feet of water off Cherbourg. The sunken vessel today is a protected site under a joint French-American authority.

The *Kearsarge* sailed from France to the Caribbean to continue its offensive against Confederate raiders. The ship was in port at Boston for repairs when the war ended, but it returned to sea for another thirty years of honorable service to the United States. On February 2, 1894, the *Kearsarge* ran aground and was destroyed on Roncador Reef off Central America without loss of life.

After the war, the United States demanded $101 million (about $1.13 billion today) in reparations from the British for their violation of the neutrality agreement and the damage that violation caused. The *Alabama* and its fellow raiders were evidence of the breach.

Although the *Alabama* was only one of eleven CSA raiders and accounted for $6.5 million ($73 million today) of the inflicted damages, the demands became known as the *Alabama* Claims. After several international meetings and boards, the British concurred that it had violated the rules of neutrality and in 1871 agreed to pay the U.S. $15.5 million ($174 million today).

During its raiding period as well as its sinking by the *Kearsarge*, the *Alabama* had little actual impact on the war. The *Alabama* became a symbol of the Confederacy as it carried its colors around the world. Its loss was a further blow to the Confederate morale following their defeats at Gettysburg and Vicksburg the previous year.

The duel between the *Alabama* and *Kearsarge* ended the career of the most successful and best-known raider. It, however, does not compare to the immediate and long-term influence of the battle between the *Virginia* and the *Monitor,* and its ranking comes more from its fame than from any real impact on the war.

91

JOHN SINGLETON MOSBY

Confederate Colonel

1833–1916

John Singleton Mosby earned the reputation as the South's finest guerrilla fighter for his behind-the-lines operations. Although he most frequently led fewer than thirty men, never commanded more than a cavalry regiment, and only reached the rank of colonel, he gained a lasting fame that exceeds nearly all of his fellow Confederate officers.

Born in Edgemont, Virginia, on December 6, 1833, Mosby found trouble long before he joined the Confederate army. At age fifteen he entered the University of Virginia where an argument resulted in a duel that wounded a classmate. A jury sentenced Mosby to six months in jail and a fine of $1,000 ($12,000 today), but an act passed by the state legislature suspended the punishment. Mosby returned to school, graduated in 1852, and gained admission to the state bar three years later.

At the outbreak of the Civil War, Mosby left his law practice in Bristol to enlist as a private in the 1st Virginia Cavalry. He quickly advanced in rank to lieutenant and fought in First Bull Run (10) and then joined J. E. B. Stuart (23) in the famous ride around George McClellan (51) in June 1862 during the Union's Peninsular Campaign (32).

Mosby's superiors recognized his talents as a cavalry leader, but they also experienced his resistance to operate under the strict discipline of conventional units. In January 1863, his superiors gave Mosby permission to form a company known as the Partisan Rangers, also known as Mosby's Rangers, to conduct guerrilla operations in Northern Virginia.

Operating initially with only nine men, Mosby harassed isolated Union outposts, cut supply and communication lines, and gathered intelligence on enemy troop movements. Mosby prided himself on mounting his men on the finest horses in Virginia, animals that allowed the Rangers to quickly disperse after raids and reassemble in friendly territory. He also took advantage of the local population for supplies and information.

Mosby's most spectacular raid occurred on March 9, 1863, when his force of twenty-nine men slipped through the Union lines at Fairfax Court House. Entering an enemy camp in a driving rainstorm, Mosby's men caught the Union soldiers sleeping in confidence that they were far from the dangerous front lines. Mosby himself crept into the headquarters tent and captured Brigadier General Edwin H. Stoughton, commander of the 5th New York Cavalry. The raiders then delivered Stoughton, about a hundred of his men, and their horses to the Confederate commander at Culpepper before once again melting into the countryside.

The raid earned Mosby a promotion to captain, and additional actions over the next few months saw him advance to major. On one occasion he captured a Union payroll of $173,000 ($1.9 million today). Later, when asked how he paid and supplied his troops, Mosby replied, "By courtesy of the United States quartermaster general."

In June 1863, Mosby's irregular force was redesignated Company A, 43rd Battalion Partisan Rangers. During the Gettysburg (4) Campaign, the unit acted as regular cavalry in providing reconnaissance and then returned to their raiding operations in Northern Virginia.

From late 1863 until the end of the war, Mosby, now a lieutenant colonel, so disrupted the Union occupation of Virginia's Fauquier and Loudoun counties that the region became known as Mosby's Confederacy.

His raids continued not only to destroy Union supplies and disrupt their lines of communications but also to force Union soldiers to guard rear headquarters and supply areas in case Mosby appeared. Mosby continued to supply his men in whatever manner necessary, including the confiscation of private property. Generals U. S. Grant (3) and Phil Sheridan (8) declared this action theft that violated the rules of warfare and in February 1864 declared Mosby and his men to be outlaws.

Over the next few months, several of Mosby's men were captured and hung without benefit of a trial. Mosby responded by hanging an equal number of captured Union soldiers and sent word that he would continue to do so if necessary. Grant rescinded his orders and recognized Mosby's Rangers as a formal Confederate unit.

Mosby continued his operations in northern Virginia as he advanced to colonel and increased his command to a regiment of eight companies. He dispersed his men over a wide area and focused on poorly defended rear areas rather than opposing regular frontline units.

The Rangers conducted their last raid a day after Robert E. Lee (5) surrendered at Appomattox Court House (37). Mosby never surrendered. On April 20, 1865, he held a final review of his troops at Salem, Virginia, and bid them farewell, saying, "I disband your organization in preference to surrendering. I part from you with pride in the fame of your achievements and grateful recollections of your generous kindness to myself."

Mosby, popularly known as the Gray Ghost, and his men had indeed gained fame throughout the South during the long war. He returned a hero to Warrenton, Virginia, and resumed his law practice. Mosby became one of the earliest Confederate leaders who believed the future of the South was dependent on it becoming a viable part of the preserved Union. Instead of blindly worshiping the Lost Cause, he made efforts to reunite the country. Soon after the war concluded he met Grant and the two warriors developed a lasting friendship.

The Gray Ghost joined the Republican Party, much to the dismay of many fellow former rebels, and supported Grant for the presidency in 1872. He also supported Rutherford Hayes in 1876 and served in several minor political offices before becoming the U.S. consul in Hong Kong from 1878 to 1885. He then worked in the U.S. Department of Justice from 1904 to 1910. Mosby died in Washington, D.C., on May 30, 1916.

Mosby's actions in the war made for great newspaper stories, and his daring deeds were good for the Confederate morale. Undoubtedly, he did force a huge expenditure of Union men and support to counteract his actions, but most of Mosby's operations were more a nuisance than actually influential on the war's outcome.

Grant himself best summed up Mosby's accomplishments when he said, "There were probably but few men in the South who could have commanded successfully a separate detachment in the rear of an opposing army and so near the border of hostilities as long as he did without losing his entire command."

In his memoir, written in 1887, Mosby modestly responded to both his supporters and critics, "In one sense the charge that I did not fight fair is true. I fought for success and not for display. There was no man in the Confederate army who had less of the spirit of knight-errantry in him, or who took a more practical view of the war than I did."

Mosby continued, "Having no fixed lines to guard or defined territory to hold, it was always my policy to elude the enemy when they came in search of me, and carry the war into their own camps."

About the Union feelings toward him, Mosby concluded, "I have often thought their fierce hostility to me was more on account of the sleep I made them lose than the number we killed or captured."

The passage of nearly a century and a half since the end of the Civil War has only added to the fame and legend of Mosby. A television series nearly a hundred years after Appomattox, titled *The Gray Ghost,* used the expertise of Hollywood and the small screen to elevate Mosby's Rangers to hero status. If this ranking were based on fame alone, Mosby would have to be near the top. However, since influence, not fame, is the standard, he appears near the end of this list.

92

NATHANIEL PRENTISS BANKS

Union General

1816–1894

As a general who received his stars because of his political connections rather than his military experience, Nathaniel Prentiss Banks was but yet another Union officer whose failures on the battlefield extended the length and cost of the Civil War. Despite his nearly continual record of failures in combat, Banks led Union troops throughout the war from the Shenandoah Valley of Virginia to the Red River of Louisiana and Texas.

Born in Waltham, Massachusetts, on January 30, 1816, Banks showed his intelligence and propensity for hard work as a boy. With little formal education and no family fortune or connections, Banks worked in the textile mills, earning himself the nickname of "Bobbin Boy." Self-taught, he edited a local newspaper while he also studied law and earned admission to the bar.

Banks became enamored with politics as a young man and entered several unsuccessful campaigns before being elected to the Massachusetts House of Representatives in 1849. Four years later he won a seat in the U.S. Congress, where he was known for his parliamentary skills. In 1856 he was selected Speaker of the House.

In 1858, Banks returned home to become the governor of Massachusetts but left two years later to accept the presidency of the Illinois Central Railroad in Chicago. At the outbreak of the Civil War, Banks resigned and journeyed back to Massachusetts, where he accepted a commission as a major general in the United States volunteers. His lack of military experience took a backseat to his abilities to raise money, sign up recruits, and rally support for the war.

Banks soon learned that political leadership skills did not necessarily transfer to the battlefield. His early battle experience was further compounded in that he faced the extremely competent Stonewall Jackson (36). In the Shenandoah Valley Campaign in the spring of 1862, Jackson forced Banks to retreat with the loss of 30 percent of his men. The general called himself the "Fighting Politician," but Jackson's rebels referred to him as "Commissary Banks" for all the supplies he left behind for their use as he fled the battlefield.

In August 1862, Banks had another chance at Jackson but again met defeat at

Cedar Mountain during Second Bull Run (40). President Abraham Lincoln (2) recalled Banks to Washington where the general briefly commanded the capital defenses. In December, Banks sailed for Louisiana to replace Benjamin Butler (71) in command of the Department of the Gulf.

Banks's mission was to neutralize the Confederate strongpoint at Port Hudson, which controlled the lower Mississippi River about twenty-five miles north of Baton Rouge. In May and June 1863 the soldiers commanded by Banks repeatedly attacked the fort, only to be beaten back each time. Banks then besieged Port Hudson until it finally surrendered on July 9.

Port Hudson was no great victory for Banks, and its defenders likely would not have surrendered if Vicksburg (7) had not fallen to the Union a few days before. Banks's old friends in Congress, however, finally had an excuse to honor one of their own. On January 28, 1864, Banks's political colleagues arranged for an official "Thanks of Congress" for "the skill, courage, and endurance which compelled the surrender of Port Hudson and thus removed the last obstruction to the free navigation of the Mississippi River."

Congress made no mention of the more than three thousand Union soldiers lost in the assaults against the fort. Senior military officers at the time thought—and historians since know—that of the sixteen "Thanks of Congress" awarded, Banks's was the least deserved.

In March 1864, Banks led the Union offensive in the Red River Campaign (81) to neutralize Confederate forces in western Louisiana and eastern Texas and also to serve as a show of force to the French who had recently established themselves in Mexico. Banks experienced success early in the campaign but, instead of pushing the attack to exploit his advantage, he decided to retreat.

Even his most adamant political friends and supporters could no longer excuse Banks's poor performance on the battlefield. He was relieved in May 1864 and remained without a command until the end of the war. Banks once again assumed command of the Department of the Gulf on April 22, 1865, as part of the occupation force but resigned his commission on June 3.

Returning to Massachusetts, Banks reentered politics, again being elected to the U.S. Congress, where he remained until his retirement in 1890. He died in Waltham on September 1, 1894, and is buried in Grove Hill Cemetery.

No one ever questioned the honesty and forthrightness of Banks as an individual or politician. He, however, lacked the training of a combat general and the wherewithal to learn from his mistakes and extreme casualties on the battlefield. As a politically appointed major general of volunteers, he succeeded in raising and arming an army, but was not worthy of command in battle. Experienced officers, including many graduates of West Point and veterans of the Mexican War, were available all across the army, but they remained in the lower and middle ranks under the command of men more familiar with politics than with the military. Promotion and retention of officers like Banks, based on influence rather than ability, may have been necessary to gain and continue the support of the Northern population. However, the practice of doing so prolonged the war and multiplied the dead and wounded.

Banks was both a benefactor and a victim of this "rank for politics" system. He meant well, but his expertise was in getting votes in elections, not victories in combat. Thus, much of Banks' influence in the Civil War was negative. Not only did he have a dismal record in command but also an apparent lack of self-recognition of his inadequacies. If this list were of "the best" commanders, Banks would not have been remotely considered; but he did influence the outcomes of battles and the length of war by his failures, and that alone earns him a place near the end of these rankings.

93

GEORGE EDWARD PICKETT

Confederate General

1825–1875

George Edward Pickett earned a lasting legacy in Civil War history for a single assault on the afternoon of July 3, 1863. His advance against the Union defenses at Gettysburg (4), known as Pickett's Charge, remains today as one of the conflict's most famous and remembered incidents.

Pickett was born on January 28, 1825, at Richmond into an influential family who dated their arrival in Virginia back to 1635. He studied law before entering West Point as a member of the Class of 1846. Graduating last in his class of fifty-nine cadets, Pickett accepted a commission in the infantry and fought in the campaigns of the Mexican War from Vera Cruz to Mexico City. He earned a brevet promotion for his gallantry at Churubusco in August 1847, and a month later led the attack against Chapultepec, where he tore down the enemy flag and replaced it with his regiment's colors.

After the Mexican War, Pickett earned a promotion to captain during the six years he served on the Texas frontier. In 1856 he transferred to the Northwest, where he became involved in a dispute between the U.S. and Great Britain over the boundary between Washington Territory and Canada in the San Juan Islands. From 1859 to 1861, Pickett and a company of infantrymen occupied one end of San Juan Island while the British held the other. The shooting of an errant farm animal gave the conflict the name of the Pig War, but no shots were fired by either side against the other. Ultimately Pickett's occupation led to an international agreement that placed the island within the United States.

Because of his responsibilities in the Northwest, Pickett did not resign his commission and return to Virginia until two months after the firing on Fort Sumter (50). When he did return home, he accepted a Confederate commission as a colonel in command of defenses along the Lower Rappahannock River. Promoted to brigadier general in February 1862, Pickett led a brigade against the Union's Peninsular Campaign (32) before being seriously wounded in the shoulder at Gaines's Mill on June 27, 1862.

Pickett missed the Battle of Antietam (1) as he recovered from his wound but returned as a major general to command the Confederate center division at Fredericksburg (53) in

December. After the battle, Pickett's division remained as a part of James Longstreet's (13) corps and spent most of the spring of 1863 in southeastern Virginia, refitting and gathering supplies.

In late June, Pickett and his division joined Robert E. Lee's (5) offensive into Pennsylvania where Lee met the Union army at Gettysburg on July 1. The first two days of the battle took place on the flanks while Lee occupied the center of Seminary Ridge. On Day 3, Lee ordered Longstreet's corps to advance against the Union center.

Longstreet strongly opposed the plan but was unsuccessful in changing Lee's mind. Longstreet then turned to Pickett and ordered him to form his division for the attack and then directed him to place brigades from two additional divisions with his own in the advance. By two o'clock in the afternoon, ten brigades, totaling about fifteen thousand men, moved forward under a Confederate artillery barrage. Unfortunately for Lee and the Confederates, they were advancing against the Union's strength that was protected by a stone wall and breastworks. Making matter worse, George Meade (24) had ample reserves to reinforce the attack point.

The rebel army advanced across a half-mile of open field into withering Union artillery and musket fire. A few hundred feet from the Union lines, the Confederates halted briefly to redress their lines and once again advanced. A few of Longstreet's men actually reached the wall and engaged the enemy in hand-to-hand combat before being killed or forced back. Barely a fourth of Pickett's men and the other attackers made their way safely back to Confederate lines. The "high tide of the Confederacy" had been reached, and it was marked by piles of rebel dead.

Not long after the battle, the Confederate advance on day three at Gettysburg became known as Pickett's Charge. However, there is really no reason for the name or the fame it produced for the general. In reality, Longstreet commanded the attack and Pickett was one of three division commanders to participate—his troops did not even make up the majority of the force.

Just why Pickett's Charge became the name for the attack or why it has endured is difficult to determine. The simple answer may be that the press and public needed a simple name for a most difficult battle and Pickett's Charge sufficed. Another influence, letters Pickett wrote before and after the battle, were later published in various forms.

In a letter to his fiancée before the advance he wrote, "If Old Peter's [Longstreet] nod [to attack] mean death, goodbye and God bless you little one."

A day after the battle he wrote to her again, "Well, it is all over now. The battle is lost, and many of us are prisoners, many are dead, many wounded, bleeding, and dying. Your soldier lives and mourns and but for you, my darling, he would rather, a million times rather, be back there with his dead, to sleep for all time in an unknown grave."

After Gettysburg, Pickett moved what was left of his division to a secure area of southeastern Virginia where he gathered replacements and supplies. He made a poorly planned, unsuccessful attack to take New Bern, North Carolina, in January 1864, but fought well in the Battle of Drewry's Bluff the following May.

Pickett then joined the defense of Petersburg (46) and skirmished against Phil Sheridan (8) at Dinwiddie Court House on March 31, 1865. At Five Forks the next day Union troops overran Pickett's lines. Pickett missed the early part of the battle because he was at a shad bake with fellow officers in a rear area. He hurried to the battlefront but was unable to influence its outcome.

After Five Forks, Pickett had few soldiers left to command. Lee ordered Pickett and two other generals to transfer their remaining men to other units and return home. This order was not only a sensible reorganization but also a reflection of the disfavor in which Pickett had found himself with Lee since his comments about the general's mistakes at Gettysburg. Whatever the motivation behind the decision, it became a moot point as the Confederacy had only days left to survive.

Pickett either did not receive the order to transfer his men or chose to ignore it. He was still with the army at Appomattox Court House (37) where he surrendered the eight hundred men remaining in his command.

After the war Pickett turned down an offer of a commission as a general in the Egyptian army as well as a later opportunity from U. S. Grant (3) to become a United States marshall. He chose instead to go into the insurance business where he remained until his death in Norfolk, Virginia, on July 30, 1875. He is buried in Richmond.

Pickett remained a lifelong friend of Longstreet, and he continued to express his negative feelings about the attack at Gettysburg that destroyed his division. However, his most common response to questions about why the Confederates were defeated at Gettysburg was, "I always thought the Yankees had something to do with it."

If the attack on the third day of Gettysburg had become known as Longstreet's Charge or had been named after one of the other division commanders in the attack, Pickett would not merit a ranking on this list. Although his Civil War service was honorable and meritorious, it differed little from dozens of other division commanders on both sides throughout the war. But Pickett's Charge it became, and Pickett's name remains a part of the legend about one of the war's most influential battles and the bravery and gallantry of the Lost Cause. His place on this list is near the end because, in reality, he is remembered more for his fame than for his influence.

NEW MEXICO AND ARIZONA

1861–1862

Almost all of the Civil War battles took place in the states located between the Atlantic Ocean to just beyond the Mississippi River and from the Gulf of Mexico to the Ohio River. However, war activities did extend into Texas, and, during the first two years of the conflict, the Confederacy attempted to capture New Mexico and Arizona with the ultimate goal of securing the wealth of California to support the rebellion.

After the Mexican War ended in 1847, the victorious United States took control of much of what would become the western part of the country. California became a territory and, with discovery of its gold, quickly became the thirty-first state in 1850. The United States organized what is today New Mexico, Arizona, and southern Nevada into the New Mexico Territory. While this territory also had mineral riches, they had yet to be discovered. Native Americans, especially various bands of Apaches, still controlled much of the countryside.

At the outbreak of the Civil War, nearly a quarter of all U.S. Army units were stationed on the West Coast to control the gold fields and to defend U.S. interests along the Pacific. California, admitted to the Union as a free state, also had factions that supported the Confederacy. When news of Fort Sumter (50) reached the West Coast, army officers took quick action to neutralize Confederate sympathizers and secured the state for the Union. Other Union forces along the Rio Grande from Albuquerque to Santa Fe and at Fort Yuma in far western Arizona did the same to secure the New Mexico Territory.

While President Jefferson Davis (9) and other Confederate leaders professed that they wanted to be left alone in their newly formed country, they harbored ambitions to expand the Confederacy westward. By doing so, they could expand slavery and capture the gold fields of California. They believed California could support the rebellion with gold and provide ports to replace the Union blockaded ones in the Atlantic and Gulf states.

When Texas seceded from the Union, its militia took over forts formally occupied by Union troops whom they allowed to withdraw to Union territory. Texas militiaman John Baylor secured San Antonio and marched westward with seven hundred men. Along the way he took over Forts Clark and Davis and left detachments behind to

New Mexico and Arizona Territory

hold them. By the end of June he had occupied Fort Bliss at El Paso and prepared to move northward along the Rio Grande into New Mexico.

On July 25, Baylor and 250 men reached Fort Fillmore, where they intimidated the Union commander to surrender his seven hundred men, two artillery pieces, two hundred horses, and three hundred head of cattle after only a brief skirmish. On August 1, Baylor declared the area south of the 34th parallel as the Territory of Arizona. He named Mesilla, about thirty miles north of El Paso, as the capital and himself as the governor.

On December 14, Brigadier General Henry H. Sibley arrived at Fort Bliss with thirty-seven hundred troops and plans to secure the Rio Grande all the way to Santa Fe. He also intended to send a small detachment to Tucson to claim Arizona. Meanwhile, Union Colonel E. S. B. Canby established the Federal Department of New Mexico on November 9 and prepared to defend the territory.

Sibley marched northward with twenty-six hundred men in early January 1862. The Confederates met the Union forces of about their same size at Valverde on February 21. They were in danger of being overrun before the Texans captured four Union artillery pieces and turned them on the Federals. Canby suffered 68 killed and 185 wounded or missing while Confederate losses totaled 36 dead and 150 wounded or missing.

During the next month the Confederates continued their march northward and on March 23 occupied Santa Fe, which Canby had abandoned while taking with him all supplies that might be of benefit to the rebels. The Confederates now turned eastward to take control of the Santa Fe Trail and to push the last Federal troops out of the territory at Fort Union. Canby made his stand about sixty miles east of Santa Fe at Apache Canyon near Glorieta Pass. On March 26 and again on March 28, Sibley attempted unsuccessfully to break the Union lines. Union reinforcements flanked the Confederates and destroyed their supply wagons.

Sibley, low on supplies and unable to break the Union lines, retreated back toward Texas. When criticized for not pursuing and destroying the Confederates, Canby explained that he was not prepared to secure and feed a large number of prisoners.

When Sibley began his ill-fated march northward, he also dispatched a detachment westward to Tucson under the command of Captain Sherrod Hunter. The Confederates arrived in the Arizona village on February 28, 1862, finding themselves welcomed by the locals who appreciated any additional protection, whatever uniform they wore, from local Indians.

Union officials in California recognized that Confederate occupation of New Mexico and Arizona was only a prelude in the rebel advance toward their state. To assist the Union resistance in New Mexico Territory, a force of fourteen hundred soldiers assembled at Fort Yuma on the Colorado River and marched eastward across the desert. The California Column, led by Brigadier General James H. Carleton, fought hostile Indians and the elements on their long march.

From Tucson, Captain Hunter sent out reconnaissance parties to keep up with Carleton's progress. On April 15, ten Confederates ambushed twelve Union scouts at Picacho Pass about forty-five miles northwest of Tucson. The resulting skirmish killed three Union soldiers, including their leader, Lieutenant James Barrett, and wounded three more. After less than an hour, both sides withdrew, leaving Picacho Pass the distinction of being the furthermost western battle fought in the Civil War.

With the California Column approaching, Hunter marched back toward Texas with his small detachment. Along the way the unit encountered so many hostile Indians that Hunter even armed his Union prisoners to join the fight. On May 27, 1862, Hunter finally reached the Rio Grande and joined the remaining Confederate forces in their retreat all the way back to San Antonio.

By the end of May 1862, all Confederate troops were out of the New Mexico Territory. California was secure and no further rebel threat extended beyond Texas. Later claims made Glorieta the Gettysburg (4) of the West, and while neither side lost more than a hundred men, the battle indeed marked the high tide of the Confederacy in the New Mexico Territory.

For those who fought in New Mexico and Arizona, their Civil War was just as frightening and significant as any other battles of the long conflict. In the large picture, however, New Mexico and Arizona were little more than a side show to the main event. Sibley's campaign was doomed from its beginning because of the impossibly long line of supply and communications back to San Antonio. If needed, the Union could have dispatched even more troops either overland or by sea to Fort Yuma or San Diego to control the region.

For the Confederates, New Mexico and Arizona were no more than steps toward the goal of California. However, California was important to the Union, and only the United States possessed the land and sea power to protect it. This ranking is merited by the size of the contested area, not the small battles and skirmishes fought over it.

95

HUGH JUDSON KILPATRICK

Union General

1836–1881

Hugh Judson Kilpatrick was the first regular Union army officer wounded in the Civil War. Following his recovery, he took part in nearly every major cavalry action in the eastern theater for the remainder of the conflict. Known for his recklessness on the battlefield that endangered both his men and horses, Kilpatrick led attacks and raids that gained him both praise and condemnation from his own side and hatred from his enemies.

Born the son of a farmer near Deckerstown, New Jersey, on January 14, 1836, Kilpatrick learned at an early age the importance of making influential friends. It was these connections that secured Kilpatrick an appointment to West Point where he graduated number seventeen of forty-five cadets in the Class of 1861.

Kilpatrick, commissioned in the artillery, recognized that the path to rapid promotion would be found in volunteer units rather than the Regular Army. Within days of graduation he left the regular ranks as a second lieutenant to accept a captain's commission in the 5th New York Zouaves. A month later he led a company at the war's first significant battle at Big Bethel and, although he fought with volunteers, he officially became the first Regular Army officer to be wounded in the rebellion.

Combining his aggressiveness on the battlefield with his cultivation of influential political and business leaders, Kilpatrick quickly advanced in rank to lieutenant colonel. In the fall of 1861, he served in the defense of Washington before joining General James Lane in Kansas as the chief of artillery for a planned expedition into Texas. When the campaign was cancelled, Kilpatrick returned to Virginia where he participated in the skirmishes that led to Second Bull Run (40) in August 1862.

Promoted to full colonel in command of a cavalry regiment, Kilpatrick participated in George Stoneman's (89) raid toward Richmond in June 1863. In July he took command of a cavalry division as a brigadier general and lost many of his men in a costly attack at Gettysburg (4) against the Confederate right flank after Pickett's Charge was repulsed on July 3.

For the remainder of the year, Kilpatrick continued to skirmish and fight minor battles against the rebels back in Virginia. Anxious to restore his reputation for his failed attack on the final day at Gettysburg, he received permission in February 1864 to lead a raid on Richmond to free Union prisoners in advance of U. S. Grant's (3) Overland Campaign. Kilpatrick made it to the outskirts of Richmond before Confederate forces massed to stop his advance. Later claims would be made that Kilpatrick could have successfully attacked the city if he had not lost his nerve when confronted with a sizable opponent.

More wrath was heaped upon Kilpatrick when one of his subordinates, Colonel Ulric Dahlgren, was killed. On his body the Confederates recovered papers revealing that Kilpatrick had planned to burn Richmond and assassinate Jefferson Davis (9) in addition to freeing prisoners. By the time Kilpatrick returned to Union lines, he had few friends left within the Union army and had made personal enemies in the rebel camps because of his destruction of houses and farms during his raid.

The career of the Union cavalry leader seemed to be at an end until William Sherman (6) requested that Kilpatrick take command of a division in his western Army of the Cumberland. Sherman responded to critics of the move, "I know that Kilpatrick is a hell of a damn fool, but I want just that sort of man to command my cavalry on this expedition."

Kilpatrick joined Sherman in time to be wounded on May 13 at Resaca. He recovered to rejoin his division in July and led raids behind Confederate lines to destroy railways. As Sherman neared Atlanta, Kilpatrick's division rode completely around the Confederate defenses and reported their locations to Sherman. Kilpatrick remained with Sherman on his March to the Sea (16) and then continued on the offensive northward through the Carolinas.

A few weeks after the war ended, Kilpatrick was rewarded with a brevet promotion to major general. He decided, however, not to remain in the army and resigned his commission on December 1, 1865. Again relying on powerful political friends, he secured an appointment as the minister to Chile where he served until 1868. On his return to New Jersey, he ran unsuccessfully for the U.S. Congress as a Republican and then switched parties and supported Democratic candidates. In 1881 he returned to Chile as the U.S. minister and remained there until he died in Santiago on December 4. His remains were returned to the U.S. in 1887 and buried in the West Point Cemetery.

Kilpatrick, although reasonably successful on the battlefield, was one of those commanders disliked by his own side and hated by his opponents. At parades and in battle, Kilpatrick's units always looked and acted professional. His camps, however, were known for disorder and their openness to camp followers. Kilpatrick did not drink or gamble, but he did have a great weakness for women. His tent was frequently occupied by admirers or prostitutes, and on least two occasions he was nearly captured while taking care of personal, rather than military, affairs.

His reputation as a womanizer was rather odd, considering that he was a small man with a lantern jaw. A member of George Meade's (24) staff said that it was difficult to look at Kilpatrick without laughing.

Kilpatrick garnered many nicknames, but the most widely known throughout the Union army was "Kill Cavalry." To most this name represented his reckless endangerment of his soldiers. His friends said the moniker came from his rough use of his horses. Regardless, it was one of the most unkind and damning of the war.

Yet the Southern rebels had even worse, unprintable names for Kilpatrick. They damned him for his destruction in Virginia and for his plans for Richmond and Davis. Southerners saw him as one of Sherman's most enthusiastic arsonists of houses and barns during the March to the Sea. During this latter campaign Kilpatrick repeatedly told his subordinates, "Let the men catch and kill their hogs with their sabers, a weapon that can be used equally as well to kill hogs as rebels."

Kilpatrick's moral flaws and self-promotion overshadow the fact that he was a more than adequate cavalry commander. Sherman's support, although somewhat damning, speaks for his abilities. It is remarkable that he managed to be present in and survive a majority of the war's most important campaigns. While he may not have been popular with his cavalrymen, he played a significant role in many battles and campaigns. All of these factors combine to make it difficult to rank Kilpatrick on this list, but his accomplishments, personal failures, and brutal behavior place him a position near the end of this ranking.

96

INTELLIGENCE

1861–1865

Neither the North nor the South had an intelligence service at the beginning of the war and neither developed a viable information-gathering system during the conflict. The only useful intelligence provided to Civil War field commanders came from infantry scouts and cavalry reconnaissance. All other intelligence efforts by both sides were virtual failures throughout the war, including the hiring of civilian detective agencies, the employment of aerial observation balloons, the attempts to establish spy networks, and the gleaning of information from the enemy's newspapers.

Commanders have recognized the importance of intelligence—simply defined as information about the capabilities, intentions, and vulnerabilities of an adversary—since the beginnings of warfare. However, actually gathering this information, and convincing commanders that it is accurate, has always proven difficult. The Civil War was no exception.

Despite the fact that it had existed for more than three-quarters of a century, the U.S. Army had no centralized information-gathering organization at the outbreak of the Civil War. The infant Confederate army likewise established no intelligence agency as it formed. Regimental and smaller unit commanders relied on what little information they could gather from foot scouts who ventured forward across the lines to observe. Large commands relied on cavalry units to ride along the flanks of enemy armies to report on their size and possible intentions.

Confederate cavalry, at least early in the war, proved to be superior in its mobility in shadowing the Union armies and gathering information. In the war's most famous cavalry reconnaissance, General J. E. B. Stuart (23), with a thousand Confederate horsemen, rode completely around the Union army commanded by George McClellan during the Peninsular Campaign (32) in June 1862.

During this same time, McClellan made an effort to establish a formal intelligence service by hiring a civilian detective agency headed by Allan Pinkerton. Pinkerton's Agency had established its reputation in railroad security in Chicago, where it operated under the trademark of a vigilant open eye accompanied by the slogan "We Never Sleep." McClellan's primary use of "the Pinkertons" was in determining

Confederate troop strength and unit identifications. The civilian detectives, inexperienced in military operations, proved woefully inadequate. They consistently overestimated the size of the Confederate army by two to four times and McClellan, a reluctant warrior at best, used the inflated enemy troop estimates as further rationale not to fight. His reluctance to attack a much smaller force prevented his capture of Richmond and an early end to the rebellion.

During his time with McClellan, Pinkerton and his men had no official title, but he often referred to his organization as the National Detective Agency. When Lincoln relieved McClellan from command in November 1862, Pinkerton and his subordinates departed the army and played no further role in the conflict.

McClellan proved no more effective even when he possessed a complete copy of the Confederate battle plan. In one of the greatest security failures of the war, a copy of Robert E. Lee's Special Order Number 191, which outlined the plans for his first invasion of the North—including subordinate units and their strengths—was lost by a subordinate. A Union soldier discovered the lost order and delivered it to McClellan. Despite the information, McClellan remained cautious and did not fully take advantage of his intelligence at the following Battle of Antietam (1) in September 1862.

Meanwhile in Washington, D.C., the War Department provost Marshall Lafayette C. Baker established a staff of detectives and investigators in February 1862 in what he self-named the National Detective Bureau. Although the organization survived until 1866 and Baker made later claims of establishing a spy network in the South, there is no evidence that either he or his Bureau gathered any significant intelligence or made any contributions to the war. Except for the ineffective efforts of Pinkerton and Baker, Union field commanders had no intelligence sources beyond their own organic scouts and cavalry.

Confederate intelligence efforts in the Civil War are generally credited as being superior to those of the Union, but a look below the surface reveals that the South was equally inept in the information business. Although the Confederates accomplished surprise attacks at places such as Shiloh (18) and Second Bull Run (40), their successes were more the result of superior leadership than of good intelligence. At no time in the war did the Confederacy have a centralized intelligence organization, and commanders in gray, like their counterparts in blue, had to rely on their own scouts, cavalry, and prisoner interrogation for information.

Official reports from commanders of both sides, as well as memoirs written in later years, often claim that the most useful information on their opponents came from newspapers smuggled across the lines. Both sides had war correspondents (61) accompanying their armies, and their reports revealed so much information that commanders on occasion treated them as spies and banned them from their camps.

Both sides attempted inventive methods to gather information. The North and the South experimented with gas balloons, launching observers aloft to spy on the opponent. Even though the balloons established that the concept could be effective, it was a technology whose time had not yet come. The expense of the large number of men and wagons required and the air ships' vulnerabilities to wind and weather quickly placed the observation balloon concept on the shelf.

Advances in communications (34), especially the telegraph, provided opportunities for the rapid transfer of information. This also provided a means of stealing messages by tapping into the wires, but both sides quickly learned to take countermeasures, including transmitting false information and using codes and encrypts.

Without a doubt, no aspect of Civil War intelligence has been more glorified than tales of gallant men and women stealing information at the dining tables of presidents and from the camps of generals. Tales of spies, especially of females, appeared in several postwar autobiographies, but their contents are more suited to the theater stage than to history books. While there are many stories of spies in Washington, Richmond, and indeed through the North and South, these tales are part of the romantic magnolia-and-peach-blossom myths that prevailed after the war. Despite their almost complete lack of veracity, many still endure.

Not a single battle was won or lost during the Civil War based on any intelligence beyond that which was gathered on the immediate battlefield. Stories of the accomplishments and even the presence of detectives and spies are almost wholly fabrications. The lack of respect by the services for intelligence agencies is marked by the fact that the postwar U.S. Navy made no effort to establish such an organization until 1882. The U.S. Army was even less impressed as it waited until 1885, fully two decades after the Civil War, to organize an official Information Division.

Ultimately, intelligence during the Civil War, as in American wars before and in the future, was marked by failures rather than successes. For this reason, it is included at the end of these rankings.

97

CHARLESTON HARBOR

February 17, 1864

The assault by the CSS *H. L. Hunley* on the United States blockade fleet off Charleston Harbor in the winter of 1864 marked history's first successful submarine attack. While the sinking of the USS *Housatonic* had little influence on the outcome of the Civil War, it proved the value of submarines and changed the future of naval warfare.

Experimentation with submersible watercraft predates the Civil War by more than two millennia. Aristotle wrote about an underwater craft used in 332 BC. There is also evidence that the Chinese experimented with primitive submarines as early as 200 BC. In 1578, Englishman William Borne designed a submarine complete with ballast tanks, but his idea never got beyond the drafting table. It was not until 1620 that Cornelis Drebbel successfully launched and recovered an underwater vessel in London's Thames River.

In 1776, American David Bushnell launched an egg-shaped submersible that carried a crew of one. The *Turtle,* piloted by Sergeant Ezra Lee, became the first combat submarine when it unsuccessfully attempted to place a mine on the side of the HMS *Eagle* in New York Harbor on September 6, 1776.

Robert Fulton, another American inventor, experimented with a submarine he called the *Nautilus* in 1798, but he dropped the project when he failed to receive government financial support. Engineers from other countries during this period also attempted to build submarines; Germany launched the *Sea Devil,* which made several successful voyages in 1850.

Union naval officials dabbled with submarine experiments right after the war broke out, but their efforts lacked urgency. In November 1861, the U.S. Navy launched the *Alligator* for several sea trials. However, the Union, with its far superior navy and little need for new watercrafts, did not seriously pursue advancing its submarine project. In April 1863 the Union submarine program ended when the *Alligator* sank while under tow off Cape Hatteras.

When the Confederacy broke away from the United States in 1861, the North blockaded the South with traditional vessels, preventing the export of agricultural

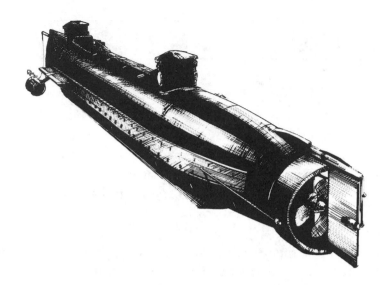

products and the import of military and other supplies. The Confederate States tried to break the blockade with an ironclad warship at Hampton Roads (72) in March 1862, but neither this nor other efforts were successful.

In 1863, Confederate inventors decided that the most practical method of breaking the blockade was with torpedo boats and submarines. Torpedo boats were not true submarines in that they could not fully submerge under the water. In late 1863, the T. Stoney Company of Charleston launched a fifty-foot-long, steam-driven, cigar-shaped vessel that rode on the surface with only a few inches of its hull exposed.

On October 5, 1863, the torpedo boat CSS *David* attacked the USS *New Ironsides* off Charleston Harbor with an explosive charge attached to the end of a spar extending from its bow. The explosion damaged the Union ship as well as the *David* but neither sank. In the spring of 1864 the repaired *David* made two more attacks on Union warships but neither was successful.

Meanwhile, in Mobile, Alabama, construction had begun on a true submarine, the CSS *H. L. Hunley,* named in honor of its principal financial backer. The *Hunley,* fashioned from an iron steam boiler, measured slightly less than forty feet long. Its design included enough space for a crew of eight to drive the hand-cranked propeller and a captain to steer the boat and control the depth. Ballast tanks on each end of the *Hunley* were flooded or emptied with hand pumps. Additional iron weights on the bottom of the boat could be released from inside if an emergency called for added buoyancy.

The submarine's only armaments were explosives attached to the end of a long bow spear. To attack, the submarine had to maneuver underwater close enough to the side of an enemy vessel to attach the explosive charge and then detonate it with a rope lanyard.

In the fall of 1863 its builders shipped the *Hunley* by rail to Charleston, South Carolina. Shortly after the submarine's arrival and launch, it attempted to attack the Union blockade of the harbor. A wave swamped the boat, drowning the entire crew save the captain, Lieutenant John Payne. The boat was recovered, only to sink twice more during sea trials in October. Two seamen survived the first sinking during the sea trials; all hands, including H. L. Hunley, died in the second.

Once again the *Hunley* was recovered. On February 17, 1864, the *Hunley*, captained by Lieutenant George Dixon, one of the submarine's builders in Alabama, pushed away from its Charleston dock, slipped below the surface, and made its way toward the Union fleet. Silently it approached the twenty-three-gun, eighteen hundred-ton Union sloop *Housatonic*.

The next day Lieutenant F. G. Higginson, U.S. Navy, wrote the following report: "Sir I…make the following report of the sinking of the U.S.S. *Housatonic*, by a rebel torpedo off Charleston, S.C., on the evening of the 17 instant. At about 8:45 p.m. the officer of the deck, acting Master J. K. Crosby, discovered something in the water about one hundred yards from and moving toward the ship. It had the appearance of a plank moving in the water. It came directly toward the ship, the time from when it was first seen till it was close alongside being about two minutes. During this time the chain was slipped, engine backed, and all hands called to quarters. The torpedo struck the ship forward of the mizzenmast on the starboard side, in a line with the magazine. Having the after pivot gun pivoted to port we were unable to bring a gun to bear upon her. About one minute after she was close alongside the explosion took place, sinking stern first and heeling to port as she sank."

Higginson included a list of his crewmen killed in the attack. He concluded with an explanation that he was making the report because his captain had been wounded by the explosion.

The *Hunley* did not return from the attack. On March 19, 1864, the assistant adjutant of the Confederate command in Charleston wrote in an official report, "I regret to say that nothing since has been heard either of Lieutenant Dixon or the torpedo boat. It is therefore feared that that gallant officer and his brave companions have perished."

The fate of the *Hunley* remained unknown for the next 131 years, until underwater archeologists discovered it on the ocean floor in 1995. Divers raised the submarine in 2000 and transported it to a special preservation tank at the Charleston Navy Yard. Since that time, the hull has been opened and artifacts and human remains recovered. The exact cause of sinking remains undetermined. On April 17, 2004, the remains of the *Hunley* crew were interred in Charleston's Magnolia Cemetery with full military honors.

Despite its loss and the inability of the Confederacy to launch subsequent underwater attacks, the *Hunley* earned the distinction of being the first submarine to sink an enemy warship. The U.S. Navy later resumed its submersible research and launched its first successful submarine, the USS *Holland,* in 1898. Other countries also noted the success of the *Hunley* and began or continued their own submarine programs. However, it was not until 1914 that a German submarine matched the *Hunley*'s success in sinking an enemy ship. From that time forward, submarines have played an important role in naval warfare. Today, the U.S. Navy nuclear-powered and armed submarines are constantly at sea.

The successful attack by the *Hunley* changed the future of naval warfare. No longer would navies fight only on the surface; after the Battle of Charleston Harbor, every sea captain had to also defend against an attack from under the waves. If this ranking was on the overall influence of an event on warfare, Charleston Bay would achieve a high ranking. However, when ranked against other battles, leaders, and events that influenced the Civil War, it only merits inclusion near the end of the list. The *Hunley* vastly changed the future of naval warfare, but it had little to no influence on the outcome of the American Civil War.

98

DANIEL BUTTERFIELD

Union General

1831–1901

Daniel Butterfield, as division and corps commander in major Eastern battles, served as the chief of staff to both Joseph Hooker (48) and George Meade (24). In addition to his leadership contributions on the battlefield, Butterfield introduced the famous bugle call "Taps" and the system of corps badges to identify units and raise morale.

Born on October 31, 1831, in Utica, New York, the future officer was the son of John Butterfield, who owned the Overland Express Company that operated stage coaches, steamships, and telegraph lines. Upon graduating from Union College in Schenectady, New York, at age eighteen, Butterfield traveled extensively in the South before joining the American Express Company, in which his father was part owner, as a division superintendent.

After the attack on Fort Sumter in April 1861, Butterfield volunteered for the "Clay Guards" in Washington, D.C., and became the unit's first sergeant. Two weeks later, on May 12, he left the Guards to accept a federal commission as a colonel in the 12th New York Militia. Despite his previous lack of significant military experience, Butterfield adapted quickly. He was the first Union commander to lead his unit into Confederate territory when he crossed Washington's Long Bridge into Virginia and fought at First Bull Run (10) in July 1861.

Promoted to brigadier general, Butterfield led his regiment in the Seven Days' Campaign in the summer of 1862, during which he was wounded at Gaines's Mill on June 27. Thirty years later, in what may have been more a political action than recognition of bravery, Congress awarded Butterfield the Medal of Honor for his actions in the battle that included seizing his unit's colors "at a critical moment and, under a galling fire of the enemy, encouraged the depleted ranks to renewed exertion."

Butterfield's unit rested at Harrison's Landing near the end of the Peninsular Campaign (32) in July 1862. There he made what may be his most lasting contribution to the military. Although many claim credit for "Taps," the best evidence shows that during this time Butterfield experimented with several bugle calls. Not happy with the various notes that ended the day, Butterfield composed what became known

as "Taps." His bugler, Oliver W. Norton, was first to play the call. Other units quickly adopted the music, and it even spread across the lines to be used by Confederate units. Commanders on both sides used the twenty-four notes of "Taps" to honor the dead at funerals as well as a regular call to end the day. By the end of the war, "Taps" was the most recognized bugle call of all times. It remains so today.

Butterfield led his brigade at Second Bull Run (40) and at Antietam (1). He then commanded a division and, after promotion to major general, led the attack of V Corps at Fredericksburg (53) in December 1862. When Joseph Hooker assumed command of the Army of the Potomac in January 1863, he selected Butterfield as his chief of staff.

Butterfield was never popular with his fellow generals and became even less so during his service with Hooker. His abrasive style of leadership and his political infighting may have angered his contemporaries, but he significantly assisted Hooker in raising the morale of the army, staggered by its loss at Fredericksburg, by improving the quality of rations, shelter, and medical support. Even so, many officers condemned Butterfield, along with Hooker, for the Union headquarters being open to alcohol and ladies of questionable reputation. Some went so far as to label the Army of the Potomac headquarters as "a combination of barroom and brothel."

Hooker and Butterfield may have run an unusual headquarters, but they also made innovative changes that increased unit morale and established a practice that continues today. As a means of identification and pride, Hooker—adapting the Philip

Kearney practice of having the soldiers in his division wear red diamond patches—directed Butterfield to create distinctive badges for each corps. Butterfield designed cloth badges about an inch and a half in width for each corps. He color-coded them to identify each division within the corps. Within a year the practice of wearing cloth badges spread throughout the Union army. Over time the badges evolved into the shoulder patches still worn by today's U.S. Army units—with many of the present corps patches the same or similar to Butterfield's original design.

George Meade was no fan of Butterfield's and considered replacing him when he took Hooker's place in June 1863 after the Union defeat at Chancellorsville (31) the previous month. He did not have time to do so before the Battle of Gettysburg (4) began only days after he assumed command. Meade's difficulties with his chief of staff were solved on the third day of the battle when an artillery fragment wounded Butterfield.

After his recovery in the fall of 1863, Butterfield rejoined Hooker, who now commanded two corps in the Army of the Cumberland. At Chattanooga (12), Butterfield again served as Hooker's chief of staff. He then took command of a division and served under William Sherman (6) in the advance against Atlanta. Near the end of the campaign, illness forced Butterfield to relinquish his command. For the remainder of the war he served in occupation and recruiting duty.

Butterfield remained in the army after the end of the war as the commander of New York Harbor. He resigned his commission in 1870 to accept an appointment from President U. S. Grant (3) as an assistant treasurer of the United States. For the rest of his life Butterfield remained active directing corporations and serving as the unofficial ambassador to several countries. He headed the Washington Centennial celebration in 1889, presided over the funeral of Sherman in 1891, and chaired the triumphant return of Admiral George Dewey after the Battle of Manila in 1899.

On July 17, 1901, Butterfield died at his summer home in Cold Spring, New York. With special permission from the War Department, he was buried in the U.S. Military Academy Cemetery, despite the fact that Butterfield never attended West Point. His headstone remains today as one of the largest and most ornate in the cemetery.

Butterfield served in many of the war's most important campaigns and battles. He performed as well as most and better than many. Still, his battle performance alone did not earn him a place on this list. He is ranked in the top one hundred because he wrote and employed the bugle call "Taps" and created unit badges. These accomplishments merit his inclusion.

99

JOHN PELHAM

Confederate Lieutenant Colonel

1838–1863

John Pelham, an innovative horse artillery leader, impressed his senior commanders with his battlefield skills, bravery, and élan. Upon his death at twenty-four, he was mourned across the South as one of its great heroes and symbols of chivalry and gallantry. Poems and books about "the Gallant Pelham" made him the war's most famous junior officer and a lasting symbol of the Lost Cause.

Born on September 14, 1838, outside Alexandria, Louisiana, Pelham grew up in an extended family headed by his physician father. He remained in Louisiana until he secured an appointment to the U.S. Military Academy as a member of the Class of 1861. He proved to be only an average student but expressed both respect and admiration for the traditions of the institution.

After the attack on Fort Sumter, Pelham wrote to his father, "I had hoped, fondly hoped, to graduate here." Despite his love for West Point, his loyalties remained with his home state and the newly declared independent Confederacy. On April 22, 1861, just weeks before graduation, he resigned from the Academy and made his way south.

Pelham, who learned the skills of an artilleryman at West Point, accepted a commission as a first lieutenant in the Confederate artillery. He joined Joseph Johnston's (17) army in Virginia and handled his guns with such daring and skill at First Bull Run (10) that he attracted the attention of his senior officers.

In November 1863, Pelham joined J. E. B. Stuart's (23) cavalry and upon directions from the general began to adapt artillery to better support the horse soldiers. Pelham, now a captain, handpicked his men and assembled a variety of types of guns and lightened their carriages by removing the seats on the limbers where the crews usually rode. Instead of riding on the guns, each crew member in Pelham's battery rode on horseback. Now his guns could keep up with the main cavalry columns. After repeated drills and training by Pelham, his men also learned to fire quickly and accurately.

Artillery, previously ponderously slow to reach the battle area and to begin firing, now rode in the midst of cavalry columns with carriages bouncing and crews joining in the rebel yell. Pelham's artillery fought bravely and efficiently at Williamsburg,

Second Bull Run (40), Antietam (1), and Shepherdstown as his fame and reputation for skill and daring increased.

Pelham joined the defense of Fredericksburg (53) in December 1862. When the Union army advanced against Stuart's men defending the Confederate southeastern flank near present Hamilton's Crossing, Pelham raced to a vantage point a half-mile in front of the lines with two guns and began pouring shot and shell into the line of advancing soldiers in blue. Soon battery after battery of Union artillery turned their guns against Pelham's detachment. When one of his crew members fell wounded, Pelham personally replaced him on the cannon. Even after Federal fire disabled one of his guns, Pelham continued to fire with his remaining piece.

For two hours Pelham's small detachment held up the advance of an entire Union corps. He did not withdraw until Stuart ordered him to, stating, "Get back from destruction, you infernal, gallant fool, John Pelham."

Pelham, now out of ammunition, followed his orders and returned to the Confederate lines, where he secured more shot and powder. For the rest of the day he maneuvered his artillery into four different positions to blunt the Union attack. By battle's end he was directing more than half of all the Confederate artillery in the battle.

After the fight ended with one of the greatest Union defeats of the war, Robert E. Lee (5) referred to the young artilleryman as "the Gallant Pelham" and noted, "It is glorious to see such courage in one so young."

Both armies after Fredericksburg went into winter quarters, and the fighting was reduced to small skirmishes for the next several months. Stories of Pelham's performance spread during this time, polishing his already shining reputation. Blue-eyed, blond, and youthfully handsome, Pelham was modest in his fame but not beyond using it to gain introduction to young, single women whenever possible. Known as a flirt to all, it was said he had a lady friend in every town he visited.

On February 17, Pelham, on Stuart's orders, rode to the Upper Rappahannock to investigate an outbreak of hoof and leg disease in horses in the cavalry commanded by Fitz Lee. During the inspection, Pelham paid a social call on Bessie Shackelford in the nearby village of Culpeper Court House. A month later, when Stuart was called to Culpeper to attend a court martial, Pelham volunteered to ride along with hopes of once again seeing Miss Shackelford.

Soon after their arrival in Culpeper, the two cavalrymen learned of an impending battle between Fitz Lee and Union cavalry at nearby Kelly's Ford. The two officers rode to the front to observe the fight. Soon after their arrival on March 17, 1863, an artillery shell fragment struck Pelham in the head. He was placed on a horse and taken to a field hospital where he died around midnight. Orders already approved for his promotion to lieutenant colonel arrived shortly after his death and were awarded posthumously.

Pelham's body was escorted to Richmond where it lay in state in the capital building—a great honor for one so young and junior in rank. It was then transported to Alabama by wagon, boat, and train. Along the rail route in his home state, young women covered the train tracks with flower petals in his honor. He lay in state again in Jacksonville, Louisiana, before his burial in City Cemetery.

It was said that at least three women donned mourning attire on Pelham's death as they would if they were his widow. Others across the South, male and female, soldier and civilian, mourned the passing of "the Gallant Pelham." Poems, articles, and books, both fact and fiction, soon appeared to add to his heroic status.

Doubtless, Pelham was daring and exceedingly brave. Just what he could have accomplished if he had lived is one of those "what ifs" that is impossible to answer. It is fact that his artillery tactics and performance enhanced Stuart's fighting abilities and significantly influenced the Battle of Fredericksburg. This aside, Pelham was much more famous, more like a "pop star" of his age, than actually influential, and his ranking cannot exceed the commanders and battles that drove the war's outcome. Nevertheless, he remains one of the war's best-known characters and a lasting symbol of all that the South thought was gallant and just.

PALMITO RANCH

May 12–13, 1865

Every war must, of course, have its last battle, and Palmito Ranch in south Texas provided the last bloodshed of the Civil War. Although it ended in a Confederate victory, it had absolutely no influence on the outcome of the war and joins this list merely because of its date rather than any other great significance.

Texas provided troops during the war mostly for the Confederacy but also for several regiments which remained loyal to the Union. More importantly, the state was a major supplier of beef and other food products to the South, and its ports were some of the last to remain open to foreign shipping. Except for Union efforts to blockade the Sabine River and to occupy the ports of Galveston and Brownsville, little combat actually took place in the vast state.

The port at Brownsville was important because it could receive shipping from the Gulf of Mexico. Its importance increased with the tightening of the Union blockade in that ships could land legally and unmolested in the Mexican port of Bagdad and then their goods could be transported to Matamoros to be shipped across the Rio Grande into Texas. After capturing Vicksburg (7) and securing the Mississippi River, the Union made efforts to cut off these last ports of entry on the Texas Gulf Coast while also pushing inland from western Louisiana in the Red River Campaign (81). The United States also had a secondary purpose of "showing the flag" to the French who had recently taken control of Mexico. The Union wanted to prevent their possible support of the rebellion.

U.S. forces that occupied Brownsville briefly in 1864 were forced to withdraw to Brazos Island at the entrance to the Rio Grande. From a camp named Brazos Santiago, the Union force settled into blockading the river. The Union commander, Colonel Theodore H. Barrett, reported to his superiors that the base was secure and requested permission to once again attack Brownsville. His commander, General Lew Wallace, turned down the request and, aware that the war was nearly over, arranged a meeting with Texas officials to pursue a separate peace. On March 11 the two sides produced an informal agreement to cease hostilities.

There were commanders for both the blue and gray who did not accept a ceasefire, including Barrett and John S. "Rip" Ford, the rebel commander in the area.

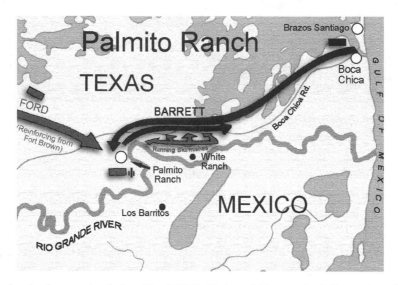

Barrett, who had organized the 62nd U.S. Colored Troops in Missouri and brought them to Texas, had little combat experience. However, he desired to prove the worth of his black troops and also harbored postwar political ambitions that would be enhanced by a successful combat record.

On the other side, Rip Ford had been fighting most of his life. Ford arrived in Texas from Tennessee in 1836 a few months after the Battle of San Jacinto. In addition to being a politician, Ford served his new home as a doctor and a lawyer. As a lawyer he occasionally acted as a judge and many accounts incorrectly claim that while on the bench he gained his nickname by signing death sentences with "Rest in Peace." Actually, he earned the name while serving as a doctor with the U.S. Army during the Mexican War where he was responsible for writing letters to families of fallen soldiers. Early in the war Ford signed the letters "Rest in Peace," but disease and battle deaths so increased his writing load that he shortened it to "RIP."

On February 28, 1848, Ford and his fellow Texas Rangers participated in the last battle of the Mexican War at the Battle of Sequaltepan. Upon returning home he remained with the Rangers to fight the Indians on the Texas frontier. When Union Colonel Barrett disobeyed the cease-fire and marched toward Brownsville, Rip Ford was prepared to fight the last land battle of the Civil War.

On May 11, 1865, Barrett's army—composed of his black soldiers, a regiment of Indiana volunteers, and a Texas cavalry unit containing whites, Indians, and Mexicans—crossed from its island fortress to the Texas mainland and headed toward Brownsville twenty-five miles away. They made it about halfway to their objective in a night march before halting for a rest at White's Ranch on the Rio Grande. Mexican civilians, or possibly a Confederate patrol that had illegally crossed the river, spotted them. Barrett immediately resumed his march and about ten miles east of Brownsville, early the next morning, attacked and scattered a small Confederate force occupying Palmito Ranch.

Additional Union forces arrived, increasing Barrett's numbers to about eight hundred men. Ford approached in the afternoon of May 12 with about half the number of troops he opposed, but he had the advantage of six twelve-pound cannons. His infantry and cavalry attack, supported by artillery, soon had Barrett on the run back to Brazos Santiago. Ford pursued for a few miles and then stopped, telling his men, "Boys, we have done finely. We will let well enough alone and retire." Some accounts claim that a few shots came into the battle area from across the Rio Grande, fired either by the Mexicans or possibly the French.

Exact casualties figures are unknown, but the Confederates later claimed only five to a dozen men were slightly wounded. Union losses were about thirty killed or wounded with another one hundred or so captured. Among the dead was Private John J. Williams of the 34th Indiana Volunteer Infantry—the last man killed in the battle, and likely the war itself, by hostile action. Barrett was proud of his soldiers, particularly those of the 62nd Colored Regiment. In his after-action report, he wrote that the operation "demonstrated the fact that the Negro soldier can march, keep order in the ranks, and be depended upon under trying circumstances."

At the time of the Battle of Palmito Ranch, it is likely that both the Confederates and the Union commands knew of Robert E. Lee's (5) surrender a month earlier. Copies of the New Orleans *Times* with the news from Virginia had arrived by steamer in Brownsville as early as May 1. Confederate commanders in the West were aware they were in their last days, but it would be early June before the final rebel units gave up. Rip Ford also knew that the Confederacy was defeated. Thirteen days after their victory at Palmito Ranch, Ford disbanded his command rather than submit to formal surrender.

Later claims that the last battle of the Civil War was fought after the conflict had already officially ended are incorrect as General Edward Kirby Smith (33) did not surrender his Texas command until June 2. But it is true that the fight at Palmito Ranch was entirely useless and had no influence on the war. It did, however, display that the fighting spirit and loyalty of its participants continued to the last days. The battle also showed that African Americans would be a continued part of the U.S. Army and did, in fact, accomplish the purpose of "showing the flag" to the French in Mexico. None of these factors gain the Battle of Palmito a place on this list. Only its being last secures it this appropriate ranking.

BIBLIOGRAPHY

Abel, E. Lawrence. *Singing the New Nation: How Music Shaped the Confederacy.* Mechanicsburg, PA: Stackpole Books, 2000.

Ambrose, Stephen E. *Halleck: Lincoln's Chief of Staff.* Baton Rouge: Louisiana State University Press, 1996.

Anders, Curt. *Henry Halleck's War: A Fresh Look at Lincoln's Controversial General-in-Chief.* Carmel, IN: Guild Press of Indiana, 1999.

Armstrong, William H. *Major McKinley: William McKinley and the Civil War.* Kent, OH: Kent State University Press, 2000.

Bacon, Benjamin. *Sinews of War: How Technology, Industry and Transportation Won the Civil War.* Navato, CA: Presidio Press, 1997.

Bailey, Ronald H. *Forward to Richmond: McClellan's Peninsular Campaign.* Virginia Beach, VA: Time-Life, 1985.

Ballard, Michael B. *Vicksburg: The Campaign That Opened the Mississippi.* Chapel Hill: University of North Carolina Press, 2004.

Banks, R. W. *The Battle of Franklin, November 30, 1864.* Dayton, OH: Morningside, 1982.

Barrett, John G. *The Civil War in North Carolina.* Chapel Hill: University of North Carolina Press, 1963.

————.*Sherman's March Through the Carolinas.* Chapel Hill: University of North Carolina Press, 1956.

Beringer, Richard E. *Why the South Lost the Civil War.* Athens: University of Georgia Press, 1986.

Berstein, Iver. *The New York City Draft Riots: Their Significance for American Society and Politics in the Age of the Civil War.* New York: Oxford University Press, 1990.

Blackford, W. W. *War Years with Jeb Stuart.* New York: Charles Scribner's Sons, 1945.

Blake, Nelson Morehouse. *William Mahone of Virginia: Soldier and Political Insurgent.* Richmond: Garret & Massie, 1935.

Boatner, Mark Mayo III. *The Civil War Dictionary.* New York: David McKay, 1959.

Bowers, John. *Chickamauga and Chattanooga: The Battles That Doomed the Confederacy.* New York: Harper Perennial, 1995.

Brooksher, William R. *Bloody Hill: The Civil War Battle of Wilson's Creek.* McLean VA: Brassey's, 1996.

———.*War along the Bayous: The 1864 Red River Campaign in Louisiana.* McLean, VA: Brassey's, 1998.

Butler, Benjamin F. *Butler's Book: Autobiography and Personal Reminiscences of Major General Benjamin F. Butler.* Boston: A. M. Thayer & Co., 1892.

Butterfield, Daniel. *Camp and Outpost Duty for Infantry, 1862.* Mechanicsburg, PA: Stackpole, 2003.

Cangemi, Joseph P. *Andersonville Prison.* Lanham, MD: University Press of America, 1992.

Cannan, John. *The Crater: Petersburg.* Cambridge, MA: Da Capo Press, 2002.

Carhart, Tom. *Lost Triumph: Lee's Real Plan at Gettysburg and Why It Failed.* New York: G. P. Putnam's Sons, 2005.

Castel, Albert. *Decision in the West: The Atlanta Campaign of 1864.* Lawrence: University Press of Kansas, 1995.

Catton, Bruce. *The Army of the Potomac.* 3 vols. New York: Doubleday & Company, 1951–1953.

———.*U. S. Grant and the American Military Tradition.* Boston: Little Brown & Company, 1972.

Chamberlain, Joshua L. *The Passing of the Armies: An Account of the Final Campaign Of the Army of the Potomac.* New York: G. P. Putnam's Sons, 1915.

Cisco, Walter Brian. *Wade Hampton: Confederate Warrior, Conservative Statesman.* Dulles, VA: Potomac Books, 2004.

Cleaves, Freeman. *Rock of Chickamauga: The Life of General George H. Thomas.* Norman: University of Oklahoma Press, 1986.

Colton, Ray C. *The Civil War in the Western Territories: Arizona, Colorado, New Mexico and Utah.* Norman: University of Oklahoma Press, 1984.

Commager, Henry Steele, editor. *The Blue and the Gray: The Story of the Civil War as Told by Participants.* Indianapolis: Bobbs-Merrill Co., 1950.

Cook, Adrian. *The Armies of the Streets: The New York City Draft Riots of 1863.* Lexington: University of Kentucky Press, 1974.

Cooling, Benjamin F. *Fort Donelson's Legacy: War and Society in Kentucky and Tennessee, 1862–1863.* Knoxville: University of Tennessee Press, 1997.

———.*Forts Henry and Donelson: The Key to the Confederate Heartland.* Knoxville: University of Tennessee Press, 1987.

———*Jubal Early's Raid on Washington, 1864.* Baltimore: Nautical and

Aviation Publishing Co., 1989.

Cooper, William J. *Jefferson Davis, American.* New York: Knopf, 2000.

Cornelius, Steven H. *Music of the Civil War Era.* Westport, CN: Greenwood Press, 2004.

Cornish, Dudley Taylor. *The Sable Arm: Negro Troops in the Union Army, 1861–1865.* New York: W. W. Norton, 1966.

Cox, Jacob D. *Sherman's Battle for Atlanta.* Cambridge, MA: Da Capo Press, 1994.

Cozzens, Peter. *General John Pope: A Life for the Nation.* Urbana: University of Illinois Press, 2005.

————.*The Military Memoirs of General John Pope.* Chapel Hill: University of North Carolina Press, 1998.

————.*The Shipwreck of Their Hopes: The Battle for Chattanooga.* Urbana: University of Illinois Press, 1994.

————.*The Terrible Sound: The Battle of Chickamauga.* Urbana: University of Illinois Press, 1996.

Current, Richard N., et al., editors. *Encyclopedia of the Confederacy.* New York: Simon & Schuster, 1993.

Daniel, Larry J. *Shiloh: The Battle That Changed the Civil War.* New York: Simon & Schuster, 1997.

Davis, Burke. *Jeb Stuart: The Last Cavalier.* New York: Gramercy, 2000.

————.*Sherman's March: The First Full Length Narrative of Sherman's Devastating March Through Georgia and the Carolinas.* New York: Vintage, 1988.

Davis, William C. *An Honorable Defeat: The Last Days of the Confederate Government.* New York: Harcourt, 2001.

————.*Battle at Bull Run: A History of the First Major Campaign of the Civil War.* Garden City, NY: Doubleday & Co., 1977.

————.*Breckinridge: Statesman, Soldier, Symbol.* Baton Rouge: Louisiana State University Press, 1992.

————.*Duel Between the Ironclads.* Garden City, NY: Doubleday & Co., 1975.

————.*Jefferson Davis: The Man and His Hour.* New York: Harper Collins, 1991.

Dixon, Susan Bullitt. *The True Story of the Missouri Compromise and Its Repeal.* Cincinnati, OH: Robert Clark, 1898.

Donald, David H. *Lincoln.* New York: Simon & Schuster, 1995.

Douglas, Henry Kyd. *I Rode with Stonewall.* Chapel Hill: University of North Carolina Press, 1987.

Downey, Fairfax. *The Guns of Gettysburg.* New York: David McKay, 1958.

Duffy, James P. *Lincoln's Admiral: The Civil War Campaigns of David Farragut.* Hoboken, NJ: Wiley, 1997.

Duncan, Richard R. *Lee's Endangered Left: The Civil War in Western Virginia, Spring of 1864.* Baton Rouge: Louisiana State University Press, 1998.

Dyer, John P. *From Shiloh to San Juan: The Life of Fightin' Joe Wheeler.* Baton Rouge: Louisiana State University Press, 1992.

Early, Jubal A. *Autobiographical Sketch and Narrative of the War Between the States.* Philadelphia: J. B. Lippincott Co., 1912.

Eckenrode, H. J. and Bryan Conrad. *James Longstreet: Lee's War Horse.* Chapel Hill: University of North Carolina Press, 1999.

Edrington, Thomas S. and John Taylor. *The Battle of Glorieta Pass: A Gettysburg in the West, March 26–28, 1862.* Albuquerque: University of New Mexico Press, 1998.

Eicher, John H. and David J. *Civil War High Commands.* Palo Alto, CA: Stanford University Press, 2001.

Eisenhower, John S. D. *Agent of Destiny: The Life and Times of General Winfield Scott.* New York: Free Press, 1997.

Engle, Stephen D. *Yankee Dutchman: The Life of Franz Sigel.* Baton Rouge: Louisiana State University Press, 1999.

Evans, David. *Sherman's Horsemen: Union Cavalry Operations in the Atlanta Campaign.* Bloomington: Indiana University Press, 1996.

Farwell, Byron. *Stonewall: A Biography of General Thomas J. Jackson.* New York: W. W. Norton, 1993.

Finkleman, Paul. *Dred Scott v. Sandford.* New York: St. Martin's, 1997.

Flood, Charles B. *Grant and Sherman: The Friendship That Won the Civil War.* New York: Farrar, Straus and Giroux, 2005.

Fordney, Ben Fuller. *Stoneman at Chancellorsville: The Coming of Age of Union Cavalry.* Shippenburg, PA: White Mane, 1999.

Frassanito, William A. *Antietam: The Photographic Legacy of America's Bloodiest Day.* New York: Charles Scribner's Sons, 1978.

———.*Early Photography at Gettysburg.* Gettysburg, PA: Thomas Publications, 1995.

Freeman, Douglas Southall. *Lee.* New York: Scribner's, 1997.

———.*Lee's Lieutenants: A Study in Command.* 3 vols. New York: Charles Scribner's Sons, 1942–1944.

———.*R. E. Lee: A Biography.* New York: Charles Scribner's Sons, 1934–1935.

Freemantle, Arthur J. L. *Three Months in the Southern States: April-June 1863.*

Lincoln: University of Nebraska Press, 1991.

Friend, Jack. *West Wind, Flood Tide: The Battle of Mobile Bay.* Annapolis: Naval Institute Press, 2004.

Furgurson, Ernest B. *Chancellorsville, 1863: The Souls of the Brave.* New York: Alfred Knopf, 1992.

———.*Not War But Murder: Cold Harbor 1864.* New York: Vintage, 2001.

Futch, Ovid L. *History of Andersonville Prison.* Gainesville: University of Florida Press, 1968.

Gallagher, Gary W., editor. *Chancellorsville: The Battle and Its Aftermath.* Chapel Hill: University of North Carolina Press, 1996.

———.*The Fredericksburg Campaign: Decision on the Rappahannock.* Chapel Hill: University of North Carolina Press, 1995.

———.*The Richmond Campaign of 1862: The Peninsula and the Seven Days.* Chapel Hill: University of North Carolina Press, 2000.

———.*The Spotsylvania Campaign.* Chapel Hill: University of North Carolina Press, 1998.

———.*Struggle for the Shenandoah: Essays on the 1864 Valley Campaign.* Kent, OH: Kent State University Press, 1991.

———.*The Wilderness Campaign.* Chapel Hill: University of North Carolina Press, 1997.

Gallaway, B. P., editor. *Texas: The Dark Corner of the Confederacy.* Lincoln: University of Nebraska Press, 1994.

Garfield, James A. *The Wild Life of the Army: Civil War Letters of James A. Garfield.* East Lansing: Michigan State University Press, 1994.

Glatthaar, Joseph T. *The March to the Sea and Beyond: Sherman's Troops in the Savannah and Carolinas Campaigns.* New York: New York University Press, 1985.

Goodwin, Doris Kearns. *Team of Rivals: The Political Genius of Abraham Lincoln.* New York: Simon & Schuster, 2005.

Gordon, Lesley J. *General George E. Pickett in Life and Legend.* Chapel Hill: University of North Carolina Press, 1998.

Gott, Kendall D. *Where the South Lost the War: An Analysis of the Fort Henry-Fort Donelson Campaign.* Mechanicsburg, PA: Stackpole, 2003.

Grant, Ulysses S. *Personal Memoirs of U. S. Grant.* New York: Modern Library, 1999.

Guelzo, Allen C. *Lincoln's Emancipation Proclamation: The End of Slavery in America.* New York: Simon & Schuster, 2004.

Hall, Martin Hardwick. *Sibley's New Mexico Campaign.* Albuquerque: University of

New Mexico Press, 2000.

Hassler, William W. *A. P. Hill: Lee's Forgotten General.* Chapel Hill: University of North Carolina Press, 1987.

———.*Colonel John Pelham: Lee's Boy Artillerist.* Chapel Hill: University of North Carolina Press, 1995.

Hatch, Thom. *Clashes of Cavalry: The Civil War Careers of George Armstrong Custer and Jeb Stuart.* Mechanicsburg, PA: Stackpole, 2001.

Hattaway, Herman and Archer Jones. *How the North Won: A Military History of the Civil War.* Urbana: University of Illinois Press, 1983.

Hearn, Chester G. *Admiral David Glasgow Farragut: The Civil War Years.* Annapolis: Naval Institute Press, 1998.

———.*Mobile Bay and the Mobile Campaign: The Last Great Battles of the Civil War.* Jefferson, NC: McFarland & Co., 1993.

———.*Rebels and Yankees: Naval Battles of the Civil War.* San Diego: Thunder Bay Press, 2000.

———.*When the Devil Came Down to Dixie: Ben Butler in New Orleans.* Baton Rouge: Louisiana State University Press, 1997.

Hebert, Walter H. *Fighting Joe Hooker.* Lincoln: University of Nebraska Press, 1999.

Heck, Frank Hopkins. *Proud Kentuckian: John C. Breckinridge, 1821–1875.* Lexington: University of Kentucky Press, 1976.

Hennessy, John J. *Return to Bull Run: The Campaign and Battle of Second Manassas.* New York: Simon & Schuster, 1993.

Henry, Robert Selph. *Nathan Bedford Forrest: First with the Most.* New York: Mallard Press, 1991.

Hirshon, Stanley P. *The White Tecumseh: A Biography of General William T. Sherman.* Hoboken, NJ: Wiley, 1998.

Hoehling, A. A. *Thunder at Hampton Roads.* Cambridge, MA: Da Capo Press, 1993.

Hollandsworth, James G. Jr. *Pretense of Glory: The Life of General Nathaniel P. Banks.* Baton Rouge: Louisiana State University Press, 2005.

Holzer, Harold and Tim Mulligan. *The Battle of Hampton Roads: New Perspectives on the USS Monitor and the CSS Virginia.* New York: Fordham University Press, 2005.

Hood, John Bell. *Advance and Retreat: Personal Experiences in the United States and Confederate States Armies.* Cambridge, MA: Da Capo Press, 1993.

Horn, John. *The Petersburg Campaign: June 1864–April 1865.* Cambridge, MA: Da Capo Press, 2000.

Horn, Stanley Fitzgerald. *The Decisive Battle of Nashville.* Knoxville: University of Tennessee Press, 1956.

Hughes, Nathaniel C., Jr. *Bentonville: The Final Battle of Sherman and Johnston.* Chapel Hill: University of North Carolina Press, 1996.

Hunt, Jeffery W. *The Last Battle of the Civil War.* Austin: University of Texas Press, 2002.

Hurst, Jack. *Nathan Bedford Forrest: A Biography.* New York: Vintage, 1994.

Jamison, Perry D. *Winfield Scott Hancock: Gettysburg Hero.* Abilene, TX: McWhinney Foundation Press, 2003.

Johnson, Ludwell H. *Red River Campaign: Politics and Cotton in the Civil War.* Kent, OH: Kent State University Press, 1993.

Johnson, Timothy D. *Winfield Scott: The Quest for Military Glory.* Lawrence: University Press of Kansas, 1998.

Johnston, William Preston. *The Life of Gen. Albert Sidney Johnston.* Abilene, TX: State House Press, 1997.

Jones, James Pickett. *Yankee Blitzkrieg: Wilson's Raid Through Alabama and Georgia.* Athens: University of Georgia Press, 1987.

Jordan, David M. *Winfield Scott Hancock: A Soldier's Life.* Bloomington: University of Indiana Press, 1996.

Kauffman, Michael W. *American Brutus: John Wilkes Booth and the Lincoln Conspiracies.* New York: Random House, 2004.

Klein, Maury. *Days of Defiance: Sumter, Secession, and the Coming of the War.* New York: Alfred A. Knopf, 1997.

Krick, Robert K. *Conquering the Valley: Stonewall Jackson at Port Republic.* New York: William Morrow, 1996.

Kunhardt, Philip B., Jr. *A New Birth of Freedom: Lincoln at Gettysburg.* Boston: Little, Brown & Co., 1983.

Lanning, Michael Lee. *Senseless Secrets: The Failures of U.S. Military Intelligence: From George Washington to the Present.* New York: Birch Lane, 1996.

———. *The African American Soldier: From Crispus Attucks to Colin Powell.* New York: Birch Lane Press, 1995.

———. *The Battle 100: The Stories Behind History's Most Influential Battles.* Naperville, IL: Sourcebooks, 2003.

———. *The Military 100: A Ranking of the Most Influential Military Leaders in History.* New York: Citadel Press, 1996.

Large, George R. and Joe A. Swisher. *Battle of Antietam: The Official History of the Antietam Battlefield Board.* Shippensburg, PA: White Mane, 1998.

Lepa, Jack H. *The Shenandoah Valley Campaign of 1864.* Jefferson, NC: McFarland & Co., 2003.

Longacre, Edward G. *Army of Amateurs: General Benjamin F. Butler and the Army of the James.* Mechanicsburg, PA: Stackpole Press, 1997.

————.*Fitz Lee: A Military Biography of Major General Fitzhugh Lee, C.S.A.* Cambridge, MA: De Capo Press, 2005.

————.*Gentleman and Soldier: A Biography of Wade Hampton.* Nashville, TN: Rutledge Hill Press, 2003.

————.*Grant's Cavalryman: The Life and Wars of General James H. Wilson.* Mechanicsburg, PA: Stackpole, 1996.

————.*Leader of the Charge: A Biography of General George E. Pickett, C.S.A.* Shippensburg, PA: White Mane, 1995.

Lyman, Theodore. *Meade's Headquarters, 1863–1865: Letters of Colonel Theodore Lyman from the Wilderness to Appomattox.* Boston: Atlantic Monthly Press, 1922.

Marszalek, John F. *Commander of All Lincoln's Armies: A Life of General Henry W. Halleck.* Cambridge, MA: Belnap Press, 2004.

————.*Sherman: A Soldier's Passion for Order.* New York: Free Press, 1993.

————.*Sherman's March to the Sea.* Abilene, TX: McWhiney Foundation Press, 2005.

Martin, Samuel J. *Kill-Cavalry: The Life of Union General Hugh Judson Kilpatrick.* Mechanicsburg, PA: Stackpole Books, 2000.

Marvel, William. *Andersonville: The Last Depot.* Chapel Hill: University of North Carolina Press, 1994.

————.*Burnside.* Chapel Hill: University of North Carolina Press, 1991.

————. *Lee's Last Retreat: The Flight to Appomattox.* Chapel Hill: University of North Carolina Press, 2002.

Matter, William D. *If It Takes All Summer: The Battle of Spotsylvania.* Chapel Hill: University of North Carolina Press, 1988.

McCague, James. *The Second Rebellion: The Story of the New York City Draft Riots.* New York: Doubleday, 1968.

McClellan, George B. *Civil War Papers of George B. McClellan.* Cambridge, MA: Da Capo Press, 1992.

McDonald, Joanna M. *We Shall Meet Again: The First Battle of Manassas (Bull Run) July 18–21, 1861.* Shippensburg, PA: White Mane, 1998.

McDonough, James Lee. *Chattanooga: A Death Grip on the Confederacy.* Knoxville: University of Tennessee Press, 1984.

————.*Shiloh, In Hell Before Night.* Knoxsville: University of Tennessee Press,1977.

————.*War in Kentucky: From Shiloh to Perryville.* Knoxville: University of Tennessee Press, 1994.

McDonough, James Lee and Thomas Connelly. *Five Tragic Hours: The Battle of Franklin.* Knoxville: University of Tennessee Press, 1983.

McHenry, Robert. editor. *Webster's American Military Biographies.* Springfield, MA: G. & C. Merriam, 1978.

McKinney, Francis F. *Education in Violence: The Life of George H. Thomas and the History of the Army of the Cumberland.* Chicago: Americana House, 1991.

McMurry, Richard M. *John Bell Hood and the War for Southern Independence.* Lincoln: University of Nebraska Press, 1992.

McPherson, James M. *Battle Cry of Freedom: The Civil War Era.* New York: Oxford University Press, 1988.

————.*Crossroads of Freedom: Antietam.* New York: Oxford University Press, 2004.

McWhiney, Grady and Judith Lee Hallock. *Braxton Bragg and Confederate Defeat.* Tuscaloosa: University of Alabama Press, 1991.

Mercer, Philip. *The Gallant Pelham.* Wilmington, NC: Broadfoot Publishing Co., 1995.

Morris, Roy, Jr. *Sheridan: The Life and Wars of General Philip Sheridan.* New York: Crown, 1992.

Mosby, John S. *The Memoirs of Colonel John S. Mosby.* Bloomington: Indiana University Press, 1959.

Murfin, James V. *The Gleam of Bayonets: The Battle of Antietam and Robert E. Lee's Maryland Campaign.* New York: Thomas Yoseloff, 1965.

Newell, Clayton R. *Lee vs. McClellan: The First Campaign.* Washington, D. C.: Regnery Publishing, 1996.

Newton, Steven H. *Joseph E. Johnston and the Defense of Richmond.* Lawrence: University Press of Kansas, 1998.

Noles, James L. *John Pelham: The Gallant Pelham.* Birmingham, AL: Seacoast Publishing, 2004.

Oates, Stephen B. *To Purge This Land with Blood: A Biography of John Brown.* New York: Harper & Row, 1970.

O'Reilly, Francis A. *The Fredericksburg Campaign: Winter War on the Rappahannock.* Baton Rouge: Louisiana State University Press, 2002.

Osborne, Charles C. *Jubal: The Life and Times of General Jubal A. Early, CSA, Defender of the Lost Cause.* Baton Rouge: Louisiana State University Press, 1994.

Osburn, Thomas Ward. *The Fiery Trail: A Union Officer's Account of Sherman's Last Campaigns.* Knoxville: University of Tennessee Press, 1986.

Panzer, Mary and Jeana Kae Foley. *Mathew Brady and the Image of History.* Washington, D. C.: Smithsonian Books, 1997.

Parks, Joseph H. *General Edmund Kirby Smith, C.S.A.* Baton Rouge: Louisiana

University Press, 1954.

———.*General Leonidas Polk, C.S.A.: The Fighting Bishop.* Baton Rouge: Louisiana University Press, 1962.

Parrish, Michael. *General P. G. T. Beauregard.* New York: Random House, 1994.

Perry, James M. *A Bohemian Brigade: Civil War Correspondents—Mostly Rough, Sometimes Ready.* Hoboken, NJ: Wiley, 2000.

Peskin, Allan. *Winfield Scott and the Profession of Arms.* Kent, OH: Kent State University Press, 2003.

Peterson, Merrill D. *John Brown: The Legend Revisited.* Charlottesville: University of Virginia Press, 2002.

Pickenpaugh, Roger. *Rescue by Rail: Troop Transfer and the Civil War in the West.* Lincoln: University of Nebraska Press, 1998.

Pickett, George E. *Soldier of the South: General Pickett's War Letters to His Wife.* Boston: Houghton Mifflin Co., 1928.

Pinnegar, Charles. *Brand of Infamy: A Biography of John Buchanan Floyd.* Westport, CT: Greenwood Press, 2002.

Piston, William Garrett and Richard W. Hatcher III. *Wilson's Creek: The Second Battle of the Civil War and the Men Who Fought It.* Chapel Hill: University of North Carolina Press, 2000.

Power, J. Tracy. *Lee's Miserables: Life in the Army of Northern Virginia from the Wilderness to Appomattox.* Chapel Hill: University of North Carolina Press, 1998.

Pritchard, Russ A., Jr. *Civil War Weapons and Equipment.* Guilford, CT: Lyons Press, 2003.

Prushankin, Jeffery S. *A Crisis in Confederate Command: Edmund Kirby Smith, Richard Taylor, and the Army of the Trans-Mississippi.* Baton Rouge: Louisiana State University Press, 2005.

Pullen, John J. *Joshua Chamberlain: A Hero's Life and Legacy.* Mechanicsburg, PA: Stackpole, 1999.

Rafuse, Ethan Sepp. *George Gordon Meade and the War in the East.* Abilene, TX: McWhiney Foundation Press, 2003.

———.*McClellan's War: The Failure of Moderation in the Struggle for the Union.* Bloomington: Indiana University Press, 2005.

Ramage, James A. *A Rebel Raider: The Life of General John Hunt Morgan.* Lexington: University of Kentucky Press, 1986.

———.*Gray Ghost: The Life of Colonel John Singleton Mosby.* Lexington: University of Kentucky Press, 1999.

Reardon, Carol. *Pickett's Charge in History and Memory.* Chapel Hill: University of

North Carolina Press, 1997.

Reynolds, David S. *John Brown, Abolitionist: The Man Who Killed Slavery, Sparked the Civil War, and Seeded Civil Rights.* New York: Knopf, 2005.

Rhea, Gordon C. *Cold Harbor: Grant and Lee, May 26–June 3, 1864.* Baton Rouge: Louisiana State University Press, 2002.

———. *The Battle of the Wilderness, May 5–6, 1864.* Baton Rouge: Louisiana State University Press, 1997.

Robertson, James I., Jr. *General A. P. Hill: The Story of a Confederate Warrior.* New York: Random House, 1987.

Robinson, Charles M, III. *Hurricane of Fire: The Union Assault on Fort Fisher.* Annapolis: Naval Institute Press, 1998.

Robinson, William Glen. *Back Door to Richmond: The Bermuda Hundred Campaign, April–June 1864.* Baton Rouge: Louisiana State University Press, 1991.

Roland, Charles Pierce. *Albert Sidney Johnston: Soldier of Three Republics.* Lexington: University of Kentucky Press, 2001.

———. *Jefferson Davis's Greatest General: Albert Sidney Johnston.* Abilene, TX: McWhiney Foundation Press, 2000.

Rosser, Thomas L. *Riding With Rosser.* Shippensburg, PA: Burd Street Press, 1997.

Russell, William Howard. *My Diary North and South.* New York: Harper & Bros., 1954.

Sanders, Charles W. Jr. *While in the Hands of the Enemy: Military Prisons of the Civil War.* Baton Rouge: Louisiana State University Press, 1995.

Sauers, Richard A. *Meade: Victor at Gettysburg.* Dulles, VA: Potomac, 2004.

Schultz, Duane P. *The Most Glorious Fourth: Vicksburg and Gettysburg, July 4, 1863.* New York: W. W. Norton, 2001.

Schurz, Wallace and Walter N. Trenerry. *Abandoned by Lincoln: A Military Biography of John Pope.* Urbana: University of Illinois Press, 1990.

Scott, Robert Garth. *Into the Wilderness with the Army of the Potomac.* Bloomington: Indiana University Press, 1985.

Sears, Stephen W. *Chancellorsville.* Boston: Houghton Mifflin Co., 1996.

———. *George B. McClellan: The Young Napoleon.* New York: Tecknor & Fields, 1988.

———. *To the Gates of Richmond.* Boston: Houghton Mifflin, 2001.

Sedgwick, John. *Correspondence of John Sedgwick, Major General.* Baltimore: Butternut and Blue, 1999.

Shea, William L. and Earl J. Hess. *Pea Ridge: Civil War Campaign in the West.* Chapel Hill: University of North Carolina Press, 1997.

Sheridan, Phillip H. *Personal Memoirs of P. H. Sheridan: General, United States Army.* Cambridge, MA: Da Capo Press, 1992.

Sherman, William Tecumseh. *Memoirs of General W. T. Sherman.* New York: Library of America, 1990.

Sibler, Irwin. *Songs of the Civil War.* Mineola, NY: Dover, 1995.

Silverstone, Paul H. *Warships of the Civil War.* Annapolis: Naval Institute Press, 1989.

Smith, Gene. *Allegiance: Fort Sumter, Charleston, and the Beginning of the Civil War.* New York: Harvest Books, 2002.

Speer, Lonnie R. *Portals to Hell: Military Prisons of the Civil War.* Mechanicsburg, PA: Stackpole Books, 1997.

Spruill, Matt. *Guide to the Battle of Chickamauga.* Lawrence: University Press of Kansas, 1993.

Stockdale, Paul H. *Death of an Army: The Battle of Nashville and Hood's Retreat.* Saint Petersburg, FL: Southern Heritage Press, 1992.

Stowe, Harriet Beecher. *Uncle Tom's Cabin.* New York: Oxford University Press, 2002.

Sullivan, George. *In the Wake of Battle: The Civil War Images of Mathew Brady.* London: Prestel, 2004.

Sword, Wiley. *Embrace an Angry Wind, The Confederacy's Last Hurrah: Spring Hill, Franklin, and Nashville.* New York: HarperCollins, 1992.

———.*Mountains Touched with Fire: Chattanooga Besieged, 1863.* New York: St. Martin's Press, 1995.

———.*Shiloh: Bloody April.* New York: William Morrow & Co., 1974.

Symonds, Craig L. *Joseph E. Johnston: A Civil War Biography.* New York: W. W. Norton & Co., 1992.

Tanner, Robert G. *Stonewall in the Valley: Thomas J. "Stonewall" Jackson's Shenandoah Valley Campaign, Spring 1862.* Mechanicsburg, PA: Stackpole, 1996.

Taylor, John. *Bloody Valverde: A Civil War Battle on the Rio Grande.* Albuquerque: University of New Mexico Press, 1995.

Thomas, Edison H. *John Hunt Morgan and His Raiders.* Lexington: University of Kentucky Press, 1985.

Thomas, Emory M. *Bold Dragoon: The Life of J. E. B. Stuart.* New York: Harper & Row, 1986.

———.*Robert E. Lee: A Biography.* New York: W. W. Norton & Co., 1995.

Thomason, John W., Jr. *Jeb Stuart.* Lincoln: University of Nebraska Press, 1994.

Thornton, Mark. *Tariffs, Blockades, and Inflation: The Economics of the Civil War.* Lanham: MD: SR Books, 2004.

Trulock, Alice Rains. *In the Hands of Providence: Joshua L. Chamberlain and the American Civil War.* Chapel Hill: University of North Carolina Press, 1992.

Tucker, Philip Thomas. *The Final Fury: Palmito Ranch, the Last Battle of the Civil War.*

Mechanicsburg, PA: Stackpole, 2001.

Urwin, Gregory J. W. *Custer Victorious: The Civil War Battles of General George Armstrong Custer.* Lincoln: University of Nebraska Press, 1990.

Vandiver, Frank E. *Jubal's Raid: General Early's Famous Attack on Washington in 1864.* New York: McGraw-Hill, 1960.

Warner, Ezra J. *Generals in Blue: Lives of the Union Commanders.* Baton Rouge: Louisiana State University Press, 1964.

———.*Generals in Gray: Lives of the Confederate Commanders.* Baton Rouge: Louisiana State University Press, 1959.

Wert, Jeffery D. *From Winchester to Cedar Creek: The Shenandoah Campaign of 1864* Carlisle, PA: South Mountain Press, 1987.

———.*General James Longstreet: The Confederacy's Most Controversial Soldier.* New York: Simon & Schuster, 1993.

———.*Little Phil: A Reassessment of the Civil War Leadership of Gen. Philip H. Sheridan.* Dulles, VA: Potomac Books, 2003.

———.*Mosby's Rangers.* New York: Simon & Schuster, 1990.

Wiley, Bell Irwin. *The Road to Appomattox.* Baton Rouge: Louisiana State University Press, 1994.

Williams, T. Harry. *P. G. T. Beauregard: Napoleon in Gray.* Baton Rouge: Louisiana State University Press, 1955.

Wills, Brian Steel. *A Battle From the Start: The Life of Nathan Bedford Forrest.* New York: HarperCollins, 1992.

Wills, Garry. *Lincoln at Gettysburg: The Words That Remade America.* New York: Simon & Schuster, 1991.

Wink, Jay. *April 1865: The Month That Saved America.* New York: Harper Prennial, 2002.

Wise, Stephen R. *Lifeline of the Confederacy: Blockade Running During the Civil War.* Columbia: University of South Carolina Press, 1991.

Woodworth, Steven E. *Nothing But Victory: The Army of the Tennessee 1861–1865.* New York: Knopf, 2005.

Wyeth, John Allan. *That Devil Forrest: Life of General Nathan Bedford Forrest.* Baton Rouge: Louisiana State University Press, 1989.

INDEX

ABOUT THE AUTHOR

Michael Lee Lanning is the author of sixteen nonfiction books on military history. More than a million copies of his books are in print in fifteen countries, and editions have been translated into eleven languages. A graduate of Texas A&M University, Lanning is a veteran of more than twenty years in the U.S. Army and is a retired lieutenant colonel. During the Vietnam War he served as an infantry platoon leader, reconnaissance platoon leader, and rifle company commander. He currently resides in Phoenix, Arizona.